(Tolstoy is cool.)

トルストイって
ステキ

藤崎 竜

I received a letter from a reader who lives in Tamagawa Gakuen, Machida-shi, Tokyo (Fujisaki used to live there too) which said that "paope" used as slang means "middle-aged woman" or "weirdo."

...n kind of impressed that "paope human" ...ould then mean "middle-aged woman."

Ryu Fujisaki

Ryu Fujisaki's *Worlds* came in second place for the prestigious 40th Tezuka Award. His *Psycho +*, *Wāqwāq* and *Hoshin Engi* have all run in *Weekly Shonen Jump* magazine, and *Hoshin Engi* anime is available on DVD in Japan and North America. A lover of science fiction, literature and history, Fujisaki has made *Hoshin Engi* a mix of genres that truly showcases his amazing art and imagination.

HOSHIN ENGI VOL. 6
The SHONEN JUMP Manga Edition

STORY AND ART BY RYU FUJISAKI

Based on the novel *Hoshin Engi*, translated by Tsutomu Ano,
published by Kodansha Bunko

Translation & Adaptation/Tomo Kimura
Touch-up Art & Lettering/HudsonYards
Design/Matt Hinrichs
Editor/Jonathan Tarbox

Editor in Chief, Books/Alvin Lu
Editor in Chief, Magazines/Marc Weidenbaum
VP of Publishing Licensing/Rika Inouye
VP of Sales/Gonzalo Ferreyra
Sr. VP of Marketing/Liza Coppola
Publisher/Hyoe Narita

Published by VIZ Media, LLC
P.O. Box 77010
San Francisco, CA 94107

SHONEN JUMP Manga Edition
10 9 8 7 6 5 4 3 2 1
First printing, April 2008

HOSHIN ENGI

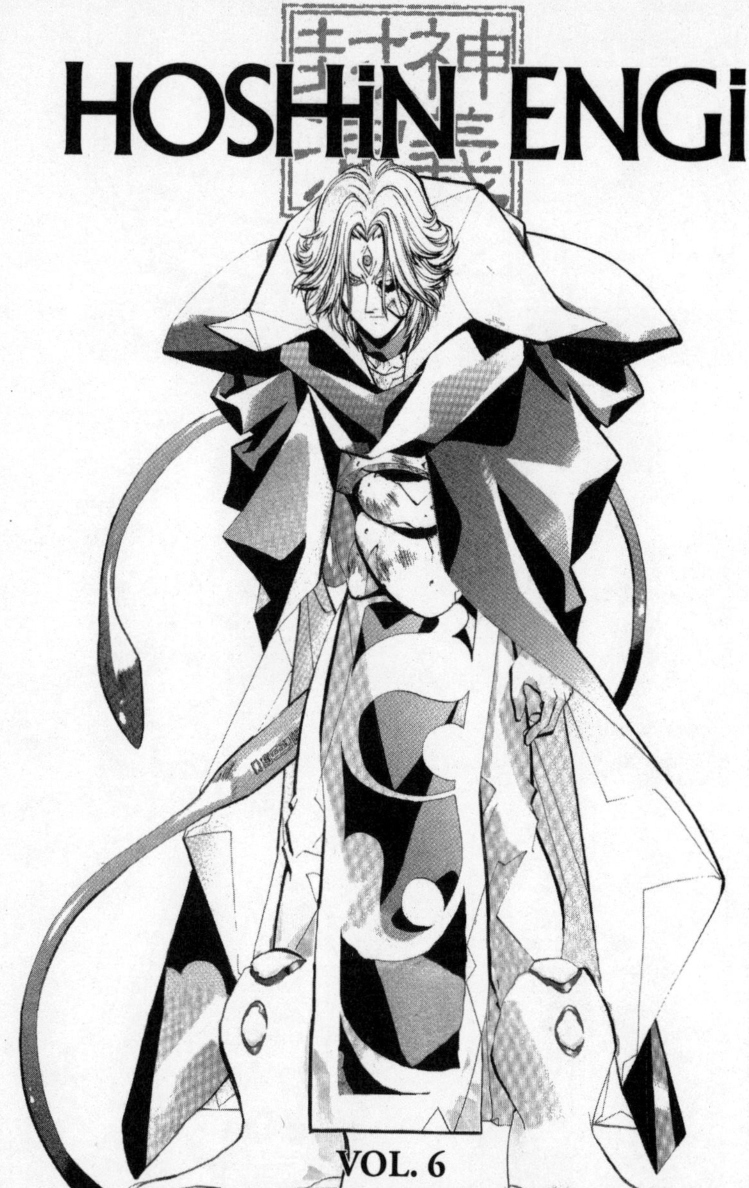

VOL. 6
THE TAISHI OF YIN

STORY AND ART BY RYU FUJISAKI

THE CHARACTERS

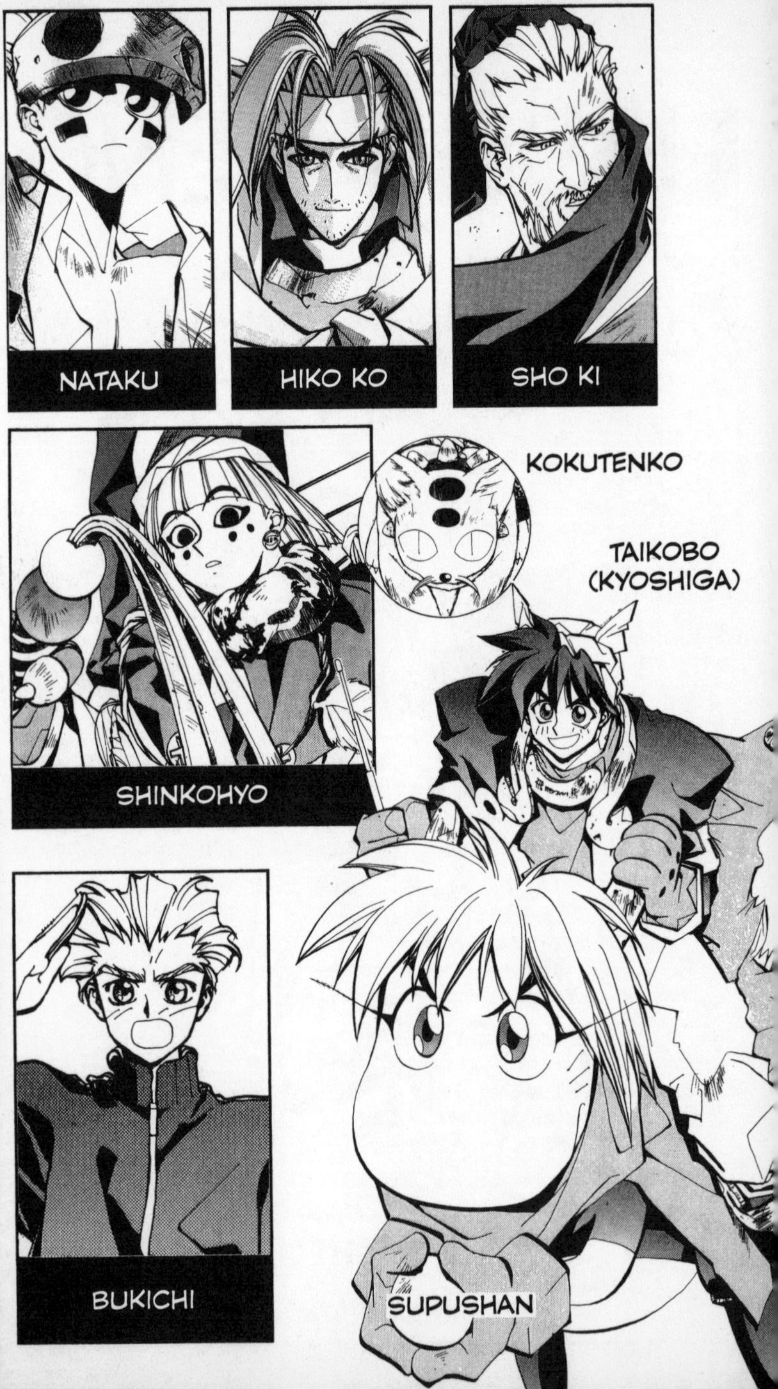
SHO KI
HIKO KO
NATAKU
KOKUTENKO
TAIKOBO (KYOSHIGA)
SHINKOHYO
SUPUSHAN
BUKICHI

KING CHU

BUNCHU

DAKKI

SHISEI

The Story Thus Far

Ancient China, over 3000 years ago. It is the era of the Yin Dynasty.

After King Chu, the emperor, married the beautiful Dakki, the good king was no longer himself, and became an unmanly and foolish ruler. Dakki, a *Sennyo* with a wicked heart, took control of Yin and the country fell into chaos.

To save the human world, the Hoshin Project was put into action. The project will seal evil Sennin and Doshi into the Shinkai, and cause Seihakuko Sho Ki to set up a new dynasty to replace Choka. Taikobo, who was chosen to execute this project, visits Sho Ki in Seiki to encourage him to be the next king.

Right after Taikobo and Sho Ki meet, the Buseio Hiko Ko rebels and abandons King Chu. Taikobo joins Hiko Ko and his clan to protect them from Dakki and Bunchu's assassins. But will Taikobo be able to stand against the deadly Shisei of the Kuryu Islands?!

VOL. 6
THE TAISHI OF YIN

CONTENTS

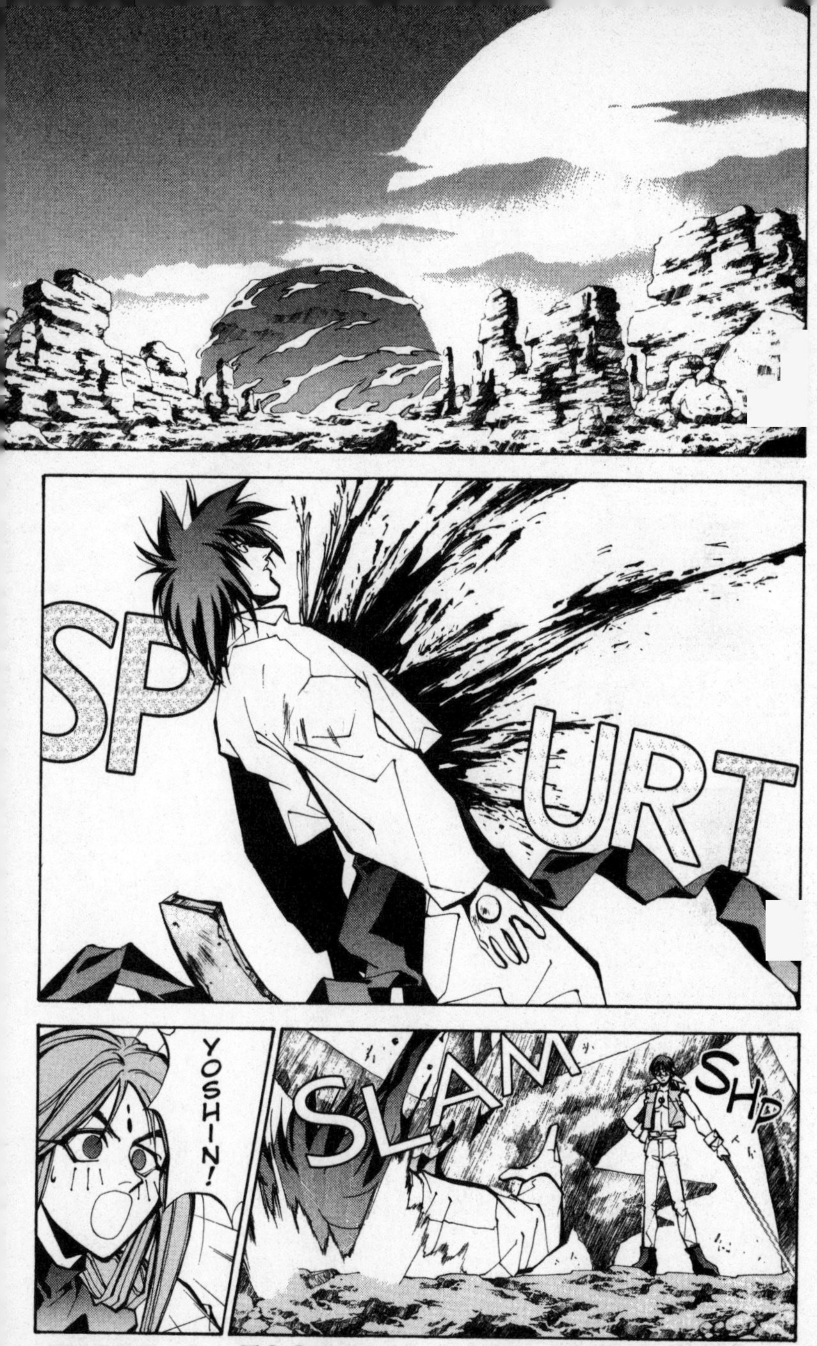
SPURT
SLAM
SHP
YOSHIN!

CHAPTER 43: TOGETHER WITH THE NIGHT

Chapter 43

TOGETHER WITH THE NIGHT

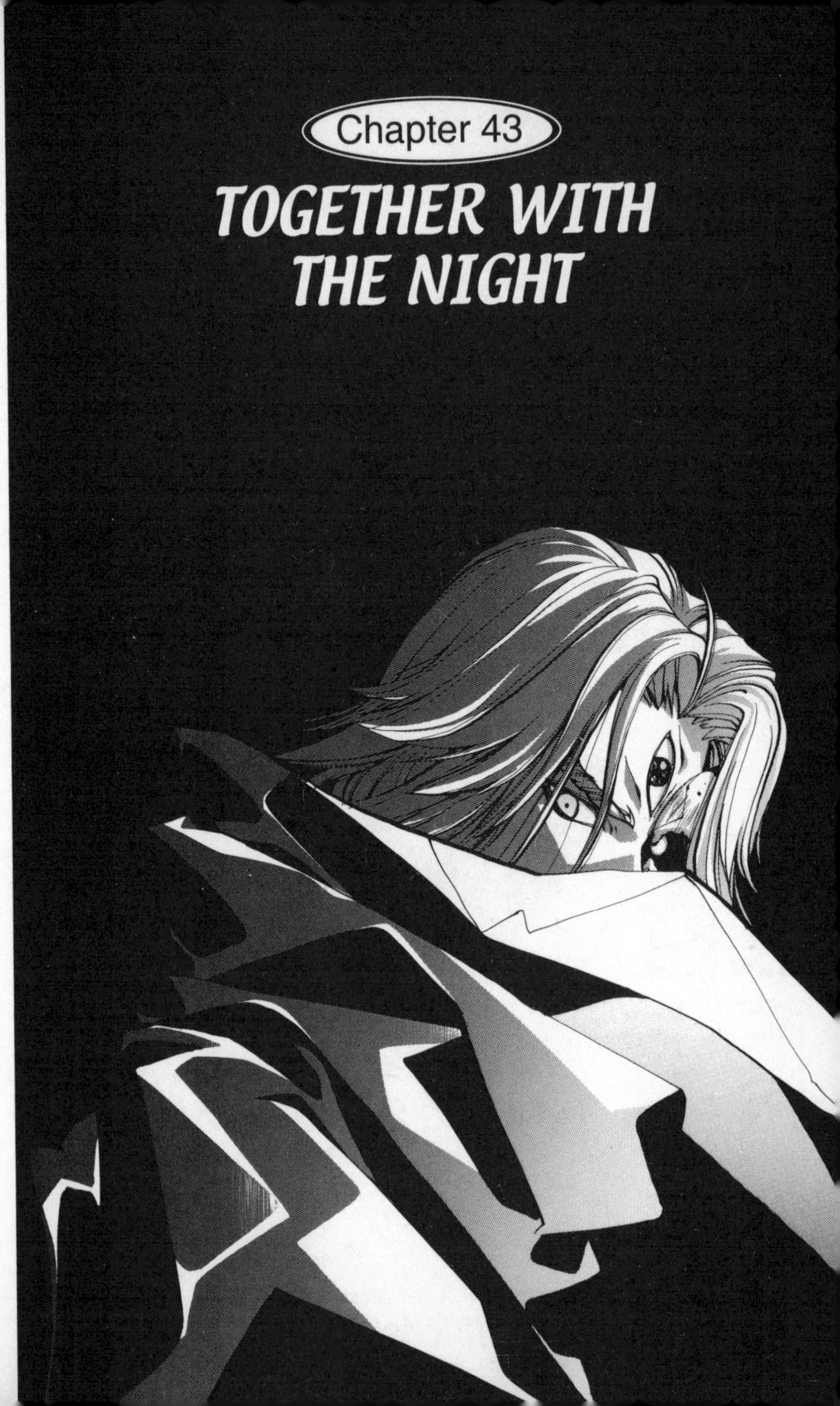

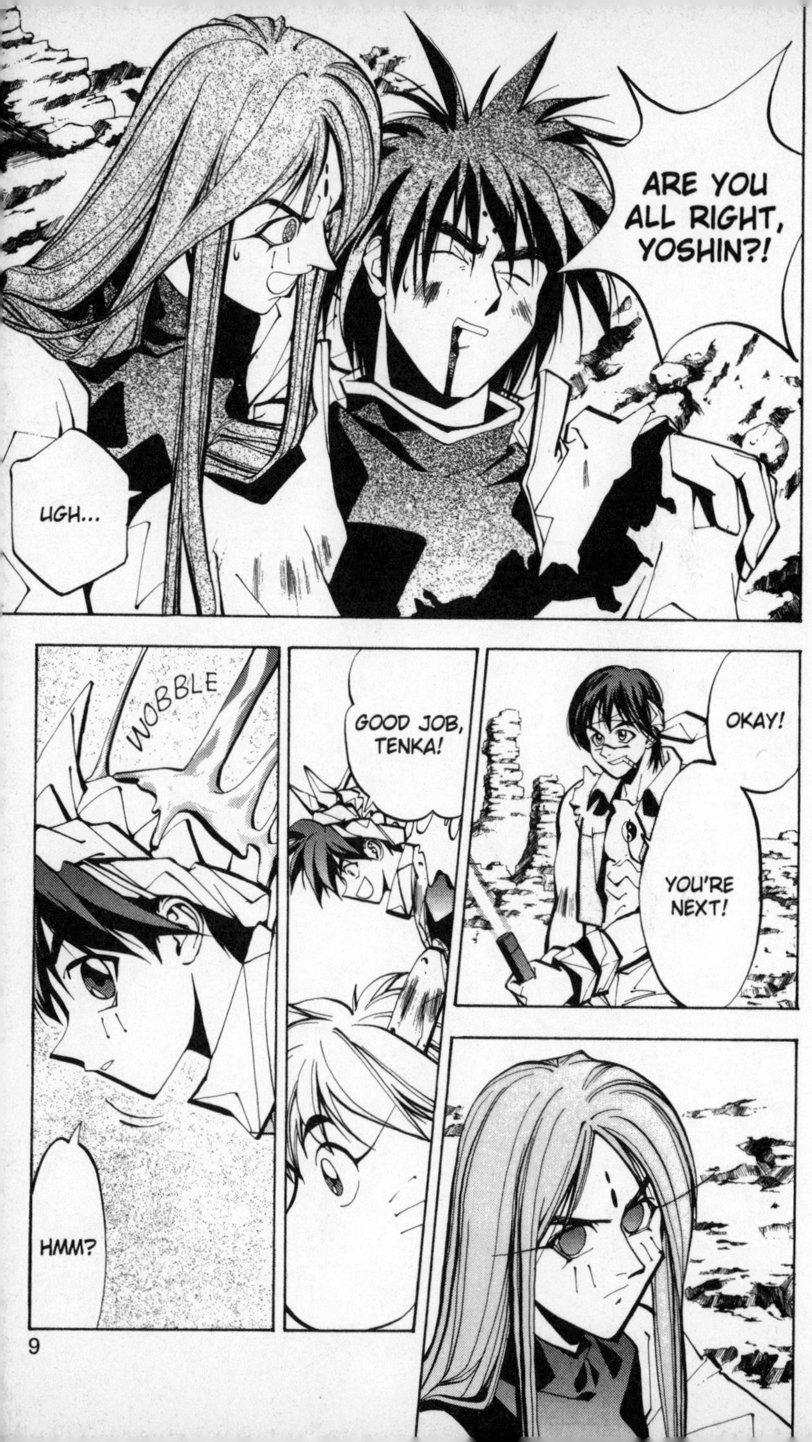
ARE YOU ALL RIGHT, YOSHIN?!
UGH...
OKAY!
YOU'RE NEXT!
GOOD JOB, TENKA!
WOBBLE
HMM?

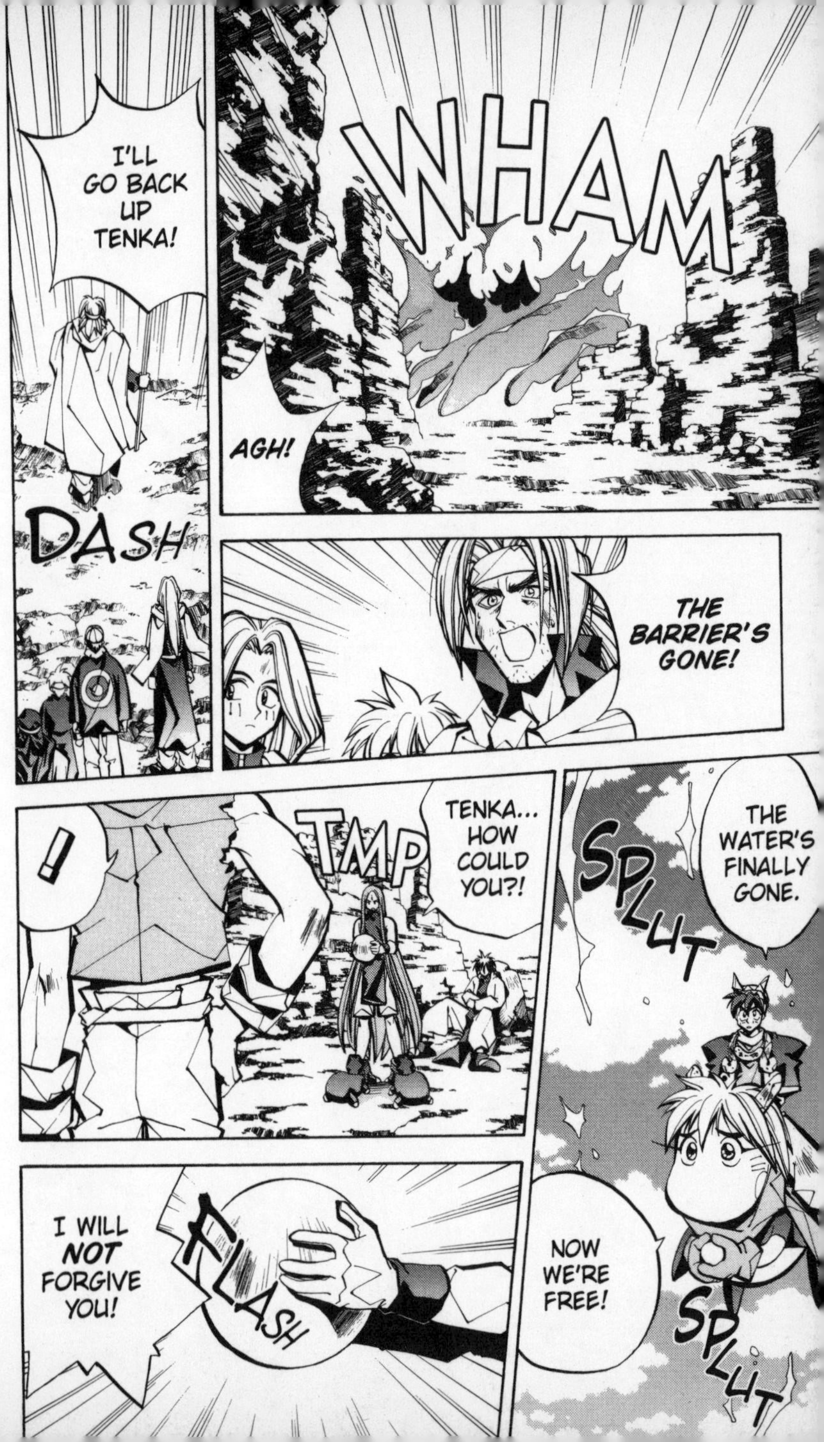
WHAM
AGH!
I'LL GO BACK UP TENKA!
THE BARRIER'S GONE!
DASH
THE WATER'S FINALLY GONE.
SPLUT
NOW WE'RE FREE!
SPLUT
TENKA... HOW COULD YOU?!
TMP
!
FLASH
I WILL *NOT* FORGIVE YOU!

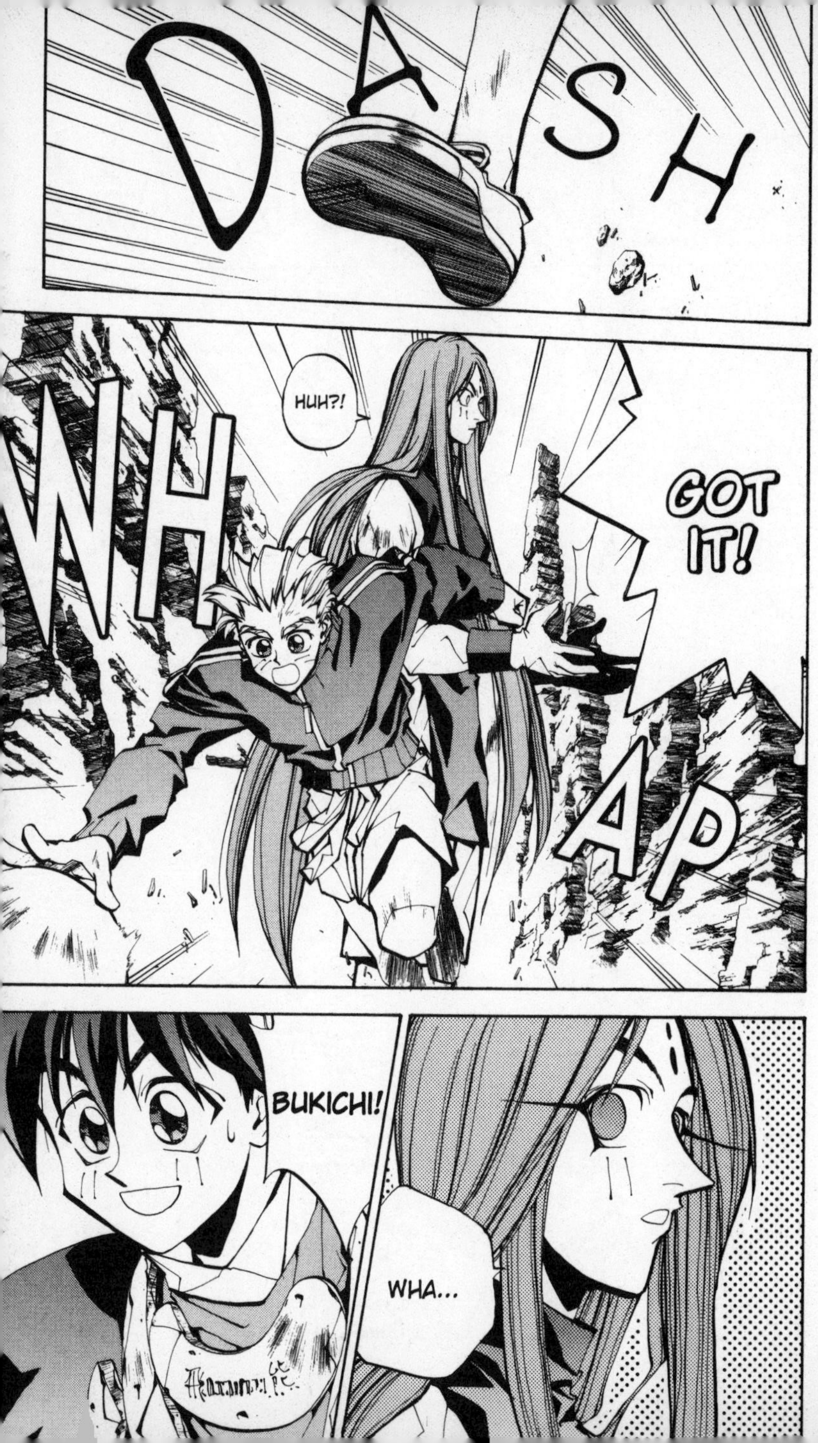
DASH
GOT IT!
HUH?!
WHAP
WHA...
BUKICHI!

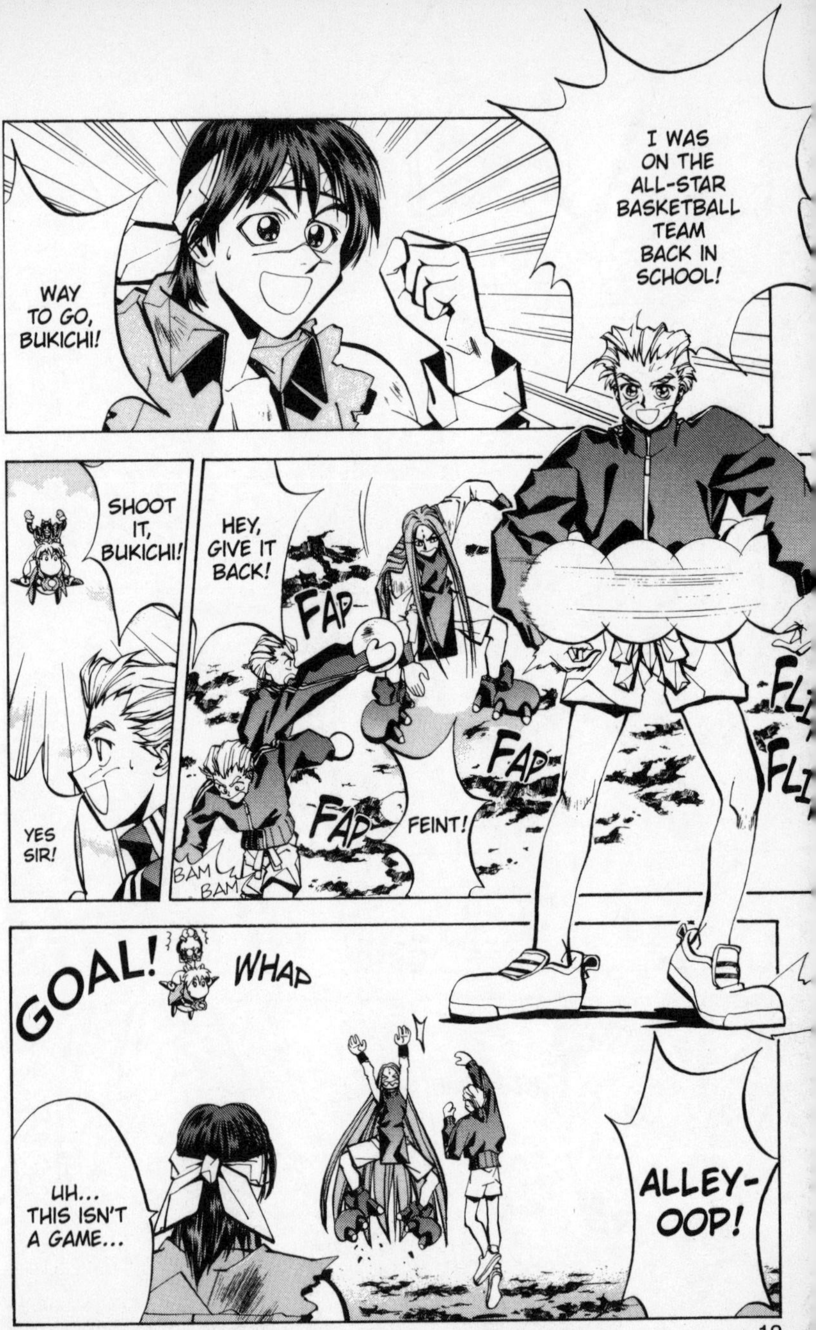
I WAS ON THE ALL-STAR BASKETBALL TEAM BACK IN SCHOOL!
WAY TO GO, BUKICHI!
HEY, GIVE IT BACK!
FAP
FAP
FAP
FEINT!
BAM BAM
SHOOT IT, BUKICHI!
YES SIR!
ALLEY-OOP!
WHAP
GOAL!
UH... THIS ISN'T A GAME...

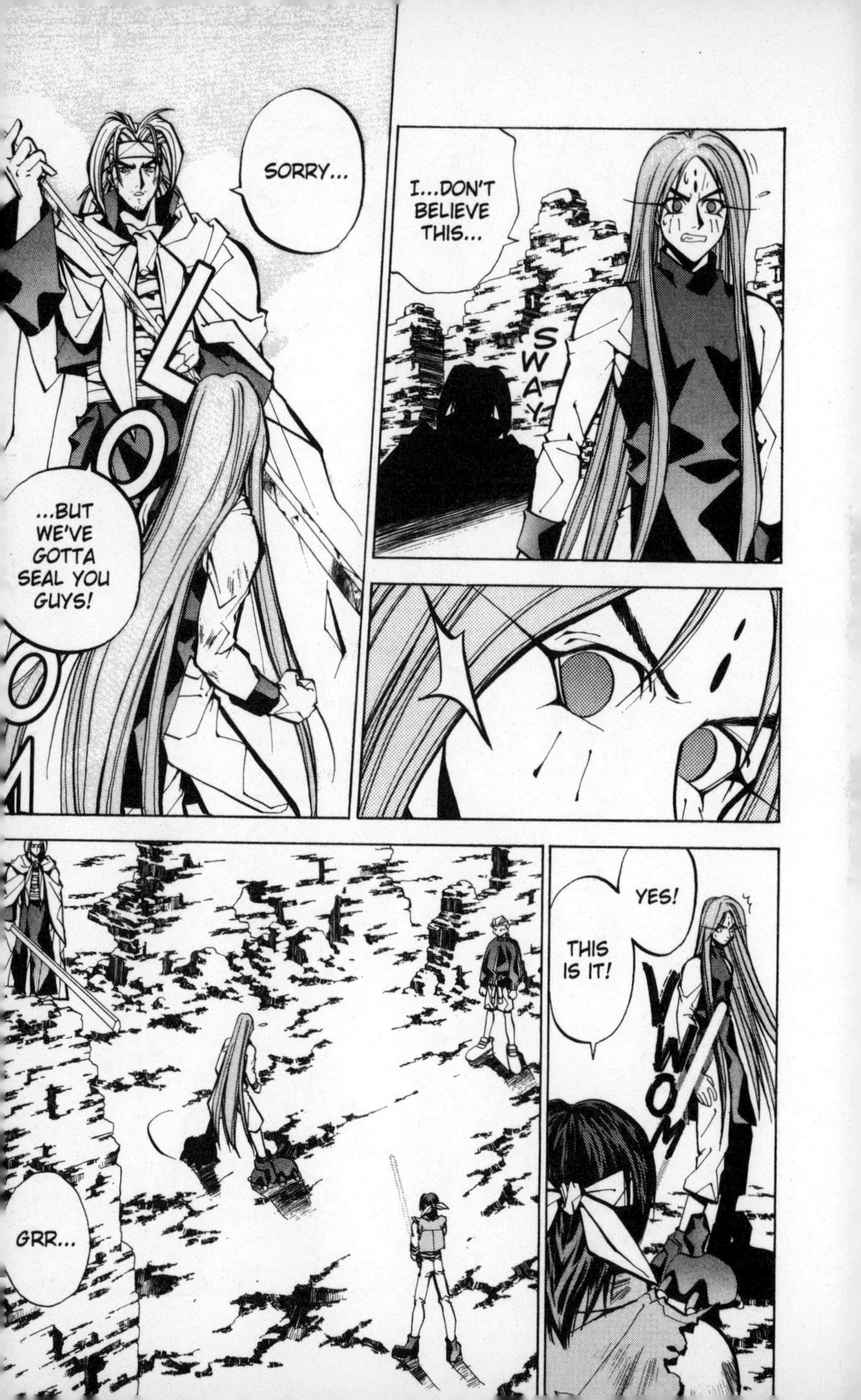
I...DON'T BELIEVE THIS...
SWAY
SORRY...
...BUT WE'VE GOTTA SEAL YOU GUYS!
YES!
THIS IS IT!
VWOM
GRR...

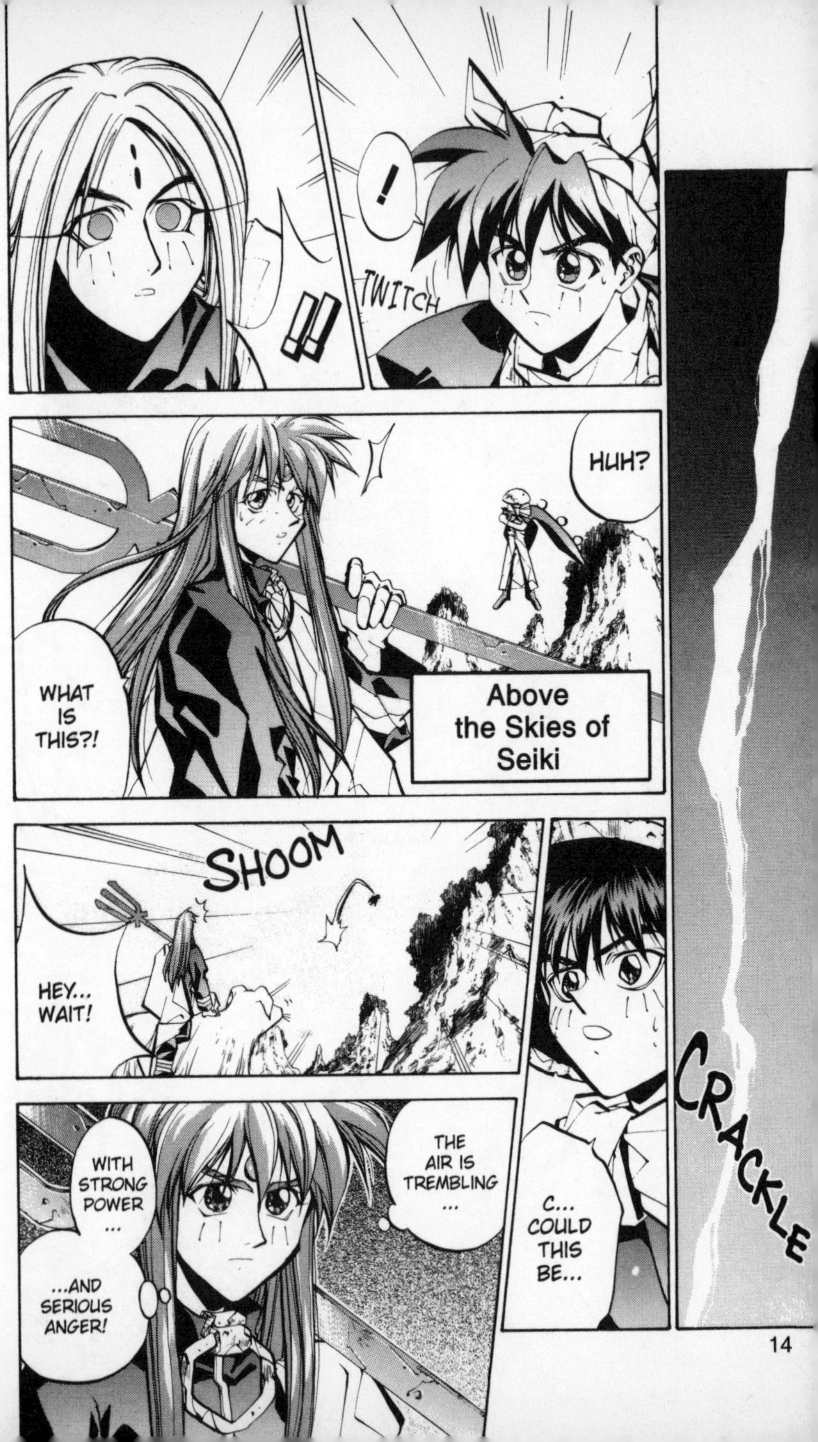
CRACKLE
!
TWITCH
!!
HUH?
Above the Skies of Seiki
WHAT IS THIS?!
C... COULD THIS BE...
SHOOM
HEY... WAIT!
THE AIR IS TREMBLING ...
WITH STRONG POWER ...
...AND SERIOUS ANGER!

READ THIS WAY

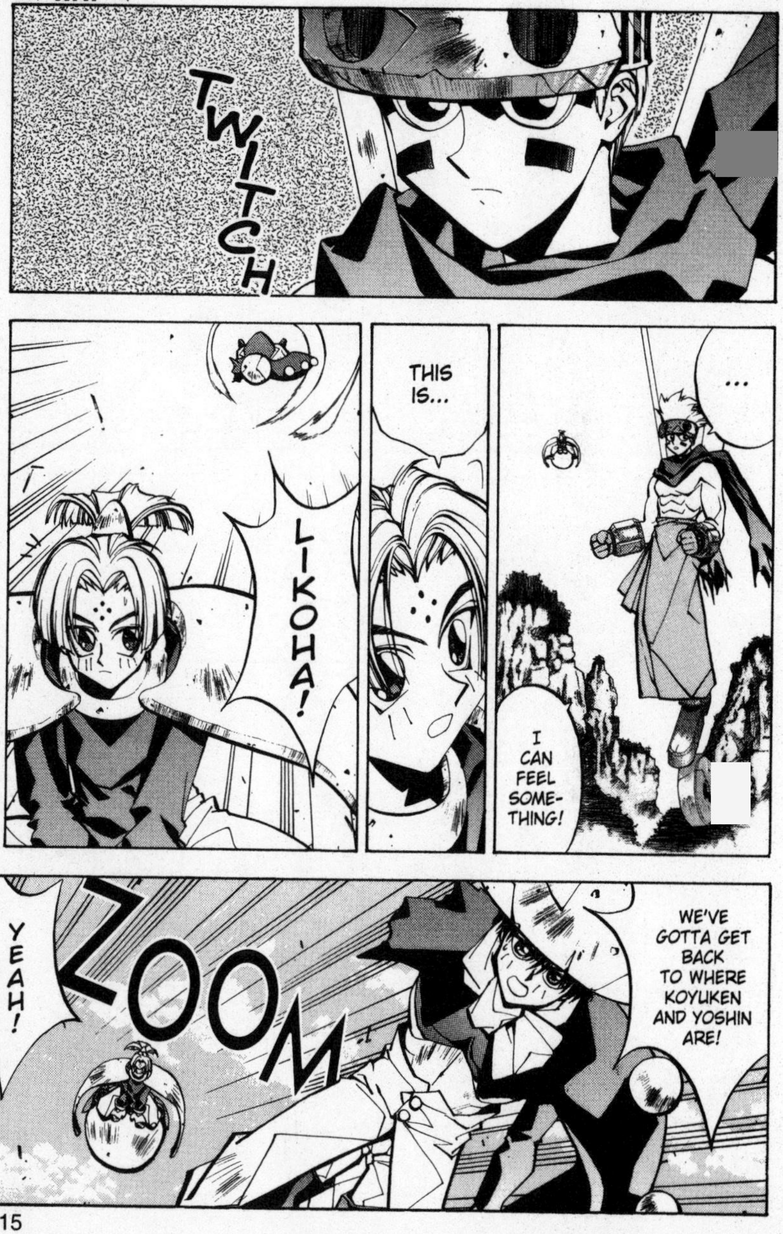
TWITCH
...
I CAN FEEL SOME-THING!
THIS IS...
LIKOHA!
WE'VE GOTTA GET BACK TO WHERE KOYUKEN AND YOSHIN ARE!
ZOOM
YEAH!

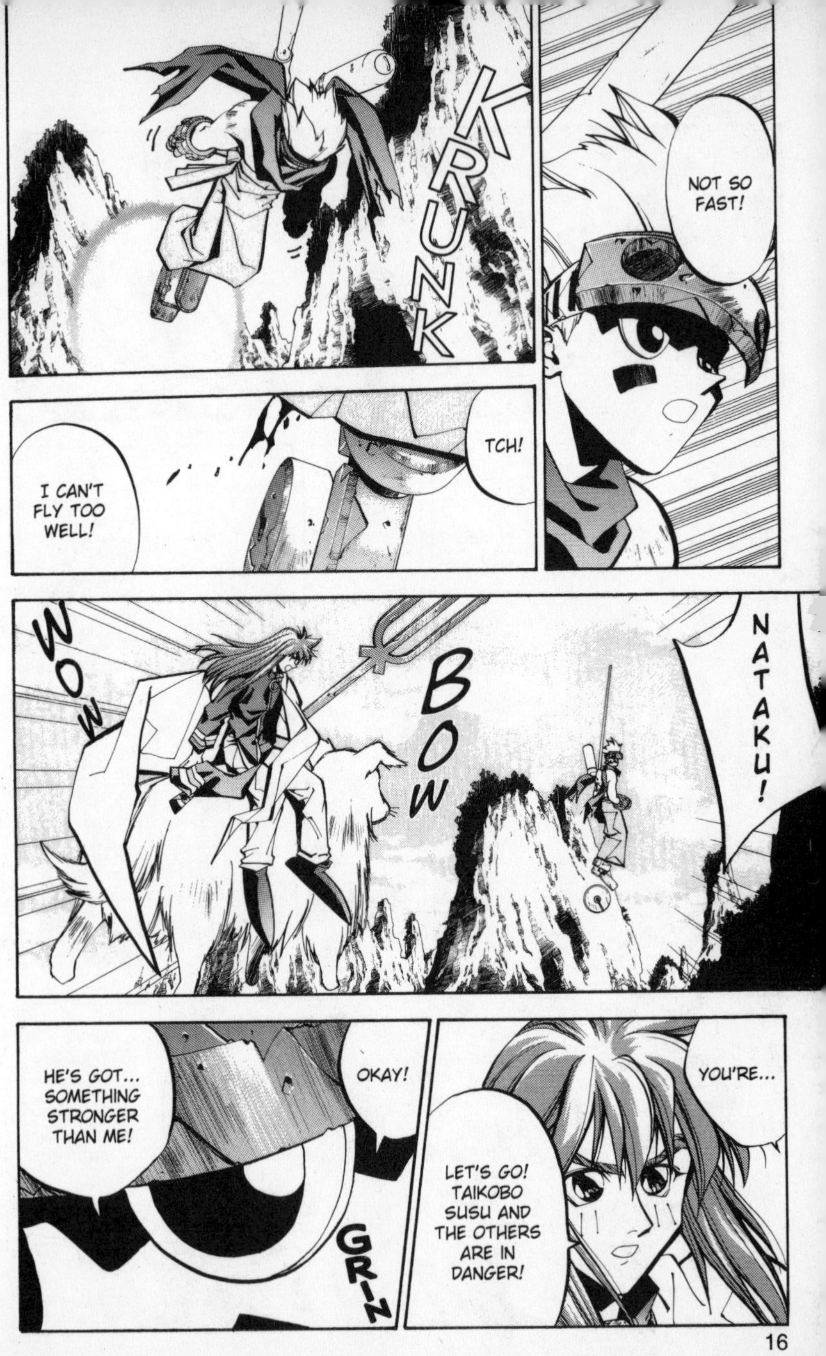
NOT SO FAST!
KRUNK
TCH!
I CAN'T FLY TOO WELL!
NATAKU!
BOW WOW
YOU'RE...
LET'S GO! TAIKOBO SUSU AND THE OTHERS ARE IN DANGER!
OKAY!
HE'S GOT... SOMETHING STRONGER THAN ME!
GRIN

READ THIS WAY

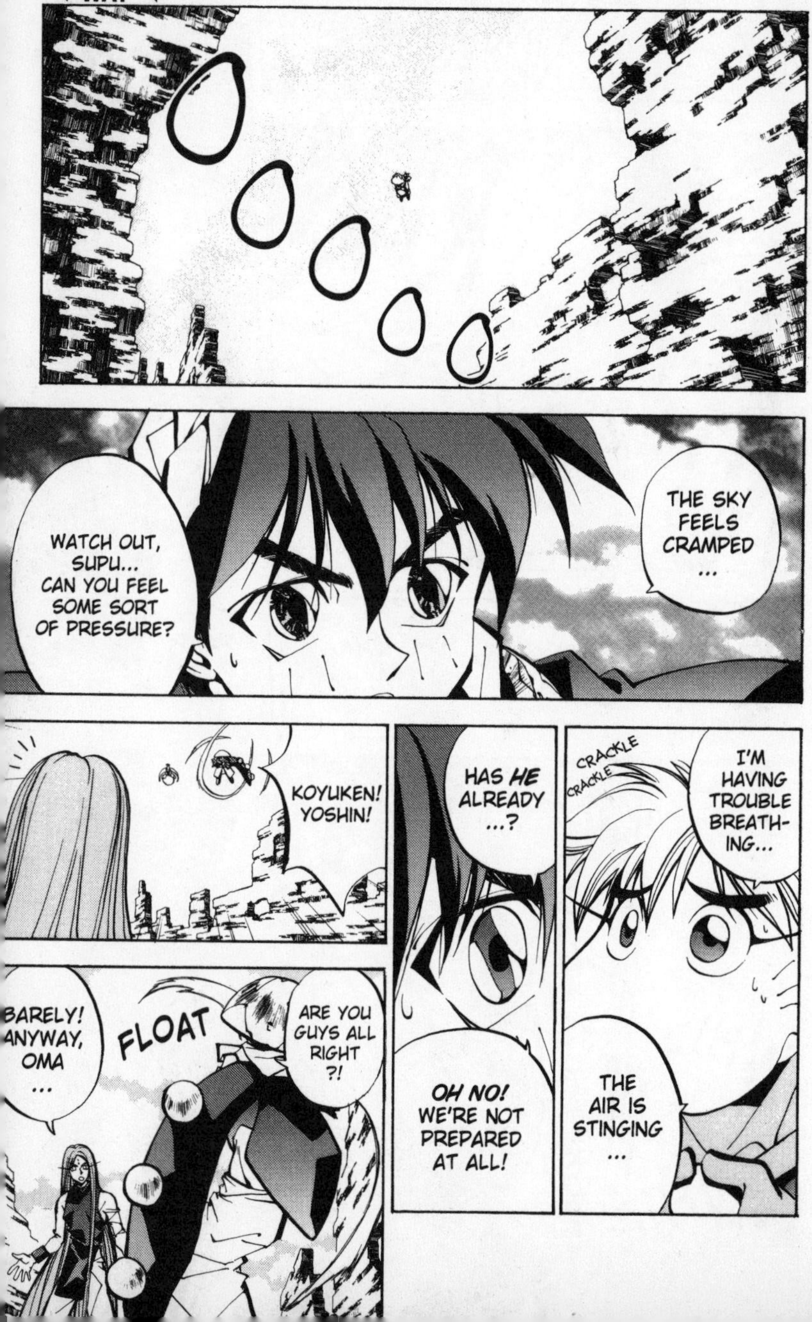
THE SKY FEELS CRAMPED ...
WATCH OUT, SUPU... CAN YOU FEEL SOME SORT OF PRESSURE?
I'M HAVING TROUBLE BREATHING...
CRACKLE CRACKLE
THE AIR IS STINGING ...
HAS *HE* ALREADY ...?
OH NO! WE'RE NOT PREPARED AT ALL!
KOYUKEN! YOSHIN!
ARE YOU GUYS ALL RIGHT ?!
FLOAT
BARELY! ANYWAY, OMA ...

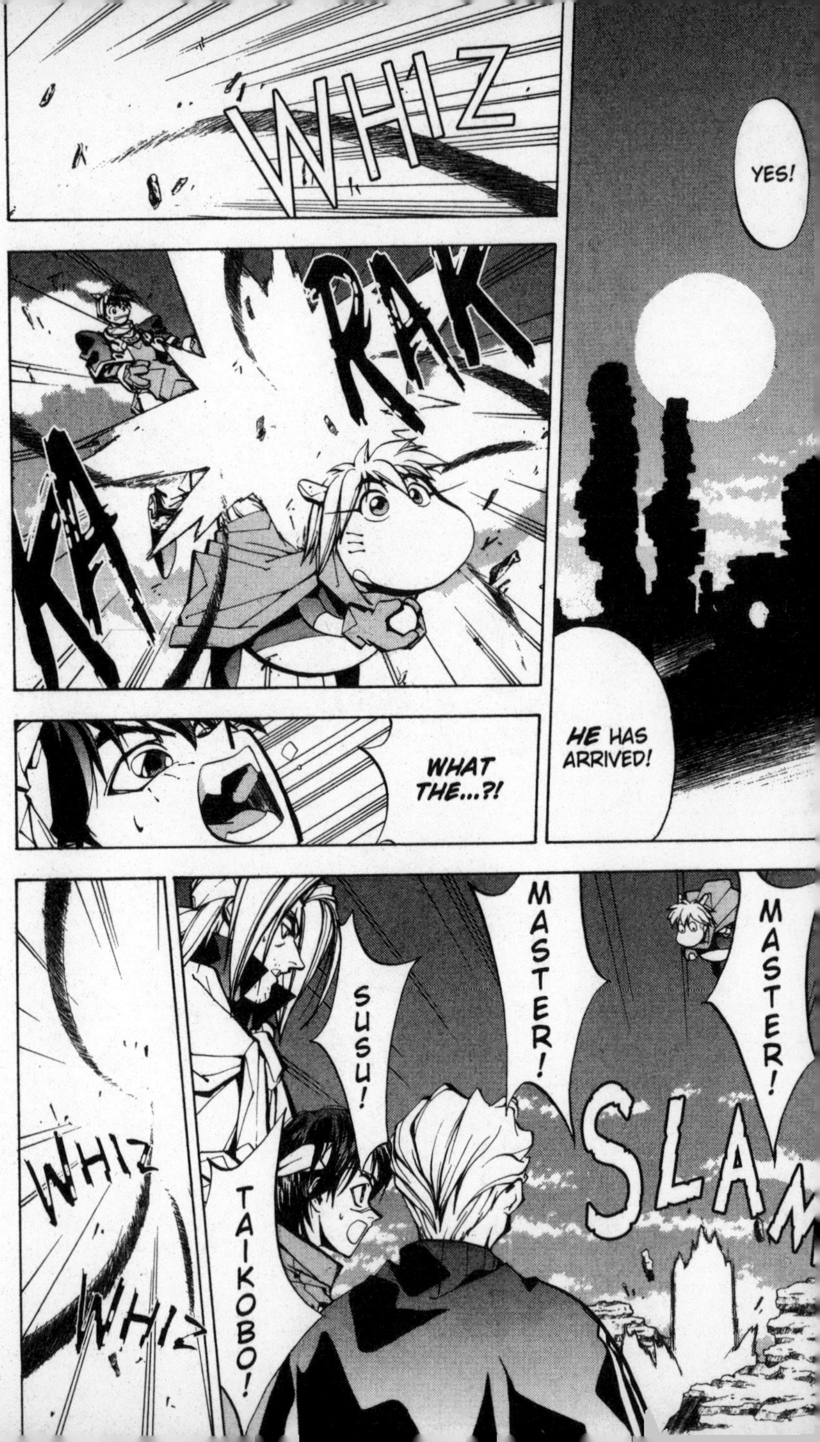
YES!
HE HAS ARRIVED!
WHIZ
RAK
KA
WHAT THE...?!
MASTER!
SLAM
MASTER!
SUSU!
TAIKOBO!
WHIZ
WHIZ

READ THIS WAY

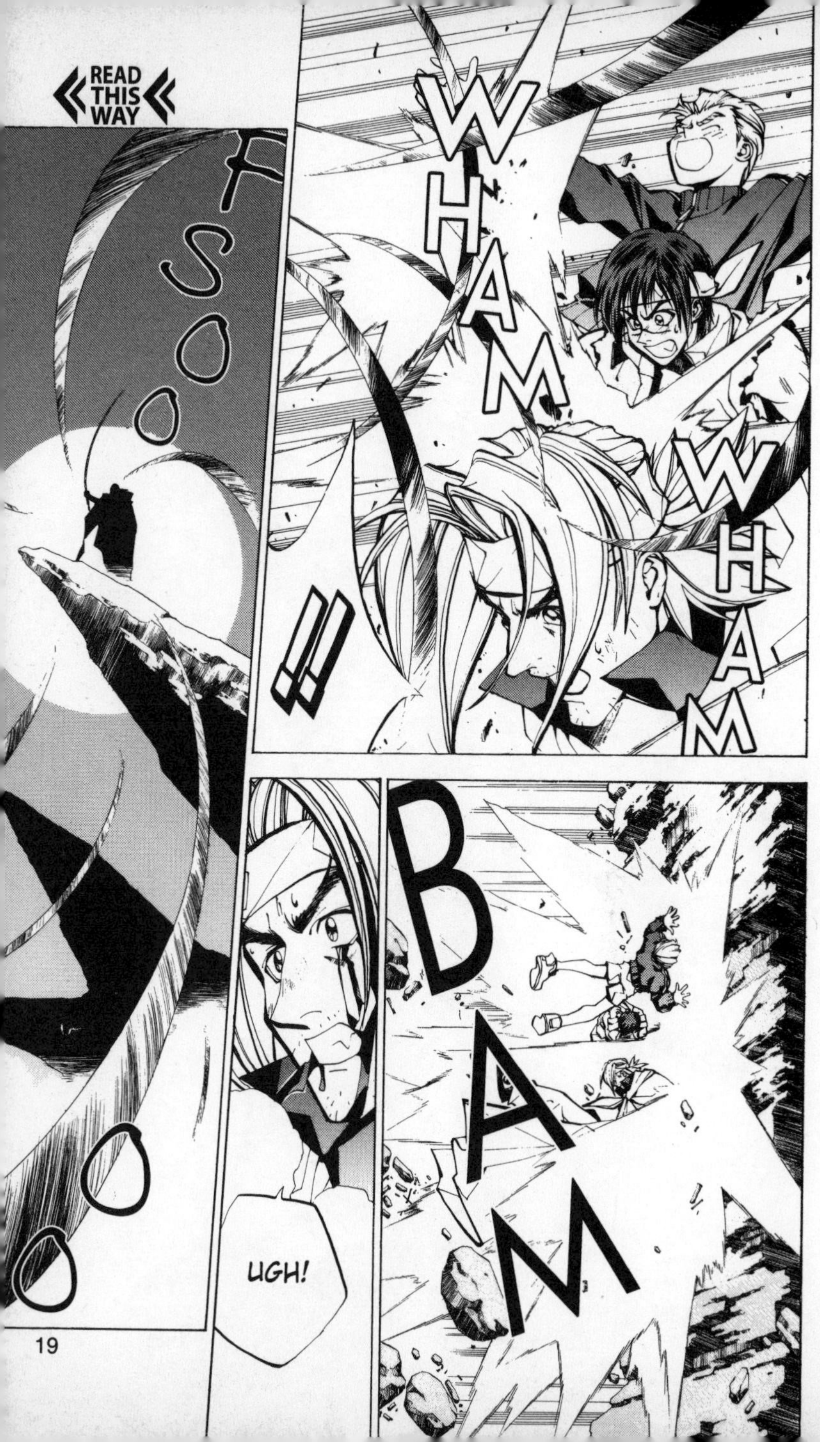

WHAM
WHAM
!!
BAM
UGH!
FSOOOOO

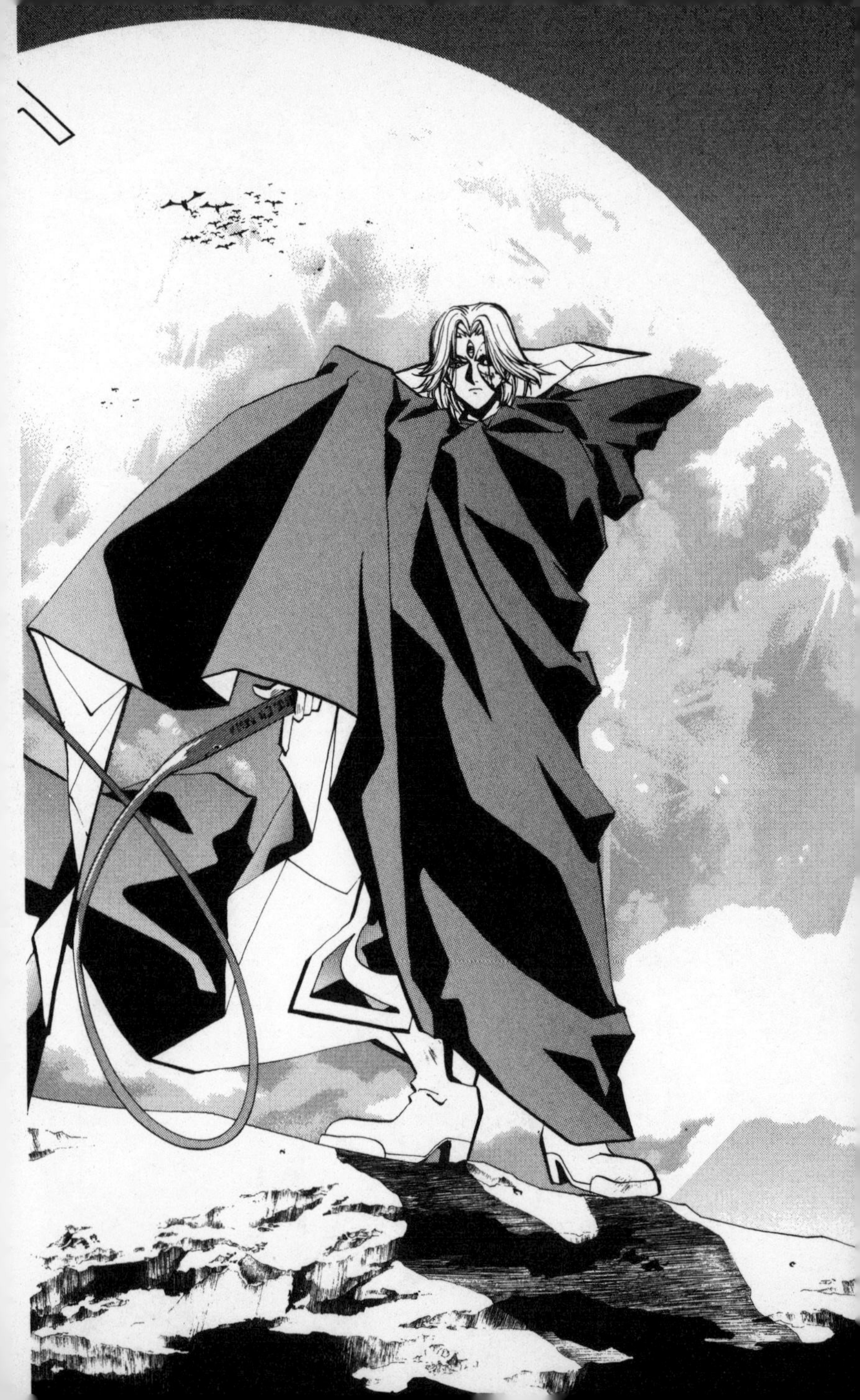

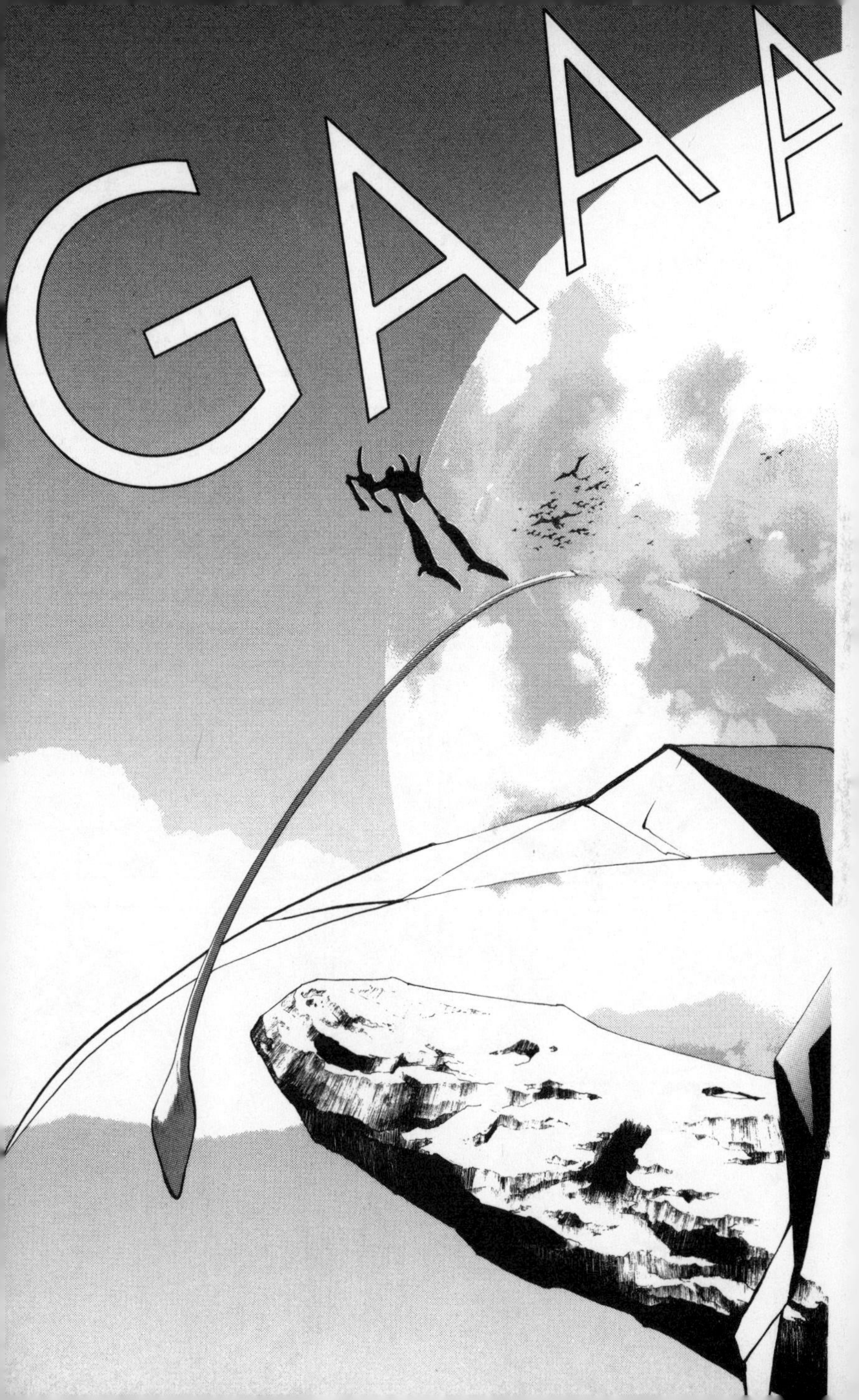
GAAA

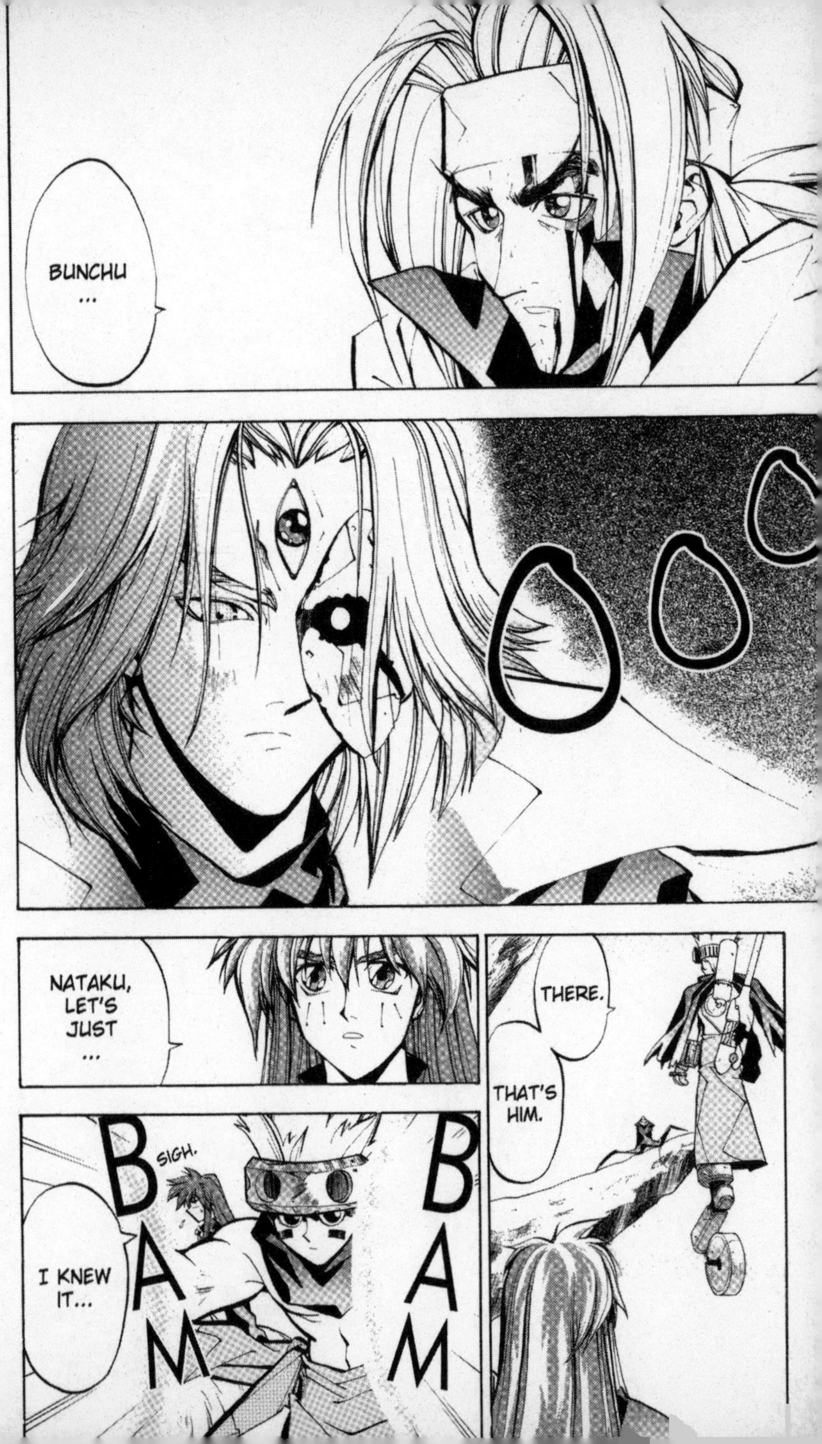
BUNCHU ...
THERE.
THAT'S HIM.
NATAKU, LET'S JUST ...
BAM
SIGH.
I KNEW IT...
BAM

READ THIS WAY

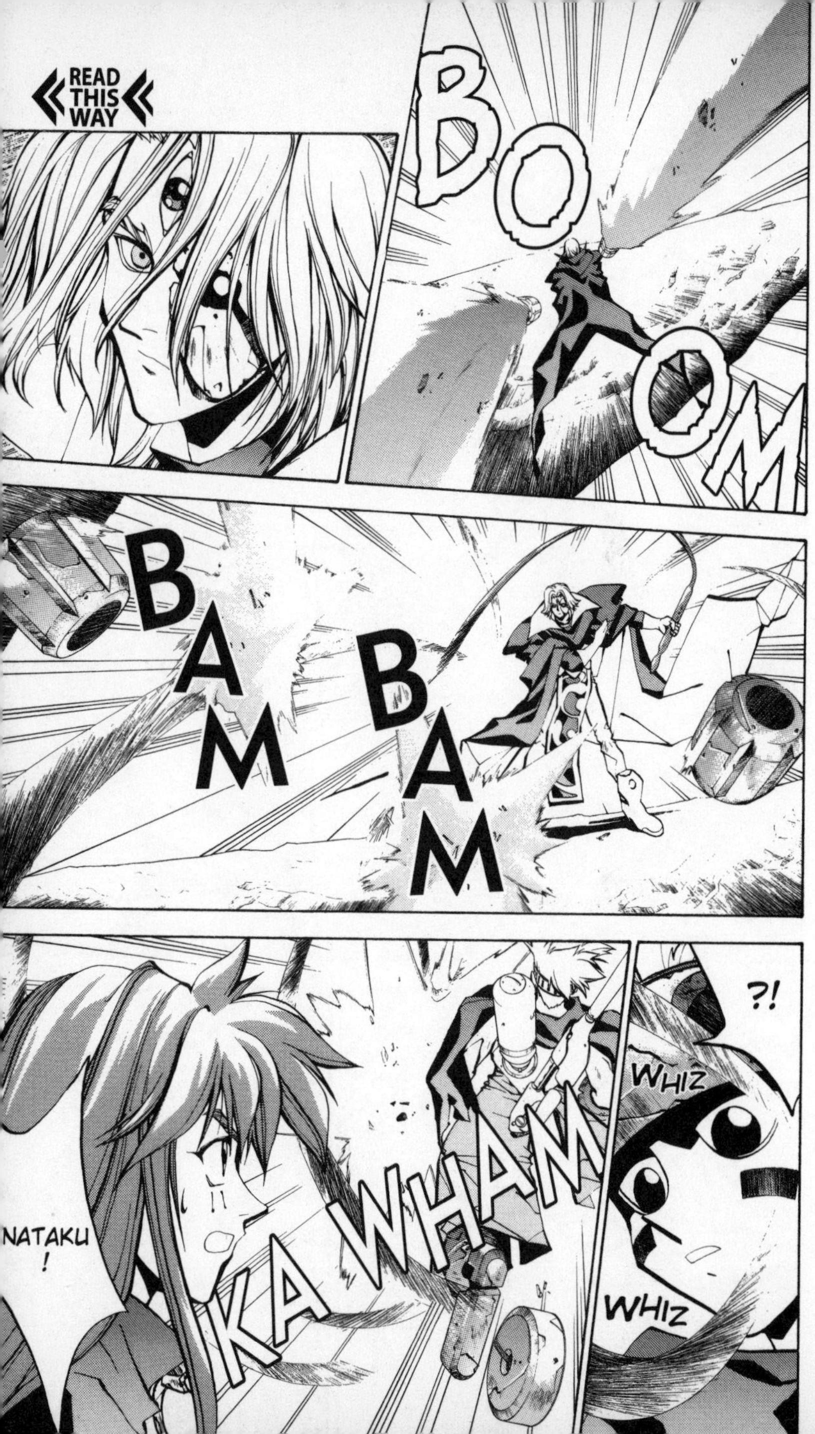
BOOM
BAM BAM
?!
WHIZ
WHIZ
KA WHAM
NATAKU!

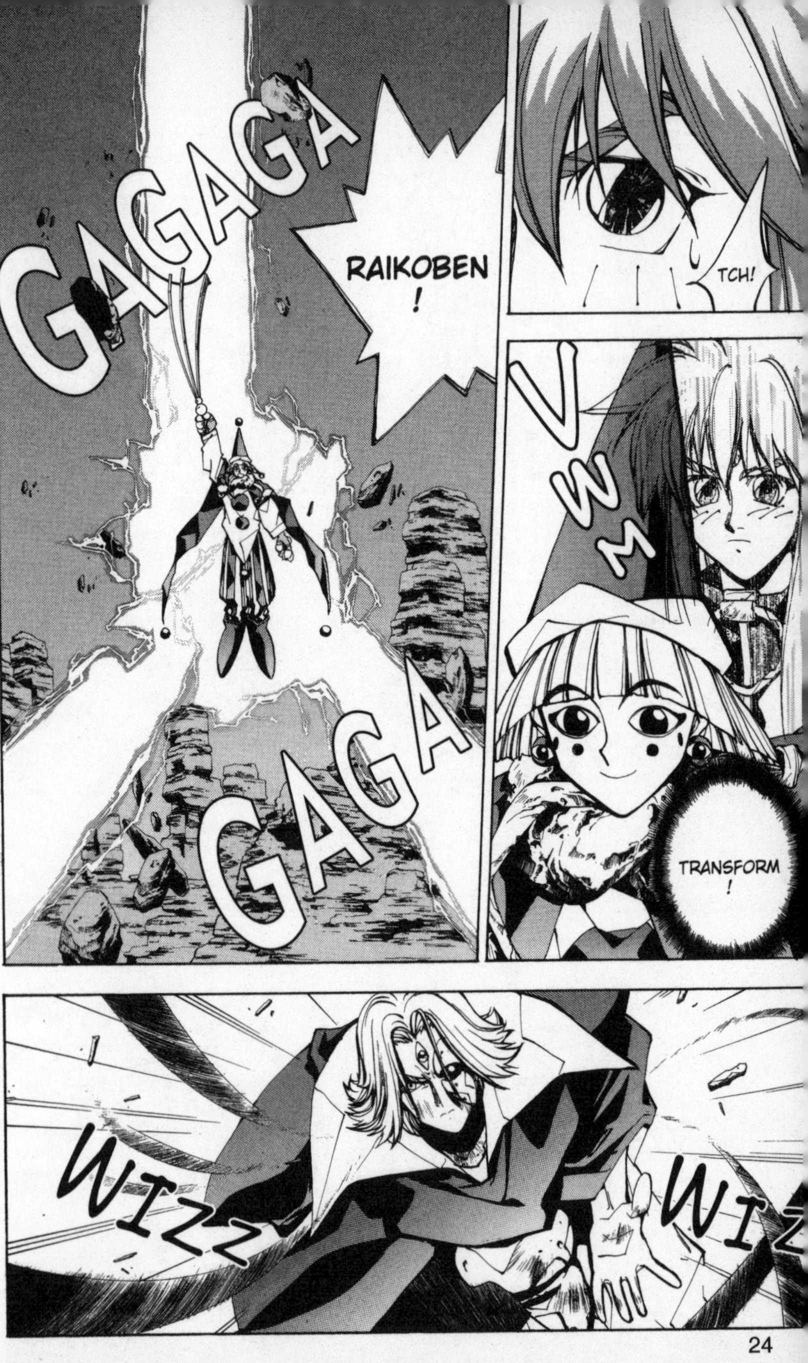
TCH!
VWM
TRANSFORM!
GAGAGA
RAIKOBEN!
GAGA
WIZ
WIZZ

READ THIS WAY

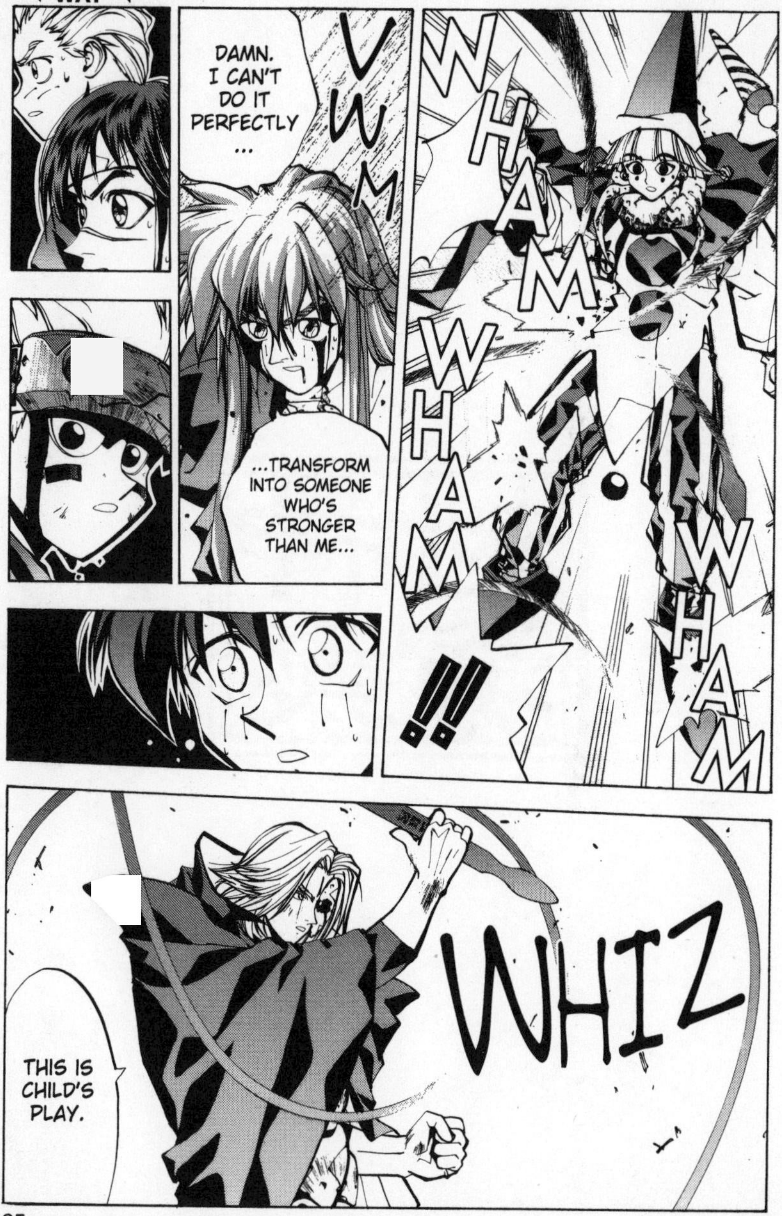
WHAM
WHAM!!
WHAM
VWM
DAMN. I CAN'T DO IT PERFECTLY ...
...TRANSFORM INTO SOMEONE WHO'S STRONGER THAN ME...
WHIZ
THIS IS CHILD'S PLAY.

封神演義

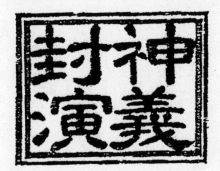

Chapter 44
THE TAISHI OF YIN

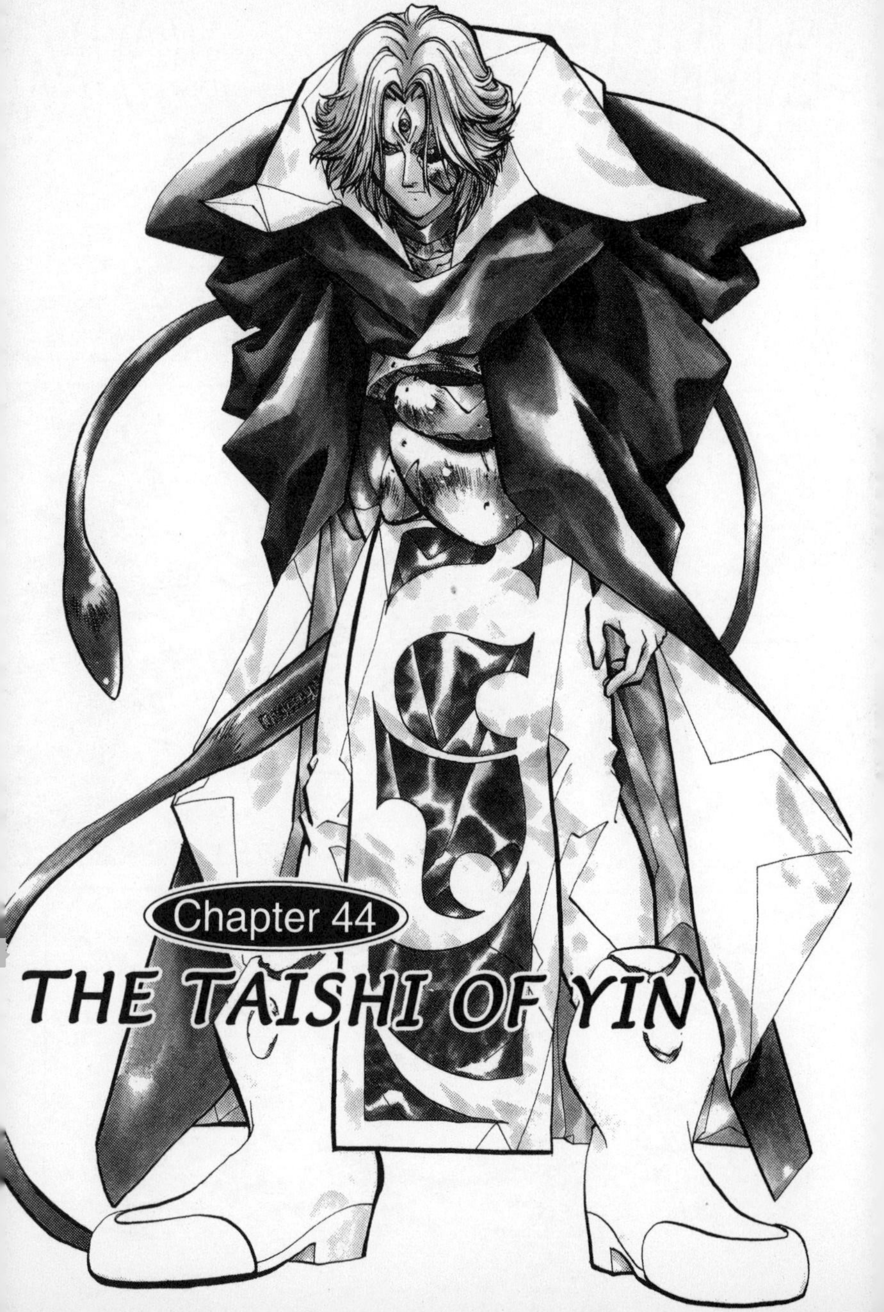

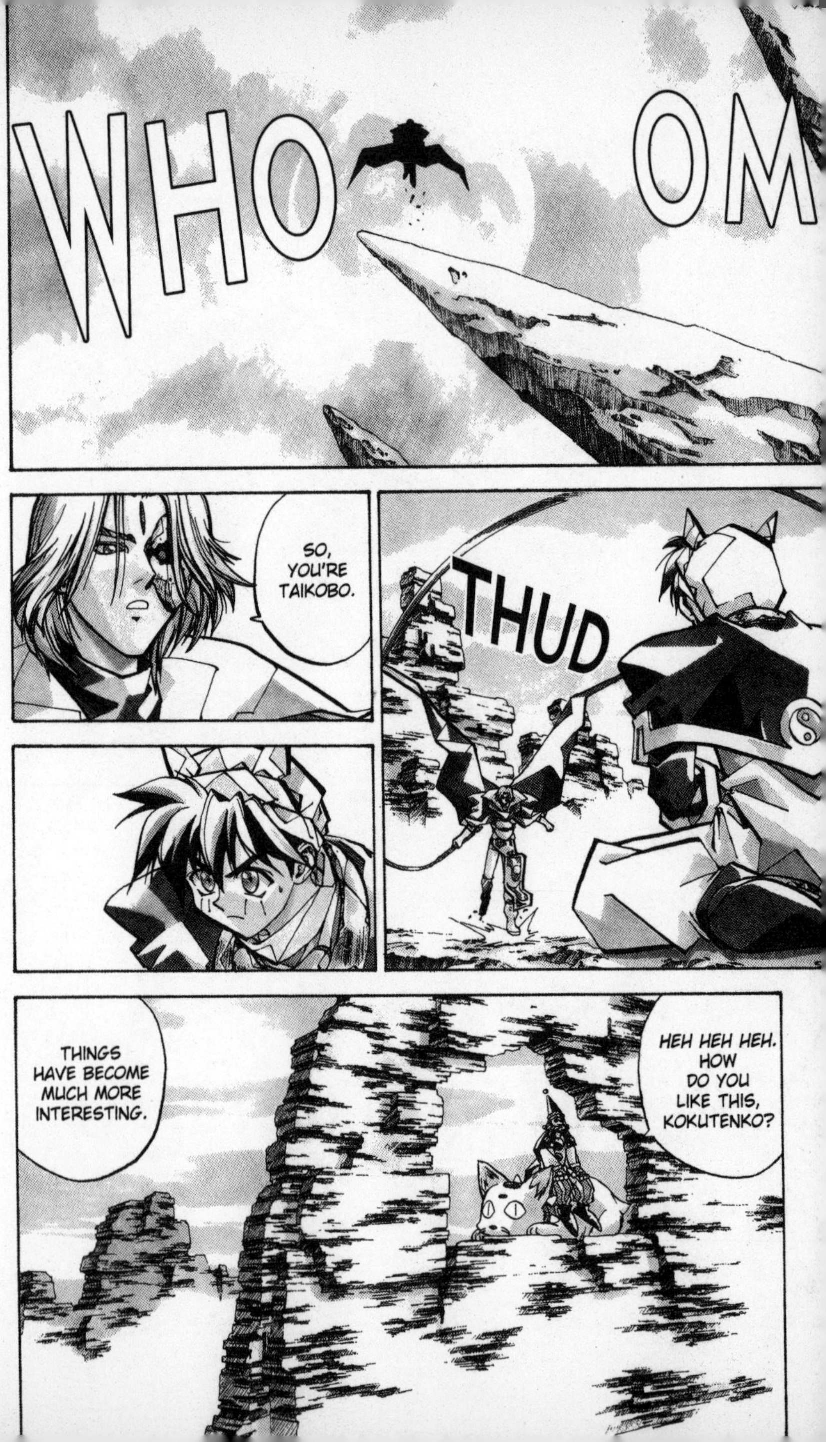
WHOOM
THUD
SO, YOU'RE TAIKOBO.
HEH HEH HEH. HOW DO YOU LIKE THIS, KOKUTENKO?
THINGS HAVE BECOME MUCH MORE INTERESTING.

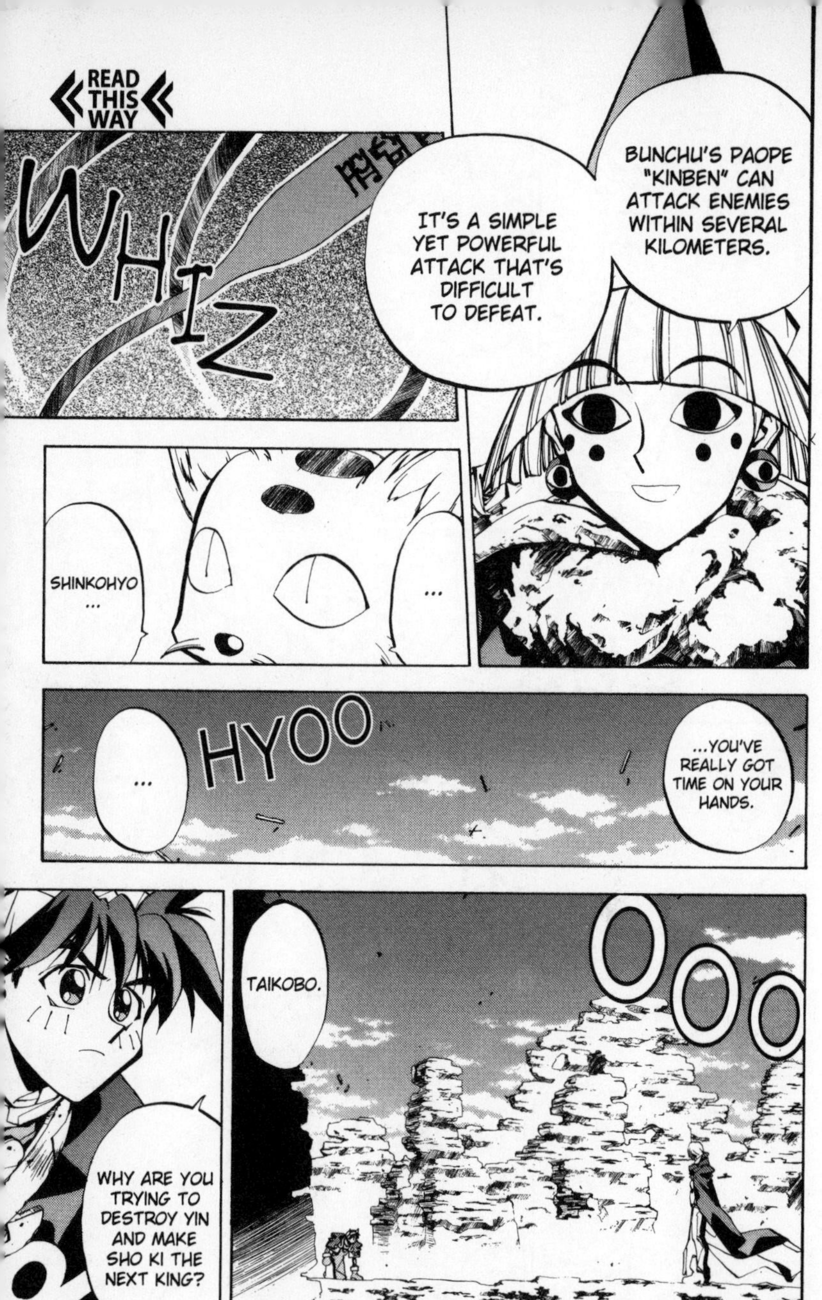
READ THIS WAY
BUNCHU'S PAOPE "KINBEN" CAN ATTACK ENEMIES WITHIN SEVERAL KILOMETERS.
IT'S A SIMPLE YET POWERFUL ATTACK THAT'S DIFFICULT TO DEFEAT.
WHIZ
...
SHINKOHYO ...
...YOU'VE REALLY GOT TIME ON YOUR HANDS.
HYOO
...
OOO
TAIKOBO.
WHY ARE YOU TRYING TO DESTROY YIN AND MAKE SHO KI THE NEXT KING?

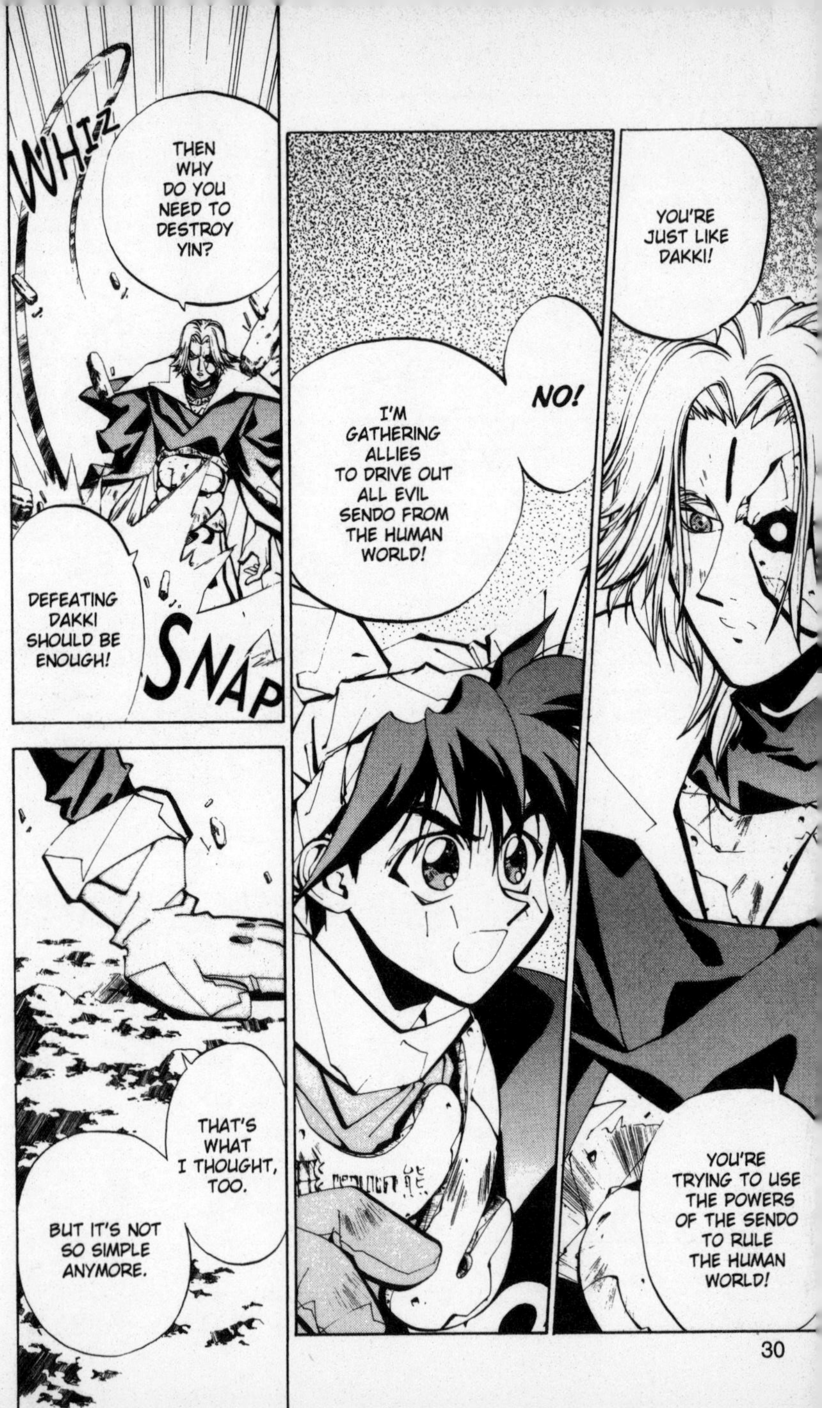
YOU'RE JUST LIKE DAKKI!
YOU'RE TRYING TO USE THE POWERS OF THE SENDO TO RULE THE HUMAN WORLD!
NO!
I'M GATHERING ALLIES TO DRIVE OUT ALL EVIL SENDO FROM THE HUMAN WORLD!
THEN WHY DO YOU NEED TO DESTROY YIN?
WHIZ
DEFEATING DAKKI SHOULD BE ENOUGH!
SNAP
THAT'S WHAT I THOUGHT, TOO.
BUT IT'S NOT SO SIMPLE ANYMORE.

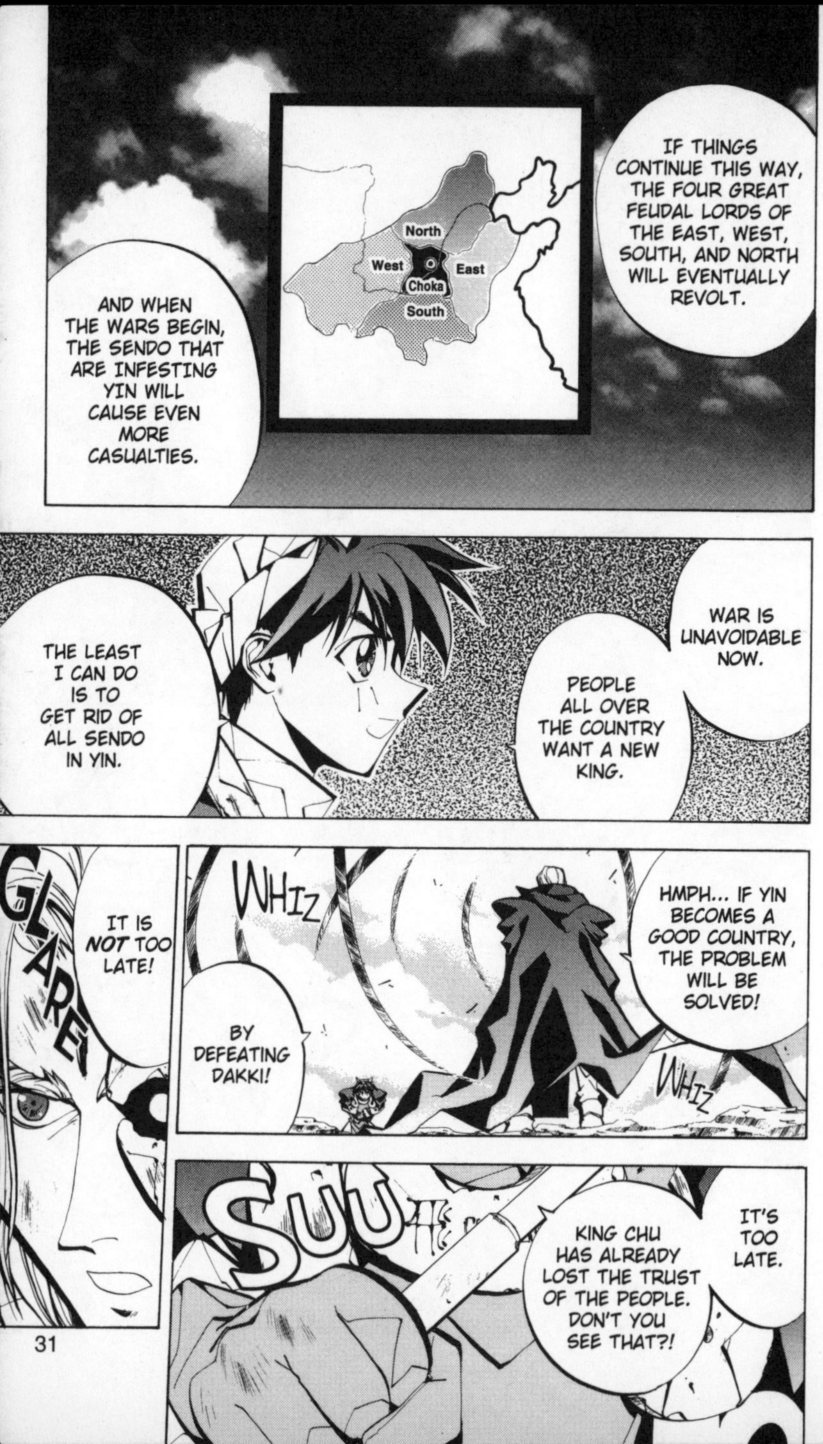
IF THINGS CONTINUE THIS WAY, THE FOUR GREAT FEUDAL LORDS OF THE EAST, WEST, SOUTH, AND NORTH WILL EVENTUALLY REVOLT.
North
West
East
Choka
South
AND WHEN THE WARS BEGIN, THE SENDO THAT ARE INFESTING YIN WILL CAUSE EVEN MORE CASUALTIES.
WAR IS UNAVOIDABLE NOW.
PEOPLE ALL OVER THE COUNTRY WANT A NEW KING.
THE LEAST I CAN DO IS TO GET RID OF ALL SENDO IN YIN.
HMPH... IF YIN BECOMES A GOOD COUNTRY, THE PROBLEM WILL BE SOLVED!
WHIZ
WHIZ
BY DEFEATING DAKKI!
IT'S TOO LATE.
KING CHU HAS ALREADY LOST THE TRUST OF THE PEOPLE. DON'T YOU SEE THAT?!
SUUU
GLARE
IT IS *NOT* TOO LATE!

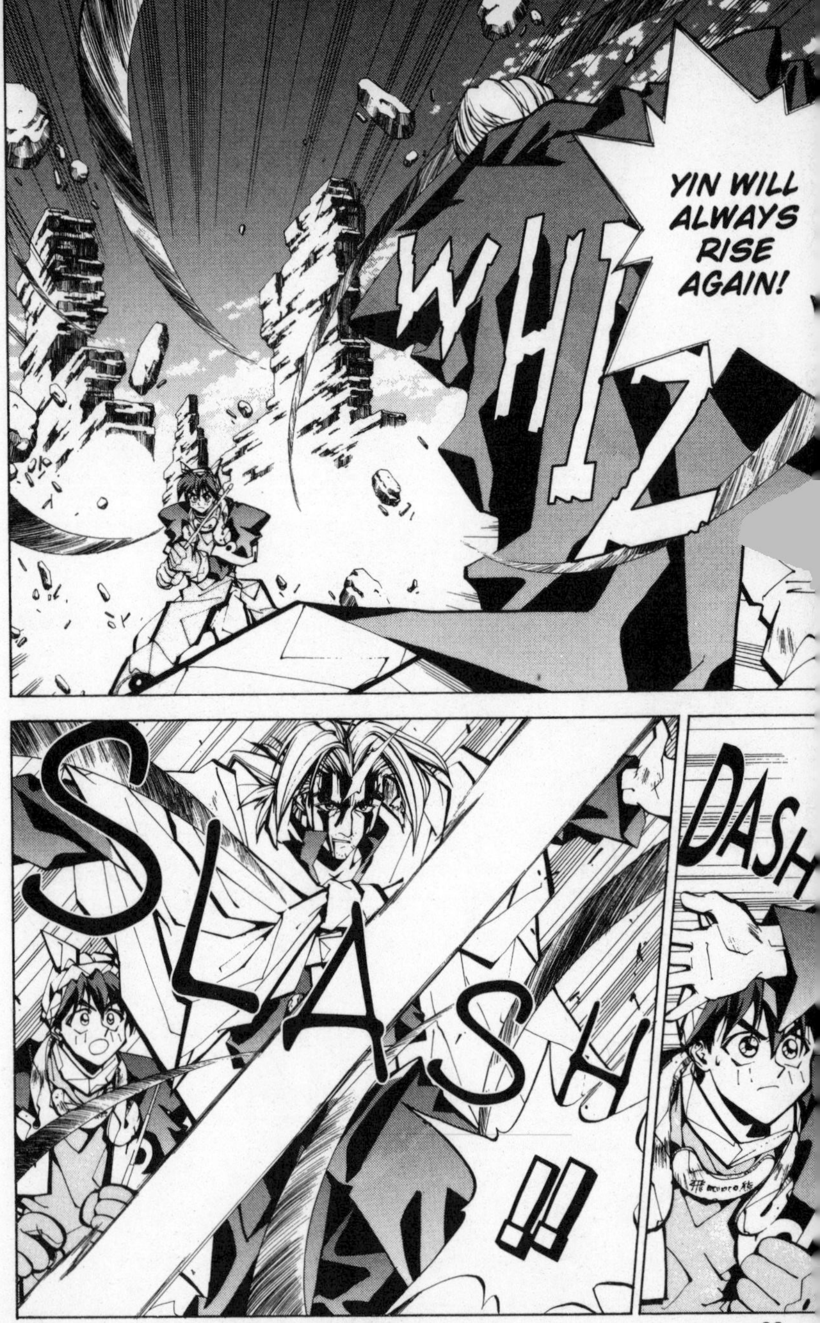
YIN WILL ALWAYS RISE AGAIN!
WHIZ
DASH
SLASH!!

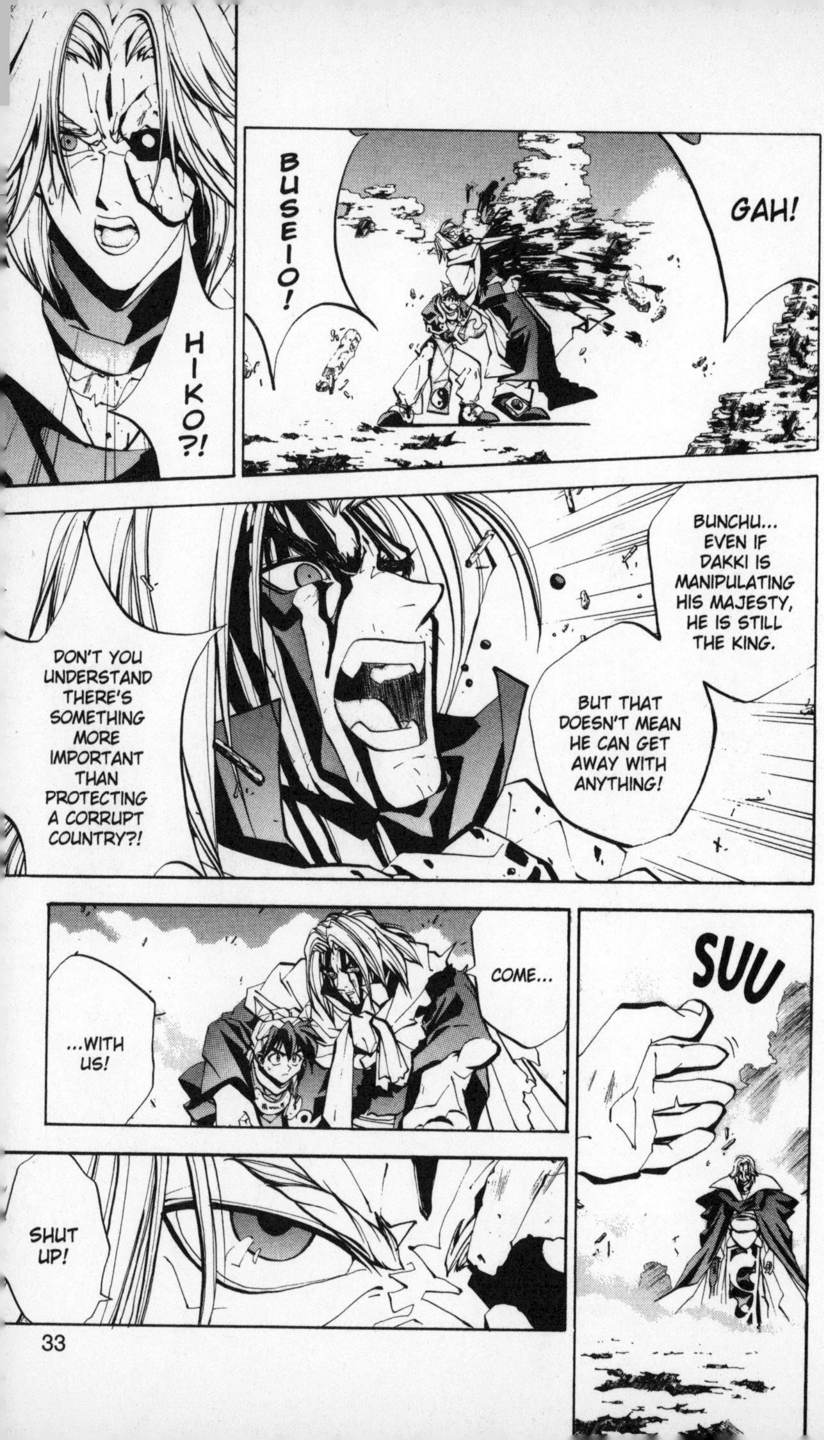
GAH!
BUSEIO!
HIKO?!
BUNCHU... EVEN IF DAKKI IS MANIPULATING HIS MAJESTY, HE IS STILL THE KING.
BUT THAT DOESN'T MEAN HE CAN GET AWAY WITH ANYTHING!
DON'T YOU UNDERSTAND THERE'S SOMETHING MORE IMPORTANT THAN PROTECTING A CORRUPT COUNTRY?!
SUU
COME...
...WITH US!
SHUT UP!

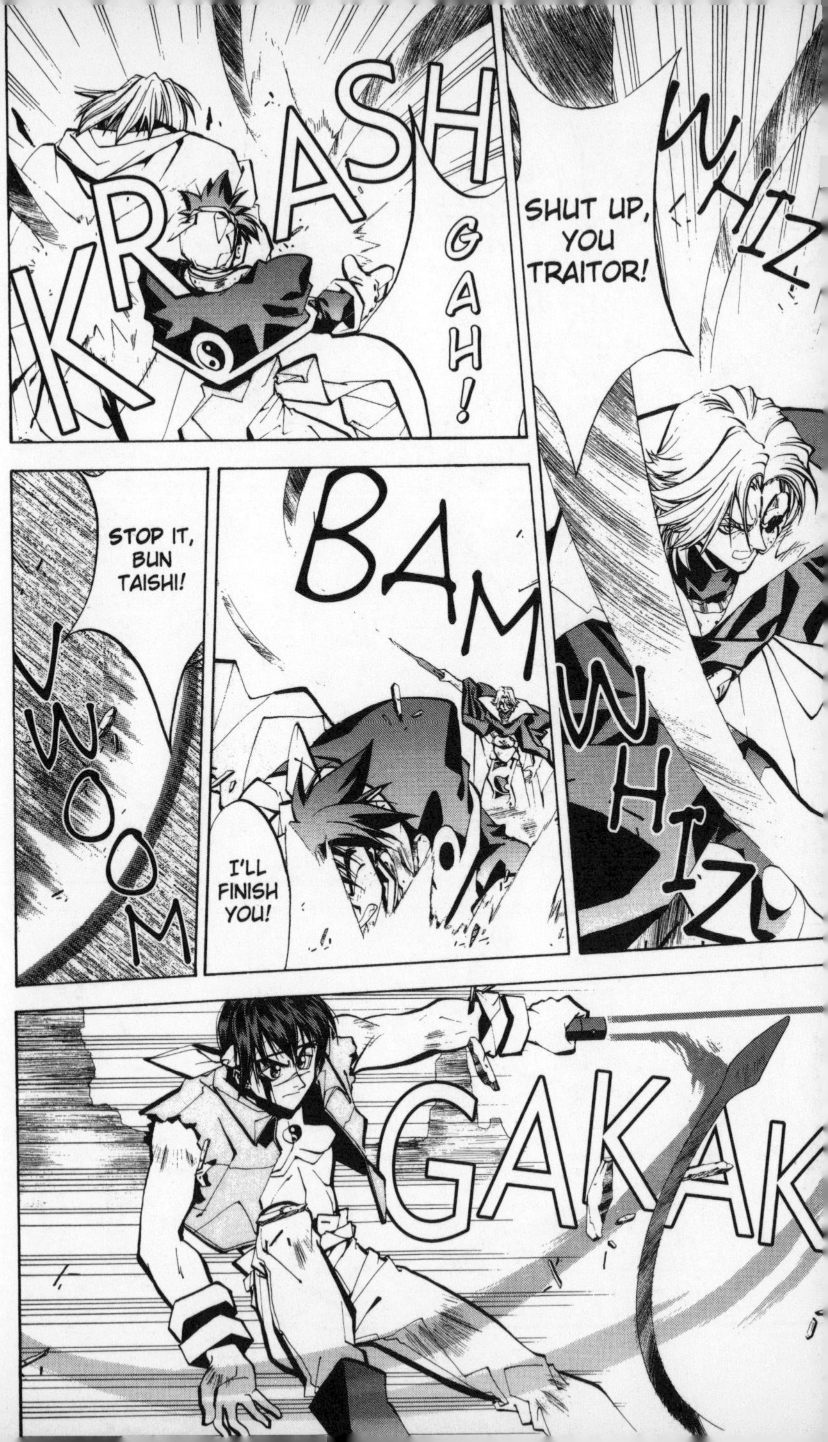
WHIZ
SHUT UP, YOU TRAITOR!
KRASH
GAH!
WHIZ
BAM
I'LL FINISH YOU!
STOP IT, BUN TAISHI!
WOOM
GAKAK

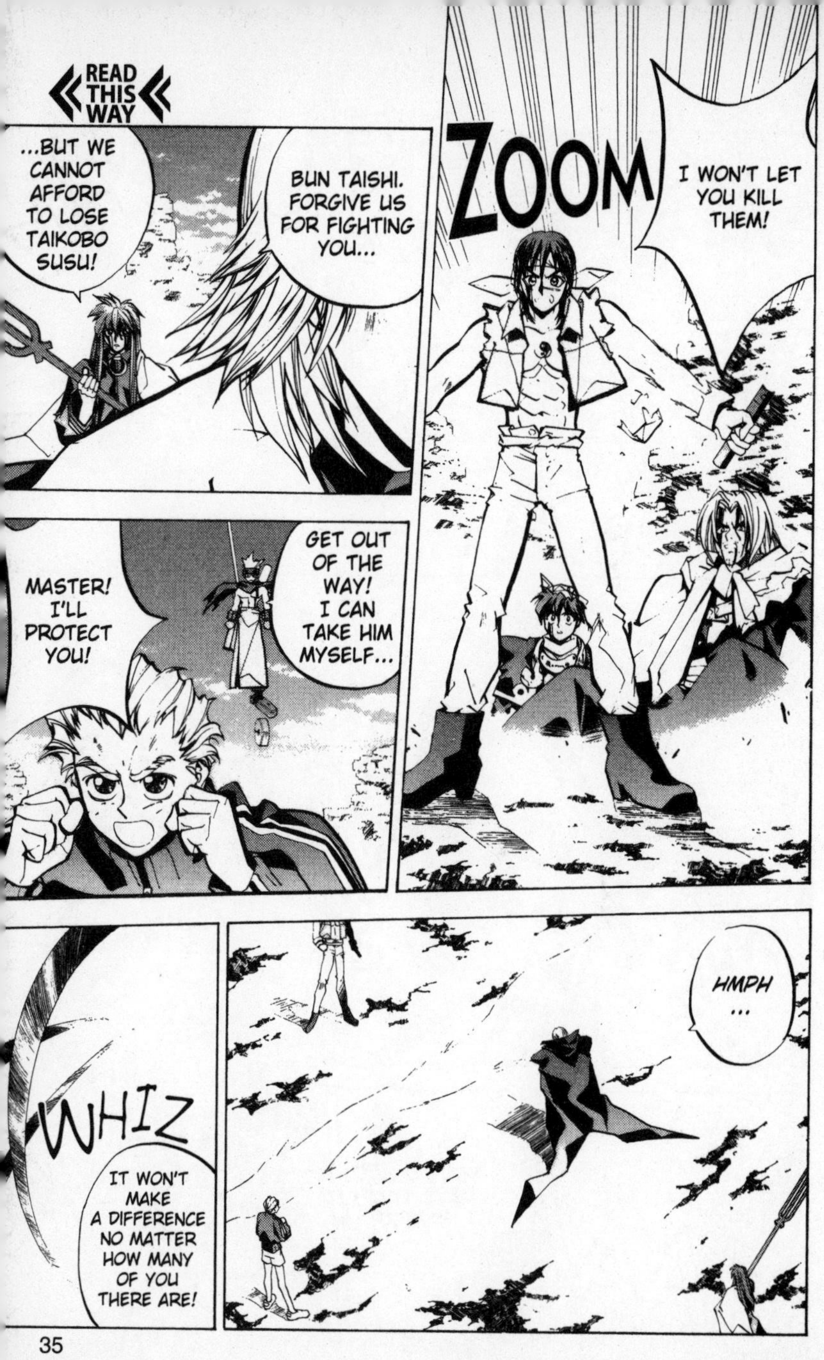
READ THIS WAY
ZOOM
I WON'T LET YOU KILL THEM!
BUN TAISHI. FORGIVE US FOR FIGHTING YOU...
...BUT WE CANNOT AFFORD TO LOSE TAIKOBO SUSU!
GET OUT OF THE WAY! I CAN TAKE HIM MYSELF...
MASTER! I'LL PROTECT YOU!
HMPH ...
WHIZ
IT WON'T MAKE A DIFFERENCE NO MATTER HOW MANY OF YOU THERE ARE!

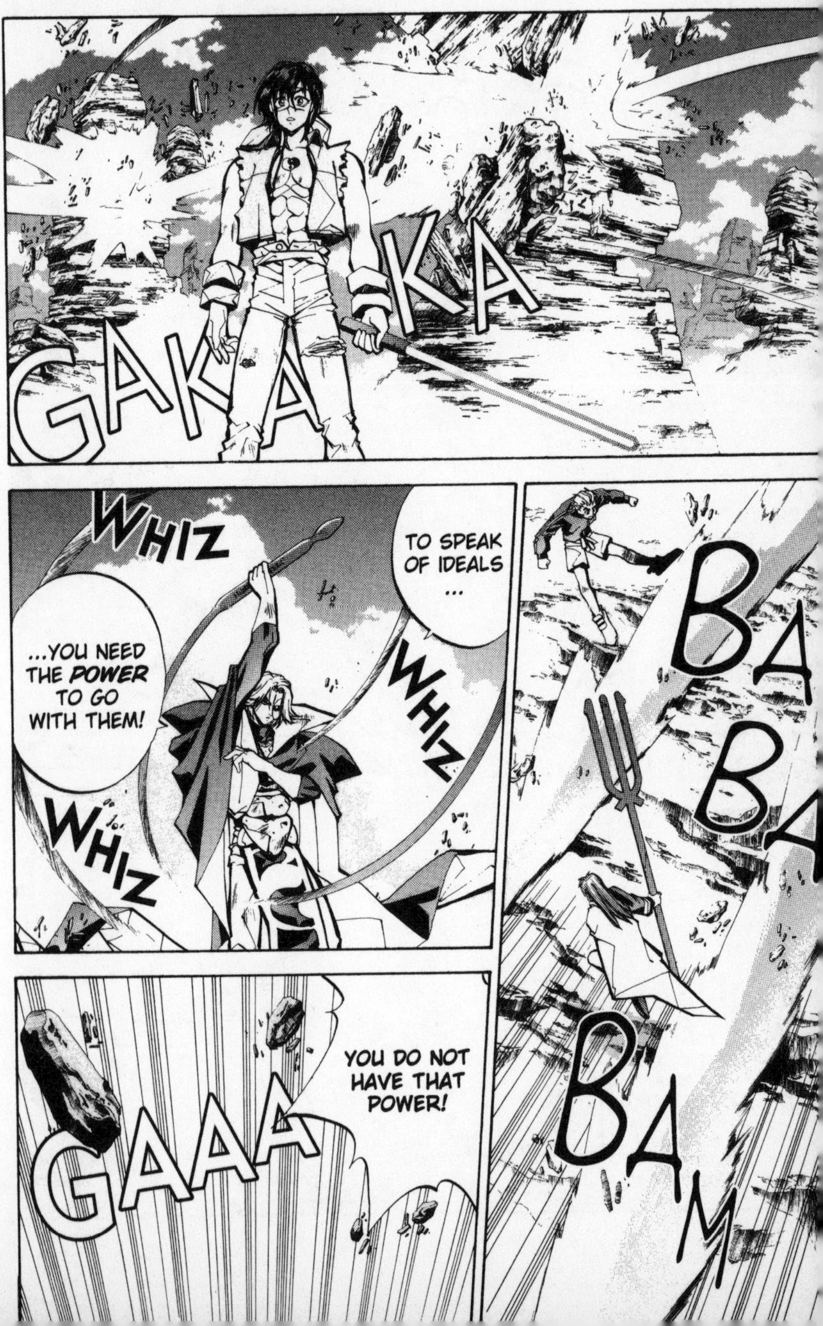
GAKAKA
BABA
BA
BAM
TO SPEAK OF IDEALS ...
WHIZ
...YOU NEED THE *POWER* TO GO WITH THEM!
WHIZ
WHIZ
YOU DO NOT HAVE THAT POWER!
GAAA

GAGAGAA

OOO

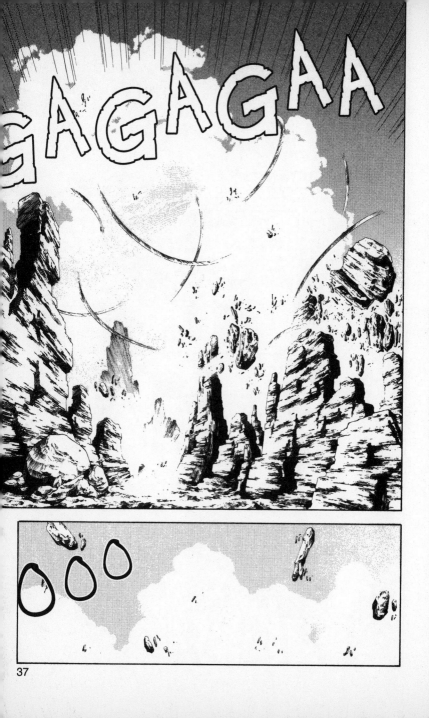

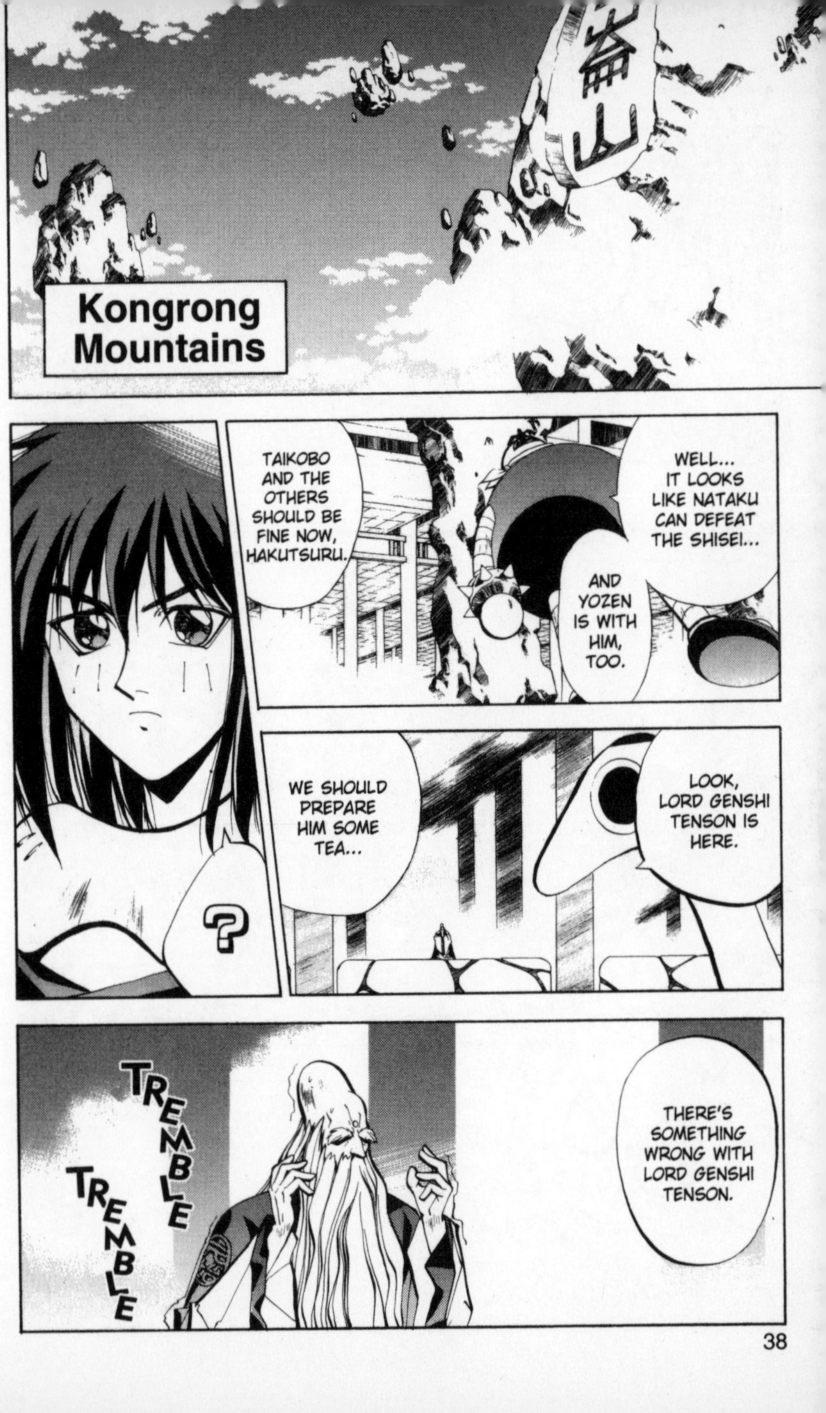
Kongrong Mountains
WELL... IT LOOKS LIKE NATAKU CAN DEFEAT THE SHISEI...
AND YOZEN IS WITH HIM, TOO.
TAIKOBO AND THE OTHERS SHOULD BE FINE NOW, HAKUTSURU.
LOOK, LORD GENSHI TENSON IS HERE.
WE SHOULD PREPARE HIM SOME TEA...
?
THERE'S SOMETHING WRONG WITH LORD GENSHI TENSON.
TREMBLE
TREMBLE

READ THIS WAY

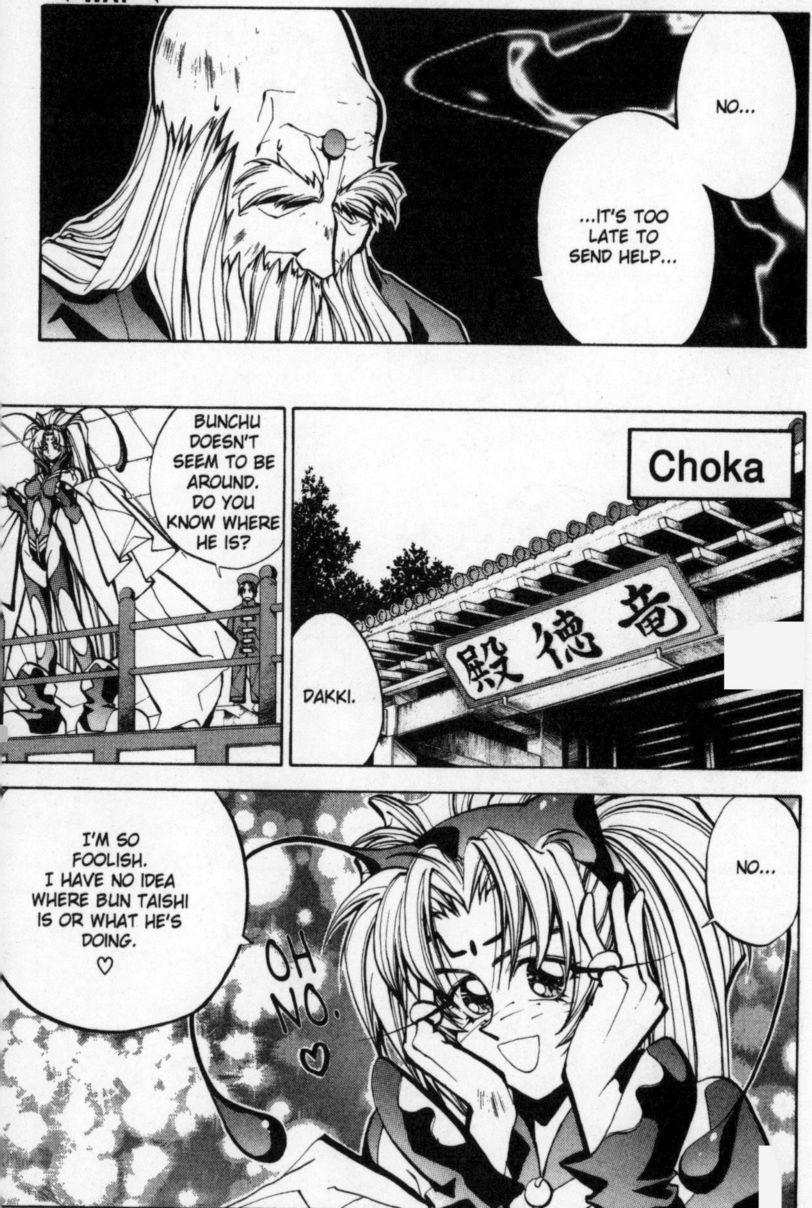

NO...
...IT'S TOO LATE TO SEND HELP...
Choka
殿徳竜
DAKKI.
BUNCHU DOESN'T SEEM TO BE AROUND. DO YOU KNOW WHERE HE IS?
NO...
OHO NO ♡
I'M SO FOOLISH. I HAVE NO IDEA WHERE BUN TAISHI IS OR WHAT HE'S DOING. ♡

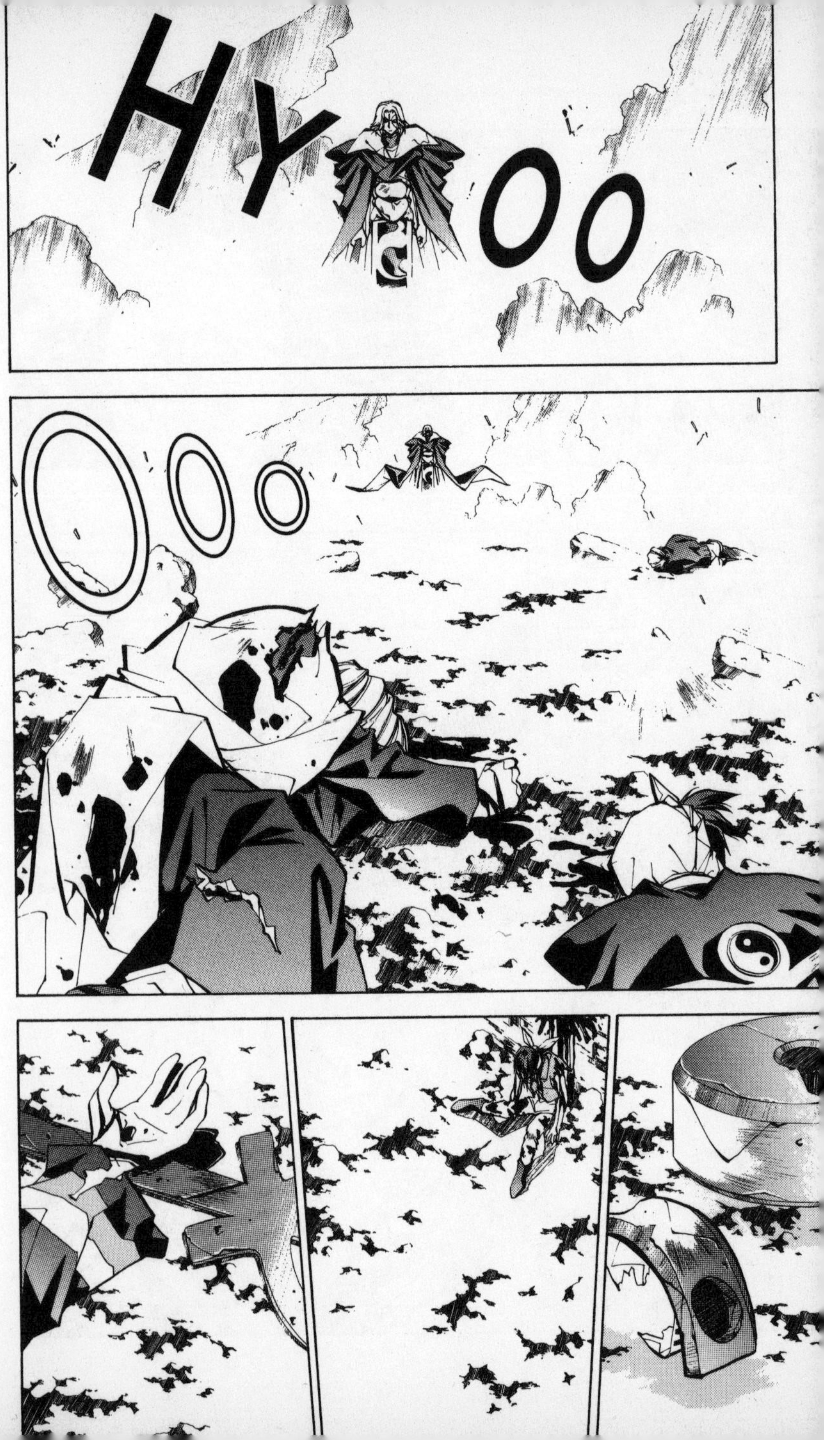
HYOOOOO

READ THIS WAY

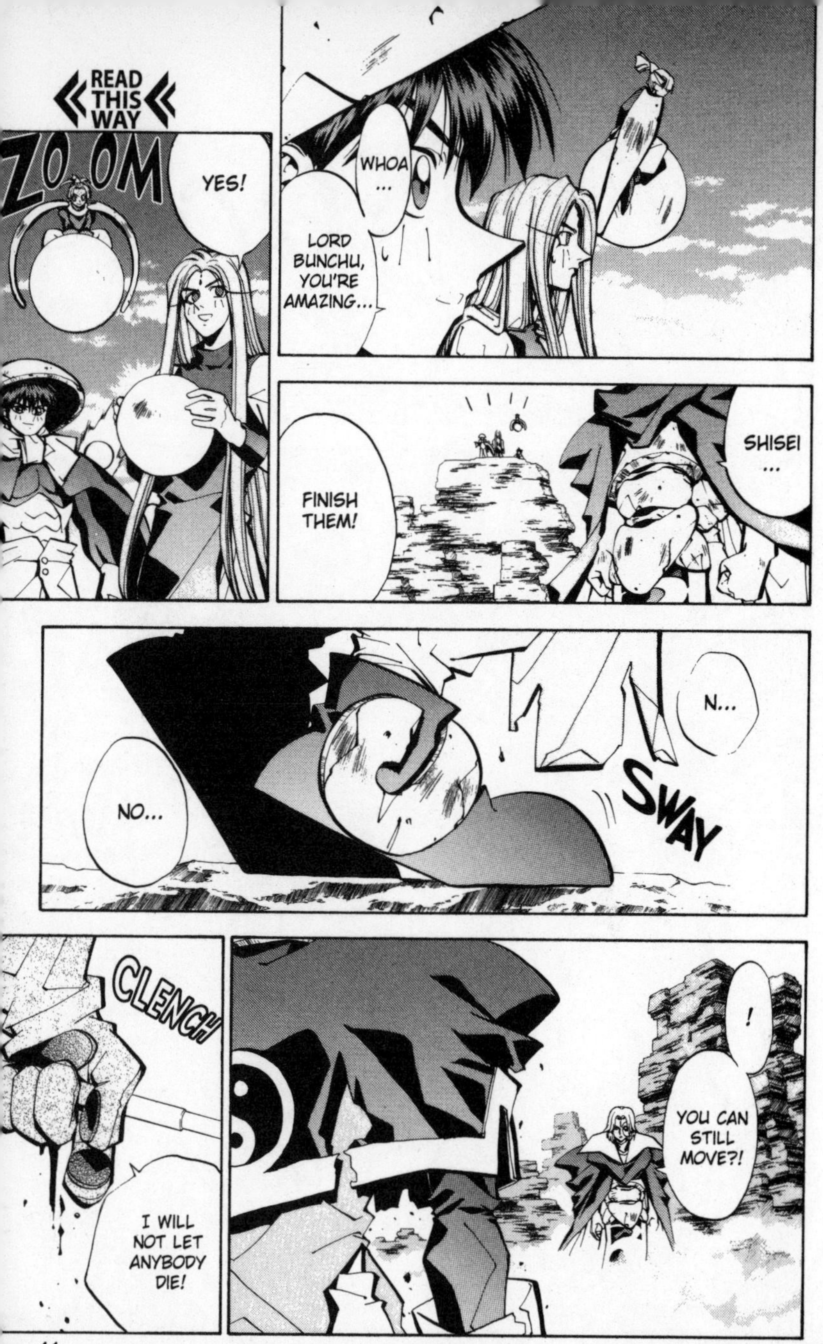

WHOA ...
LORD BUNCHU, YOU'RE AMAZING...
SHISEI ...
FINISH THEM!
ZO OM
YES!
N...
SWAY
NO...
!
YOU CAN STILL MOVE?!
CLENCH
I WILL NOT LET ANYBODY DIE!

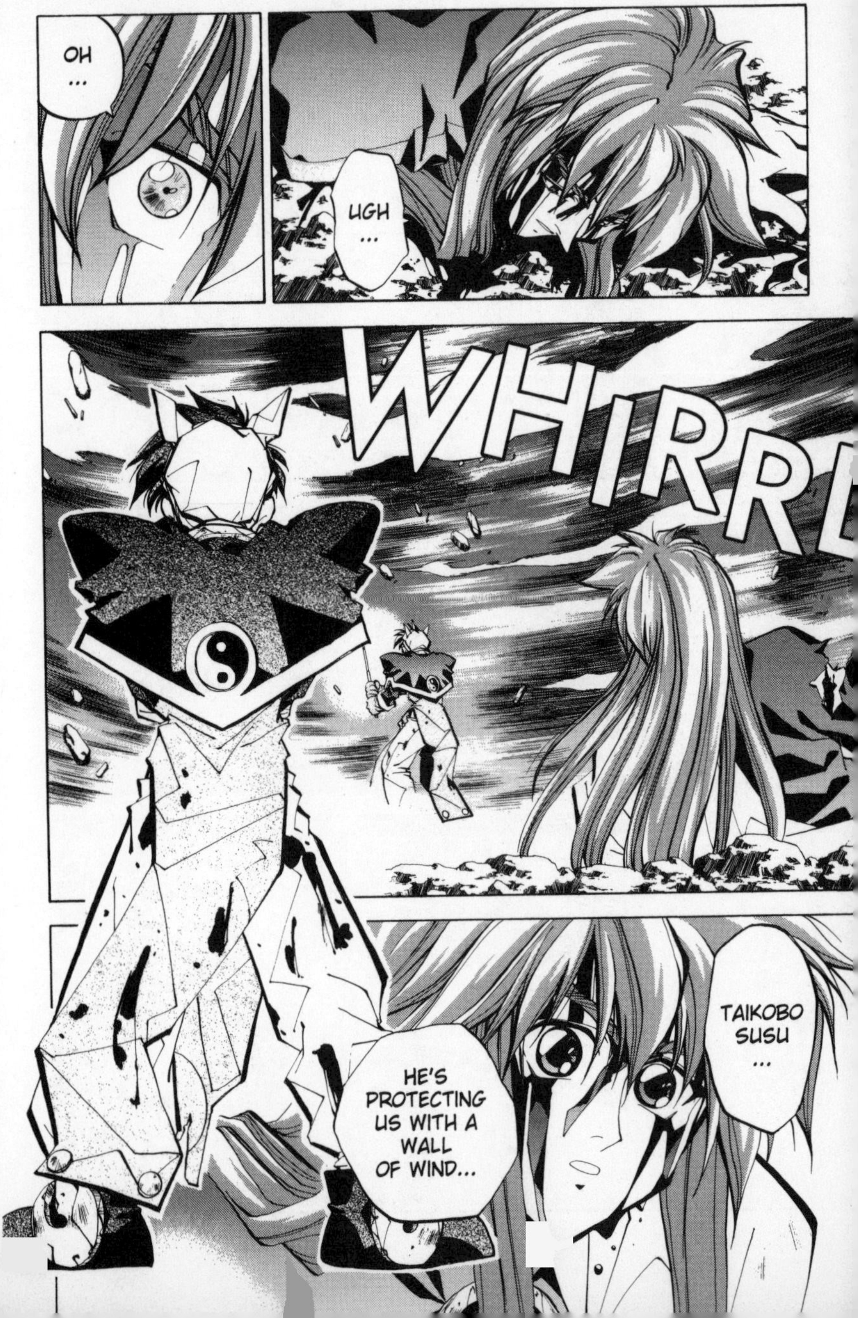
UGH ...
OH ...
WHIRRR
TAIKOBO SUSU ...
HE'S PROTECTING US WITH A WALL OF WIND...

READ THIS WAY

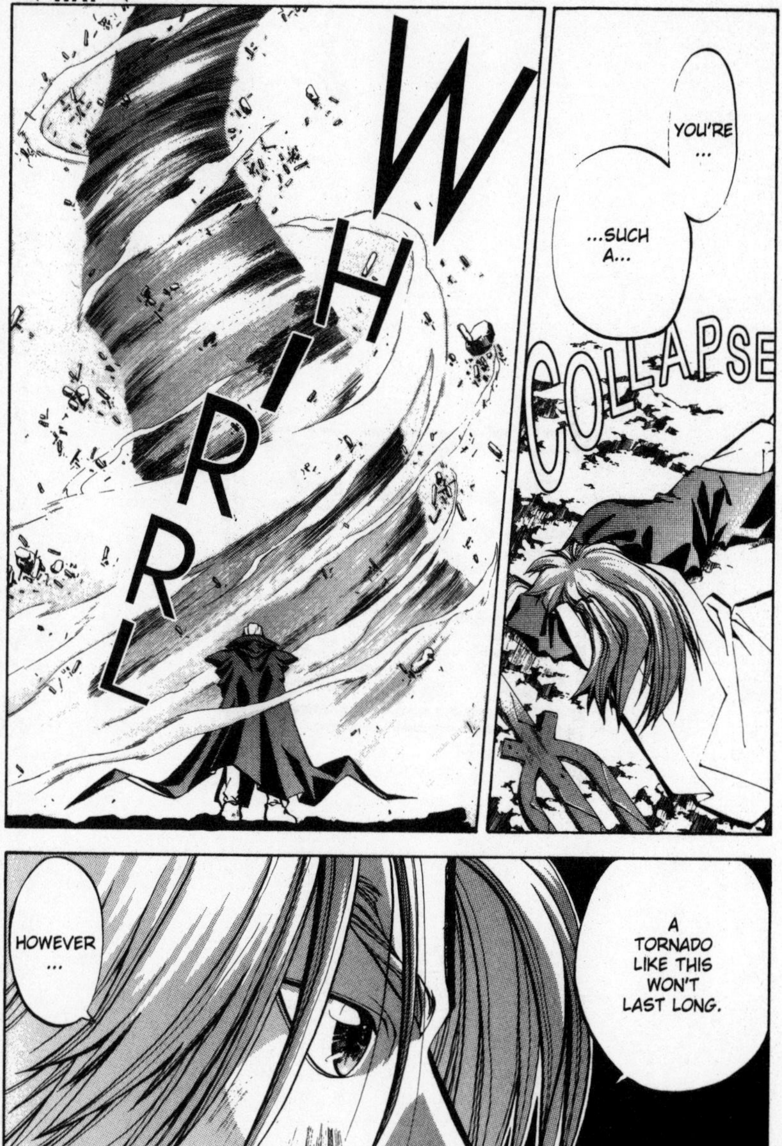

YOU'RE ...
...SUCH A...
COLLAPSE
WHIRRL
A TORNADO LIKE THIS WON'T LAST LONG.
HOWEVER ...

封神演義

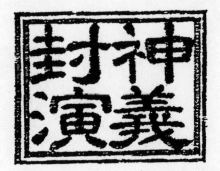

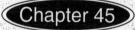

Chapter 45

TWO ALTERNATIVES

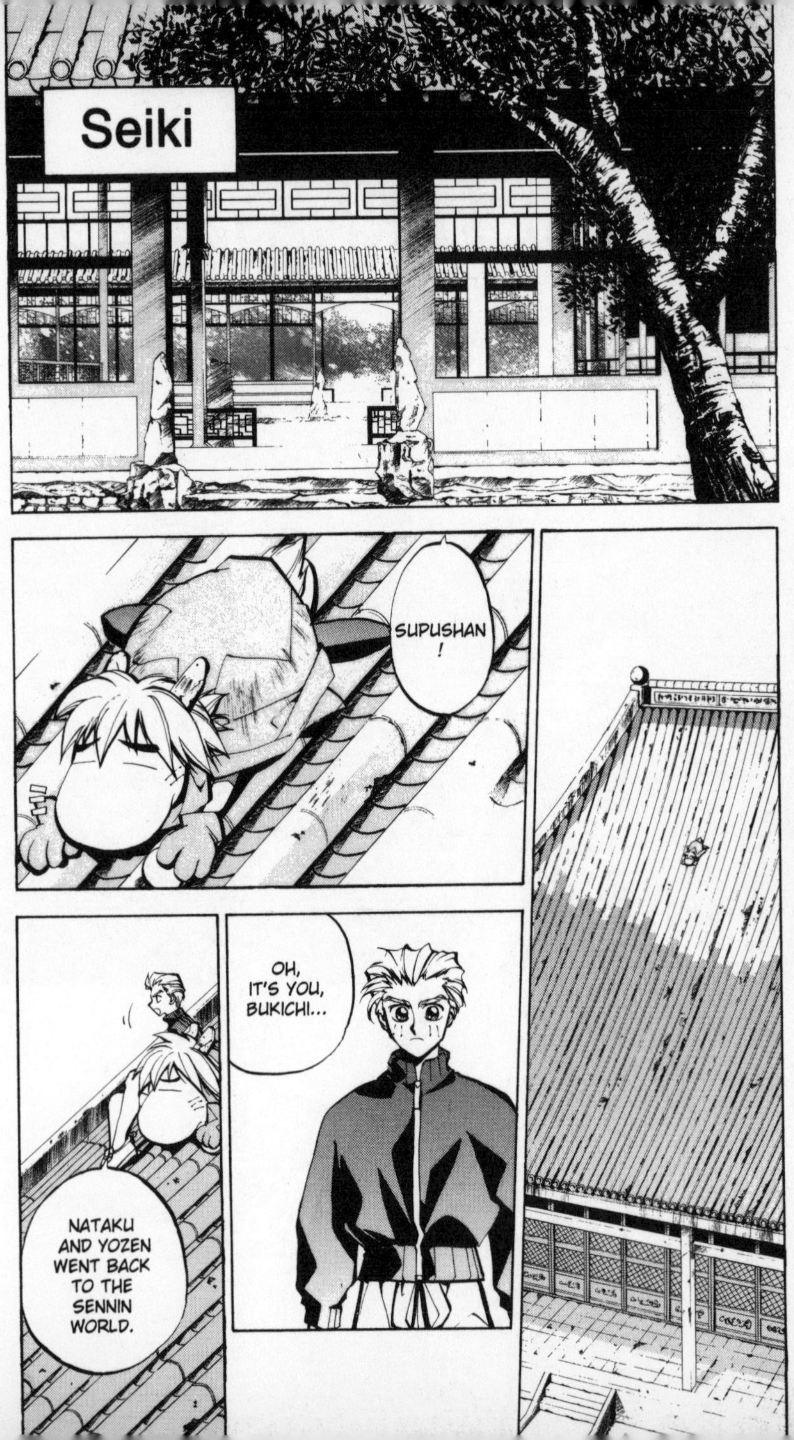
Seiki
SUPUSHAN!
OH, IT'S YOU, BUKICHI...
NATAKU AND YOZEN WENT BACK TO THE SENNIN WORLD.

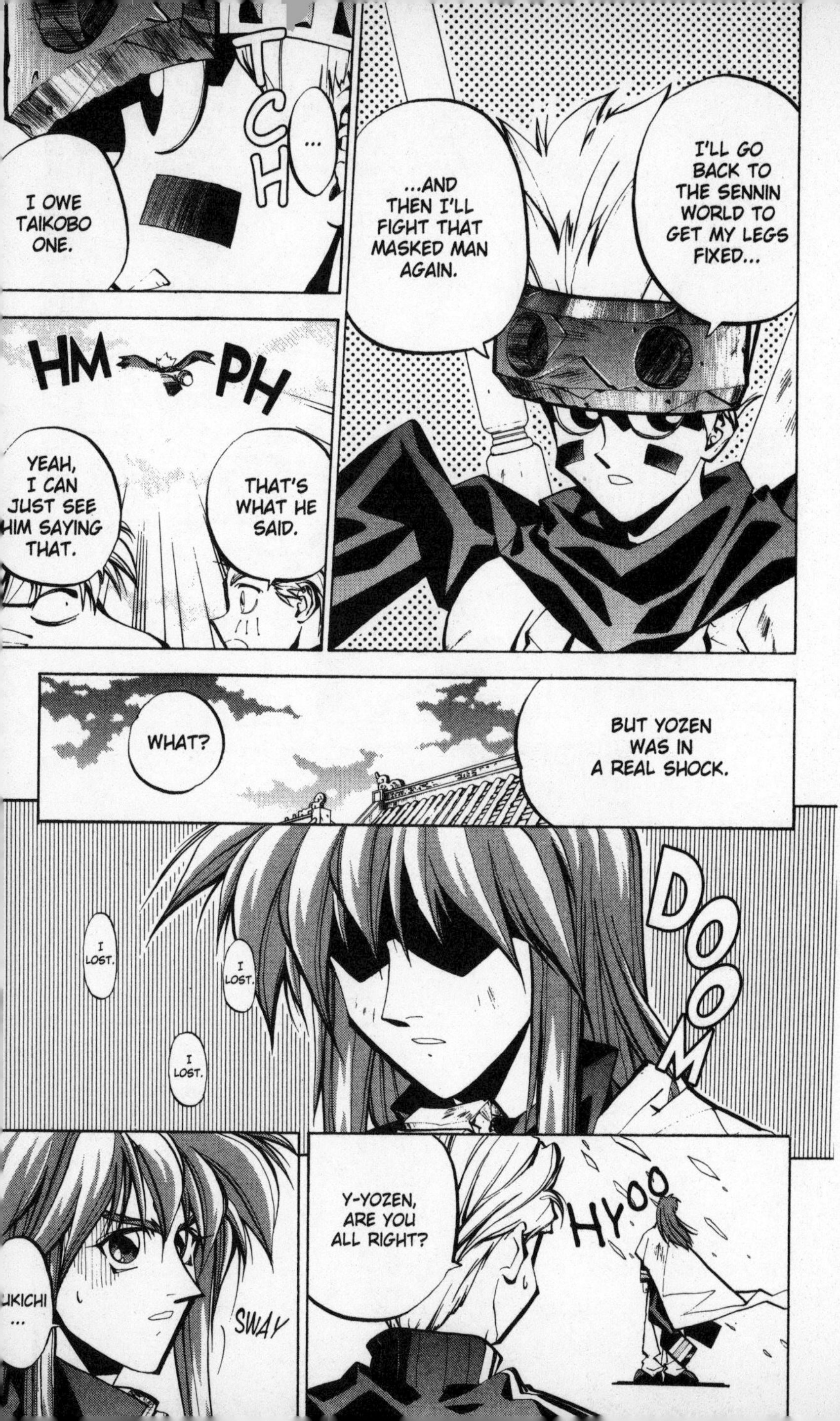
I'LL GO BACK TO THE SENNIN WORLD TO GET MY LEGS FIXED...
...AND THEN I'LL FIGHT THAT MASKED MAN AGAIN.
...
TCH
I OWE TAIKOBO ONE.
HMPH
THAT'S WHAT HE SAID.
YEAH, I CAN JUST SEE HIM SAYING THAT.
BUT YOZEN WAS IN A REAL SHOCK.
WHAT?
DOOOM
I LOST.
I LOST.
I LOST.
Y-YOZEN, ARE YOU ALL RIGHT?
HYOO
SWAY
UKICHI ...

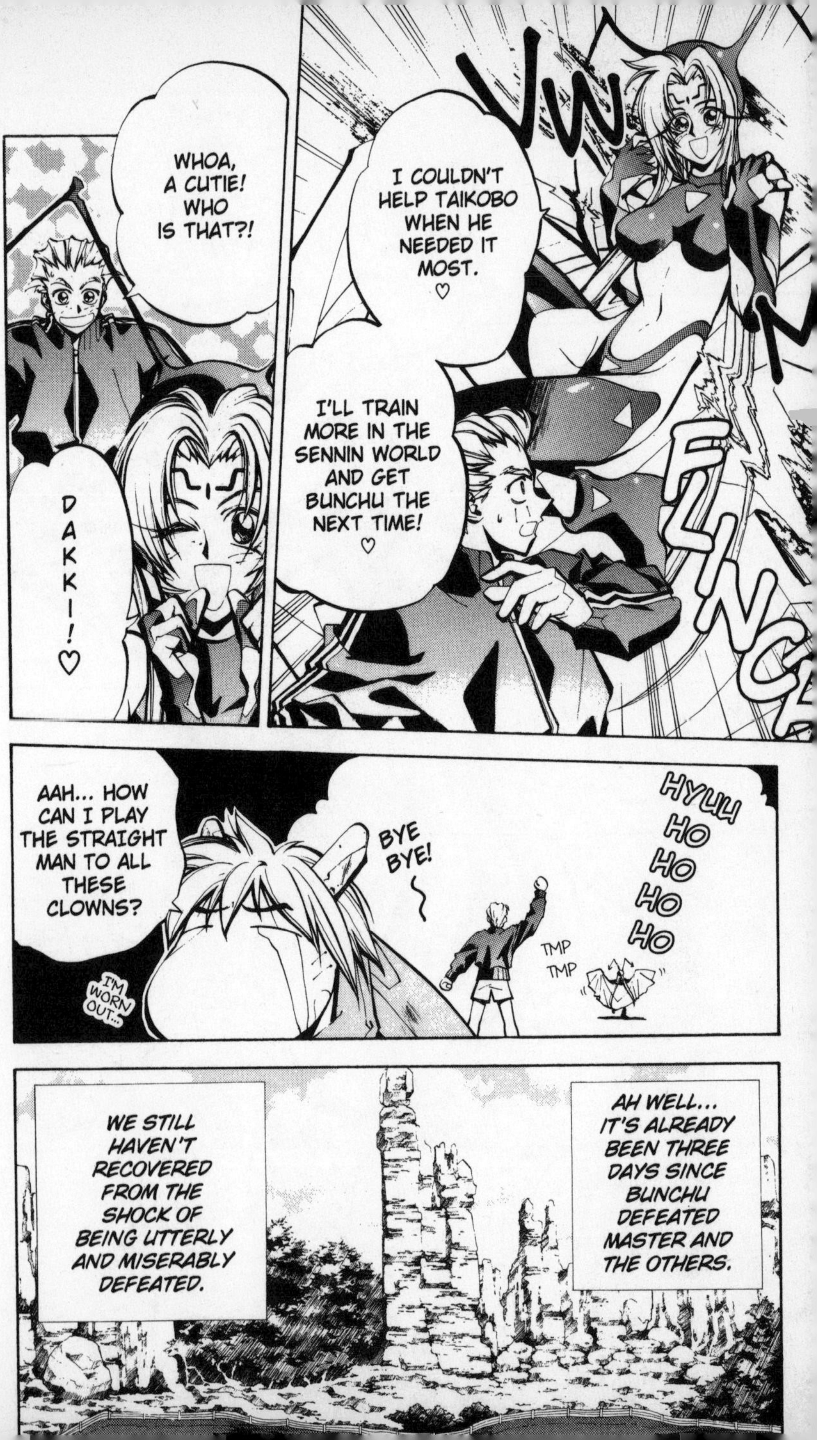
I COULDN'T HELP TAIKOBO WHEN HE NEEDED IT MOST. ♡
I'LL TRAIN MORE IN THE SENNIN WORLD AND GET BUNCHU THE NEXT TIME! ♡
WHOA, A CUTIE! WHO IS THAT?!
DAKKI! ♡
HYUU HO HO HO HO HO
TMP TMP
BYE BYE!
AAH... HOW CAN I PLAY THE STRAIGHT MAN TO ALL THESE CLOWNS?
I'M WORN OUT...
AH WELL... IT'S ALREADY BEEN THREE DAYS SINCE BUNCHU DEFEATED MASTER AND THE OTHERS.
WE STILL HAVEN'T RECOVERED FROM THE SHOCK OF BEING UTTERLY AND MISERABLY DEFEATED.

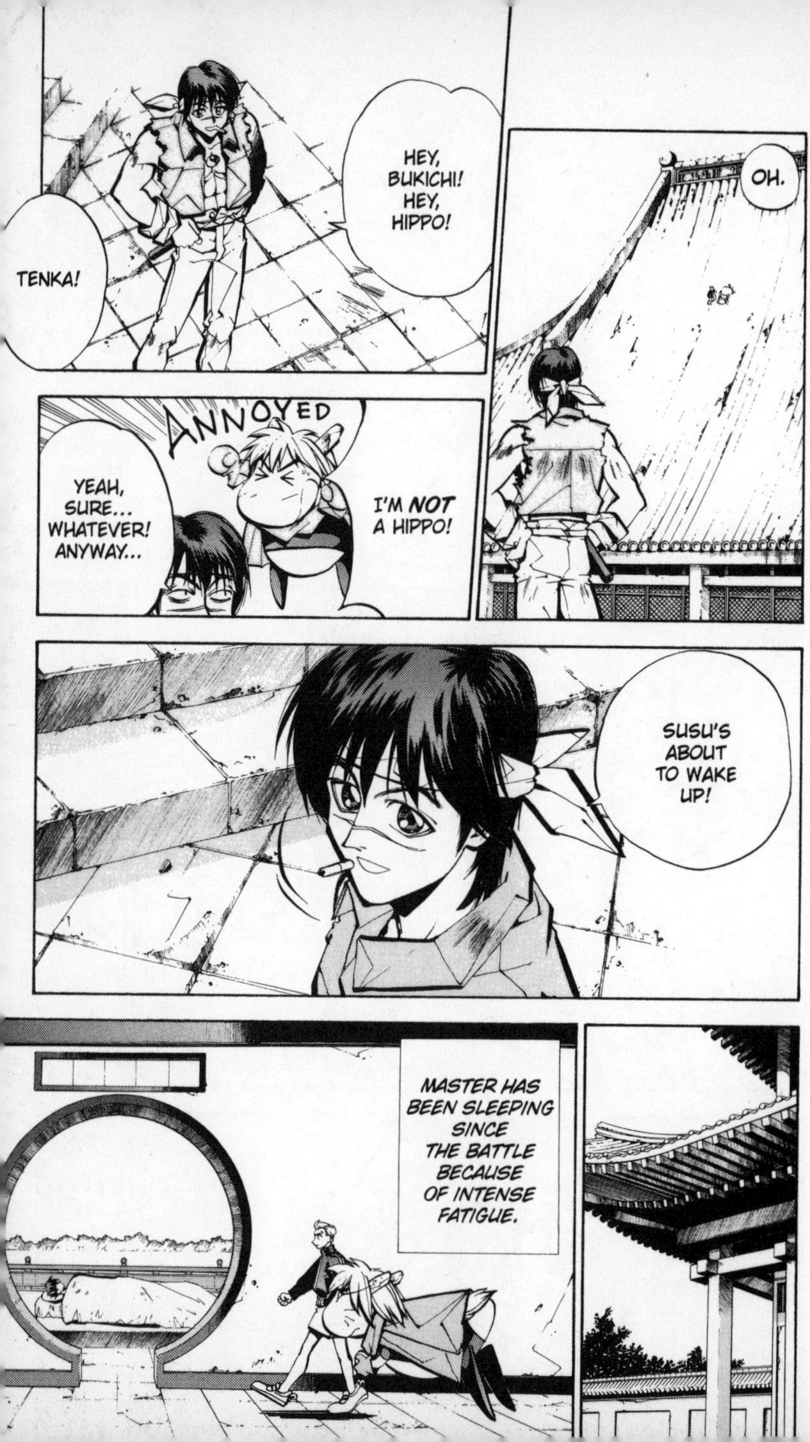
OH.
HEY, BUKICHI! HEY, HIPPO!
TENKA!
I'M NOT A HIPPO!
ANNOYED
YEAH, SURE... WHATEVER! ANYWAY...
SUSU'S ABOUT TO WAKE UP!
MASTER HAS BEEN SLEEPING SINCE THE BATTLE BECAUSE OF INTENSE FATIGUE.

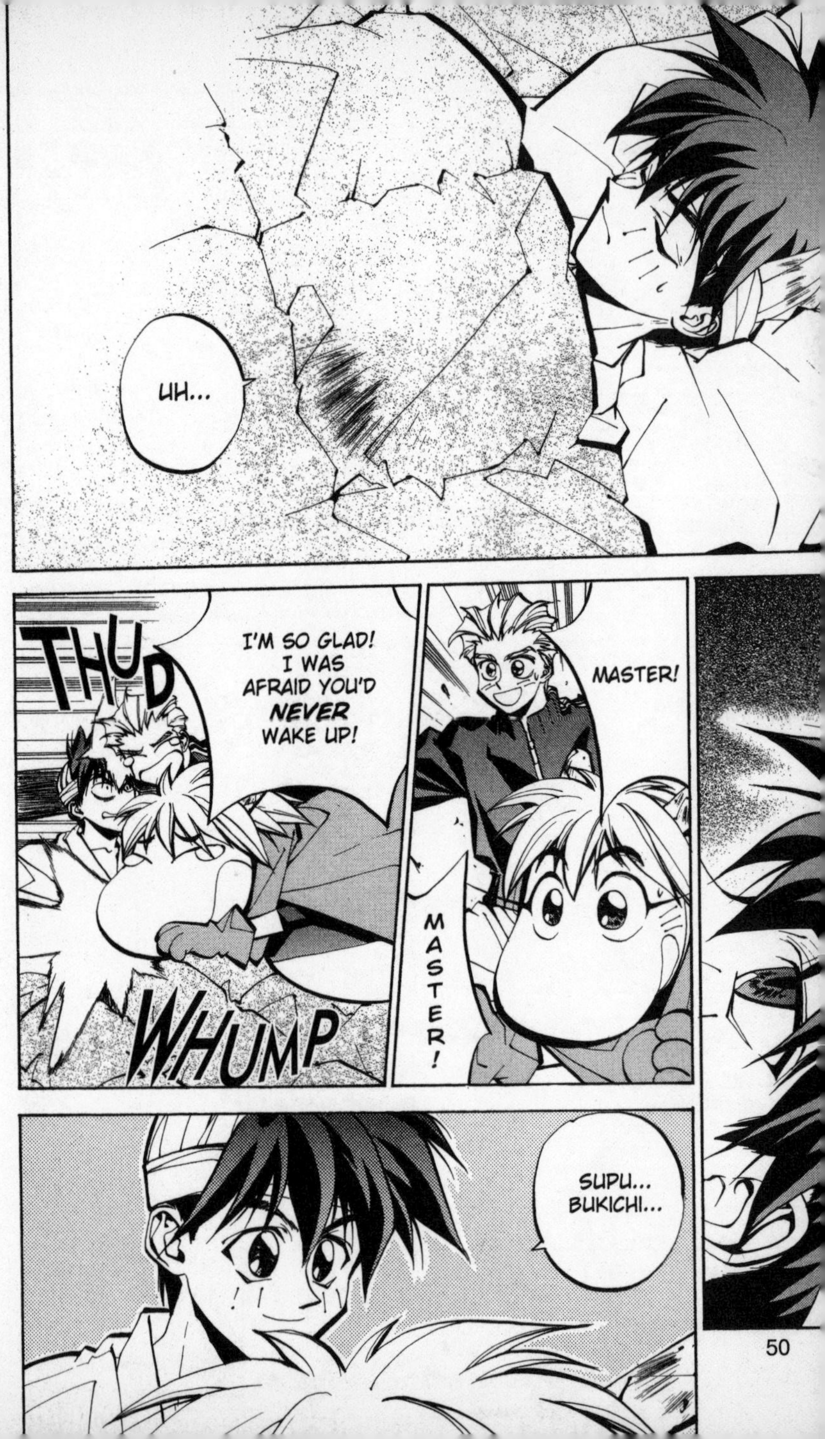
UH...
MASTER!
MASTER!
I'M SO GLAD! I WAS AFRAID YOU'D **NEVER** WAKE UP!
THUD
WHUMP
SUPU... BUKICHI...

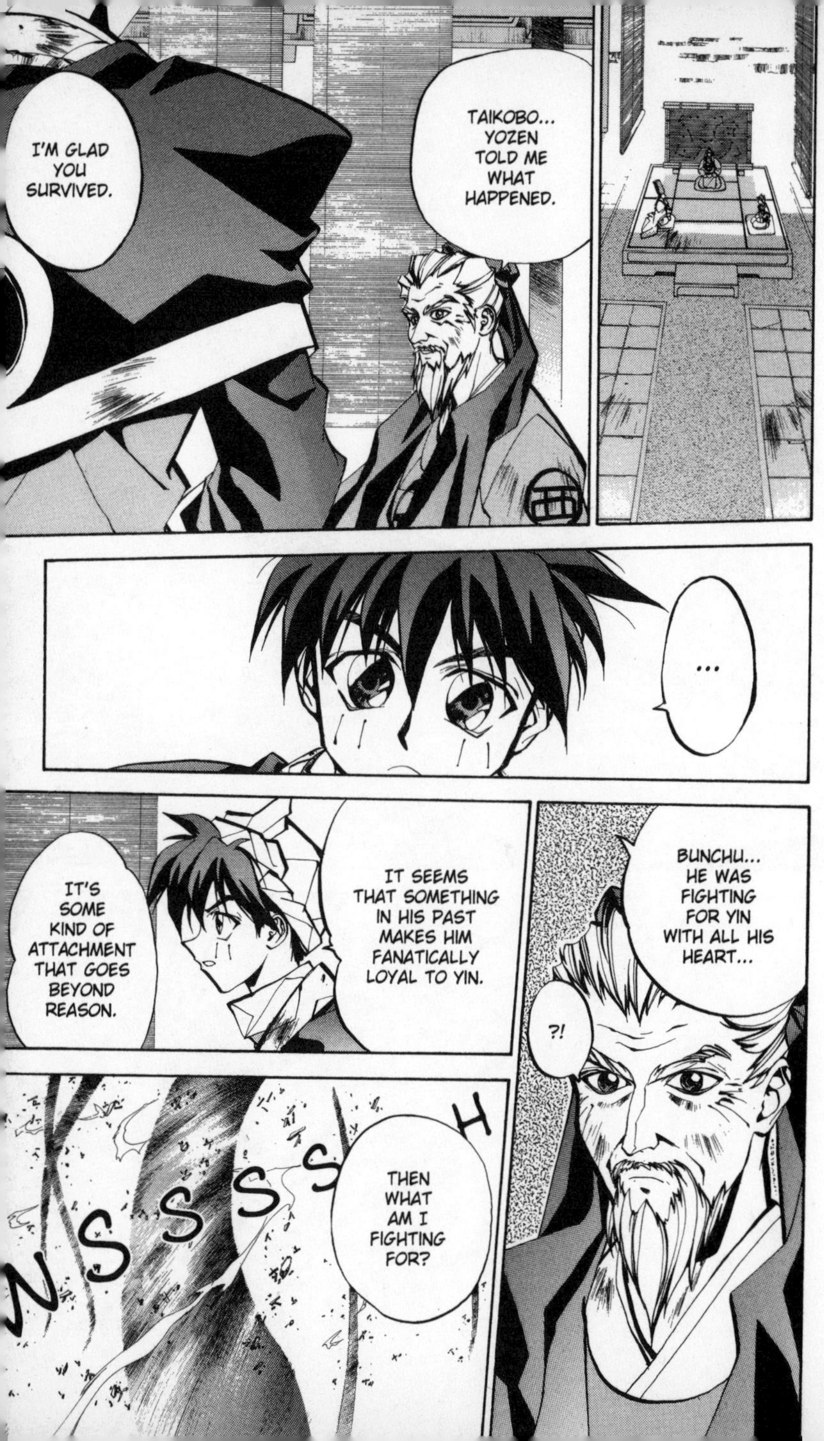
TAIKOBO... YOZEN TOLD ME WHAT HAPPENED.
I'M GLAD YOU SURVIVED.
...
BUNCHU... HE WAS FIGHTING FOR YIN WITH ALL HIS HEART...
?!
IT SEEMS THAT SOMETHING IN HIS PAST MAKES HIM FANATICALLY LOYAL TO YIN.
IT'S SOME KIND OF ATTACHMENT THAT GOES BEYOND REASON.
THEN WHAT AM I FIGHTING FOR?
WSSSSH

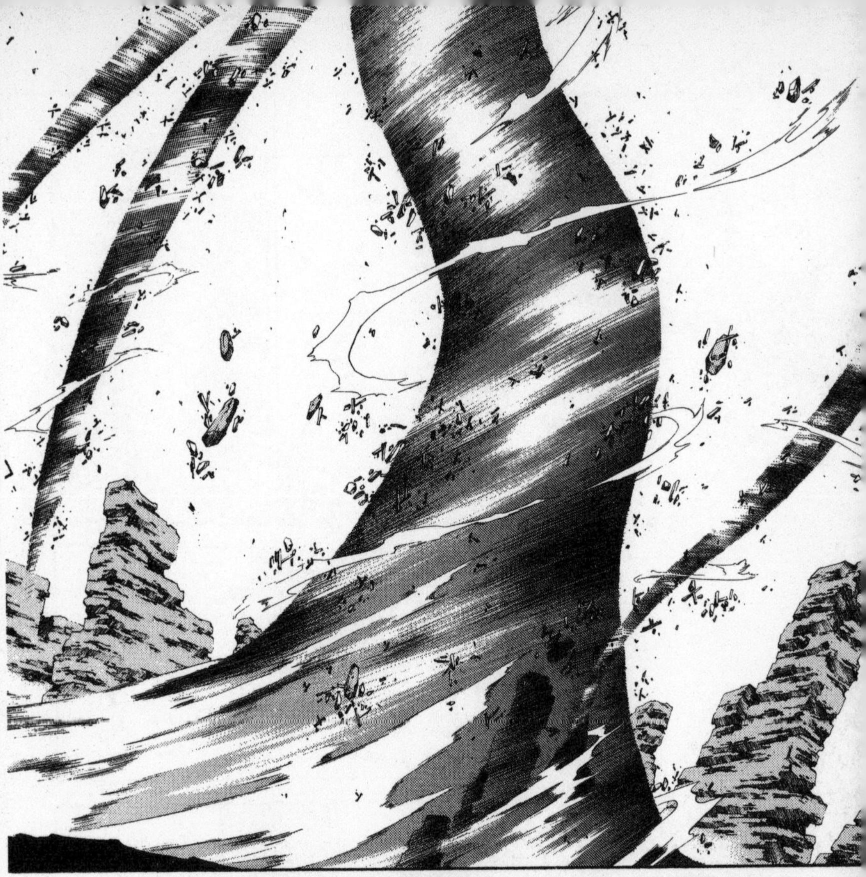

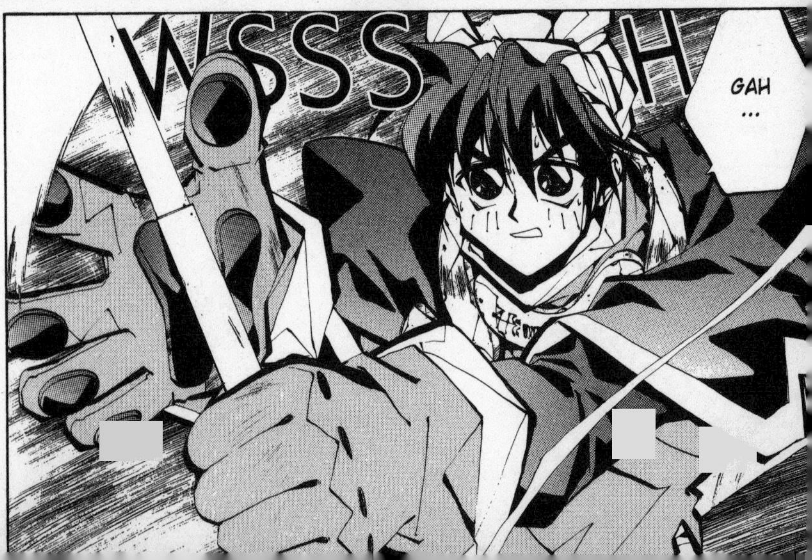
WSSSSH
GAH ...

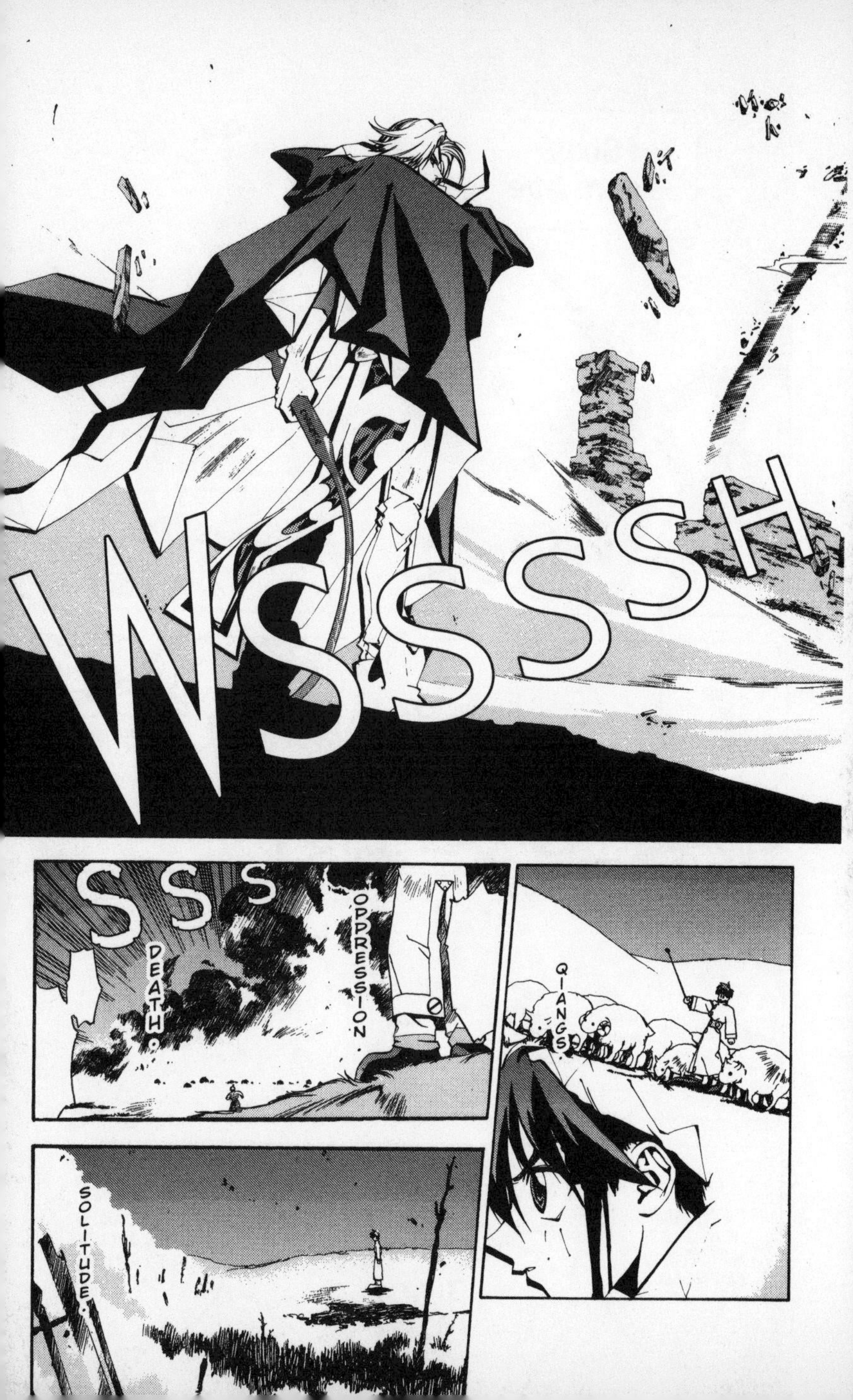
WSSSSH
QIANGS.
SSS
OPPRESSION
DEATH.
SOLITUDE.

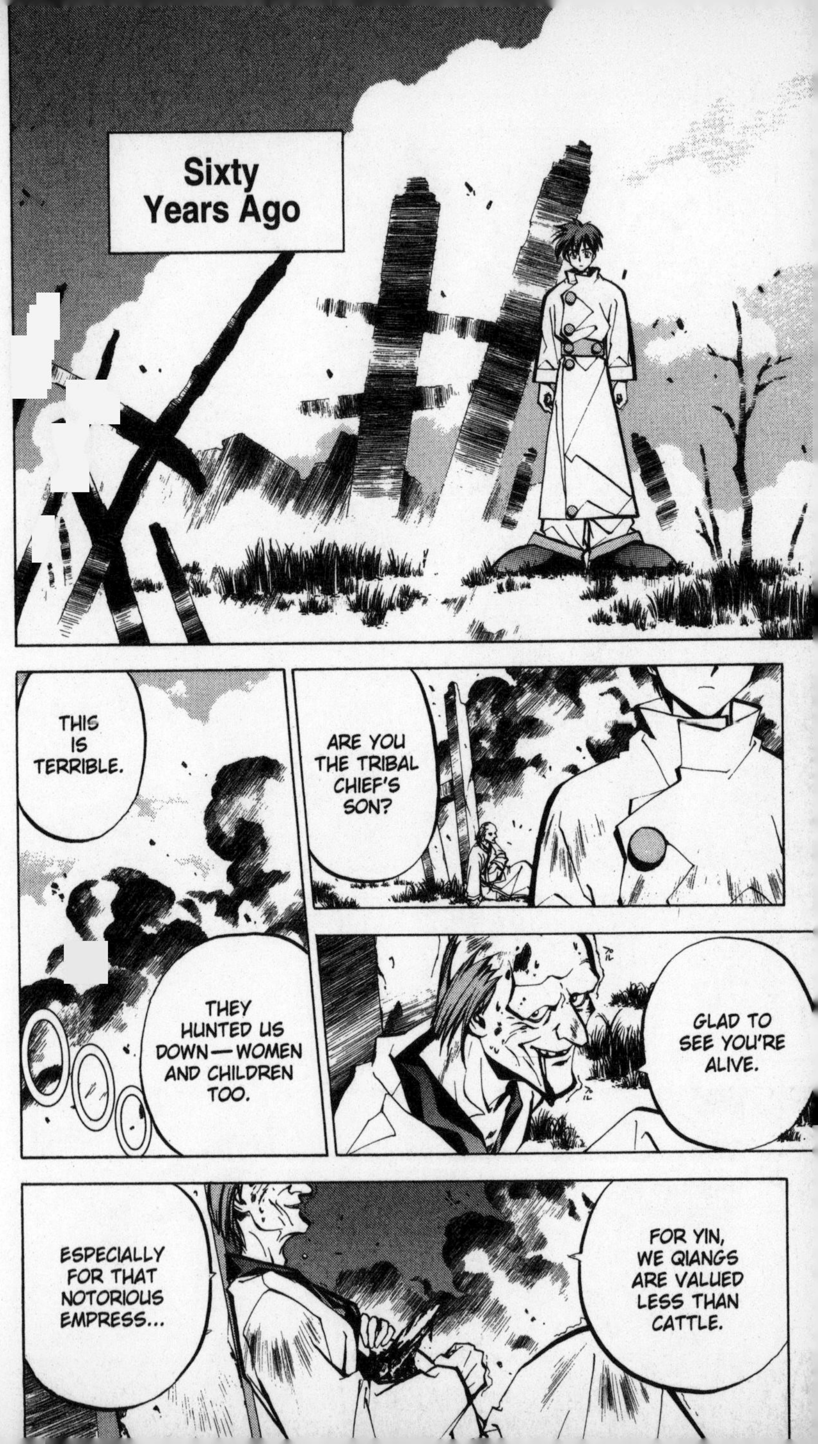
Sixty Years Ago
ARE YOU THE TRIBAL CHIEF'S SON?
GLAD TO SEE YOU'RE ALIVE.
THIS IS TERRIBLE.
THEY HUNTED US DOWN—WOMEN AND CHILDREN TOO.
FOR YIN, WE QIANGS ARE VALUED LESS THAN CATTLE.
ESPECIALLY FOR THAT NOTORIOUS EMPRESS...

READ THIS WAY

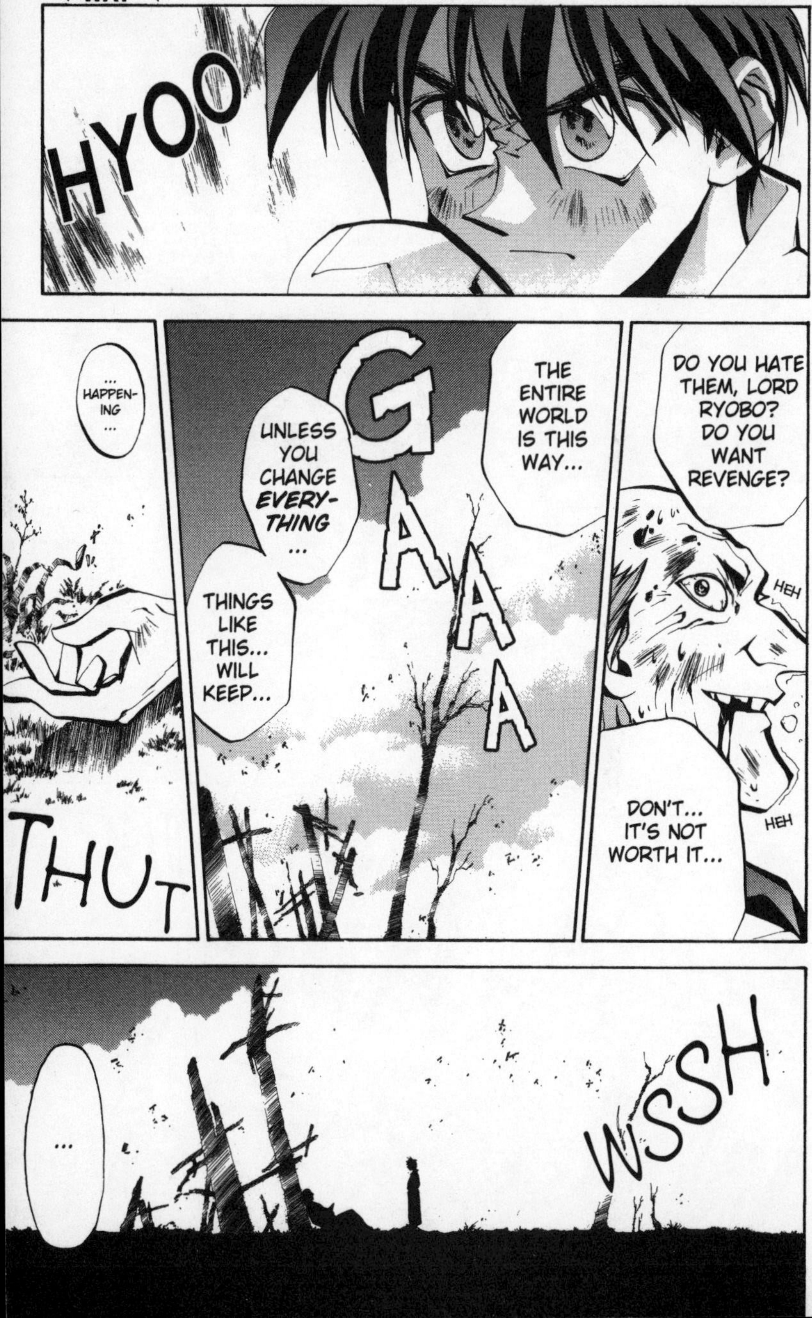
HYOO
DO YOU HATE THEM, LORD RYOBO? DO YOU WANT REVENGE?
HEH
HEH
DON'T... IT'S NOT WORTH IT...
THE ENTIRE WORLD IS THIS WAY...
GAAAA
UNLESS YOU CHANGE *EVERYTHING*...
THINGS LIKE THIS... WILL KEEP...
...HAPPENING...
THUT
WSSH
...

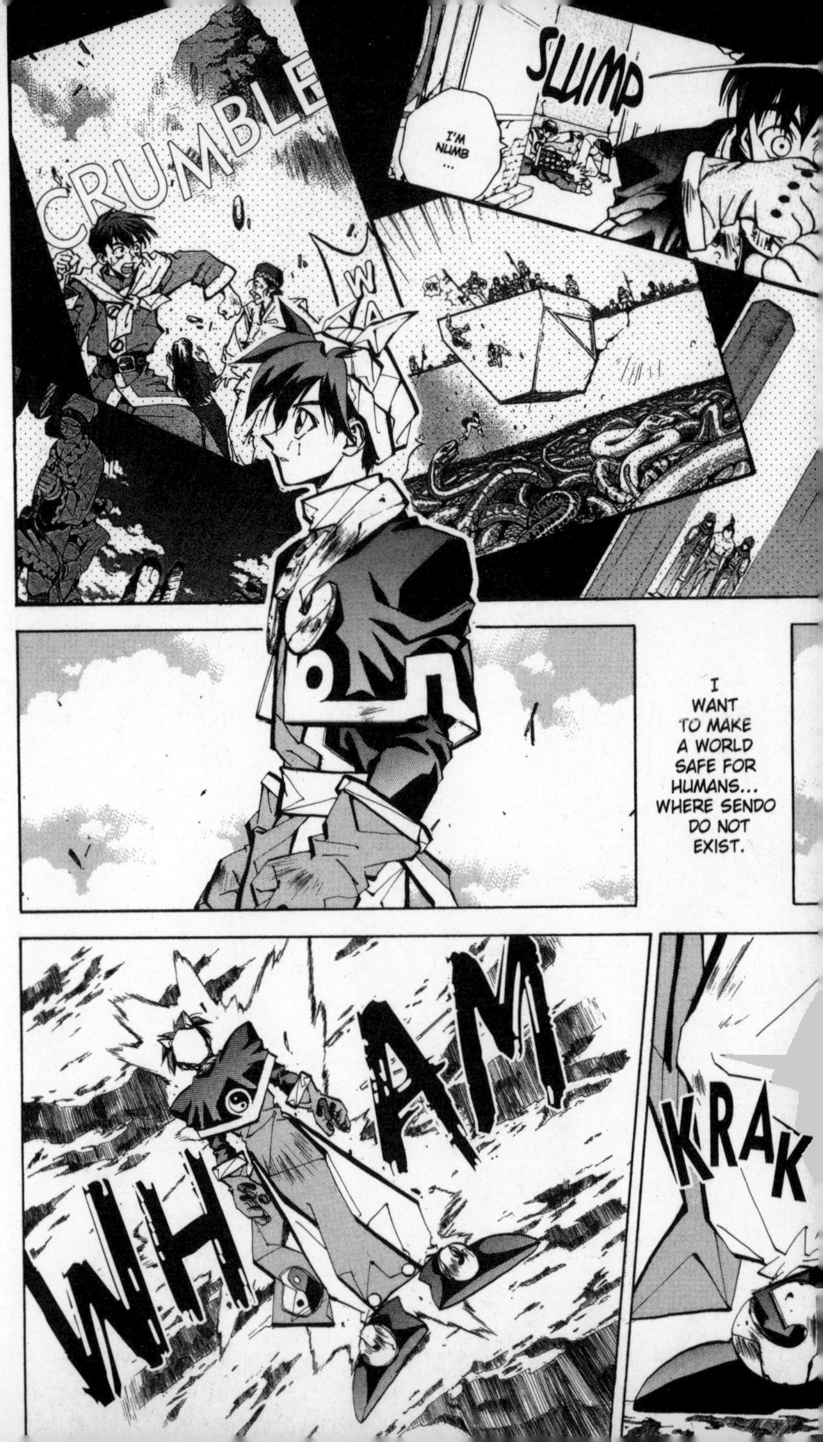
SLUMP
I'M NUMB ...
WA
CRUMBLE
I WANT TO MAKE A WORLD SAFE FOR HUMANS... WHERE SENDO DO NOT EXIST.
KRAK
WHAM

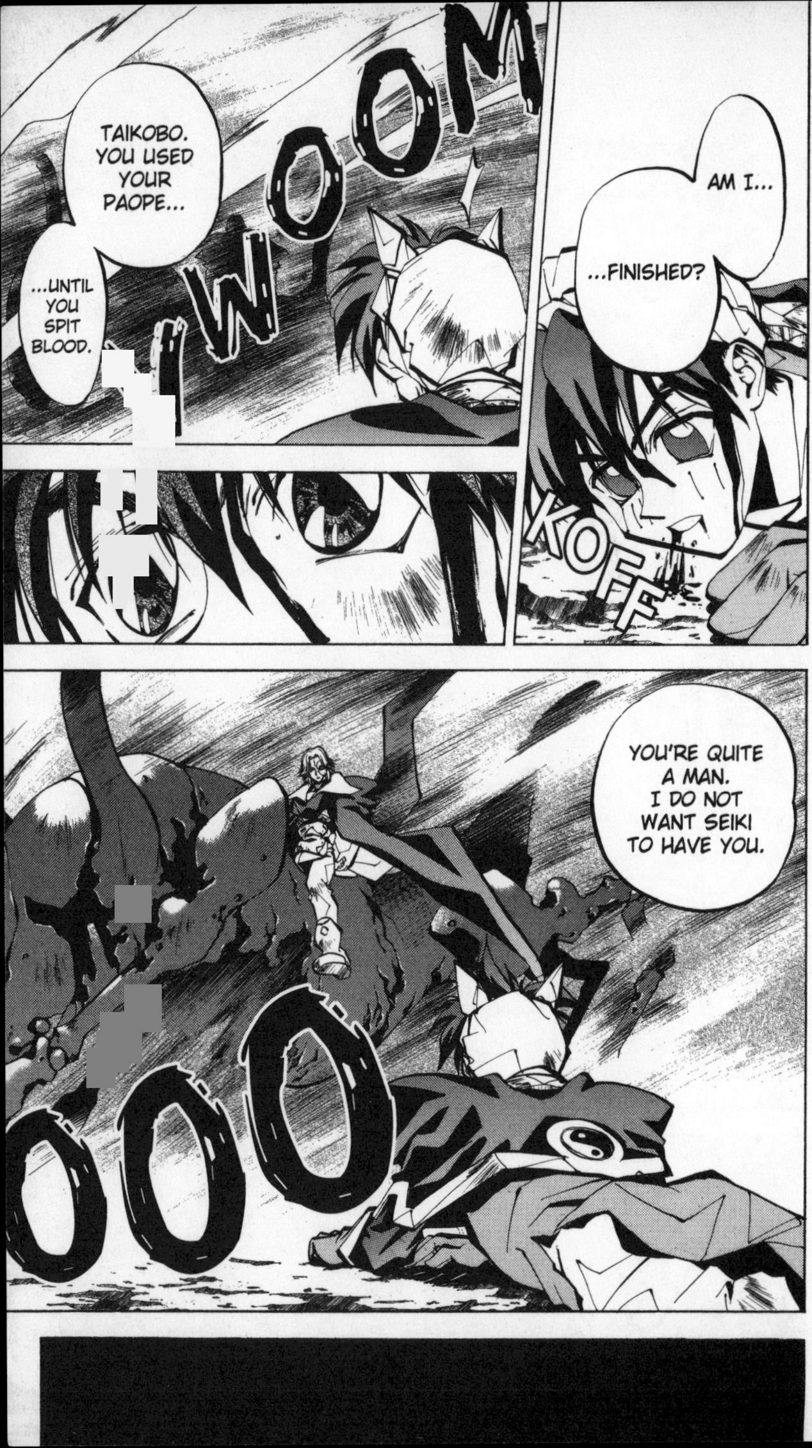
AM I...
...FINISHED?
KOFF
WOOOM
TAIKOBO. YOU USED YOUR PAOPE...
...UNTIL YOU SPIT BLOOD.
YOU'RE QUITE A MAN. I DO NOT WANT SEIKI TO HAVE YOU.
OOOO

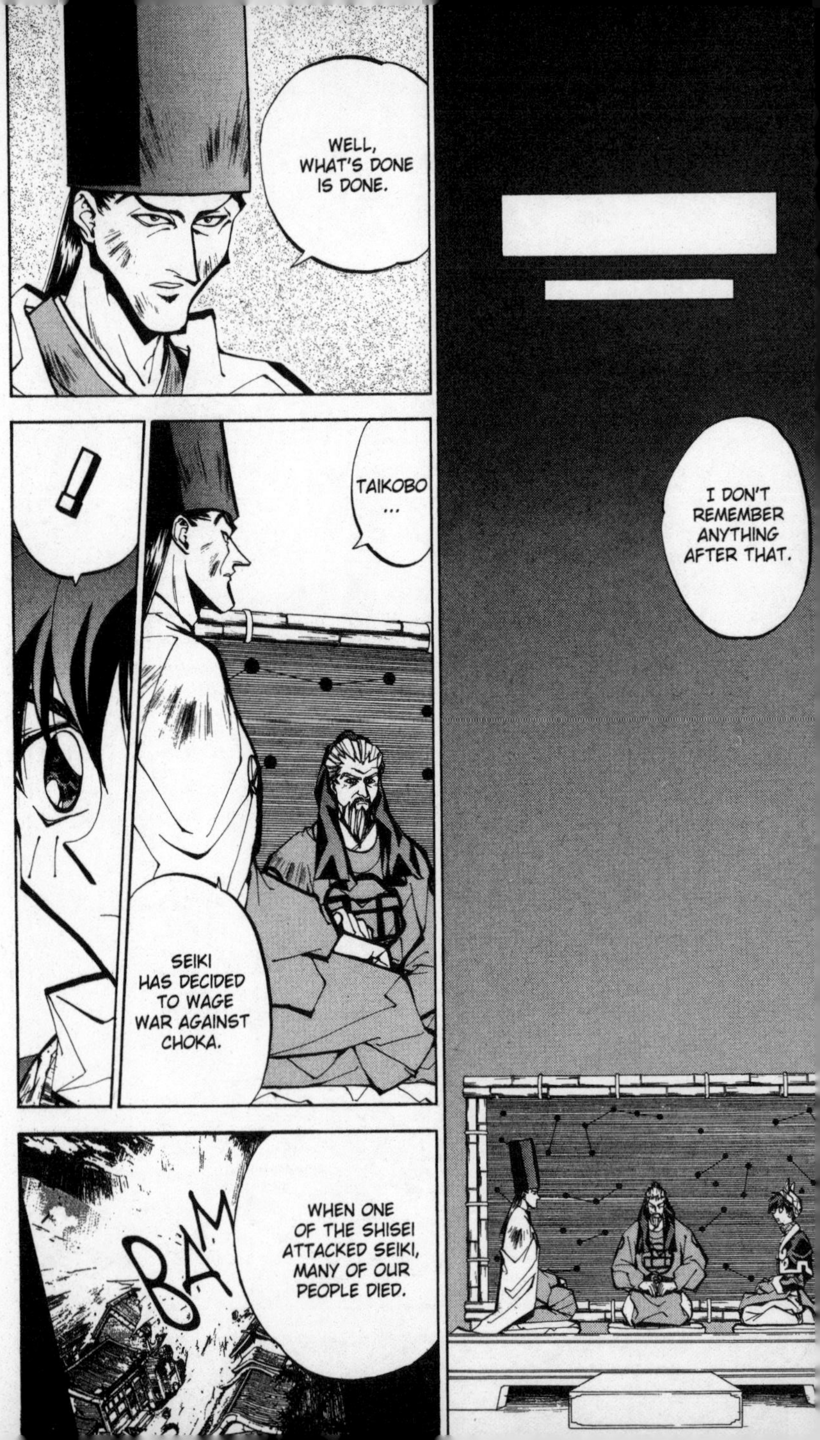
I DON'T REMEMBER ANYTHING AFTER THAT.
WELL, WHAT'S DONE IS DONE.
TAIKOBO ...
!
SEIKI HAS DECIDED TO WAGE WAR AGAINST CHOKA.
WHEN ONE OF THE SHISEI ATTACKED SEIKI, MANY OF OUR PEOPLE DIED.
BAM

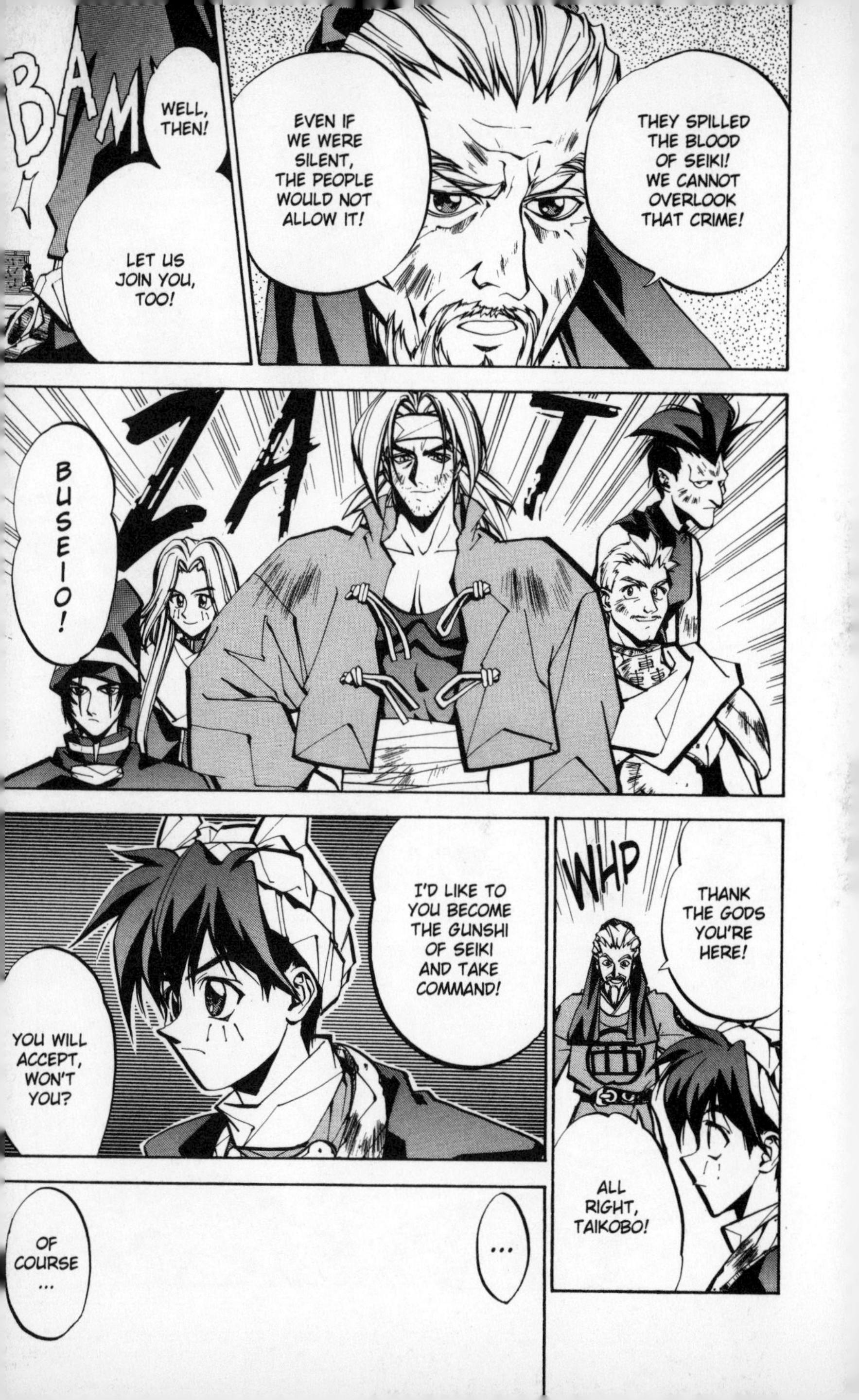
THEY SPILLED THE BLOOD OF SEIKI! WE CANNOT OVERLOOK THAT CRIME!
EVEN IF WE WERE SILENT, THE PEOPLE WOULD NOT ALLOW IT!
BAM
WELL, THEN!
LET US JOIN YOU, TOO!
ZAT
BUSEIO!
WHP
THANK THE GODS YOU'RE HERE!
ALL RIGHT, TAIKOBO!
I'D LIKE TO YOU BECOME THE GUNSHI OF SEIKI AND TAKE COMMAND!
YOU WILL ACCEPT, WON'T YOU?
...
OF COURSE ...

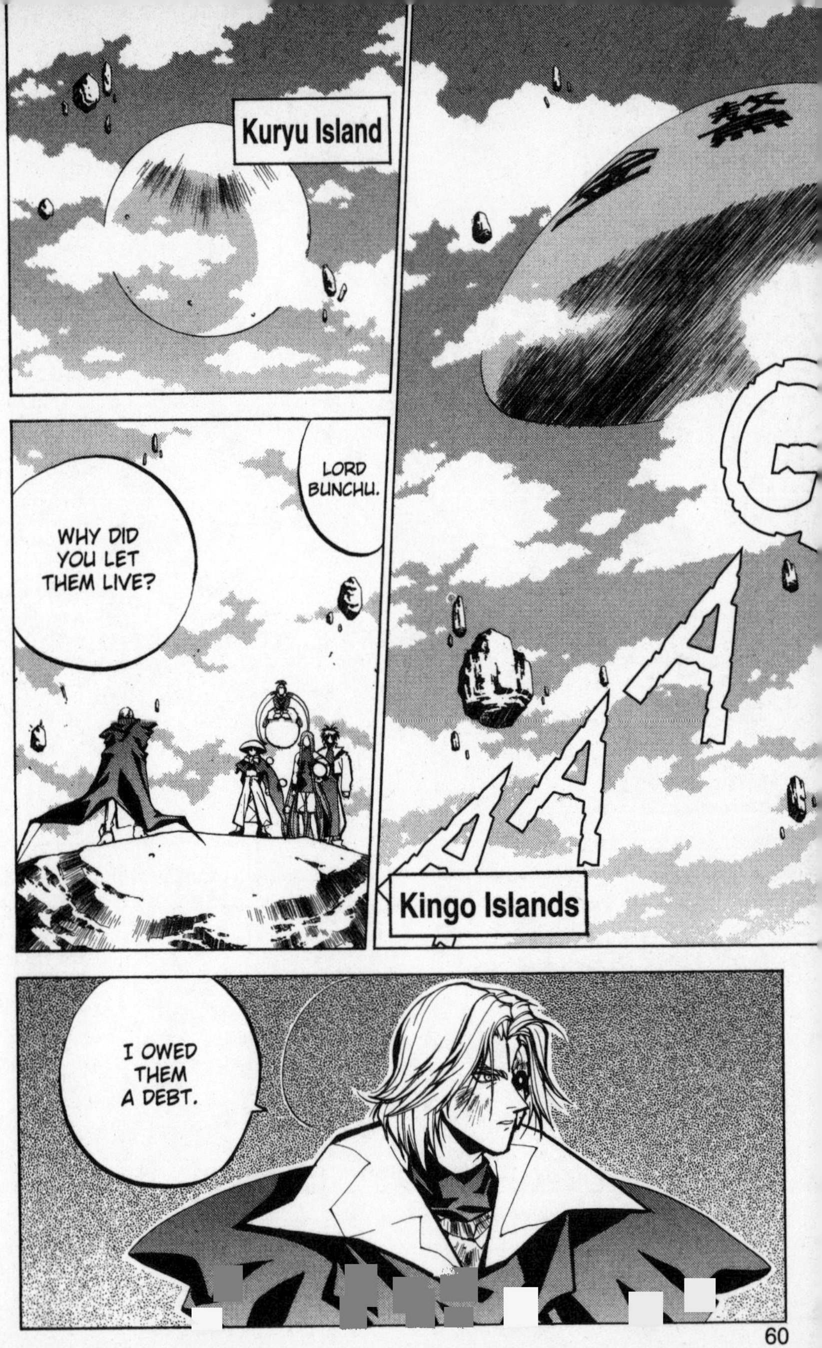
GAAAA
Kingo Islands
Kuryu Island
LORD BUNCHU.
WHY DID YOU LET THEM LIVE?
I OWED THEM A DEBT.

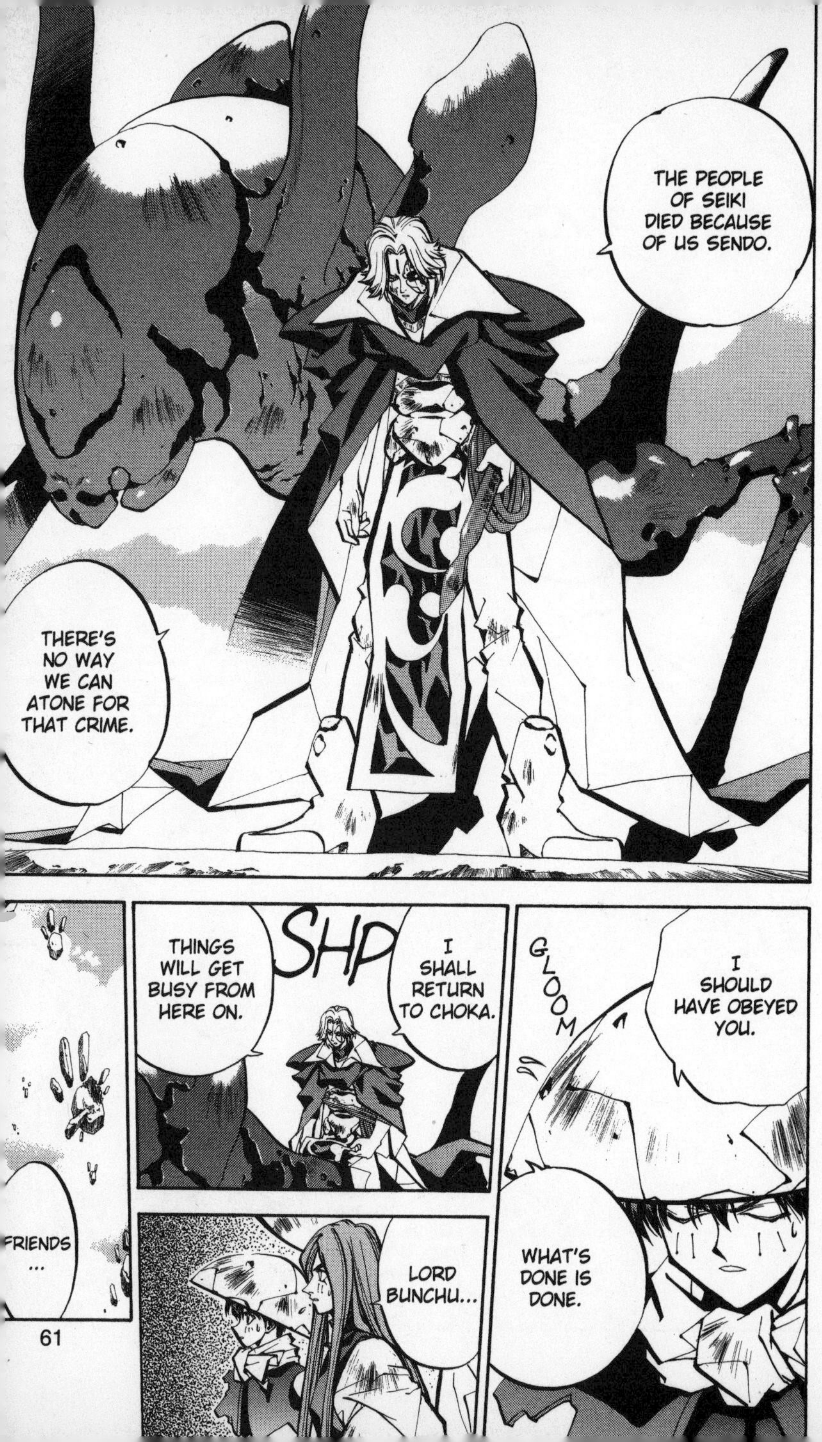
THE PEOPLE OF SEIKI DIED BECAUSE OF US SENDO.
THERE'S NO WAY WE CAN ATONE FOR THAT CRIME.
I SHOULD HAVE OBEYED YOU.
GLOOM
WHAT'S DONE IS DONE.
I SHALL RETURN TO CHOKA.
SHP
THINGS WILL GET BUSY FROM HERE ON.
LORD BUNCHU...
FRIENDS ...

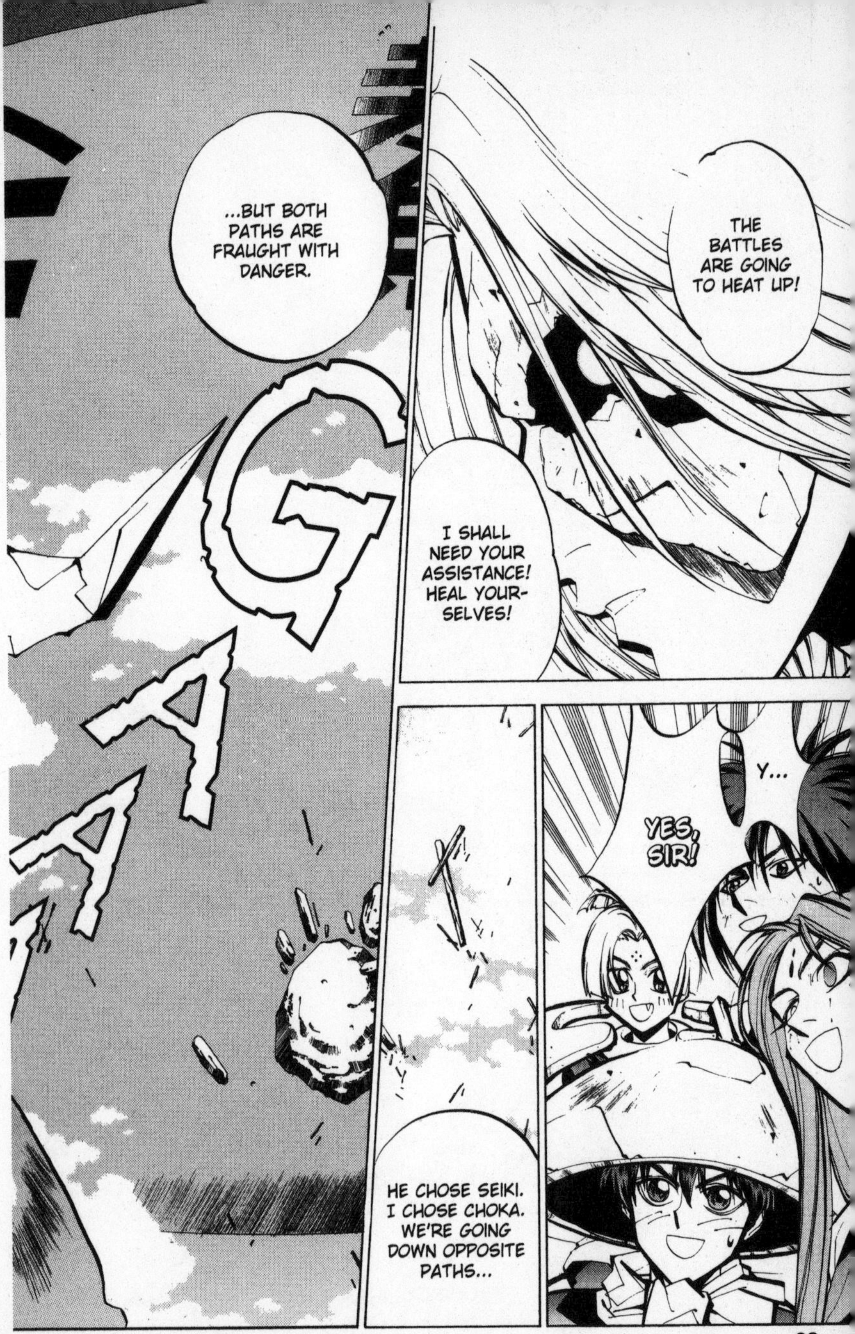
THE BATTLES ARE GOING TO HEAT UP!
I SHALL NEED YOUR ASSISTANCE! HEAL YOUR-SELVES!
Y...
YES, SIR!
HE CHOSE SEIKI. I CHOSE CHOKA. WE'RE GOING DOWN OPPOSITE PATHS...
...BUT BOTH PATHS ARE FRAUGHT WITH DANGER.
GAA

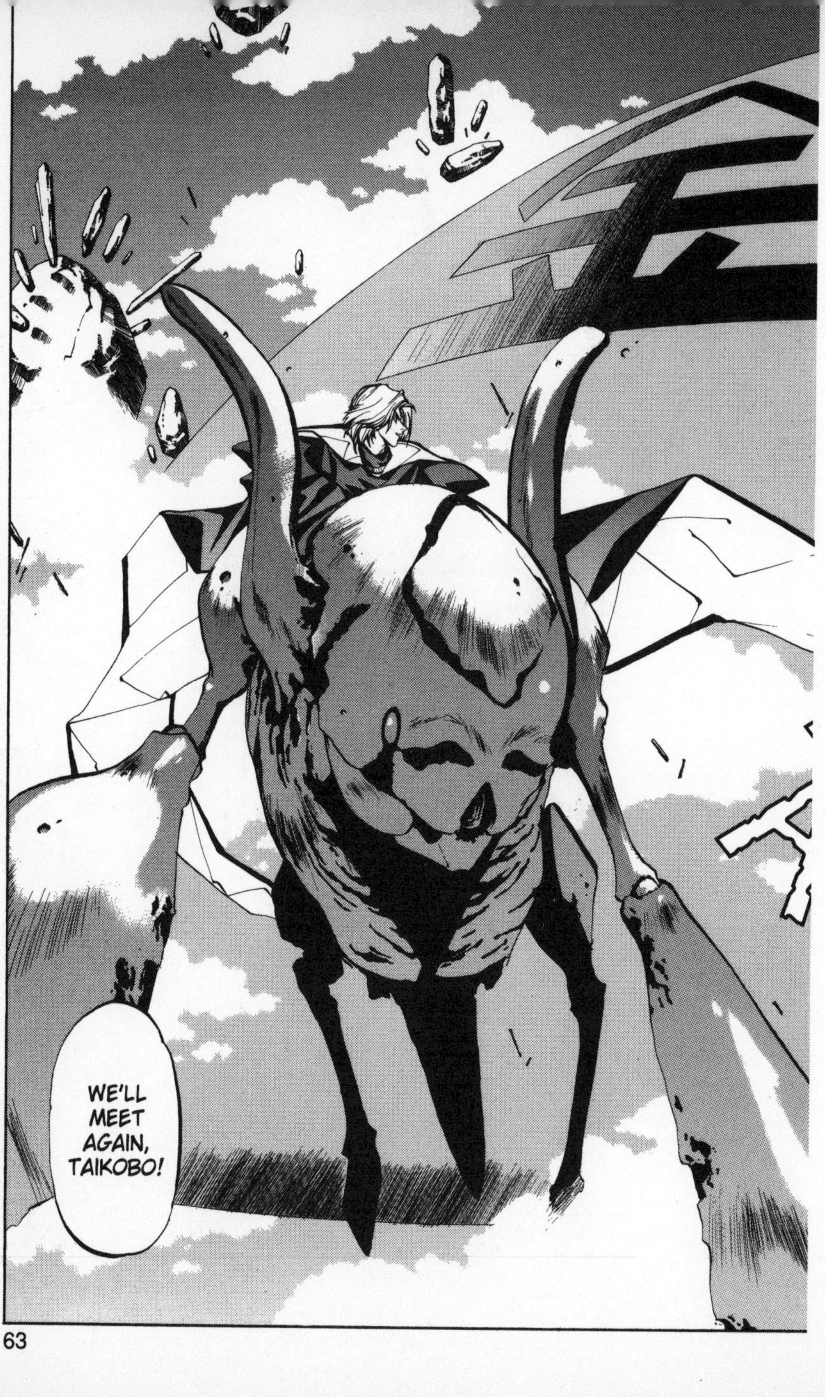
WE'LL MEET AGAIN, TAIKOBO!

封神演義

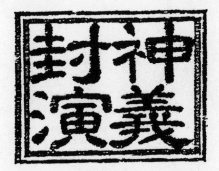

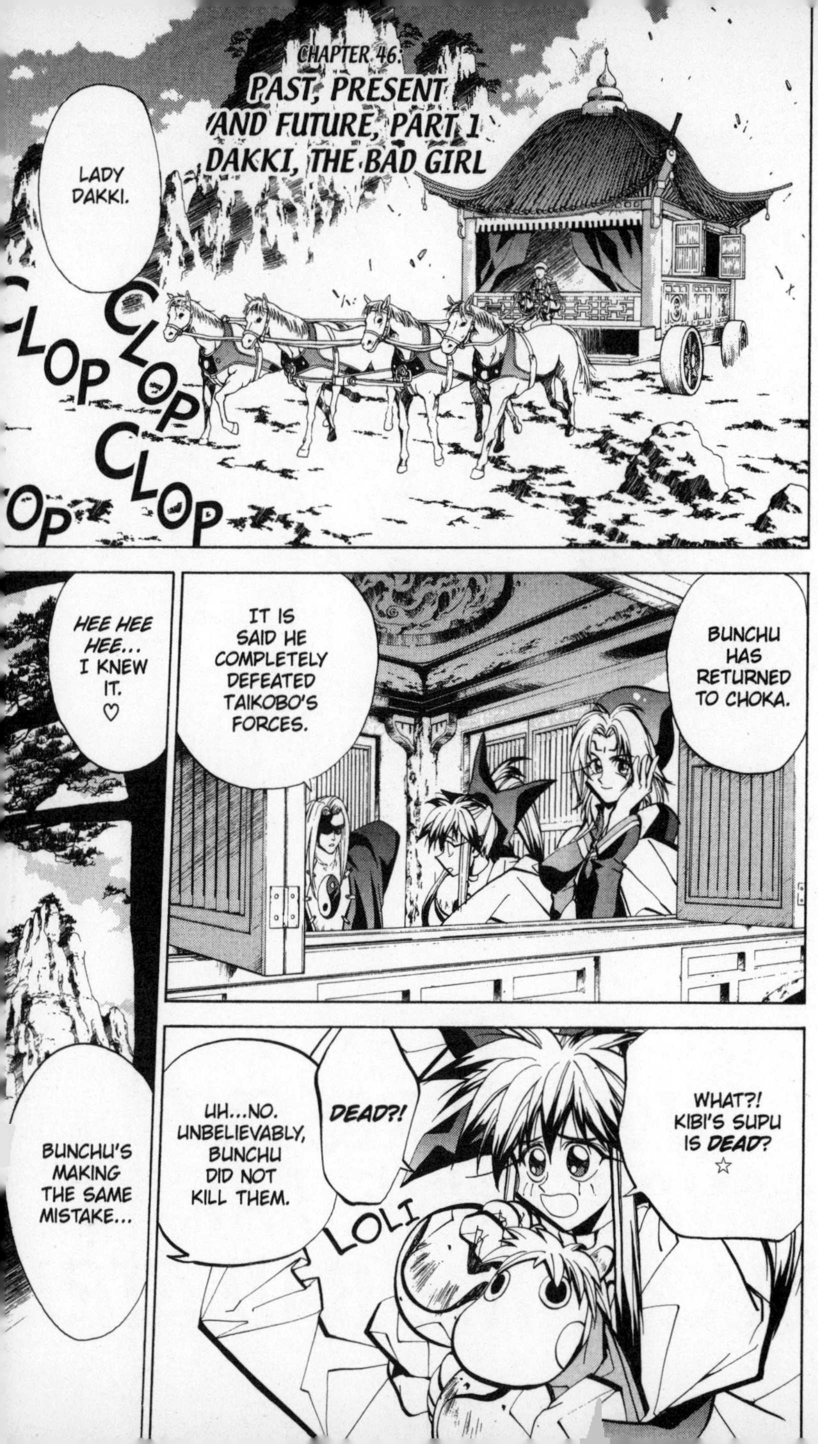
CHAPTER 46:
PAST, PRESENT AND FUTURE, PART 1
DAKKI, THE BAD GIRL
LADY DAKKI.
CLOP CLOP
CLOP CLOP
CLOP
BUNCHU HAS RETURNED TO CHOKA.
IT IS SAID HE COMPLETELY DEFEATED TAIKOBO'S FORCES.
HEE HEE HEE... I KNEW IT. ♡
WHAT?! KIBI'S SUPU IS DEAD? ☆
DEAD?!
UH...NO. UNBELIEVABLY, BUNCHU DID NOT KILL THEM.
LOLI
BUNCHU'S MAKING THE SAME MISTAKE...

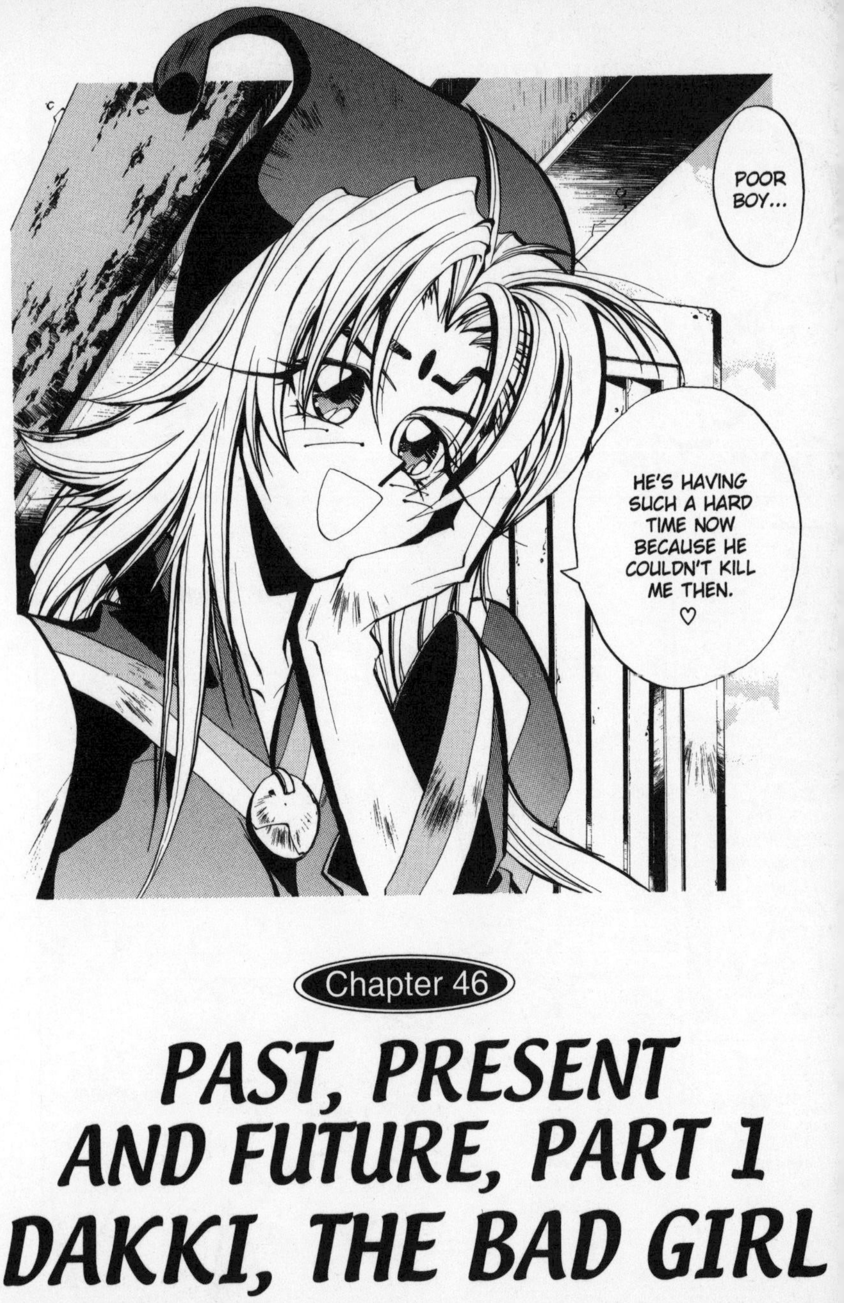
POOR BOY...
HE'S HAVING SUCH A HARD TIME NOW BECAUSE HE COULDN'T KILL ME THEN. ♡

Chapter 46

PAST, PRESENT AND FUTURE, PART 1 DAKKI, THE BAD GIRL

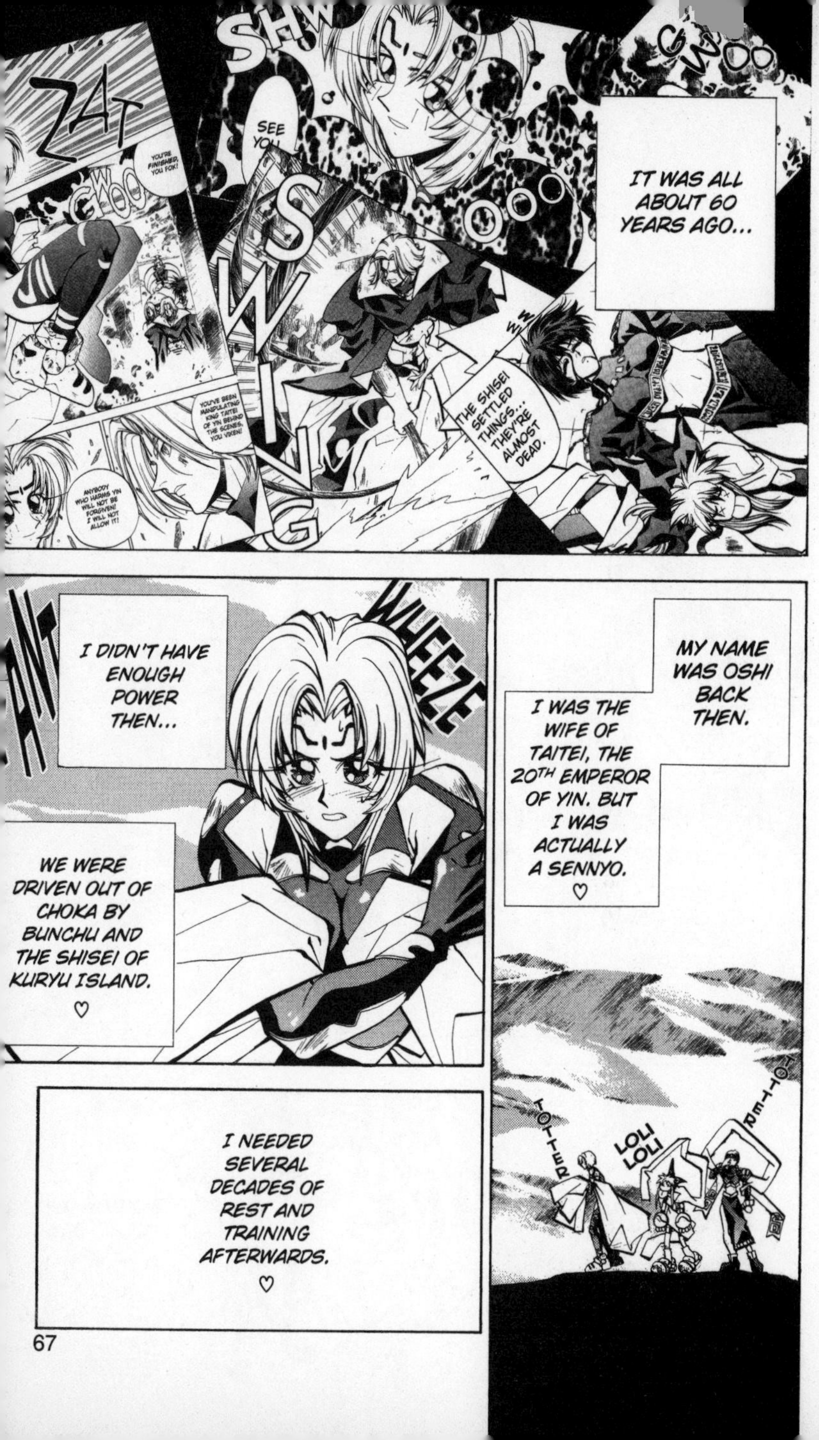

IT WAS ALL ABOUT 60 YEARS AGO...
GWOO
SHW
SEE YOU
GOOO
THE SHISEI SETTLED THINGS... THEY'RE ALMOST DEAD.
WW
SWING
ZAT
YOU'RE FINISHED, YOU FOX!
GWOO
YOU'VE BEEN MANIPULATING KING TAITEI OF YIN BEHIND THE SCENES, YOU VIXEN!
ANYBODY WHO HARMS YIN WILL NOT BE FORGIVEN! I WILL NOT ALLOW IT!
MY NAME WAS OSHI BACK THEN.
I WAS THE WIFE OF TAITEI, THE 20TH EMPEROR OF YIN. BUT I WAS ACTUALLY A SENNYO. ♡
WHEEZE
I DIDN'T HAVE ENOUGH POWER THEN...
PANT
WE WERE DRIVEN OUT OF CHOKA BY BUNCHU AND THE SHISEI OF KURYU ISLAND. ♡
TOTTER
LOLI LOLI
TOTTER
I NEEDED SEVERAL DECADES OF REST AND TRAINING AFTERWARDS. ♡

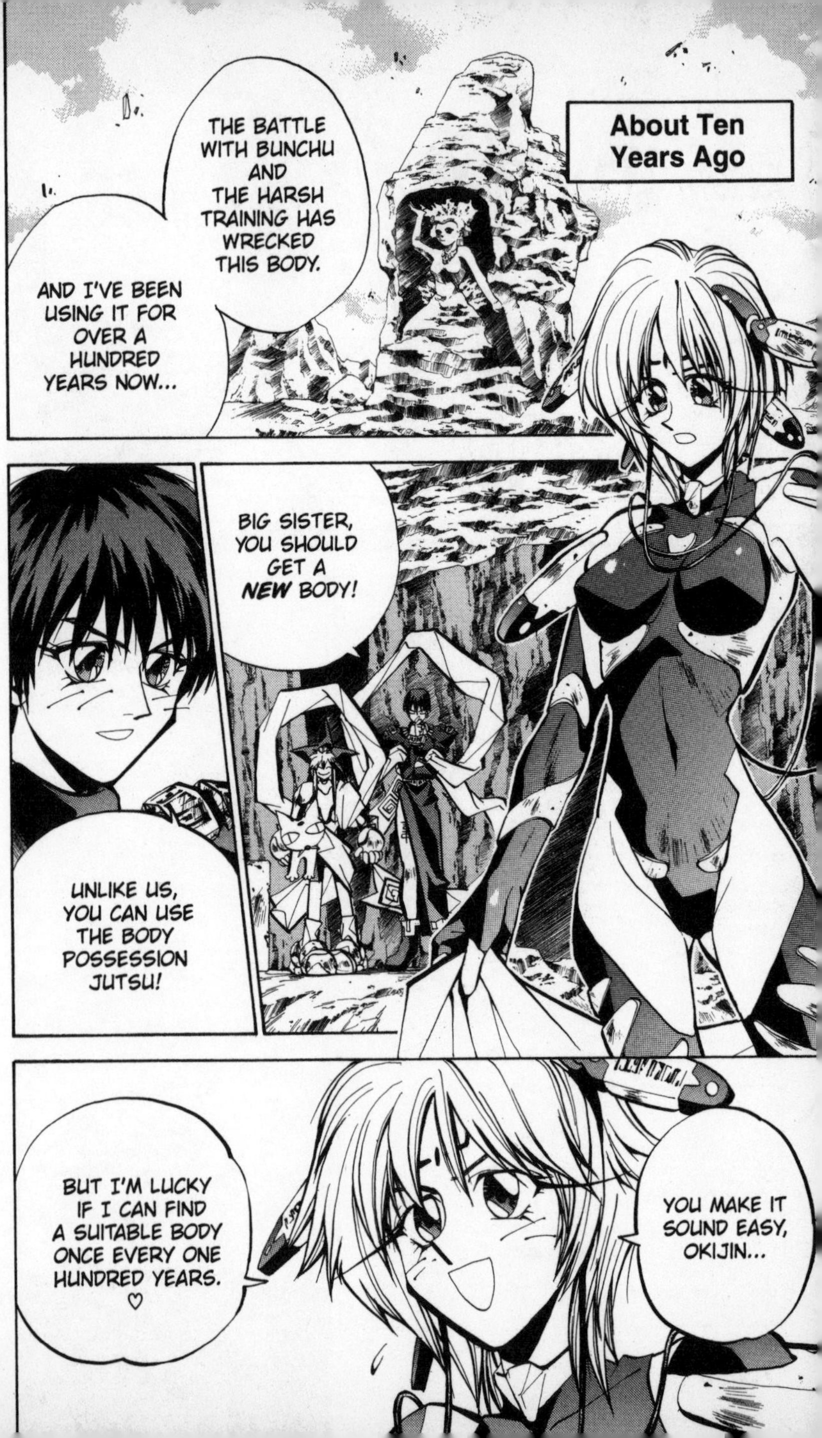
About Ten Years Ago
THE BATTLE WITH BUNCHU AND THE HARSH TRAINING HAS WRECKED THIS BODY.
AND I'VE BEEN USING IT FOR OVER A HUNDRED YEARS NOW...
BIG SISTER, YOU SHOULD GET A *NEW* BODY!
UNLIKE US, YOU CAN USE THE BODY POSSESSION JUTSU!
YOU MAKE IT SOUND EASY, OKIJIN...
BUT I'M LUCKY IF I CAN FIND A SUITABLE BODY ONCE EVERY ONE HUNDRED YEARS. ♡

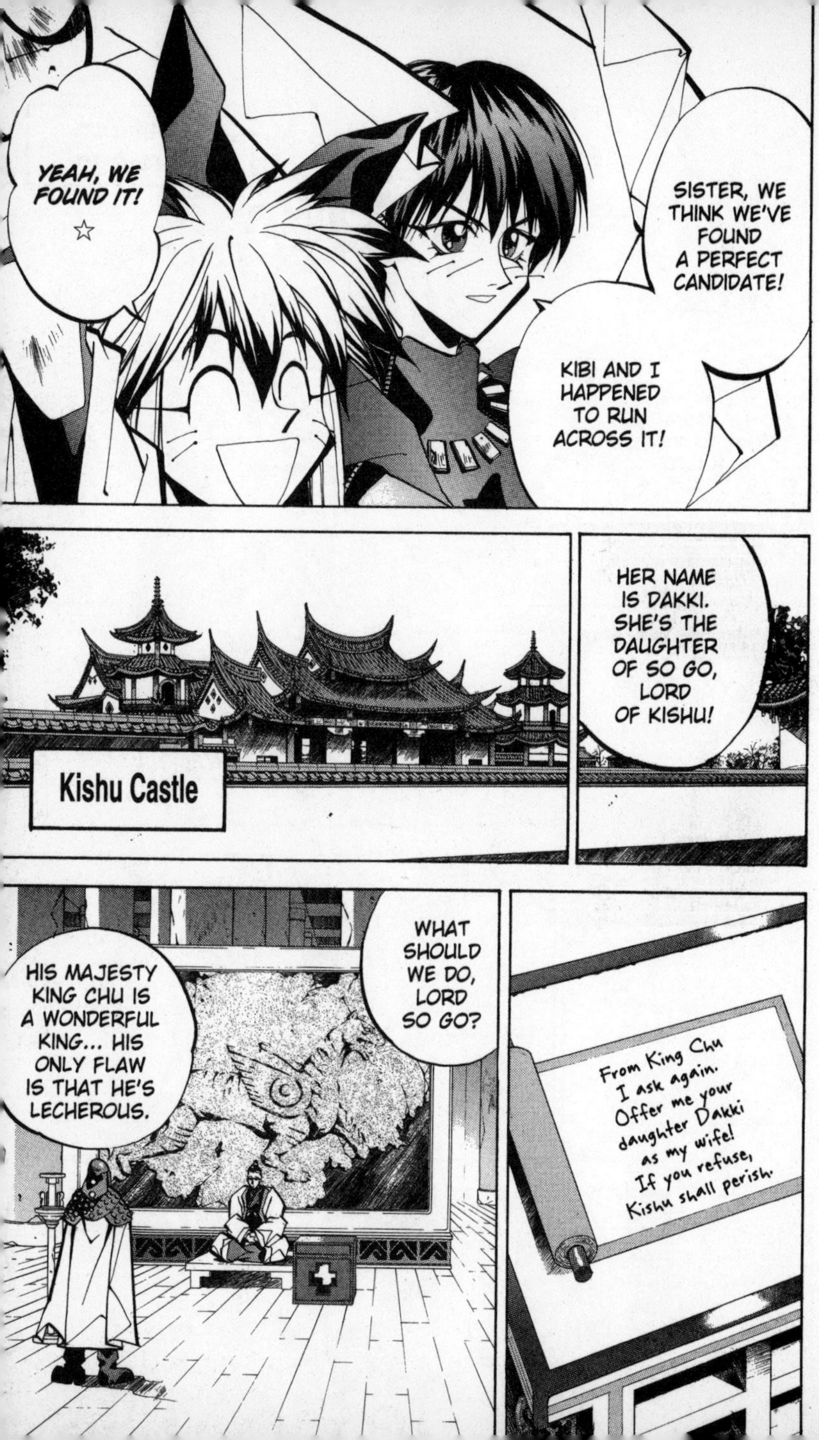
SISTER, WE THINK WE'VE FOUND A PERFECT CANDIDATE!
KIBI AND I HAPPENED TO RUN ACROSS IT!
YEAH, WE FOUND IT! ☆
HER NAME IS DAKKI. SHE'S THE DAUGHTER OF SO GO, LORD OF KISHU!
Kishu Castle
From King Chu
I ask again.
Offer me your daughter Dakki as my wife!
If you refuse, Kishu shall perish.
WHAT SHOULD WE DO, LORD SO GO?
HIS MAJESTY KING CHU IS A WONDERFUL KING... HIS ONLY FLAW IS THAT HE'S LECHEROUS.

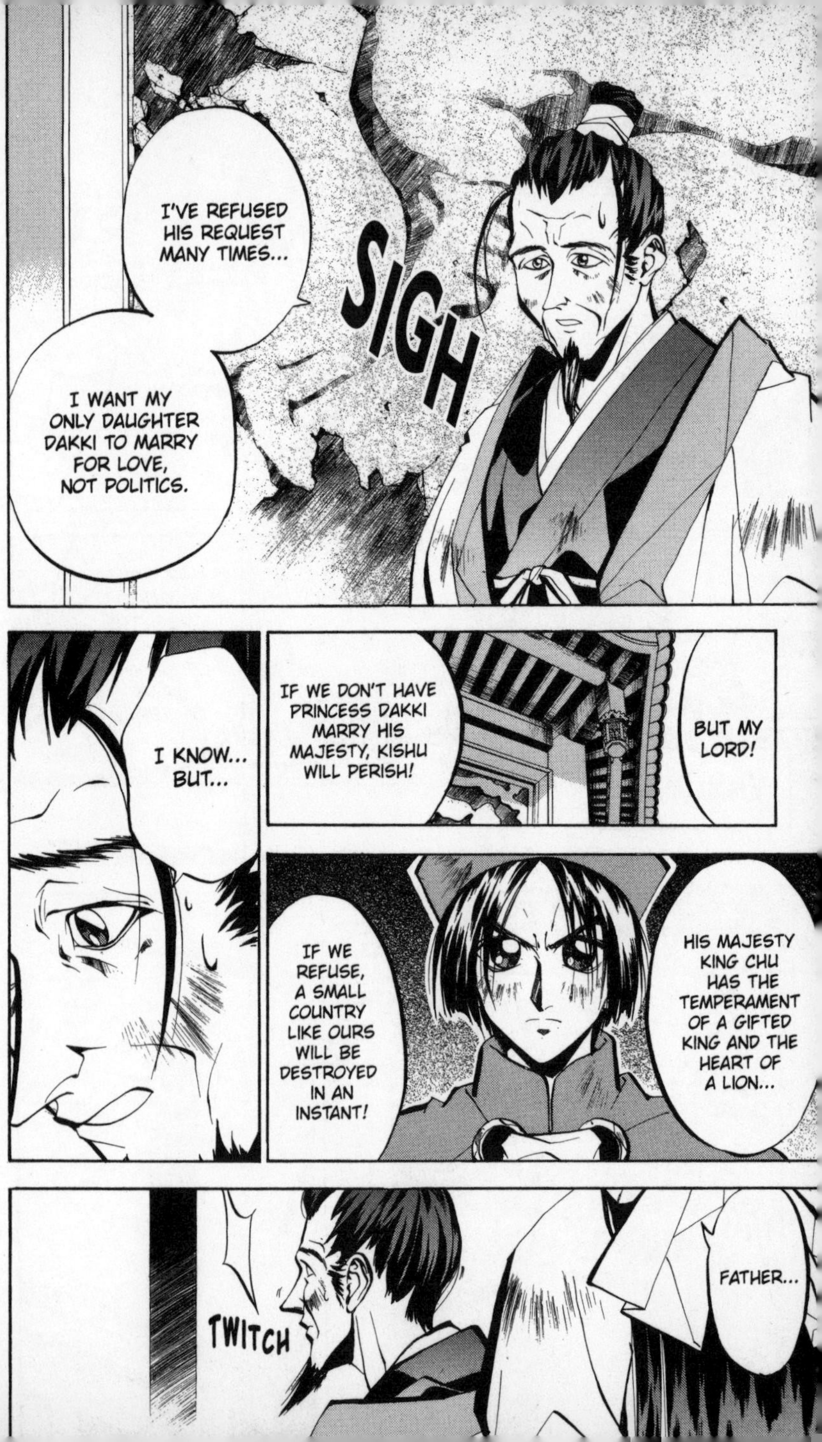

I'VE REFUSED HIS REQUEST MANY TIMES...
SIGH
I WANT MY ONLY DAUGHTER DAKKI TO MARRY FOR LOVE, NOT POLITICS.
BUT MY LORD!
IF WE DON'T HAVE PRINCESS DAKKI MARRY HIS MAJESTY, KISHU WILL PERISH!
HIS MAJESTY KING CHU HAS THE TEMPERAMENT OF A GIFTED KING AND THE HEART OF A LION...
IF WE REFUSE, A SMALL COUNTRY LIKE OURS WILL BE DESTROYED IN AN INSTANT!
I KNOW... BUT...
FATHER...
TWITCH

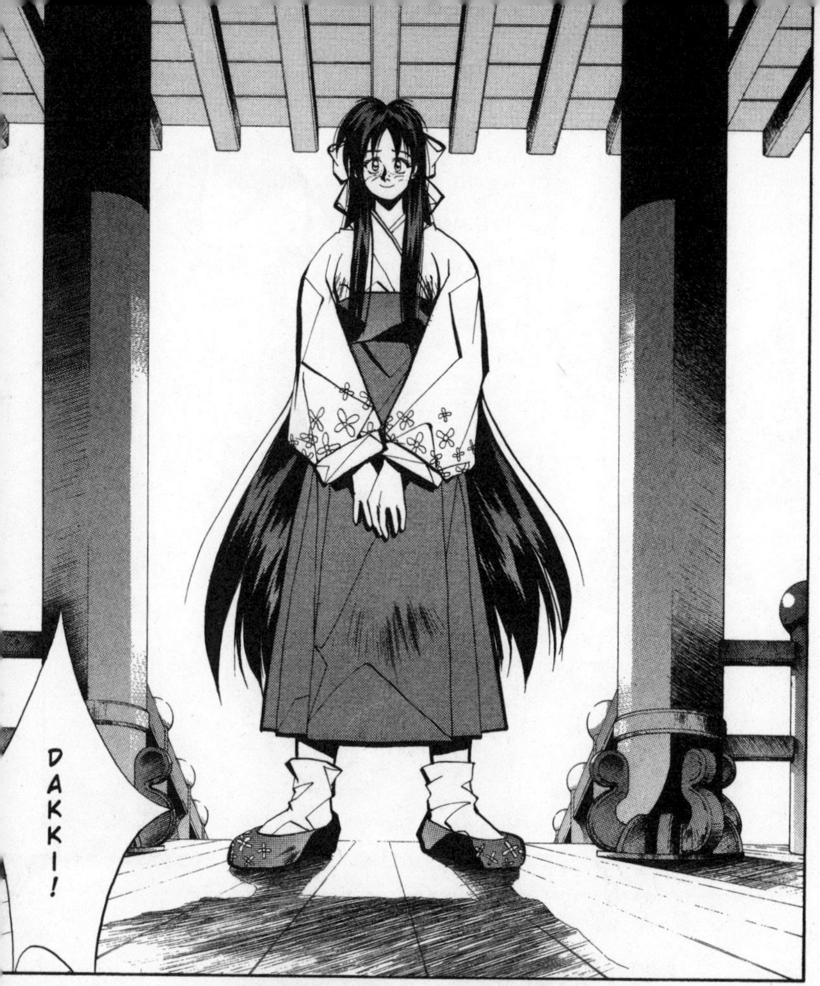
DAKKI!
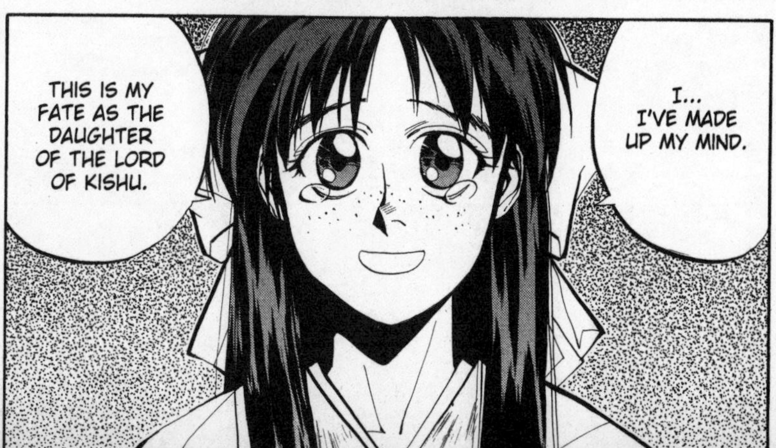
I... I'VE MADE UP MY MIND.
THIS IS MY FATE AS THE DAUGHTER OF THE LORD OF KISHU.

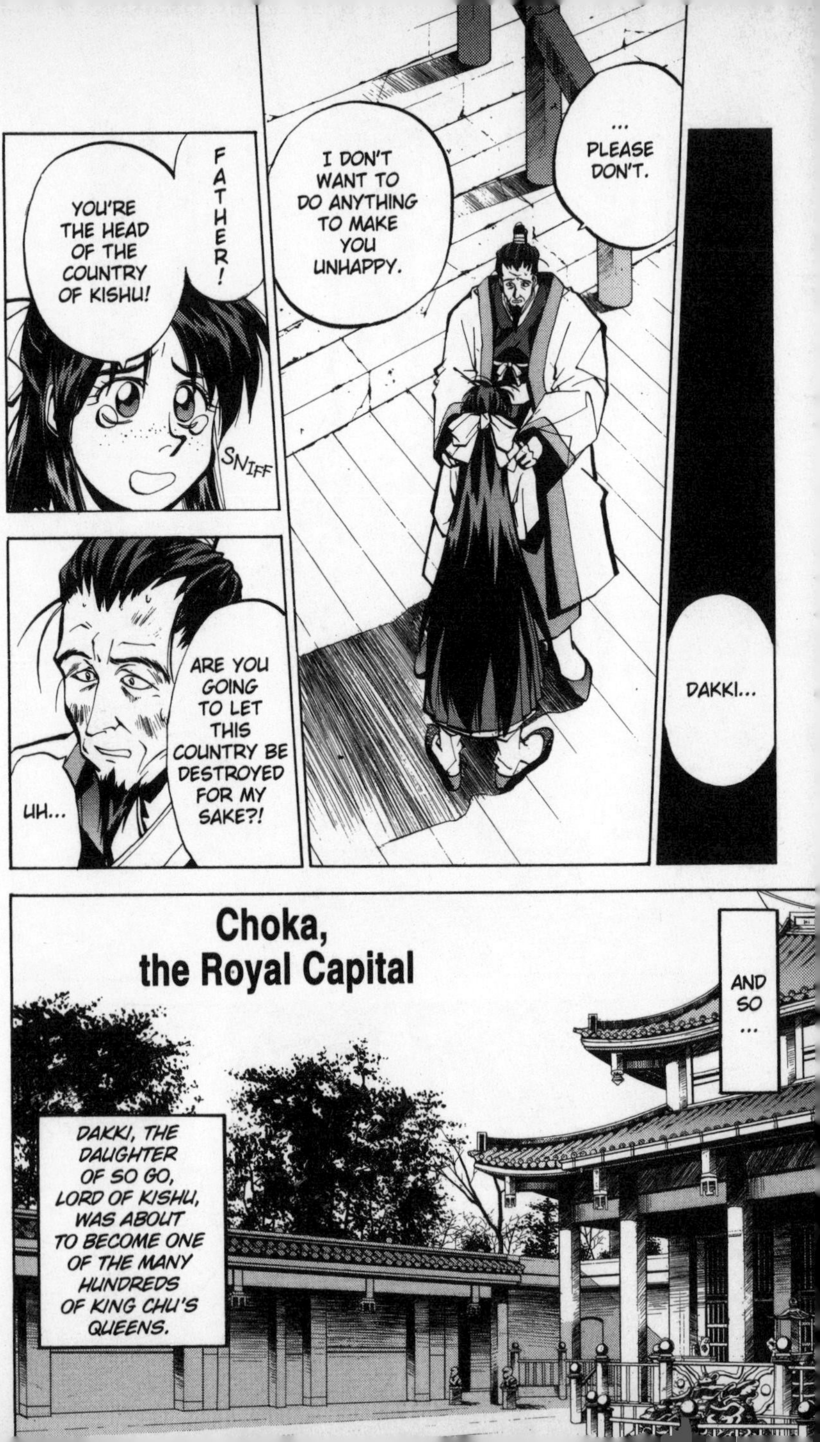
DAKKI...
... PLEASE DON'T.
I DON'T WANT TO DO ANYTHING TO MAKE YOU UNHAPPY.
FATHER!
YOU'RE THE HEAD OF THE COUNTRY OF KISHU!
SNIFF
ARE YOU GOING TO LET THIS COUNTRY BE DESTROYED FOR MY SAKE?!
UH...
AND SO ...
Choka, the Royal Capital
DAKKI, THE DAUGHTER OF SO GO, LORD OF KISHU, WAS ABOUT TO BECOME ONE OF THE MANY HUNDREDS OF KING CHU'S QUEENS.

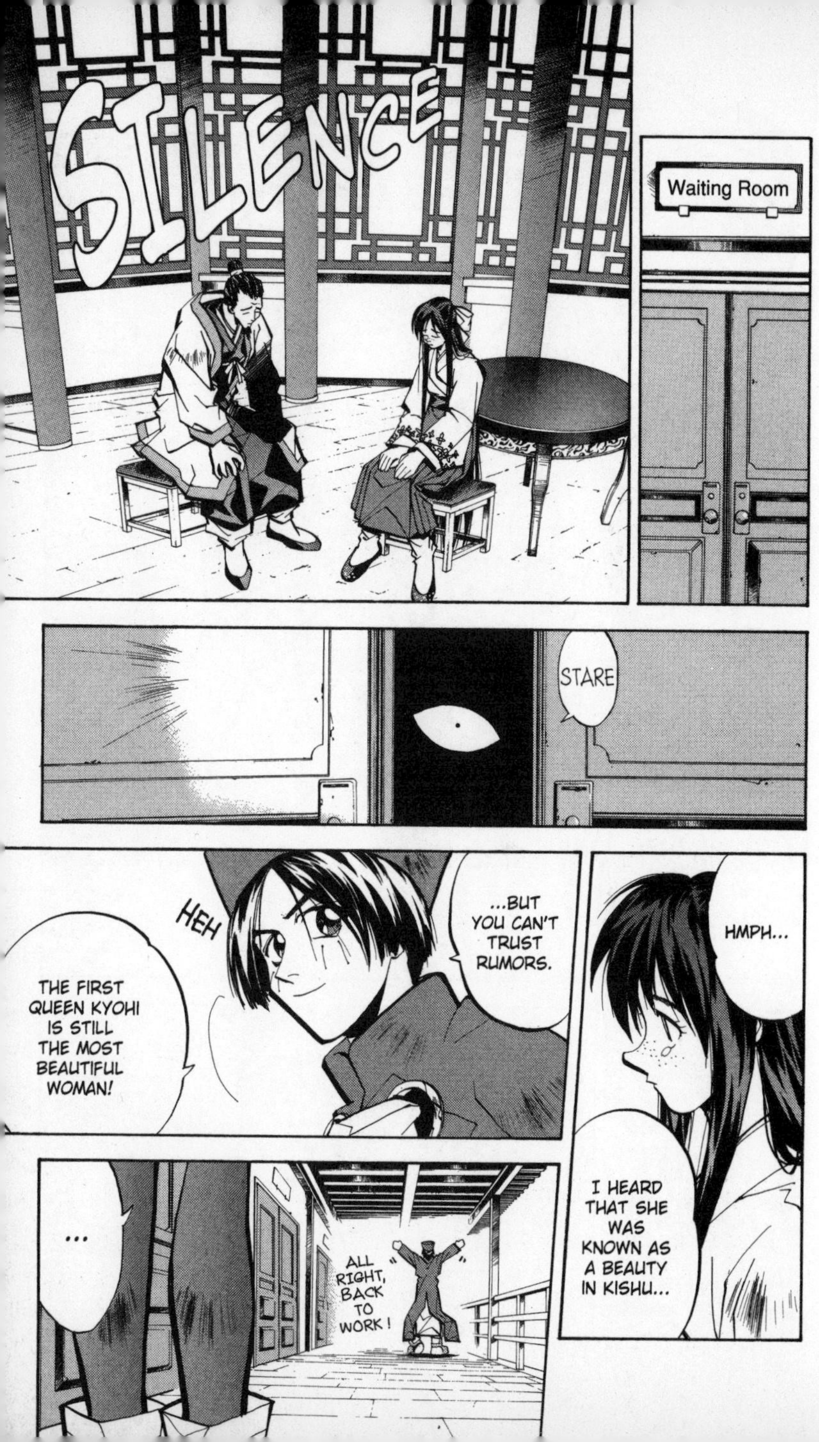
Waiting Room
SILENCE
STARE
HMPH...
I HEARD THAT SHE WAS KNOWN AS A BEAUTY IN KISHU...
...BUT YOU CAN'T TRUST RUMORS.
HEH
THE FIRST QUEEN KYOHI IS STILL THE MOST BEAUTIFUL WOMAN!
...
ALL RIGHT, BACK TO WORK!

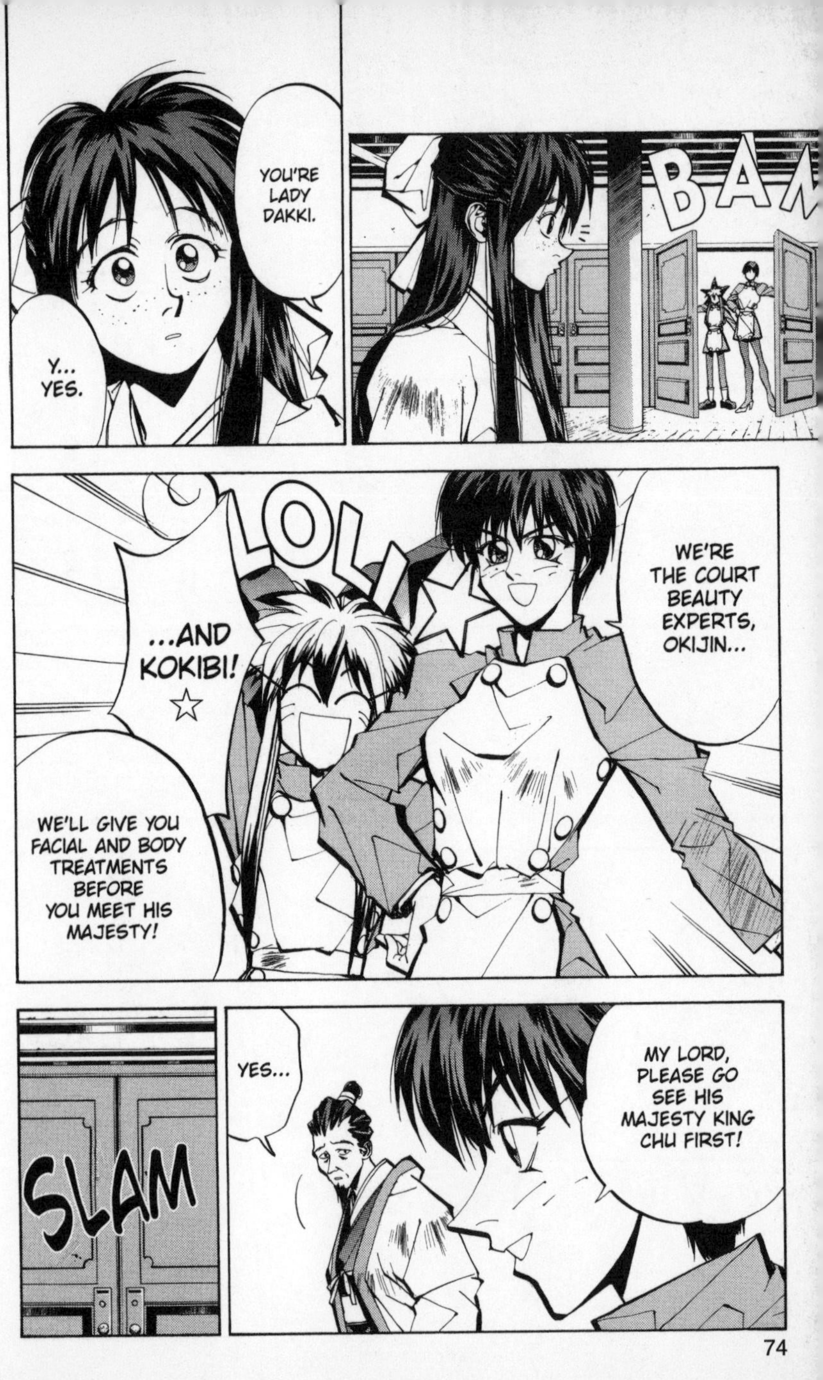
BAM
YOU'RE LADY DAKKI.
Y... YES.
WE'RE THE COURT BEAUTY EXPERTS, OKIJIN...
LOL
...AND KOKIBI! ☆
WE'LL GIVE YOU FACIAL AND BODY TREATMENTS BEFORE YOU MEET HIS MAJESTY!
MY LORD, PLEASE GO SEE HIS MAJESTY KING CHU FIRST!
YES...
SLAM

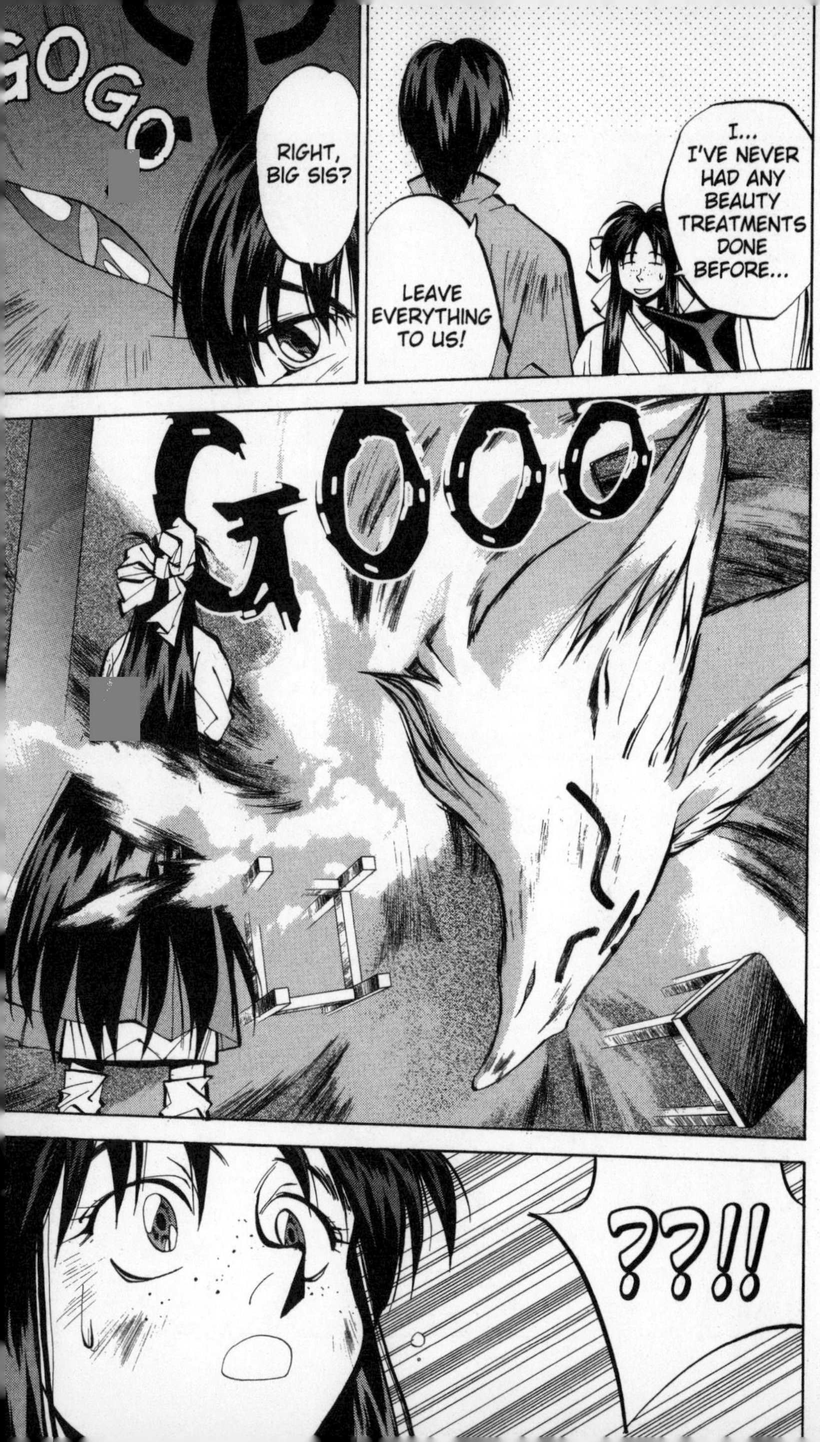
I... I'VE NEVER HAD ANY BEAUTY TREATMENTS DONE BEFORE...
LEAVE EVERYTHING TO US!
RIGHT, BIG SIS?
GOGO
GOOOO
??!!

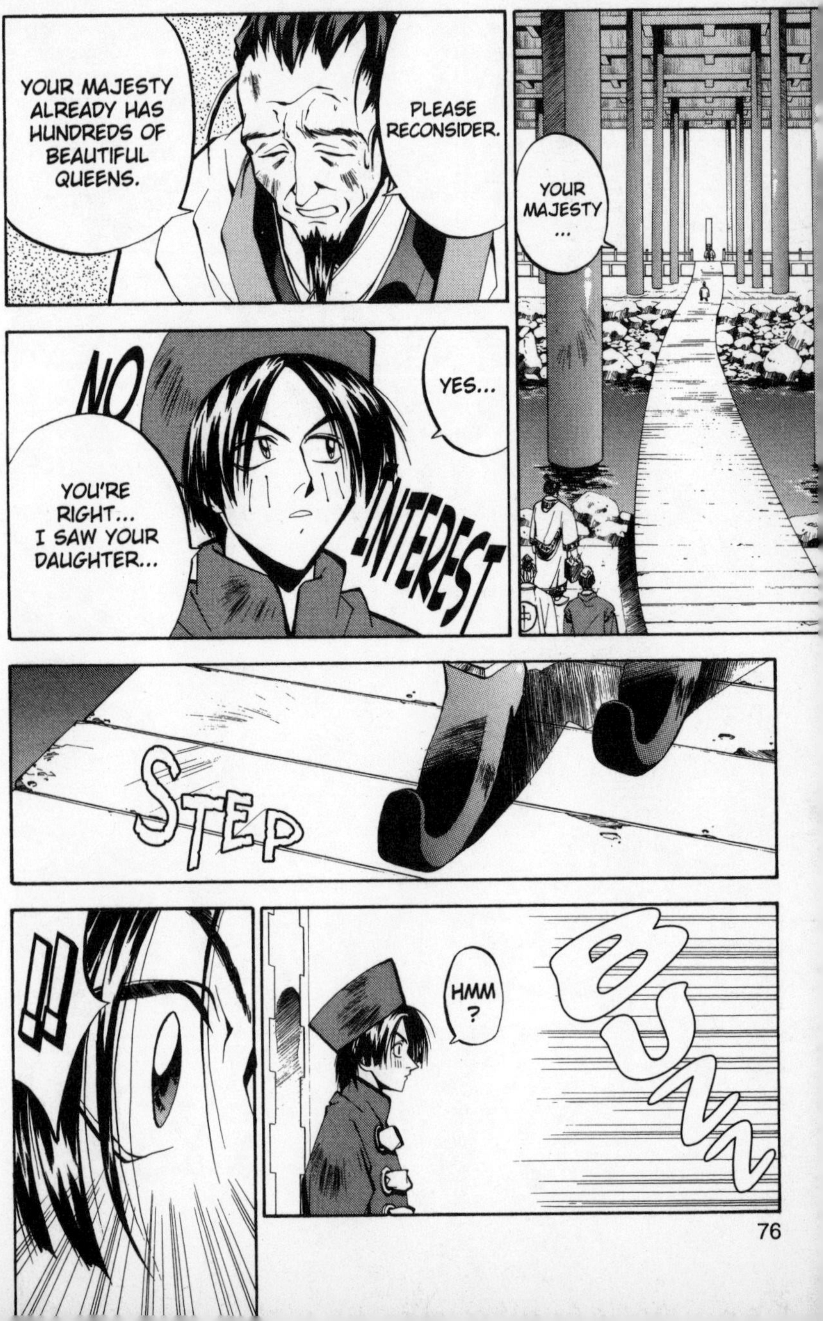
YOUR MAJESTY ...
PLEASE RECONSIDER.
YOUR MAJESTY ALREADY HAS HUNDREDS OF BEAUTIFUL QUEENS.
YES...
NO INTEREST
YOU'RE RIGHT... I SAW YOUR DAUGHTER...
STEP
BUNN
HMM ?
!!

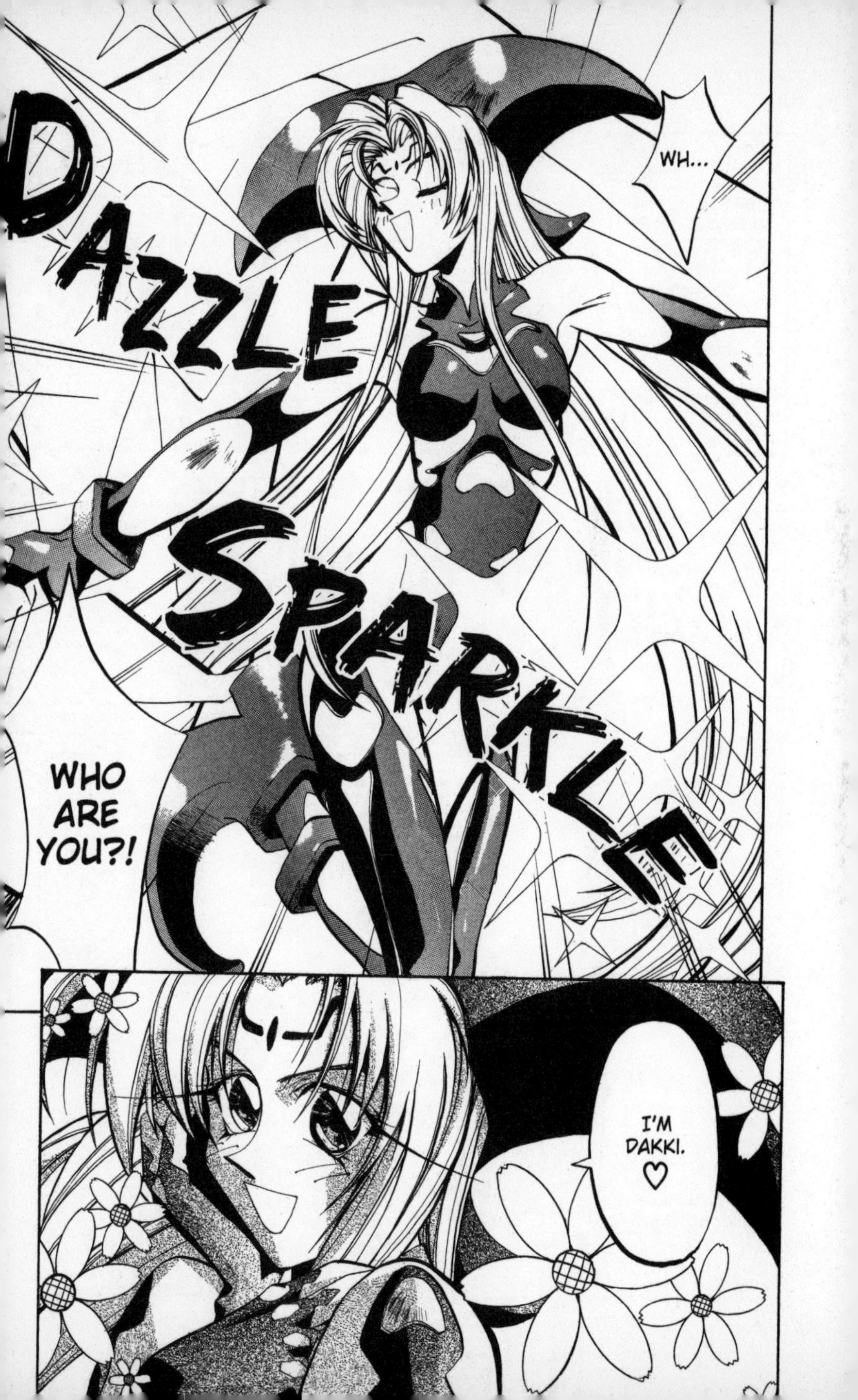
WH...
DAZZLE
SPARKLE
WHO ARE YOU?!
I'M DAKKI. ♡

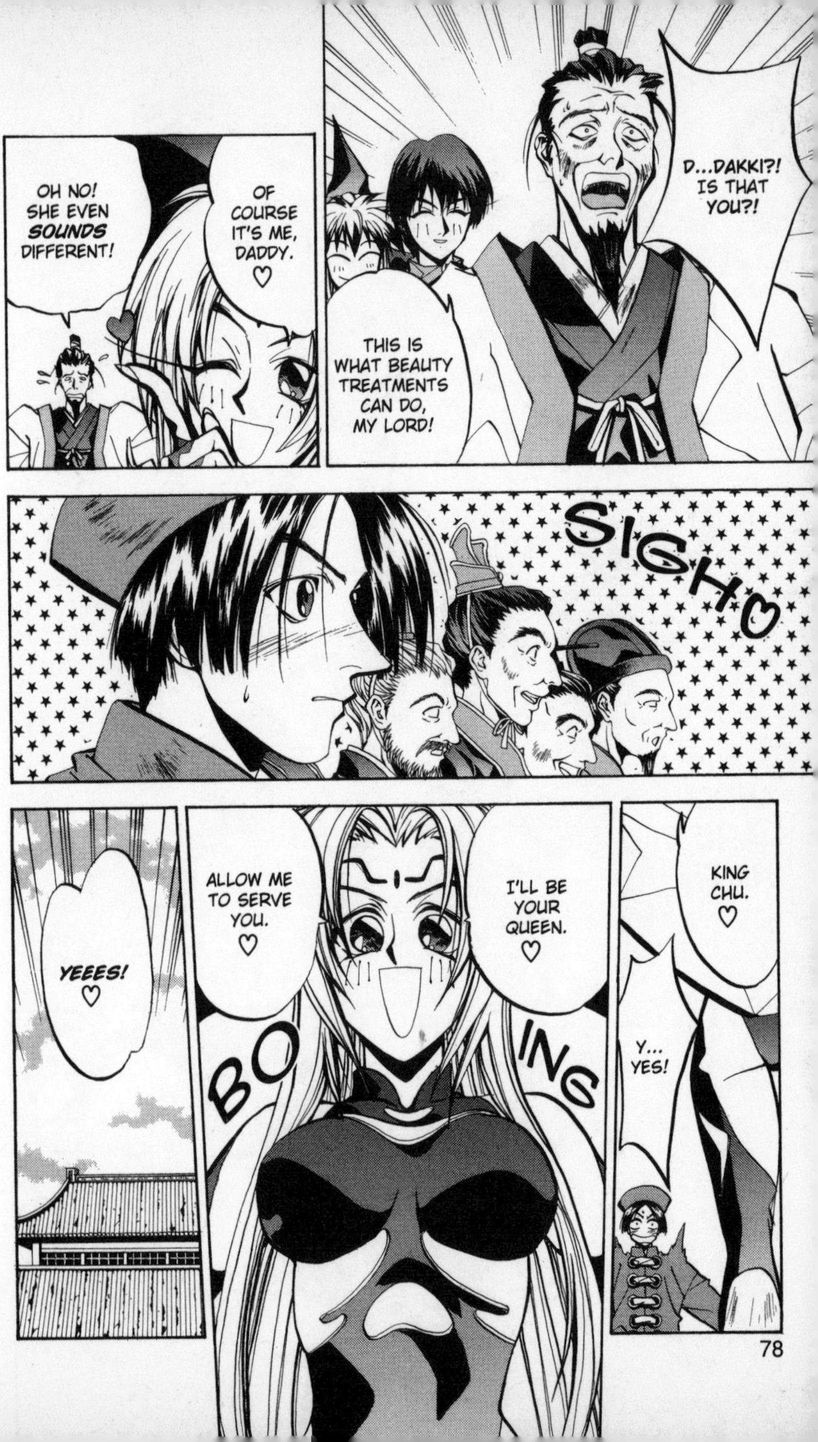
D...DAKKI?! IS THAT YOU?!
THIS IS WHAT BEAUTY TREATMENTS CAN DO, MY LORD!
OF COURSE IT'S ME, DADDY. ♡
OH NO! SHE EVEN ***SOUNDS*** DIFFERENT!
SIGH♡
KING CHU. ♡
Y... YES!
I'LL BE YOUR QUEEN. ♡
ALLOW ME TO SERVE YOU. ♡
BOING
YEEES! ♡

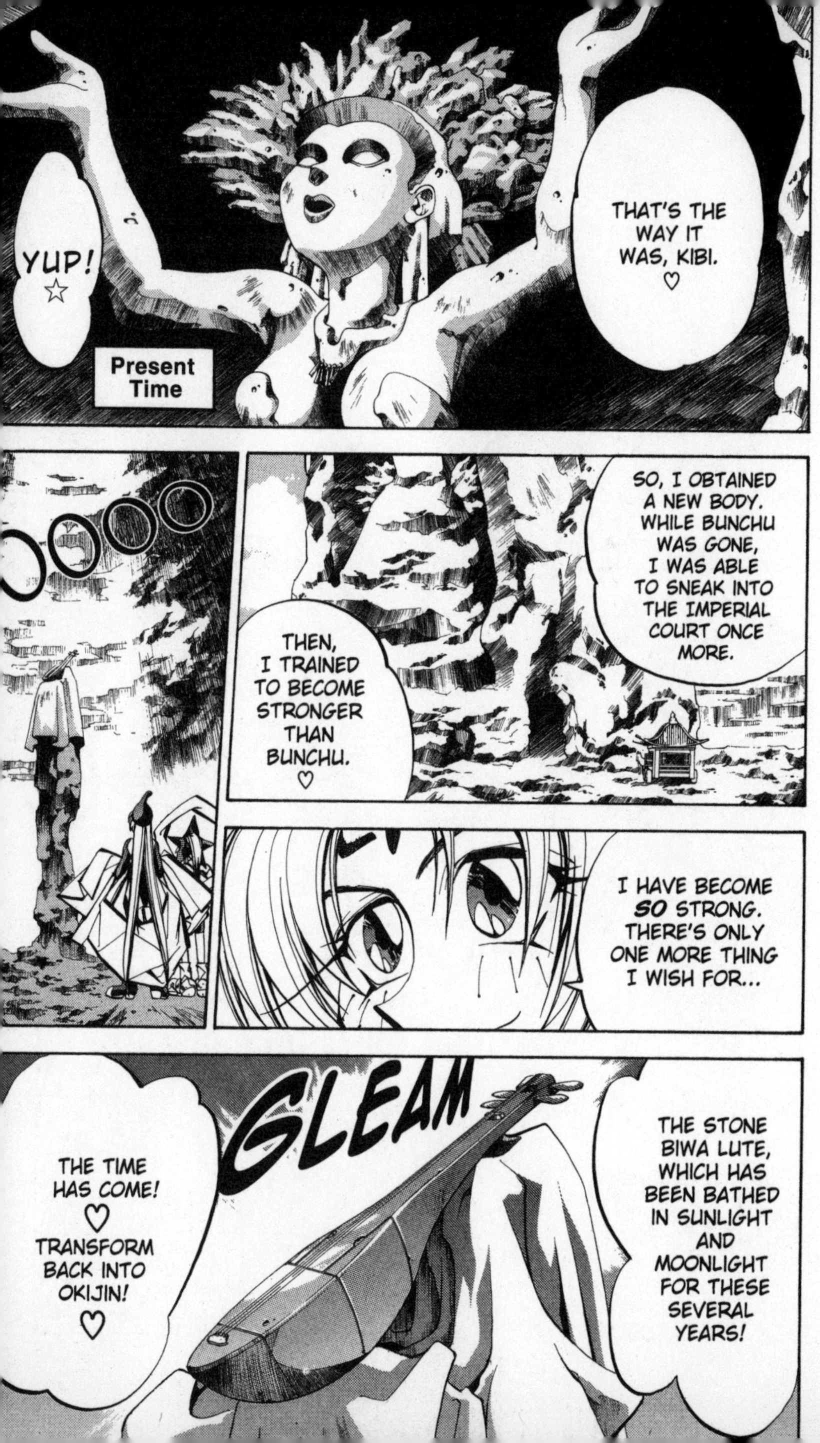
THAT'S THE WAY IT WAS, KIBI. ♡
YUP! ☆
Present Time
SO, I OBTAINED A NEW BODY. WHILE BUNCHU WAS GONE, I WAS ABLE TO SNEAK INTO THE IMPERIAL COURT ONCE MORE.
THEN, I TRAINED TO BECOME STRONGER THAN BUNCHU. ♡
I HAVE BECOME *SO* STRONG. THERE'S ONLY ONE MORE THING I WISH FOR...
GLEAM
THE STONE BIWA LUTE, WHICH HAS BEEN BATHED IN SUNLIGHT AND MOONLIGHT FOR THESE SEVERAL YEARS!
THE TIME HAS COME! ♡ TRANSFORM BACK INTO OKIJIN! ♡

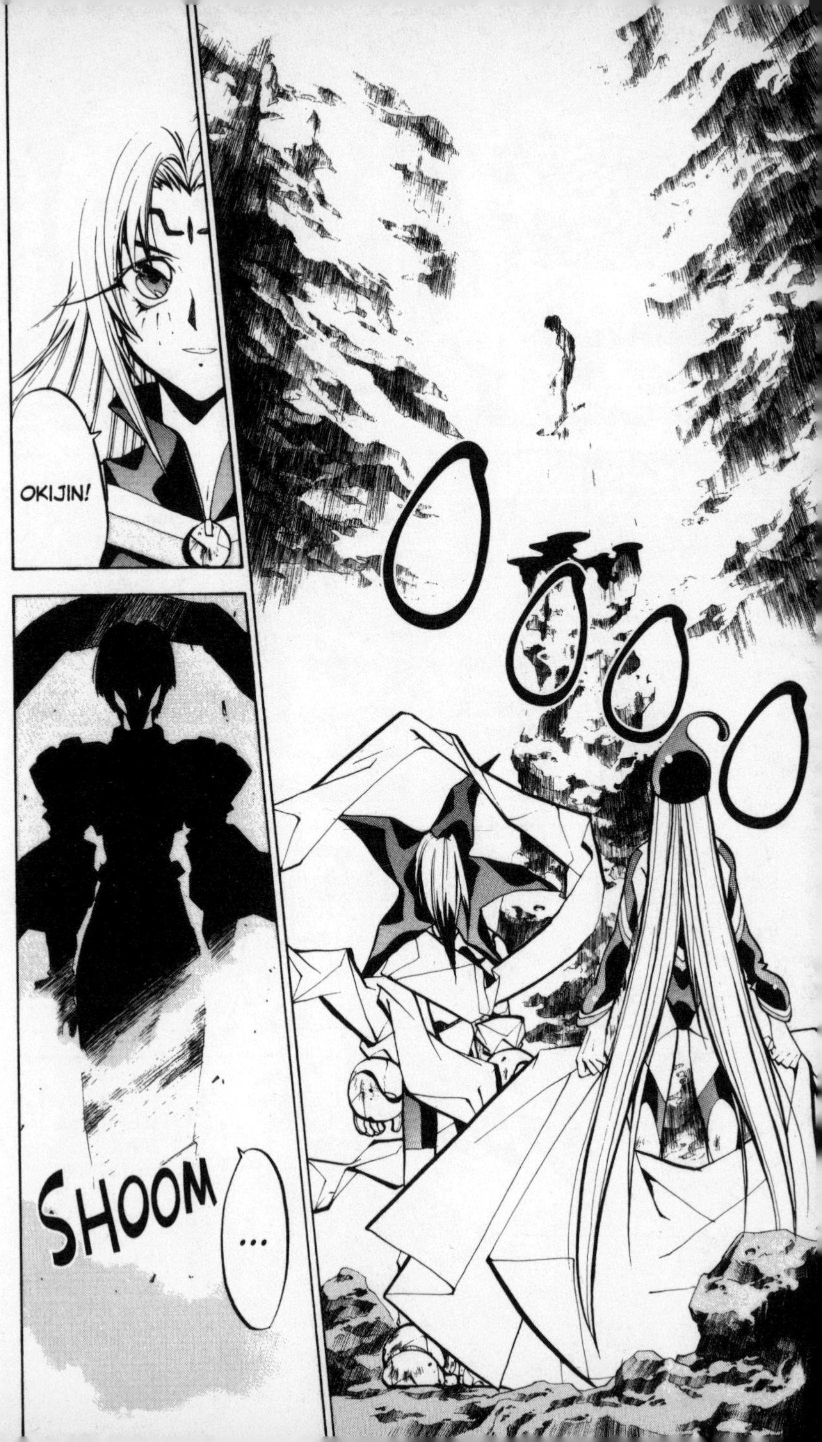
OKIJIN!
...
SHOOM

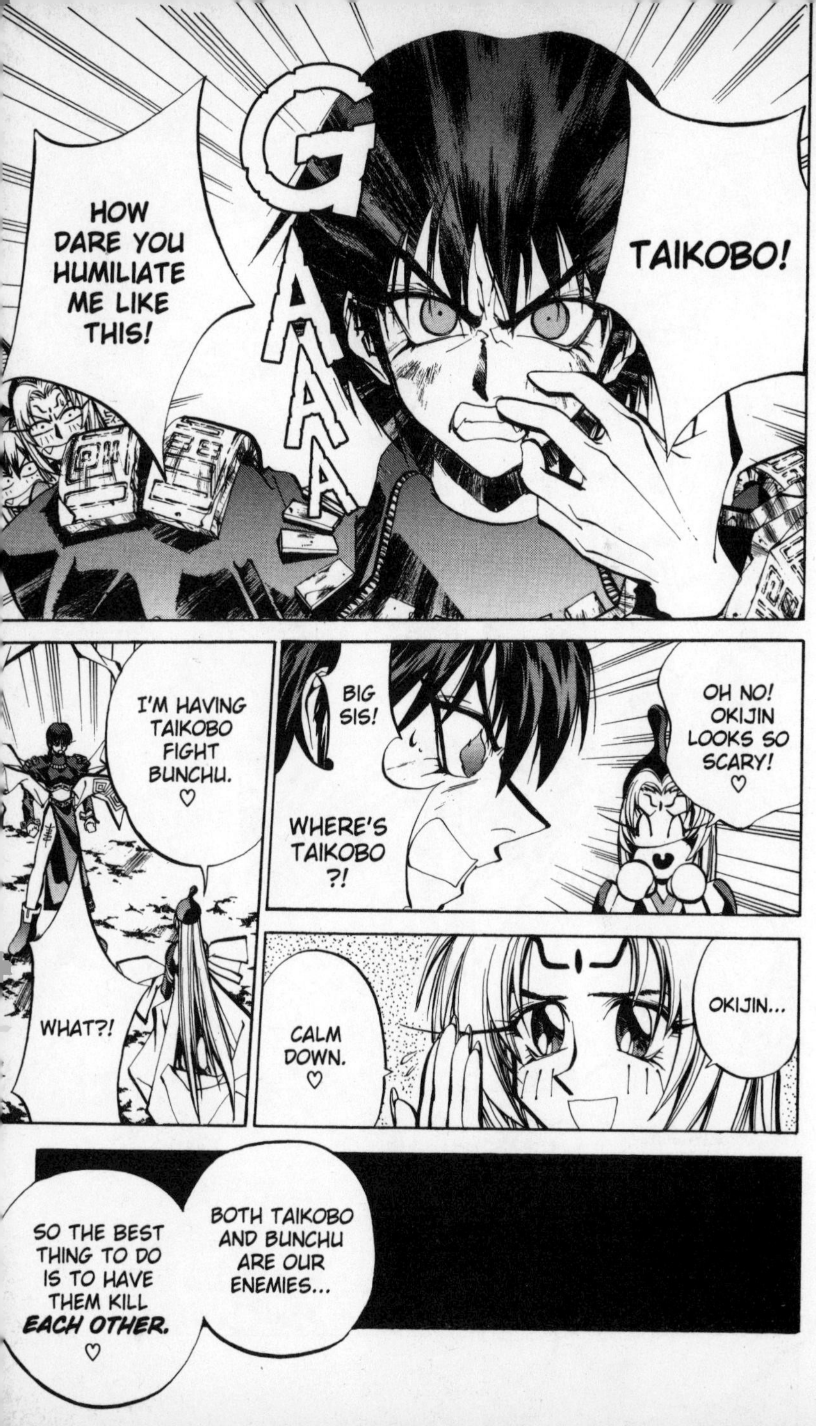
TAIKOBO!
GAAAA
HOW DARE YOU HUMILIATE ME LIKE THIS!
OH NO! OKIJIN LOOKS SO SCARY! ♡
BIG SIS!
WHERE'S TAIKOBO ?!
OKIJIN...
CALM DOWN. ♡
I'M HAVING TAIKOBO FIGHT BUNCHU. ♡
WHAT?!
BOTH TAIKOBO AND BUNCHU ARE OUR ENEMIES...
SO THE BEST THING TO DO IS TO HAVE THEM KILL ***EACH OTHER.*** ♡

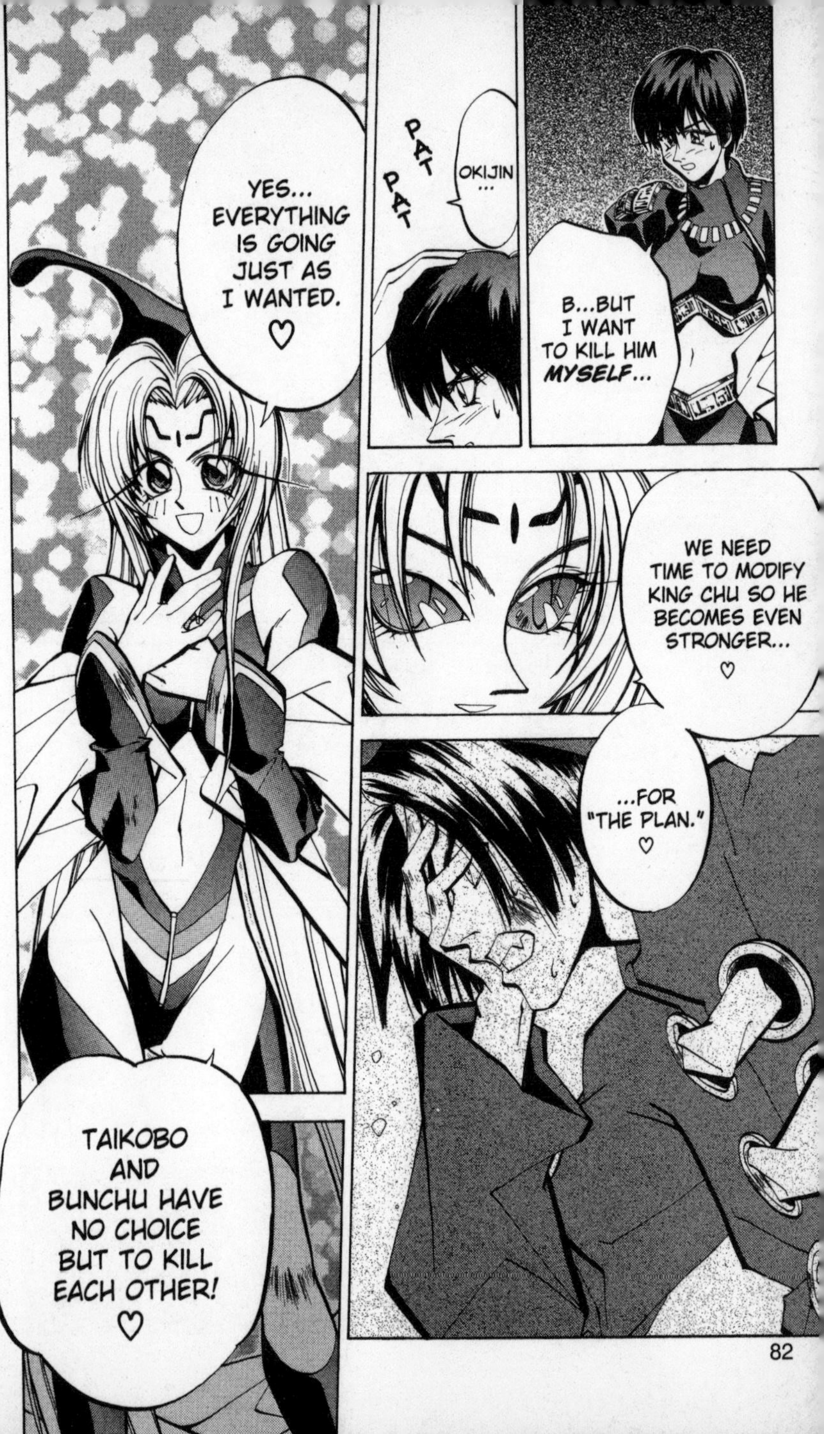
B...BUT I WANT TO KILL HIM *MYSELF*...
PAT PAT
OKIJIN...
WE NEED TIME TO MODIFY KING CHU SO HE BECOMES EVEN STRONGER... ♡
..FOR "THE PLAN." ♡
YES... EVERYTHING IS GOING JUST AS I WANTED. ♡
TAIKOBO AND BUNCHU HAVE NO CHOICE BUT TO KILL EACH OTHER! ♡

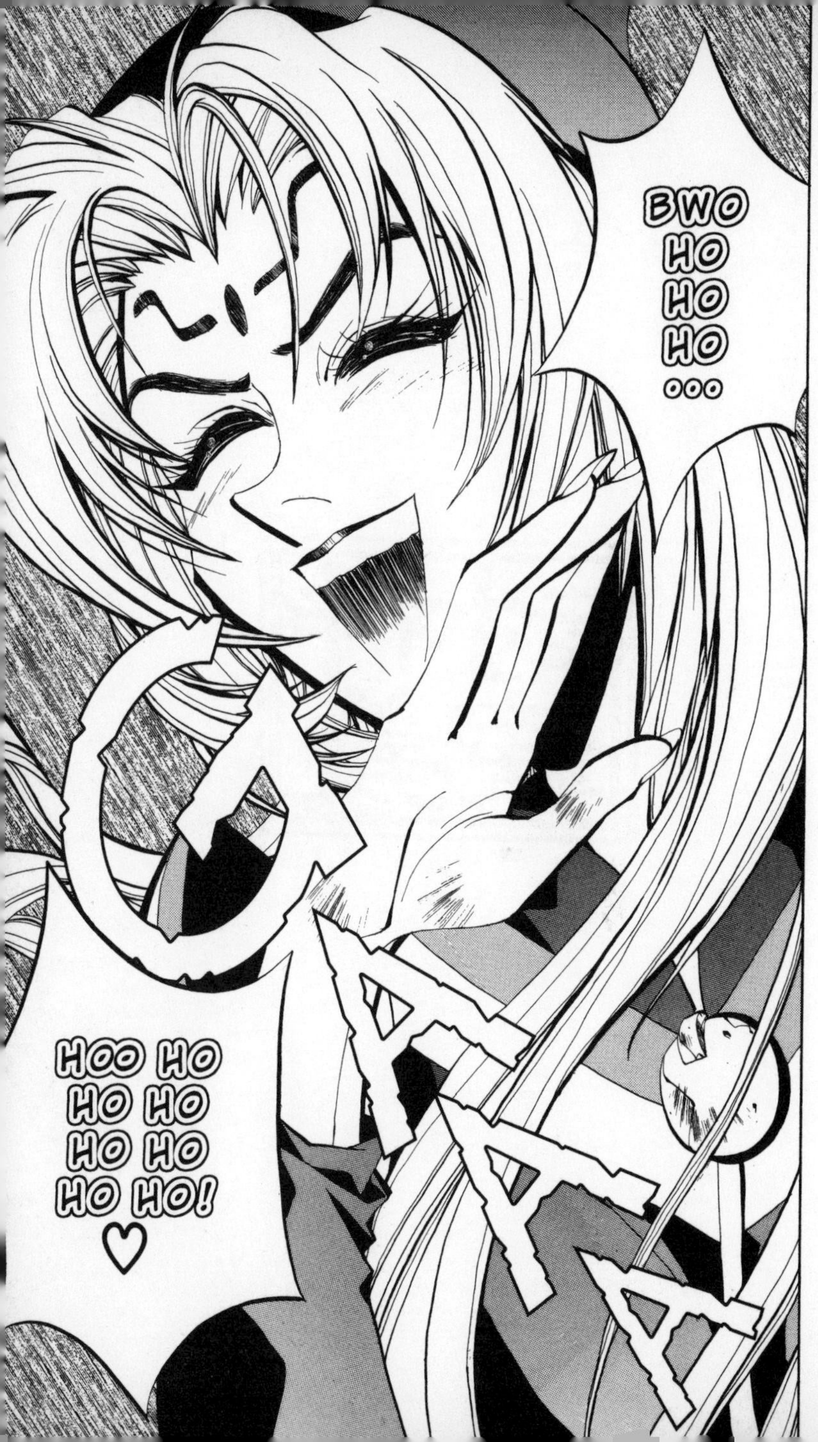
BWO HO HO HO...
HOO HO HO HO HO HO HO HO! ♥
OAAA

封神演義

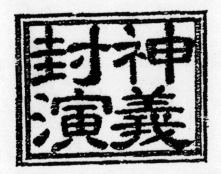

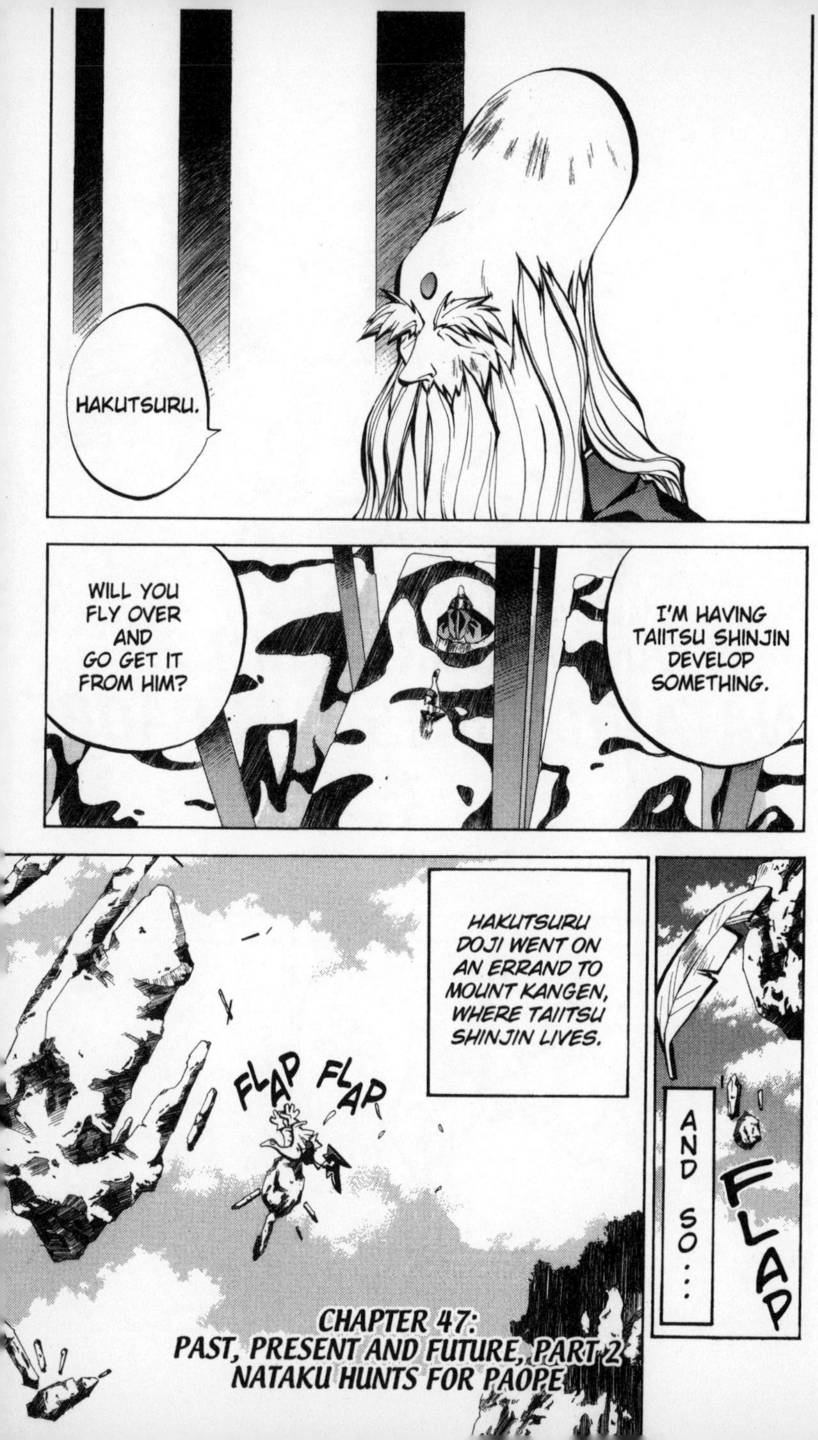
HAKUTSURU.
I'M HAVING TAIITSU SHINJIN DEVELOP SOMETHING.
WILL YOU FLY OVER AND GO GET IT FROM HIM?
AND SO...
FLAP
HAKUTSURU DOJI WENT ON AN ERRAND TO MOUNT KANGEN, WHERE TAIITSU SHINJIN LIVES.
FLAP FLAP
CHAPTER 47:
PAST, PRESENT AND FUTURE, PART 2
NATAKU HUNTS FOR PAOPE

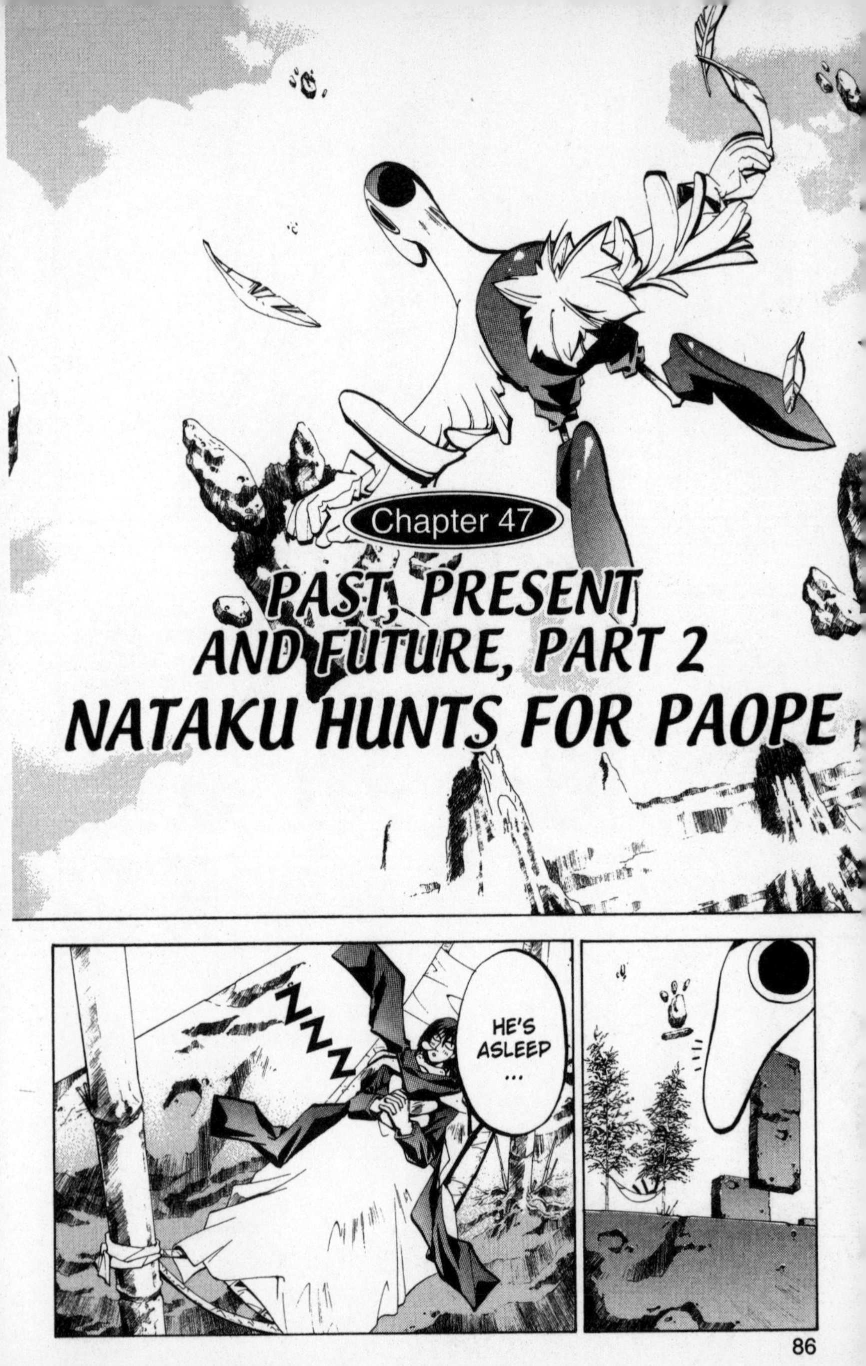
Chapter 47
PAST, PRESENT AND FUTURE, PART 2
NATAKU HUNTS FOR PAOPE
ZZZ
HE'S ASLEEP ...

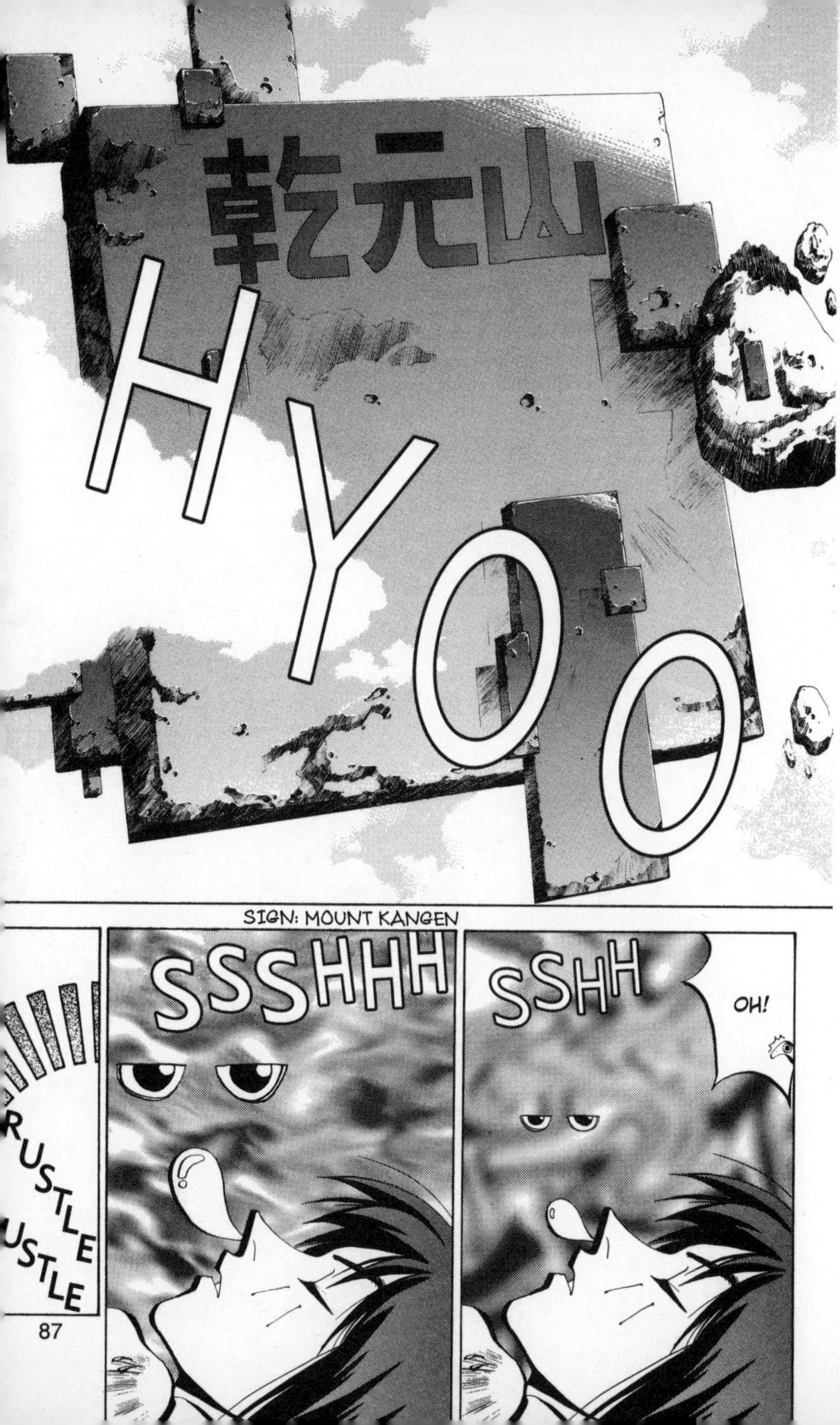
乾元山
HYOOO
SIGN: MOUNT KANGEN
SSHH
OH!
SSSHHH
RUSTLE
USTLE

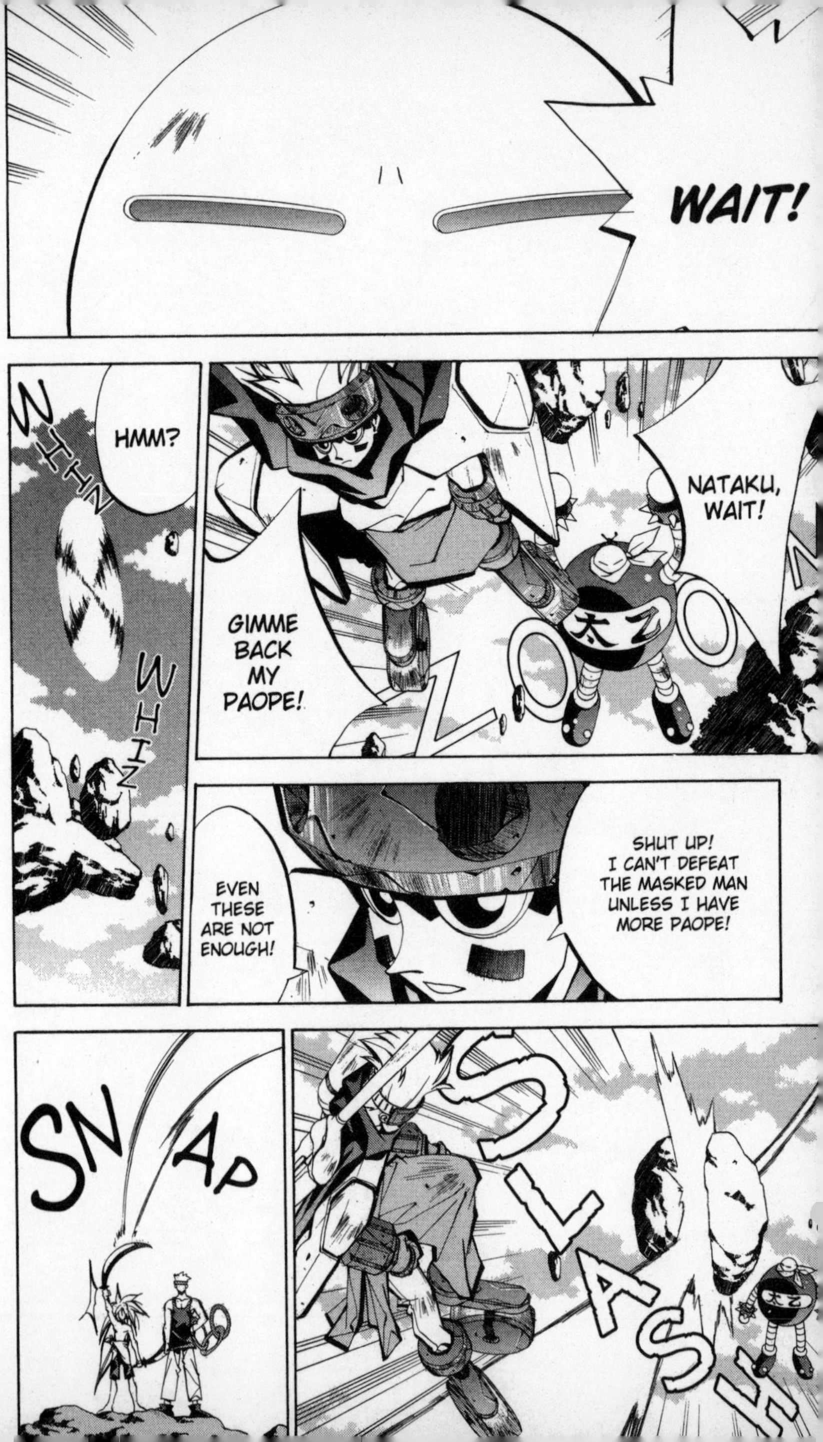
WAIT!
NATAKU, WAIT!
GIMME BACK MY PAOPE!
SHUT UP! I CAN'T DEFEAT THE MASKED MAN UNLESS I HAVE MORE PAOPE!
EVEN THESE ARE NOT ENOUGH!
HMM?
SLASH
SNAP

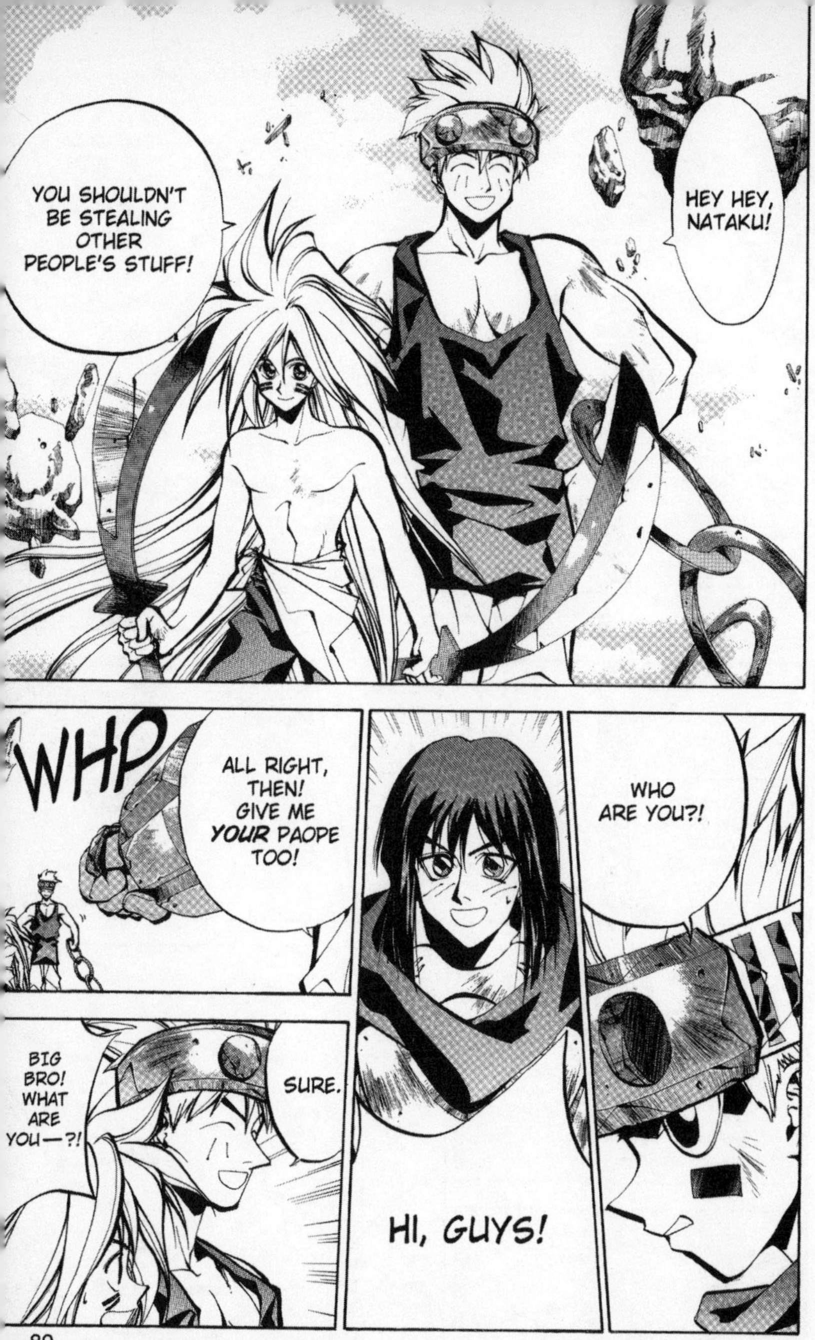
HEY HEY, NATAKU!
YOU SHOULDN'T BE STEALING OTHER PEOPLE'S STUFF!
WHO ARE YOU?!
HI, GUYS!
ALL RIGHT, THEN! GIVE ME *YOUR* PAOPE TOO!
WHP
SURE.
BIG BRO! WHAT ARE YOU—?!

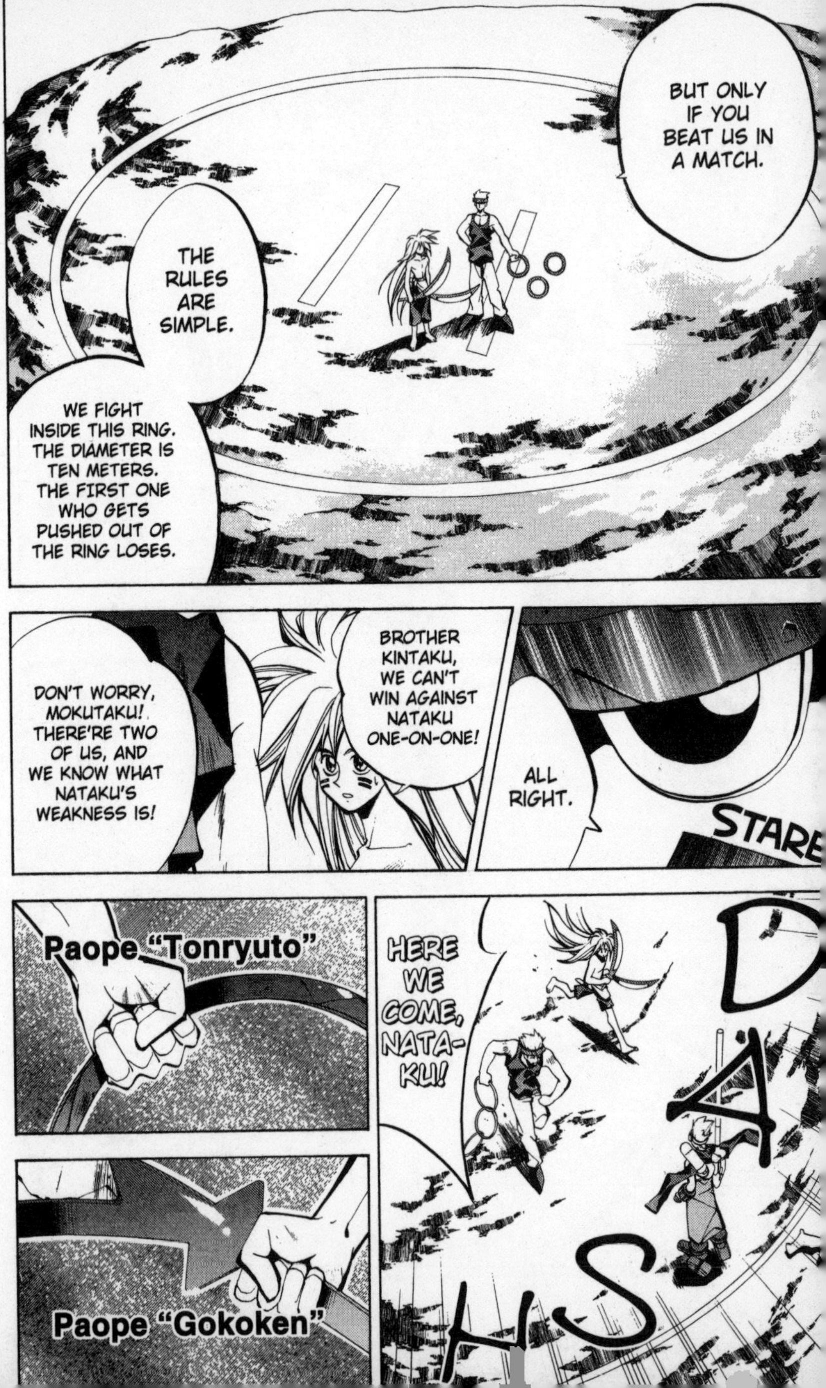
BUT ONLY IF YOU BEAT US IN A MATCH.
THE RULES ARE SIMPLE.
WE FIGHT INSIDE THIS RING. THE DIAMETER IS TEN METERS. THE FIRST ONE WHO GETS PUSHED OUT OF THE RING LOSES.
ALL RIGHT.
STARE
BROTHER KINTAKU, WE CAN'T WIN AGAINST NATAKU ONE-ON-ONE!
DON'T WORRY, MOKUTAKU! THERE'RE TWO OF US, AND WE KNOW WHAT NATAKU'S WEAKNESS IS!
HERE WE COME, NATA-KU!
DASH
Paope "Tonryuto"
Paope "Gokoken"

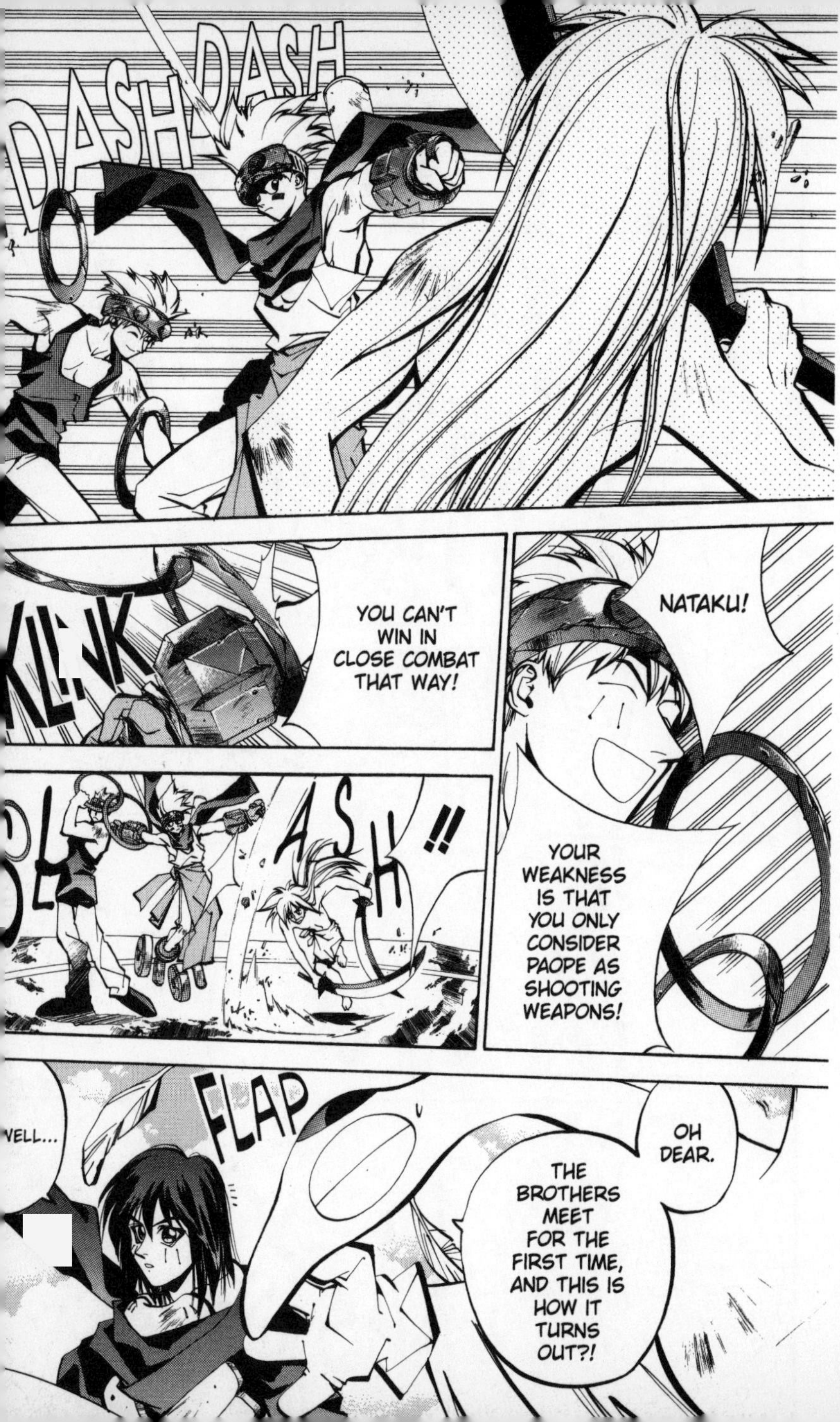
DASH DASH
NATAKU!
YOUR WEAKNESS IS THAT YOU ONLY CONSIDER PAOPE AS SHOOTING WEAPONS!
KLINK
YOU CAN'T WIN IN CLOSE COMBAT THAT WAY!
SLASH!!
OH DEAR.
THE BROTHERS MEET FOR THE FIRST TIME, AND THIS IS HOW IT TURNS OUT?!
FLAP
WELL...

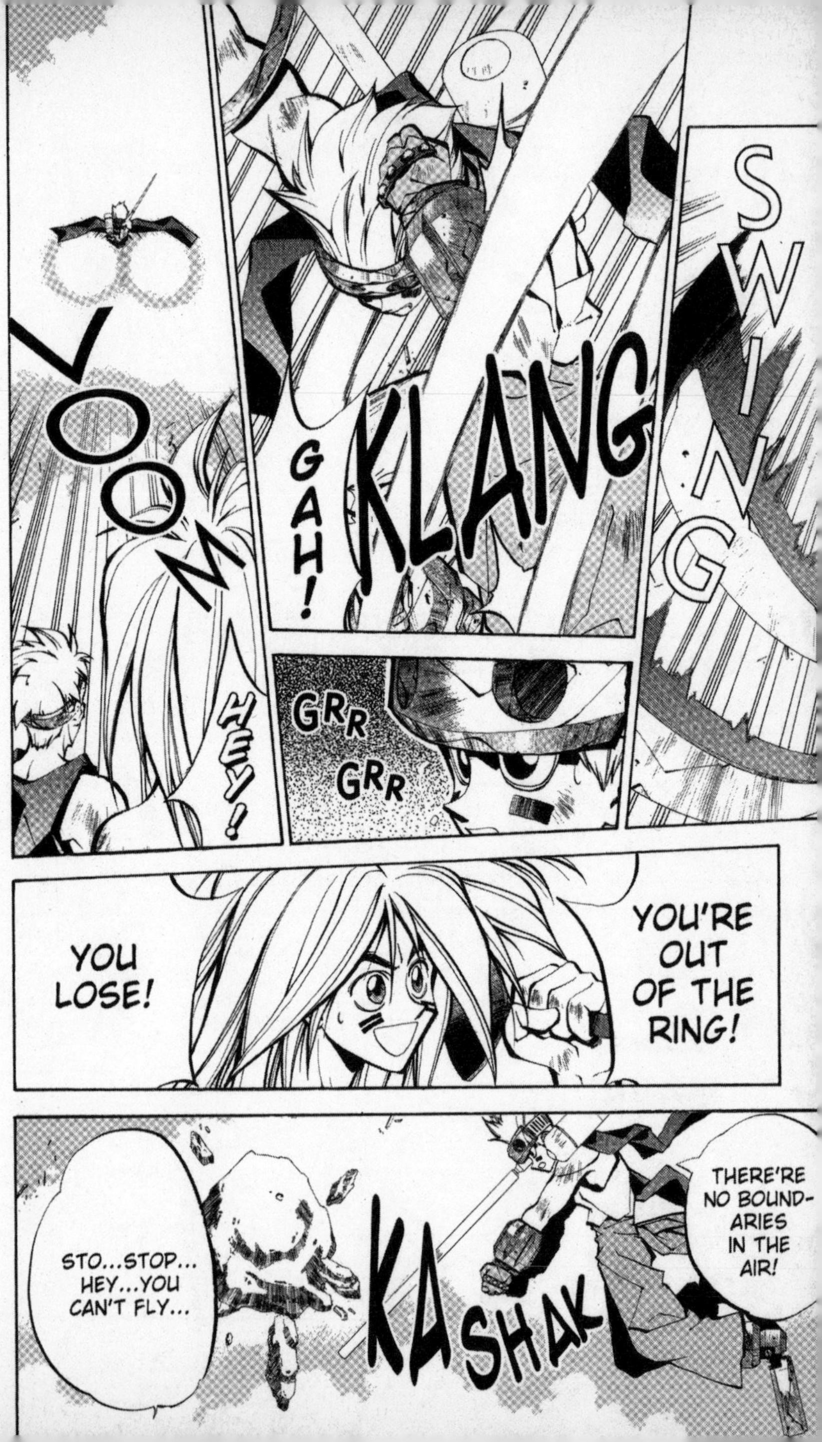
SWING
GAH!
KLANG
GRR GRR
VOOM
HEY!
YOU'RE OUT OF THE RING!
YOU LOSE!
THERE'RE NO BOUNDARIES IN THE AIR!
KASHAK
STO...STOP... HEY...YOU CAN'T FLY...

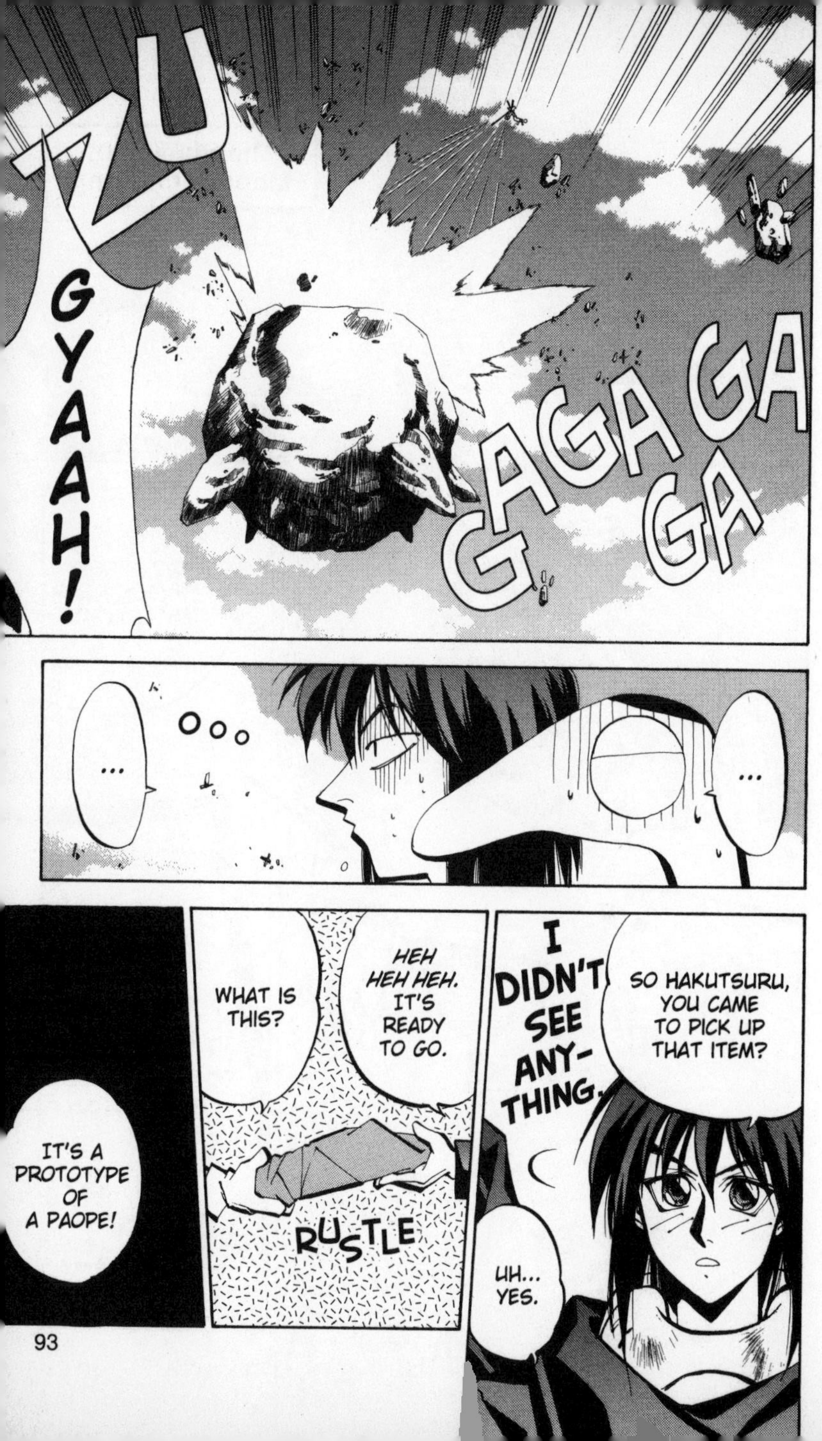
GAGAGA GA GA
ZU
GYAAH!
...
ooo
...
SO HAKUTSURU, YOU CAME TO PICK UP THAT ITEM?
I DIDN'T SEE ANY-THING.
UH... YES.
HEH HEH HEH. IT'S READY TO GO.
WHAT IS THIS?
RUSTLE
IT'S A PROTOTYPE OF A PAOPE!

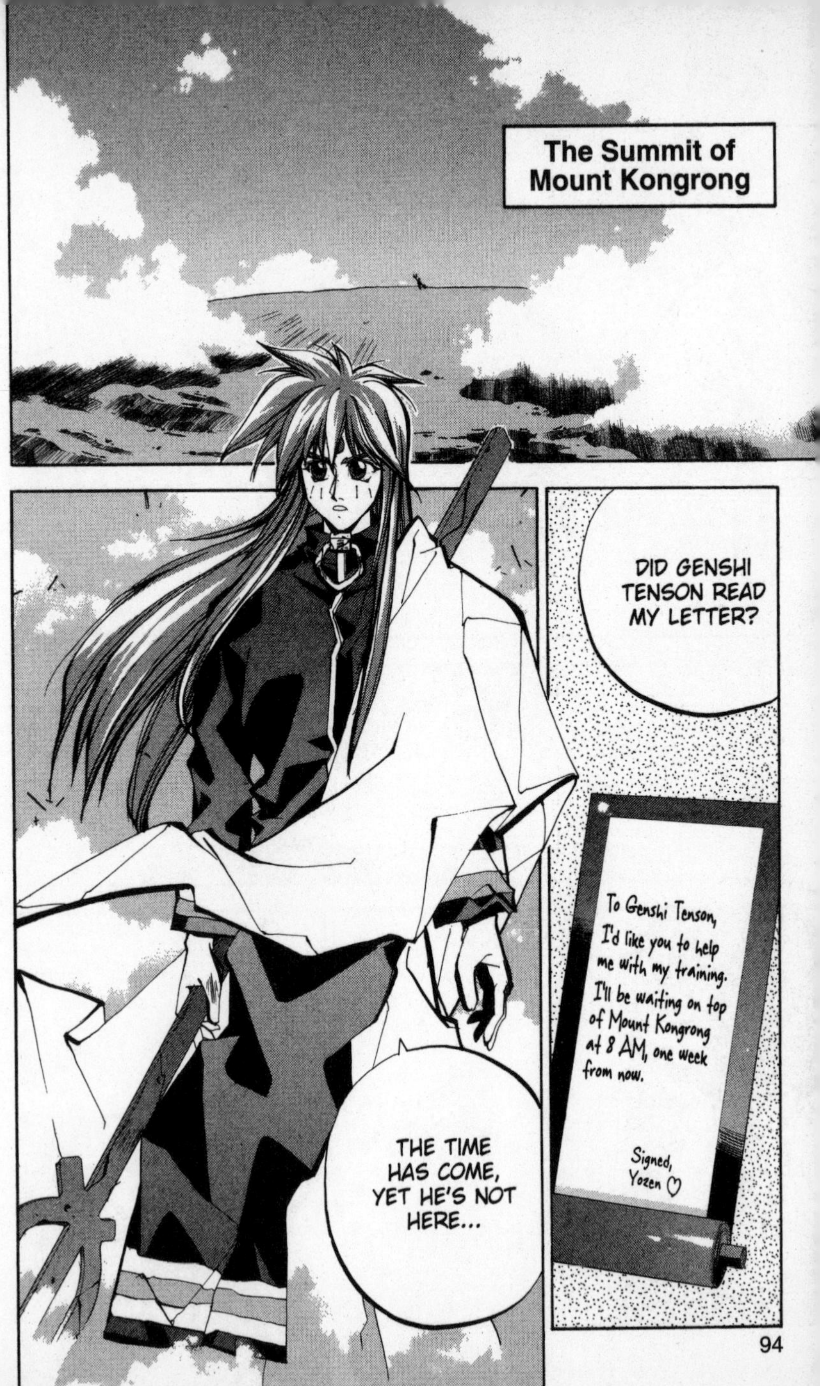
The Summit of Mount Kongrong
DID GENSHI TENSON READ MY LETTER?
To Genshi Tenson, I'd like you to help me with my training. I'll be waiting on top of Mount Kongrong at 8 AM, one week from now.
Signed, Yozen ♡
THE TIME HAS COME, YET HE'S NOT HERE...

READ THIS WAY

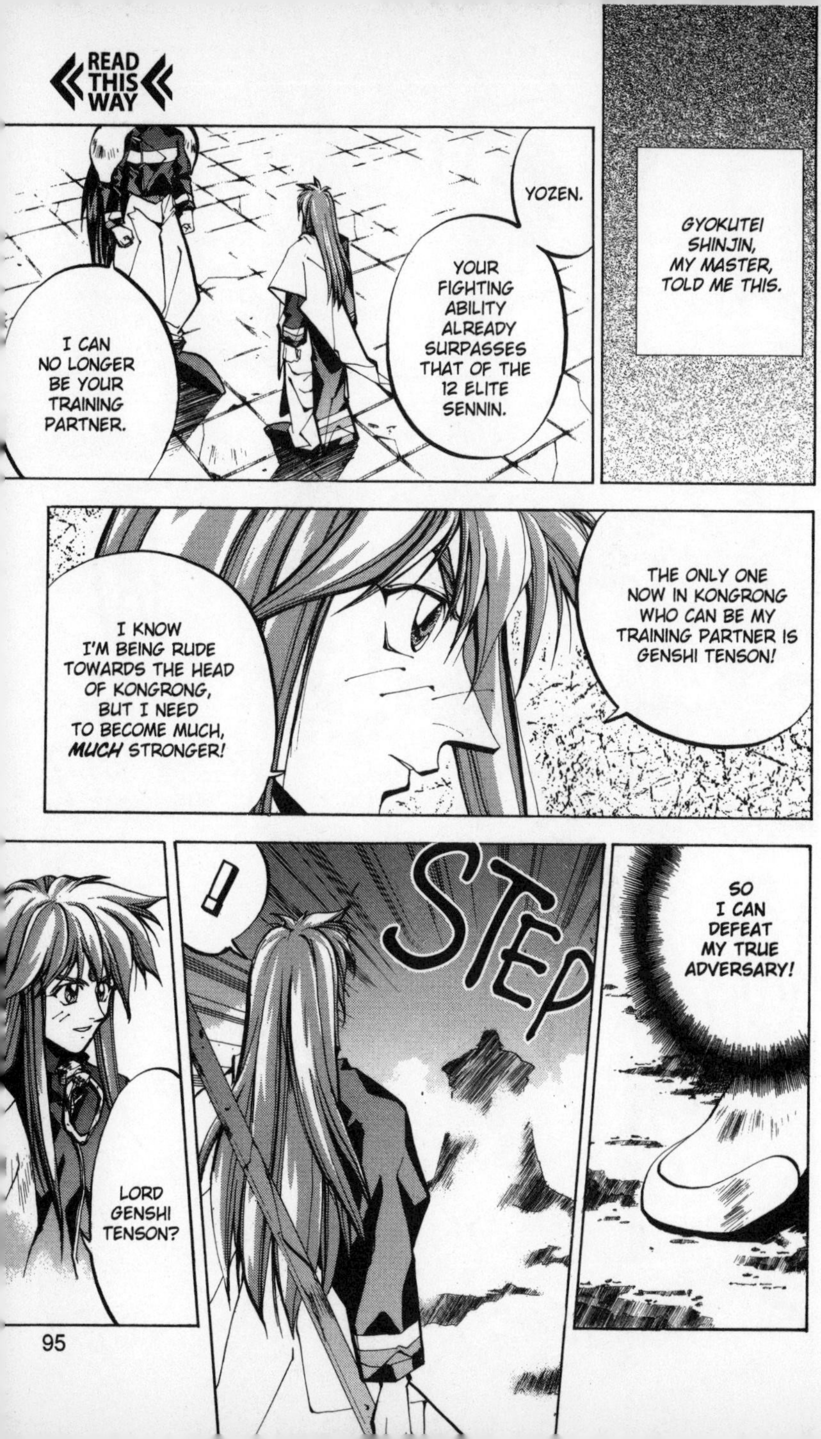
GYOKUTEI SHINJIN, MY MASTER, TOLD ME THIS.
YOZEN.
YOUR FIGHTING ABILITY ALREADY SURPASSES THAT OF THE 12 ELITE SENNIN.
I CAN NO LONGER BE YOUR TRAINING PARTNER.
THE ONLY ONE NOW IN KONGRONG WHO CAN BE MY TRAINING PARTNER IS GENSHI TENSON!
I KNOW I'M BEING RUDE TOWARDS THE HEAD OF KONGRONG, BUT I NEED TO BECOME MUCH, *MUCH* STRONGER!
SO I CAN DEFEAT MY TRUE ADVERSARY!
STEP
!
LORD GENSHI TENSON?

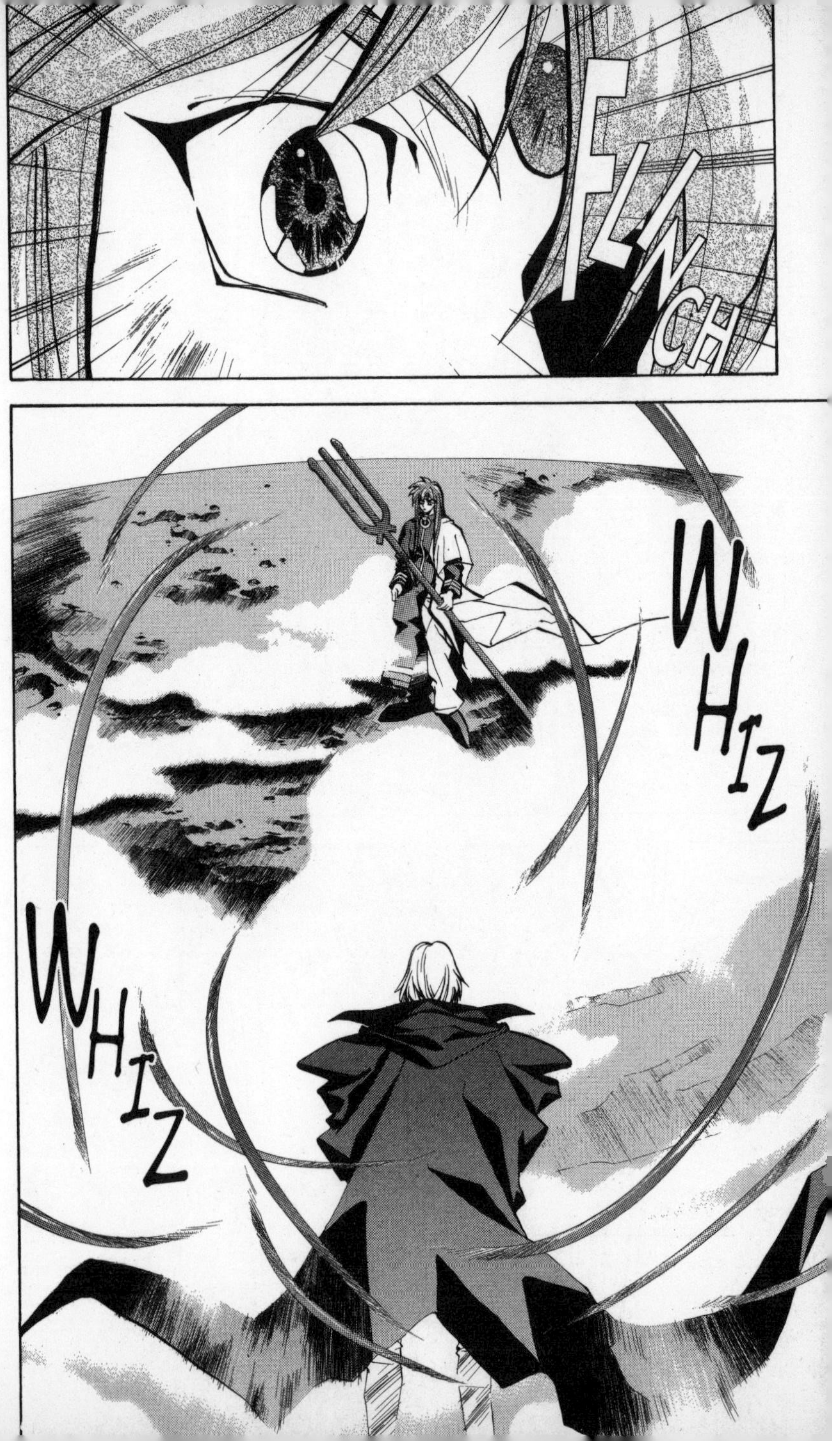
FLINCH
WHIZ
WHIZ

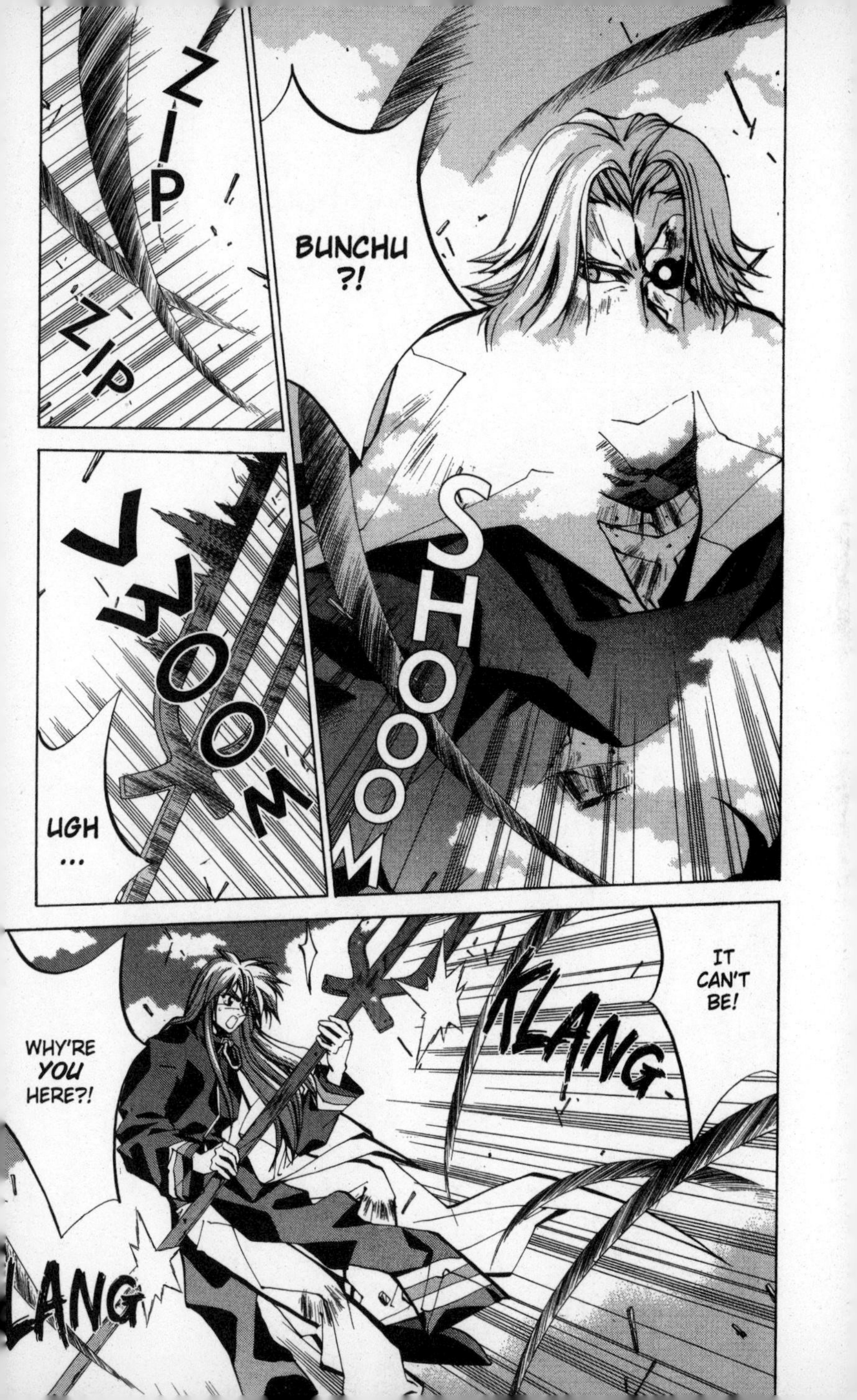
BUNCHU ?!
SHOOOOM
ZIP
ZIP
WHOOOM
UGH ...
IT CAN'T BE!
KLANG
WHY'RE *YOU* HERE?!
LANG

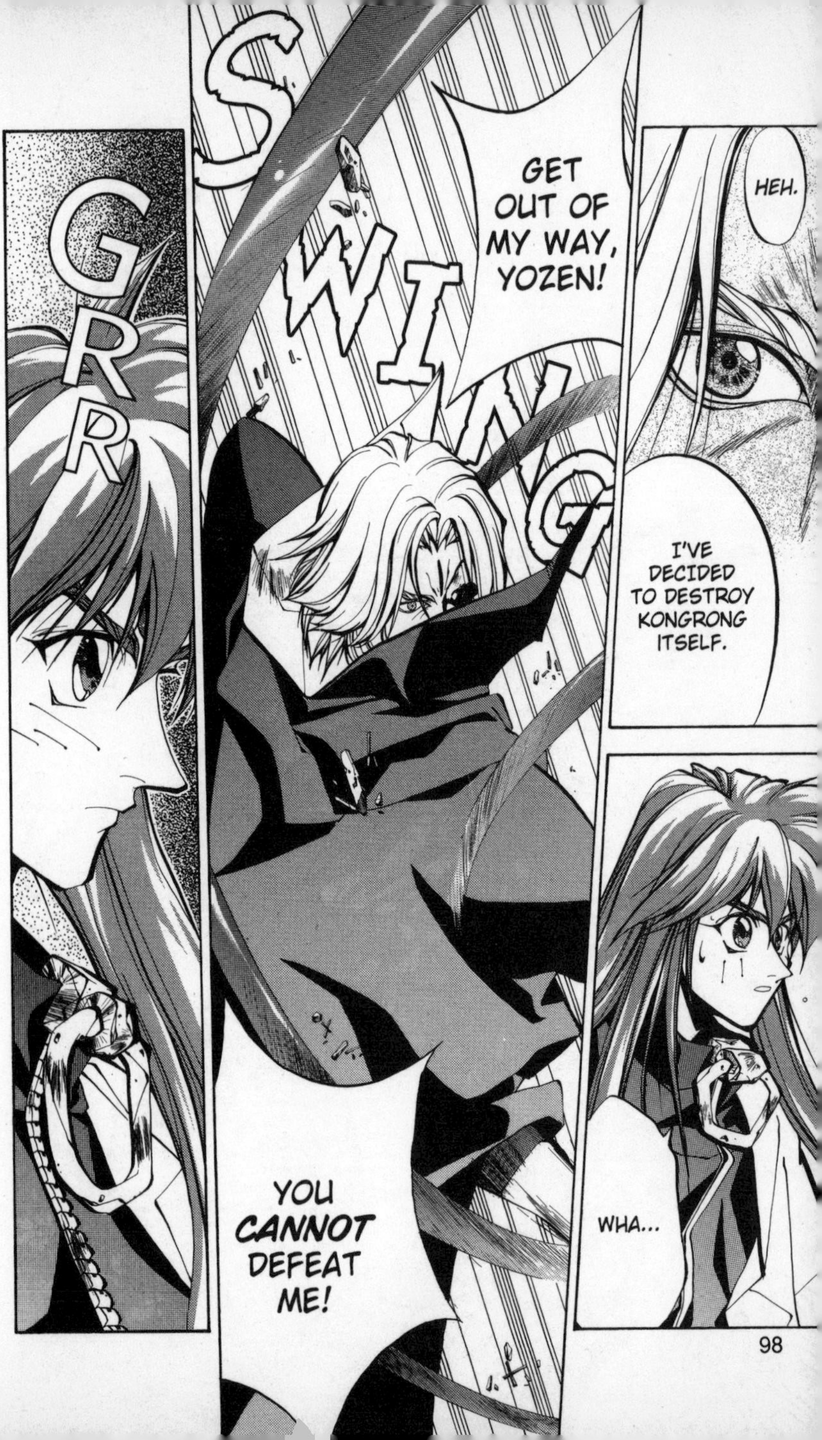
HEH.
I'VE DECIDED TO DESTROY KONGRONG ITSELF.
WHA...
SWING
GET OUT OF MY WAY, YOZEN!
YOU CANNOT DEFEAT ME!
GRR

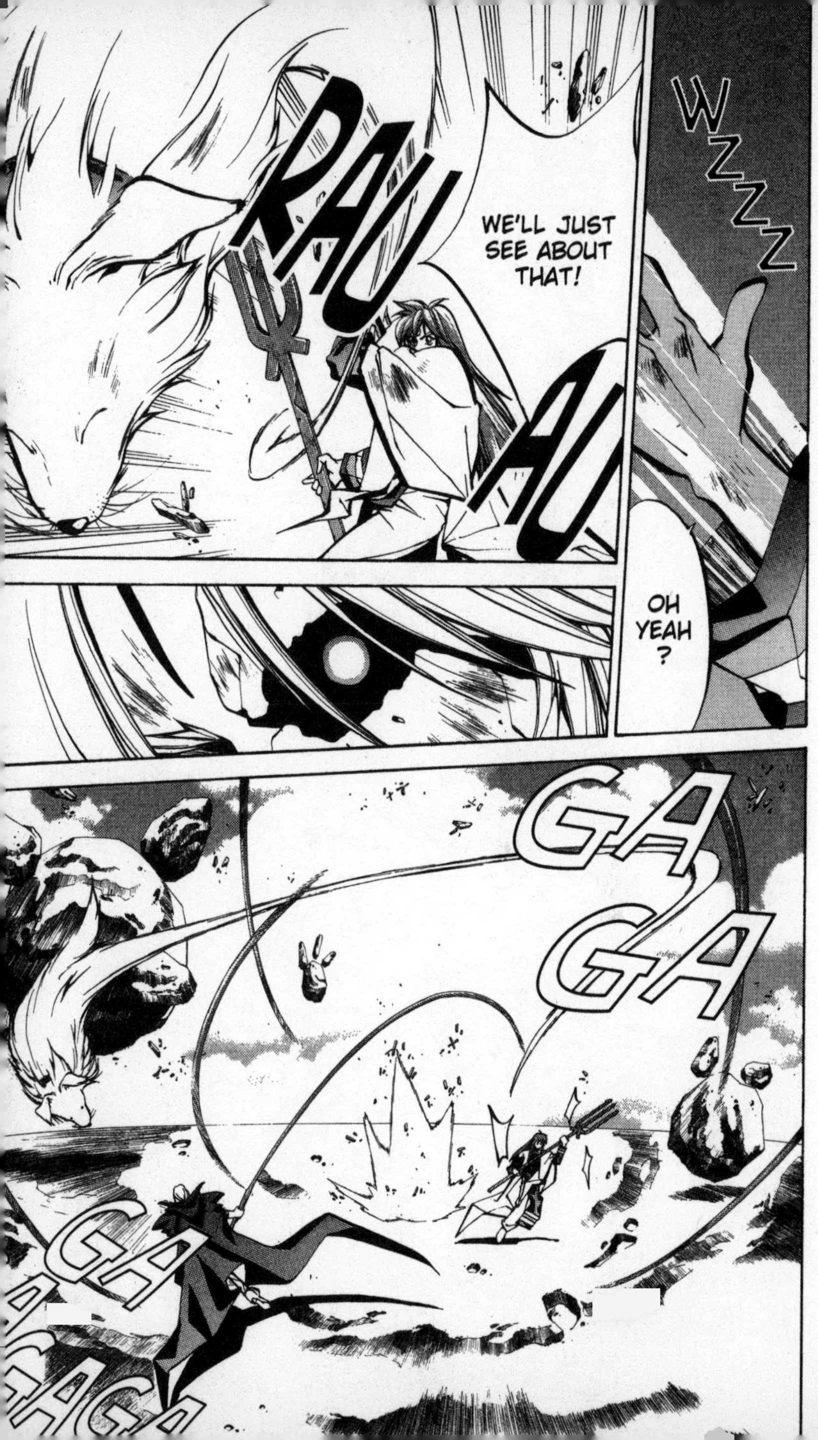
WZZZZ
OH YEAH?
RAU
WE'LL JUST SEE ABOUT THAT!
AU
GA GA
GA

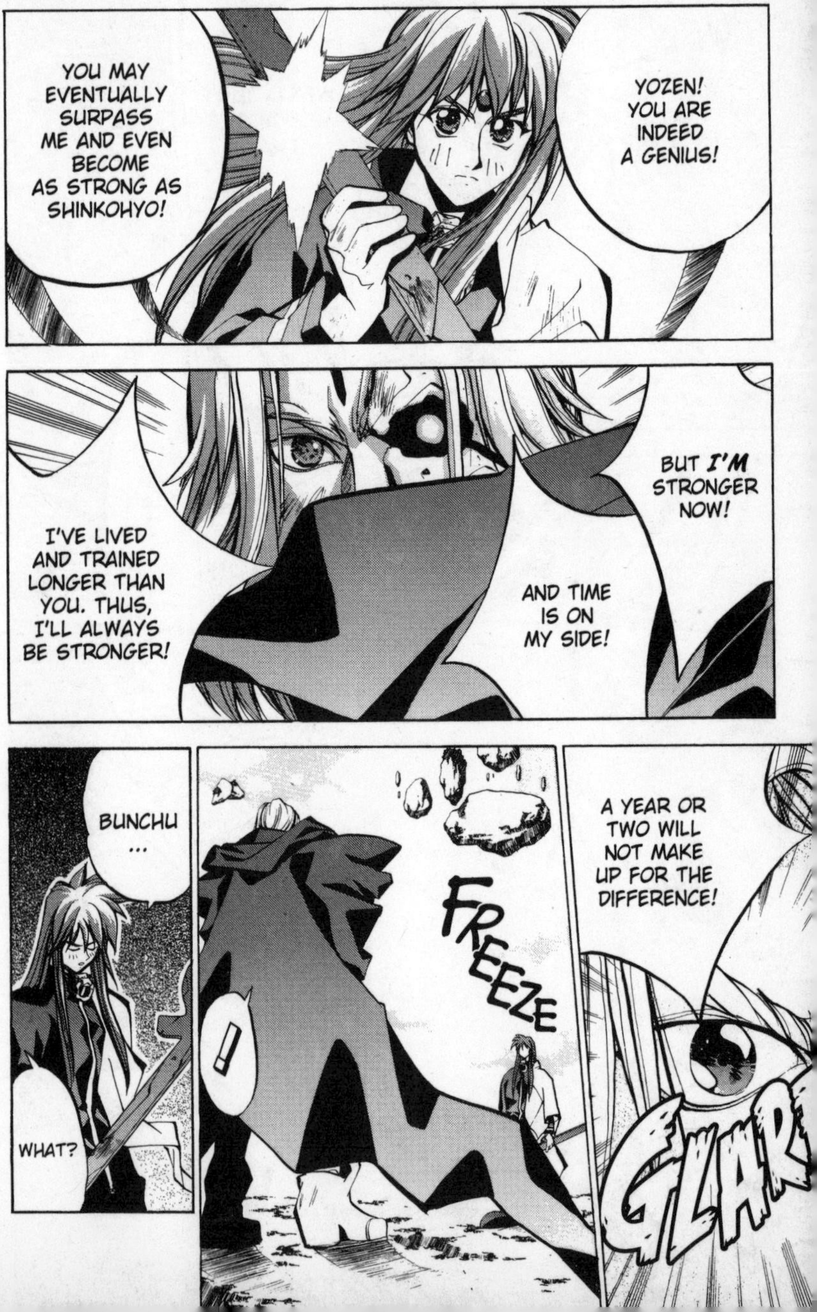
YOZEN! YOU ARE INDEED A GENIUS!
YOU MAY EVENTUALLY SURPASS ME AND EVEN BECOME AS STRONG AS SHINKOHYO!
BUT *I'M* STRONGER NOW!
I'VE LIVED AND TRAINED LONGER THAN YOU. THUS, I'LL ALWAYS BE STRONGER!
AND TIME IS ON MY SIDE!
A YEAR OR TWO WILL NOT MAKE UP FOR THE DIFFERENCE!
GLAR
FREEZE
!
BUNCHU ...
WHAT?

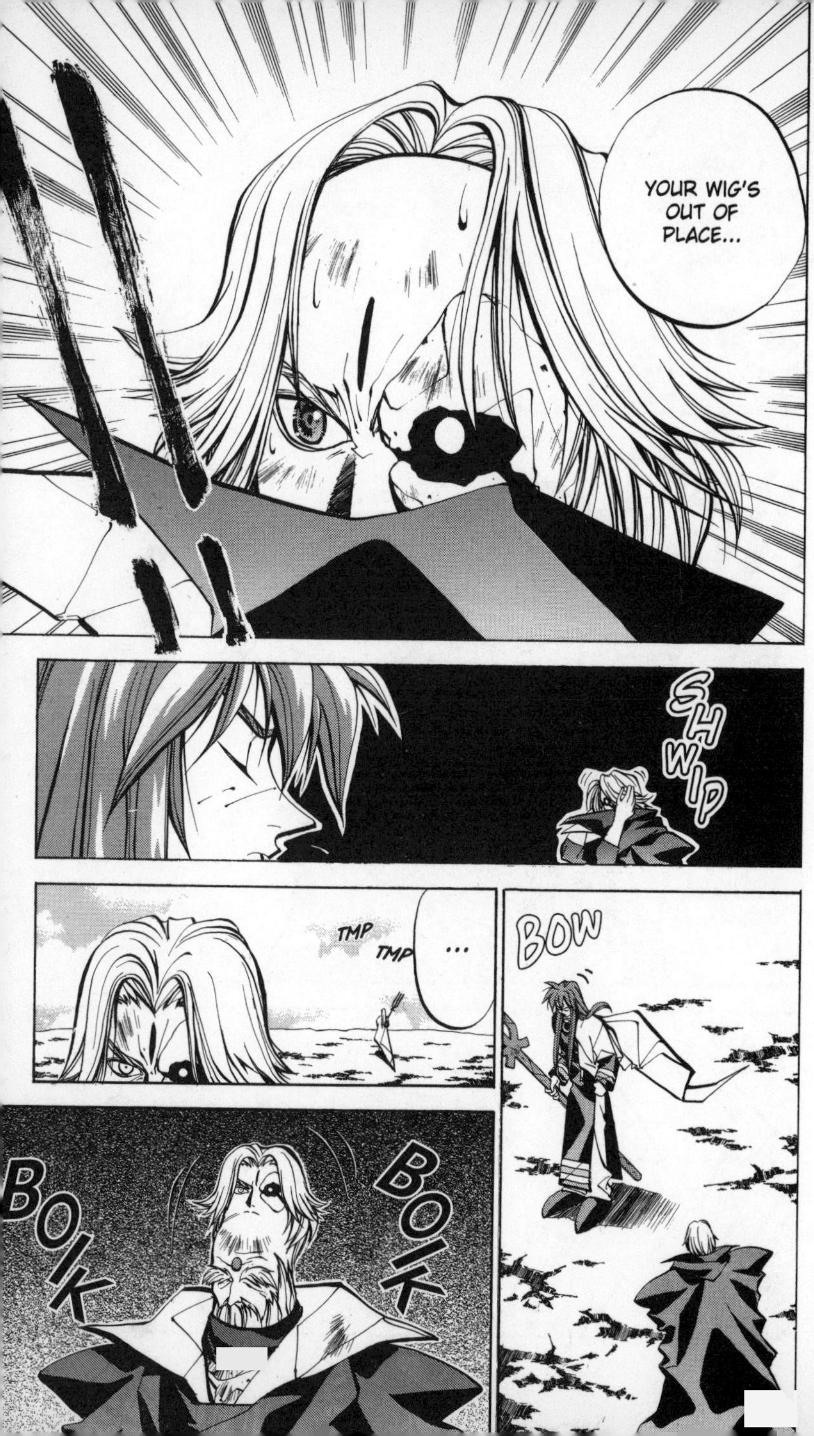
YOUR WIG'S OUT OF PLACE...
SHWIP
BOW
TMP
TMP
...
BOIK
BOIK

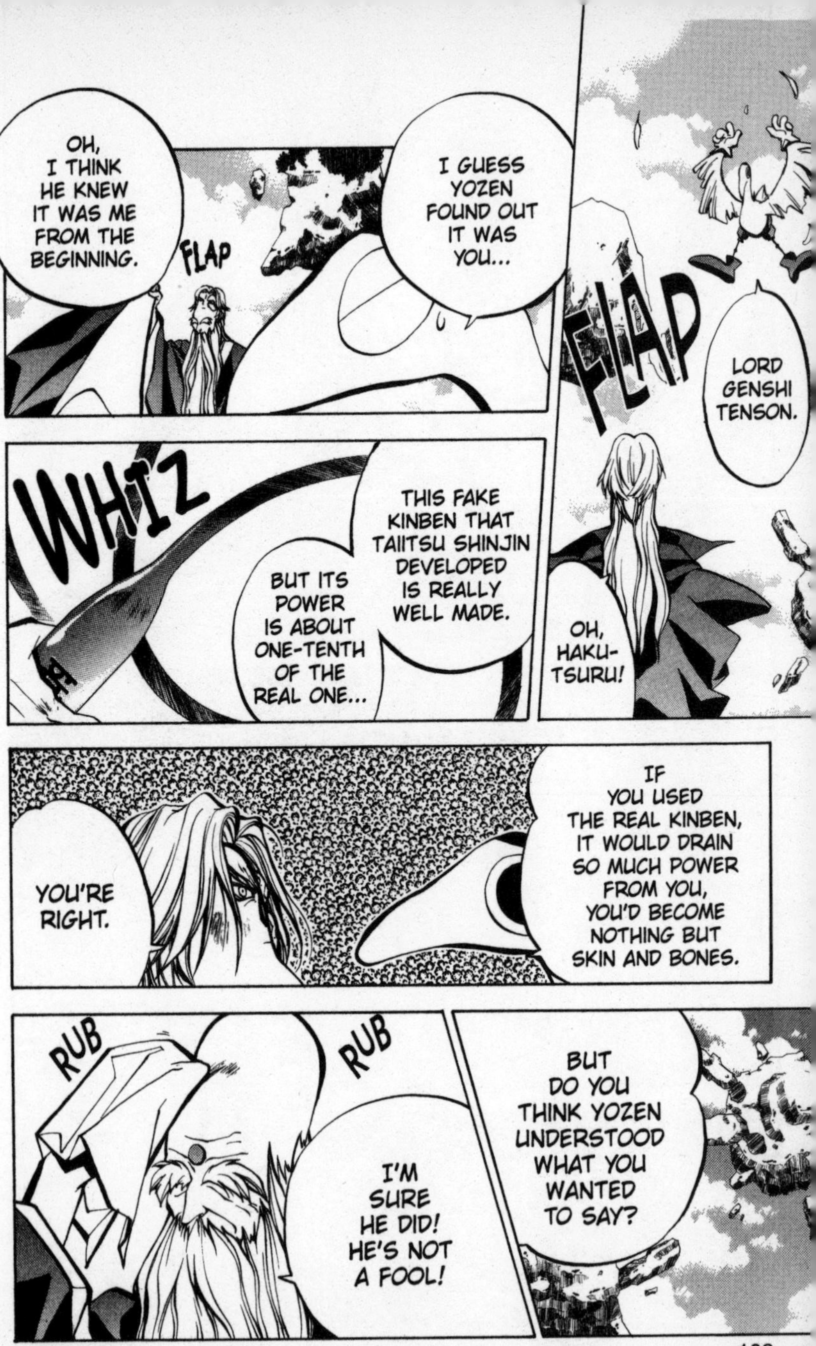
LORD GENSHI TENSON.
FLAP
OH, HAKU-TSURU!
I GUESS YOZEN FOUND OUT IT WAS YOU...
OH, I THINK HE KNEW IT WAS ME FROM THE BEGINNING.
FLAP
THIS FAKE KINBEN THAT TAIITSU SHINJIN DEVELOPED IS REALLY WELL MADE.
BUT ITS POWER IS ABOUT ONE-TENTH OF THE REAL ONE...
WHIZ
IF YOU USED THE REAL KINBEN, IT WOULD DRAIN SO MUCH POWER FROM YOU, YOU'D BECOME NOTHING BUT SKIN AND BONES.
YOU'RE RIGHT.
BUT DO YOU THINK YOZEN UNDERSTOOD WHAT YOU WANTED TO SAY?
RUB
RUB
I'M SURE HE DID! HE'S NOT A FOOL!

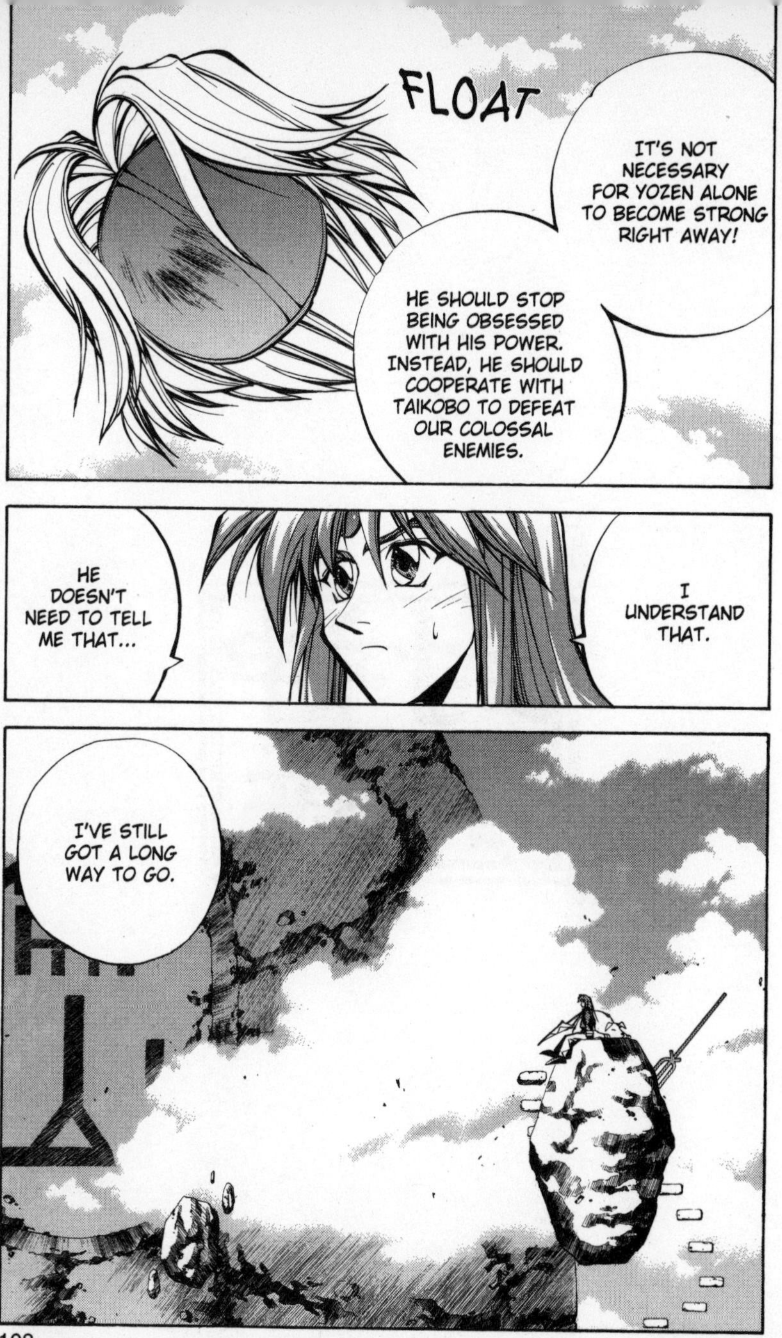
IT'S NOT NECESSARY FOR YOZEN ALONE TO BECOME STRONG RIGHT AWAY!
FLOAT
HE SHOULD STOP BEING OBSESSED WITH HIS POWER. INSTEAD, HE SHOULD COOPERATE WITH TAIKOBO TO DEFEAT OUR COLOSSAL ENEMIES.
I UNDERSTAND THAT.
HE DOESN'T NEED TO TELL ME THAT...
I'VE STILL GOT A LONG WAY TO GO.

封神演義

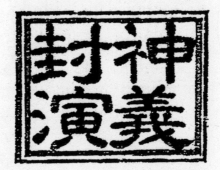

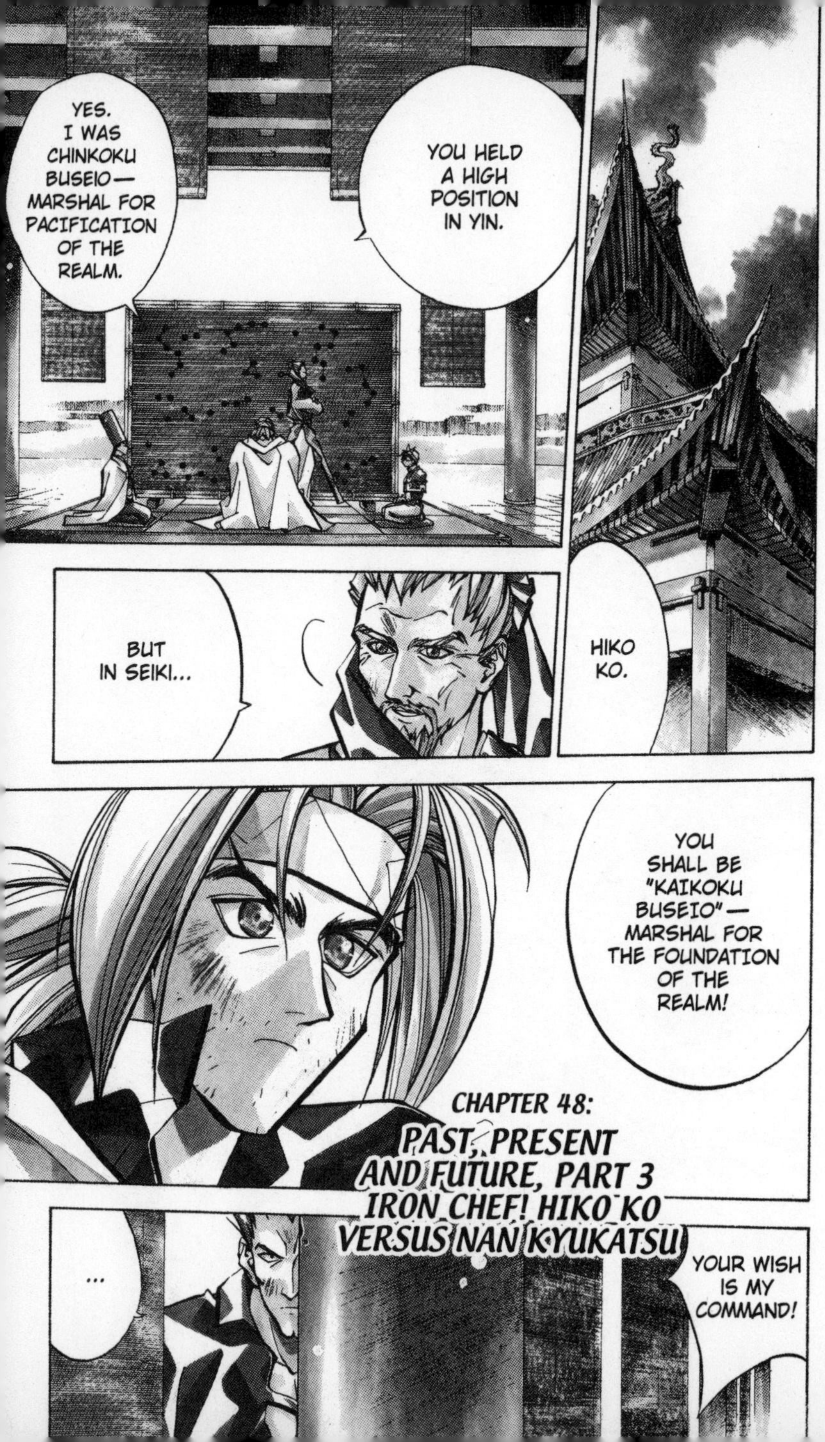
HIKO KO.
YOU HELD A HIGH POSITION IN YIN.
YES. I WAS CHINKOKU BUSEIO— MARSHAL FOR PACIFICATION OF THE REALM.
BUT IN SEIKI...
YOU SHALL BE "KAIKOKU BUSEIO"— MARSHAL FOR THE FOUNDATION OF THE REALM!
CHAPTER 48:
PAST, PRESENT AND FUTURE, PART 3
IRON CHEF! HIKO KO VERSUS NAN KYUKATSU
YOUR WISH IS MY COMMAND!
...

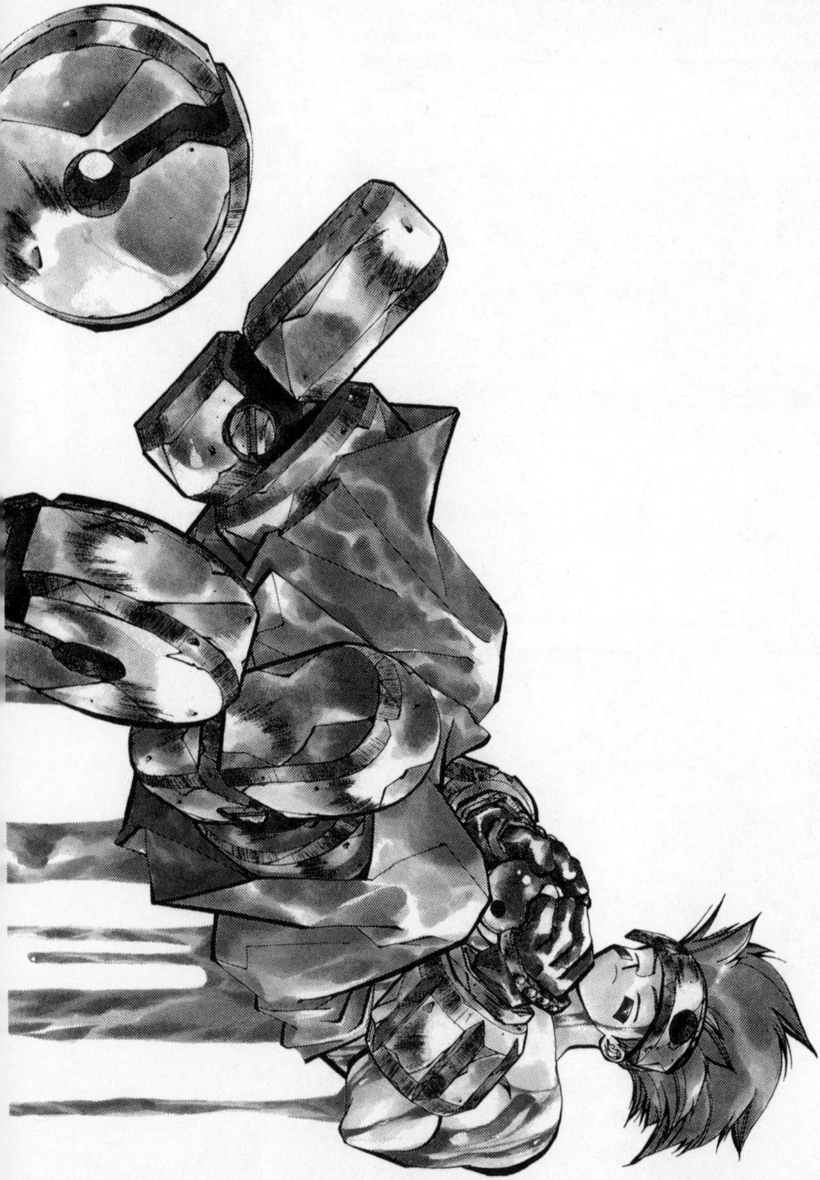

PAST, PRESENT AND FUTURE, PART 3
IRON CHEF! HIKO KO VERSUS NAN KYUKATSU

Chapter 48

YOU DON'T HAVE TO READ IT, BUT SINCE THERE'S AN EXTRA PAGE:

HACK WRITING IV

△ SOMETIMES I FEEL ANGRY ABOUT THE FACT THAT I CAN'T LOOK AT MYSELF.

△ I'M THE HUMAN THAT'S CLOSEST TO ME, YET WHY CAN'T I LOOK AT MYSELF?! MIRRORS DON'T DO THE WORK. THAT'S FAKE.

△ THERE'S NOTHING I CAN DO, AND BECAUSE THERE'S ABSOLUTELY NOTHING I CAN DO ABOUT THIS, I FEEL VERY IRRITATED.

△ BY THE WAY, WHEN I WENT TO THE BEIJING ZOO IN CHINA, I FOUND IT STRANGE THAT IT DIDN'T SMELL VERY MUCH. YOU KNOW, JAPANESE ZOOS REALLY SMELL. ESPECIALLY MONKEYS AND CAMELS. I LIKE ZOOS AND AQUARIUMS, BUT I DON'T WANT THEM TO SMELL IF THAT'S POSSIBLE. IS THIS HUMAN EGO? BUT THE BEIJING ZOO WASN'T THAT SMELLY.

△ THE REASON FOR THE DIFFERENCE IS BECAUSE BEIJING IS A VERY DRY PLACE.

△ IN JAPAN, TRAIN STATIONS AND OLD BUILDINGS SMELL DURING THE RAINY SEASON. ON THE OTHER HAND, THEY DON'T SMELL DURING SPRING (MY FAVORITE SEASON). THEREFORE,

- BEIJING IS DRY – DOESN'T SMELL
- JAPAN IS HUMID – SMELLY

WELL, THAT'S JUST NATURAL, I GUESS.

△ JAPAN IS HUMID, AND NOT MANY JAPANESE WEAR COLOGNES AND SUCH. THERE ARE PEOPLE WHO SAY, "I DON'T WANT TO SMELL LIKE ANYTHING," BUT WHEN FOREIGNERS COME TO JAPAN, THEY SMELL THE SMELL OF SOY SAUCE – THAT'S WHAT I'VE HEARD SOMEWHERE. MAYBE NOT.

UNLESS YOU BECOME SOMEBODY ELSE, YOU WOULDN'T BE ABLE TO FIGURE OUT WHAT YOU SMELL LIKE. IT'S JUST LIKE NOT BEING ABLE TO LOOK AT YOURSELF.

END OF HACK WRITING

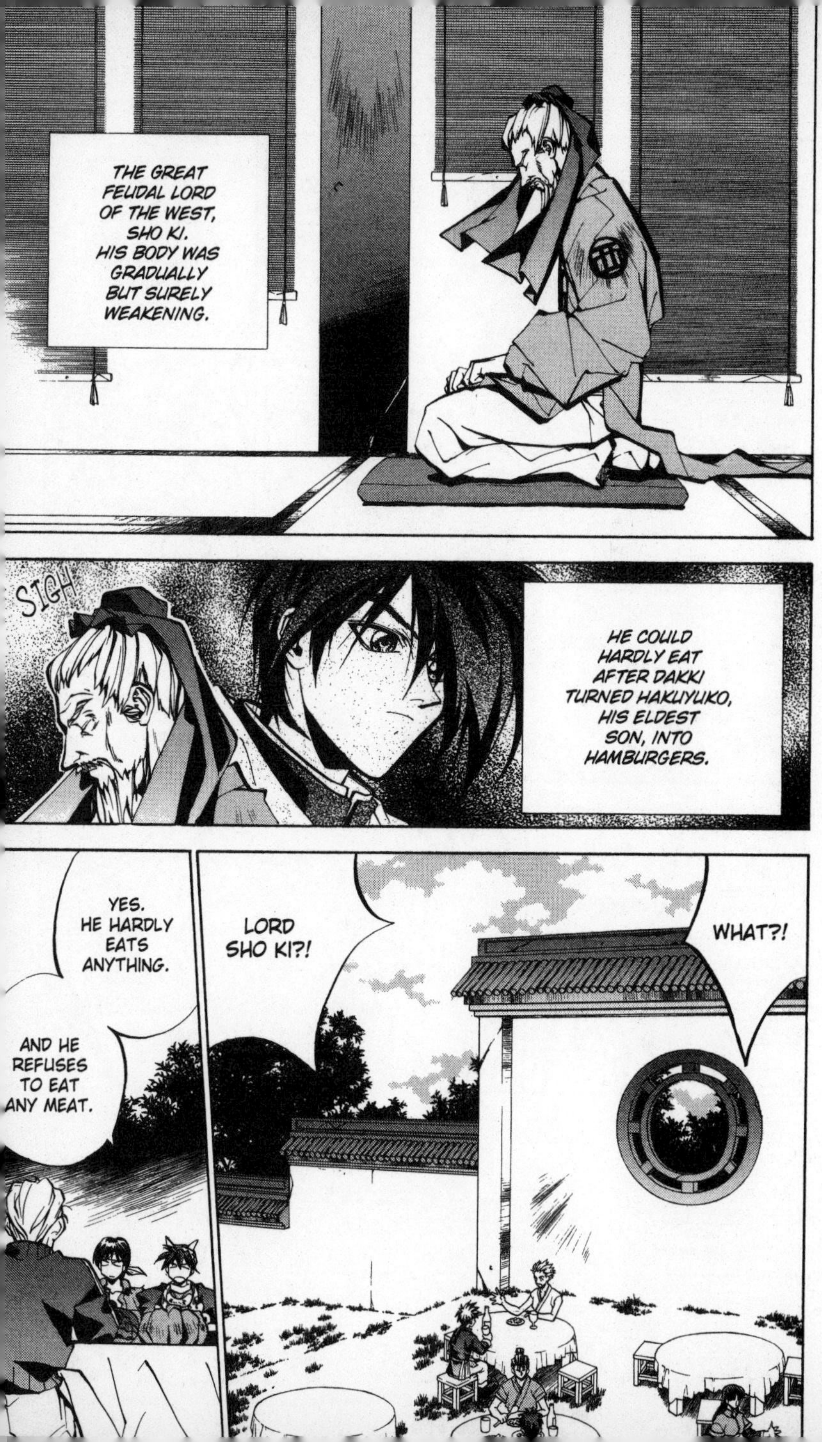
THE GREAT FEUDAL LORD OF THE WEST, SHO KI. HIS BODY WAS GRADUALLY BUT SURELY WEAKENING.
HE COULD HARDLY EAT AFTER DAKKI TURNED HAKUYUKO, HIS ELDEST SON, INTO HAMBURGERS.
SIGH
WHAT?!
LORD SHO KI?!
YES. HE HARDLY EATS ANYTHING.
AND HE REFUSES TO EAT ANY MEAT.

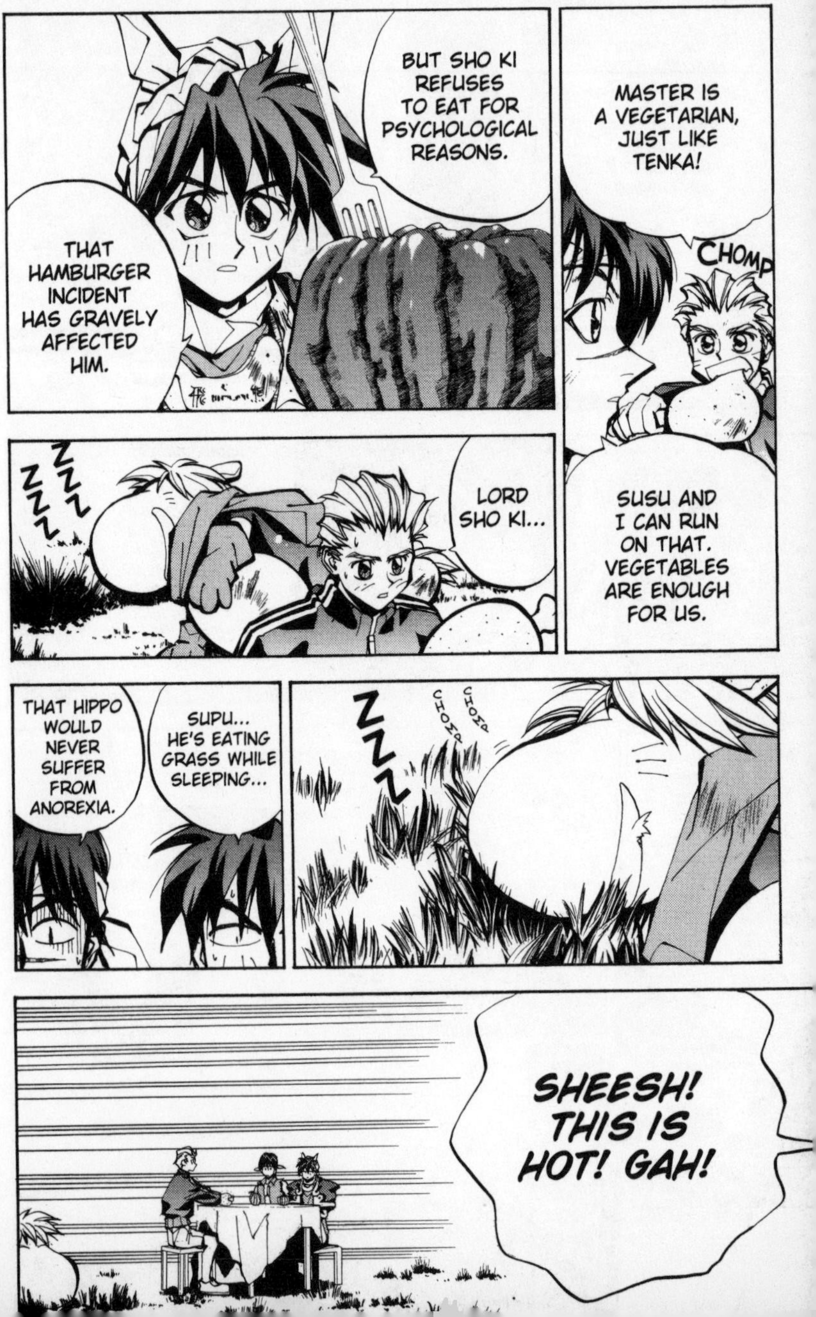
MASTER IS A VEGETARIAN, JUST LIKE TENKA!
CHOMP
SUSU AND I CAN RUN ON THAT. VEGETABLES ARE ENOUGH FOR US.
BUT SHO KI REFUSES TO EAT FOR PSYCHOLOGICAL REASONS.
THAT HAMBURGER INCIDENT HAS GRAVELY AFFECTED HIM.
LORD SHO KI...
ZZZZZZ
ZZZ
CHOMP CHOMP
SUPU... HE'S EATING GRASS WHILE SLEEPING...
THAT HIPPO WOULD NEVER SUFFER FROM ANOREXIA.
SHEESH! THIS IS HOT! GAH!

READ THIS WAY

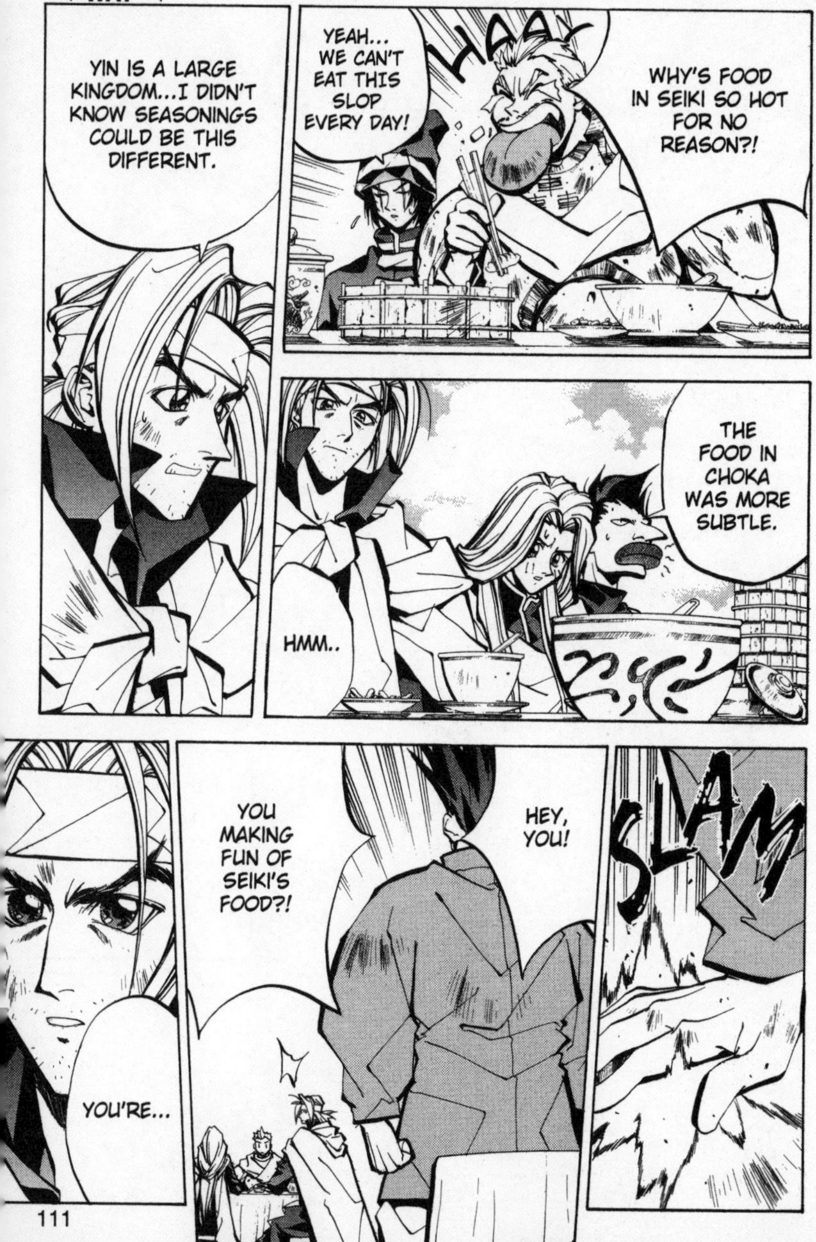
WHY'S FOOD IN SEIKI SO HOT FOR NO REASON?!
HAA
YEAH... WE CAN'T EAT THIS SLOP EVERY DAY!
THE FOOD IN CHOKA WAS MORE SUBTLE.
HMM..
YIN IS A LARGE KINGDOM...I DIDN'T KNOW SEASONINGS COULD BE THIS DIFFERENT.
SLAM
HEY, YOU!
YOU MAKING FUN OF SEIKI'S FOOD?!
YOU'RE...

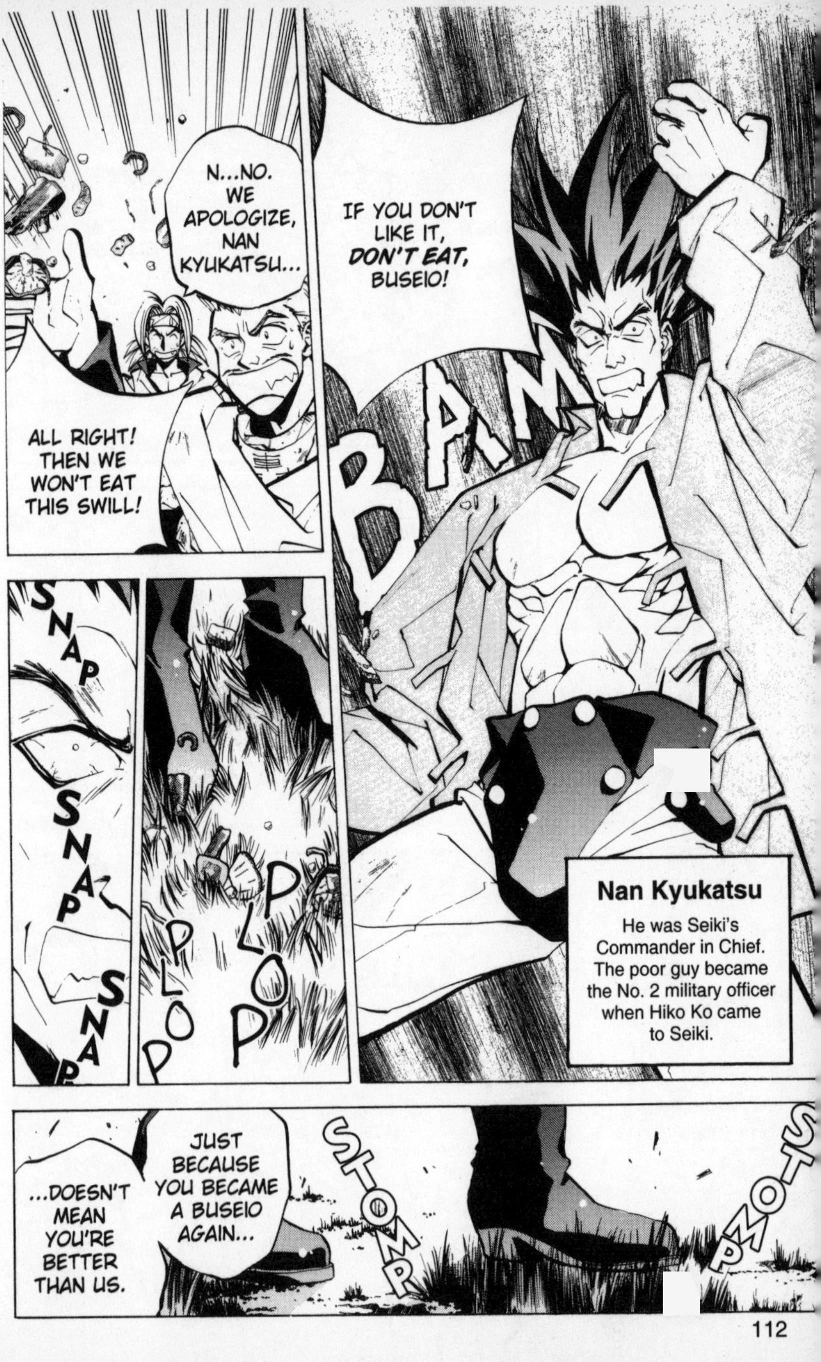
IF YOU DON'T LIKE IT, DON'T EAT, BUSEIO!
BAM
Nan Kyukatsu
He was Seiki's Commander in Chief. The poor guy became the No. 2 military officer when Hiko Ko came to Seiki.
N...NO. WE APOLOGIZE, NAN KYUKATSU...
ALL RIGHT! THEN WE WON'T EAT THIS SWILL!
PLOP PLOP
PLOP
SNAP
SNAP
SNAP
STOMP
STOMP
JUST BECAUSE YOU BECAME A BUSEIO AGAIN...
...DOESN'T MEAN YOU'RE BETTER THAN US.

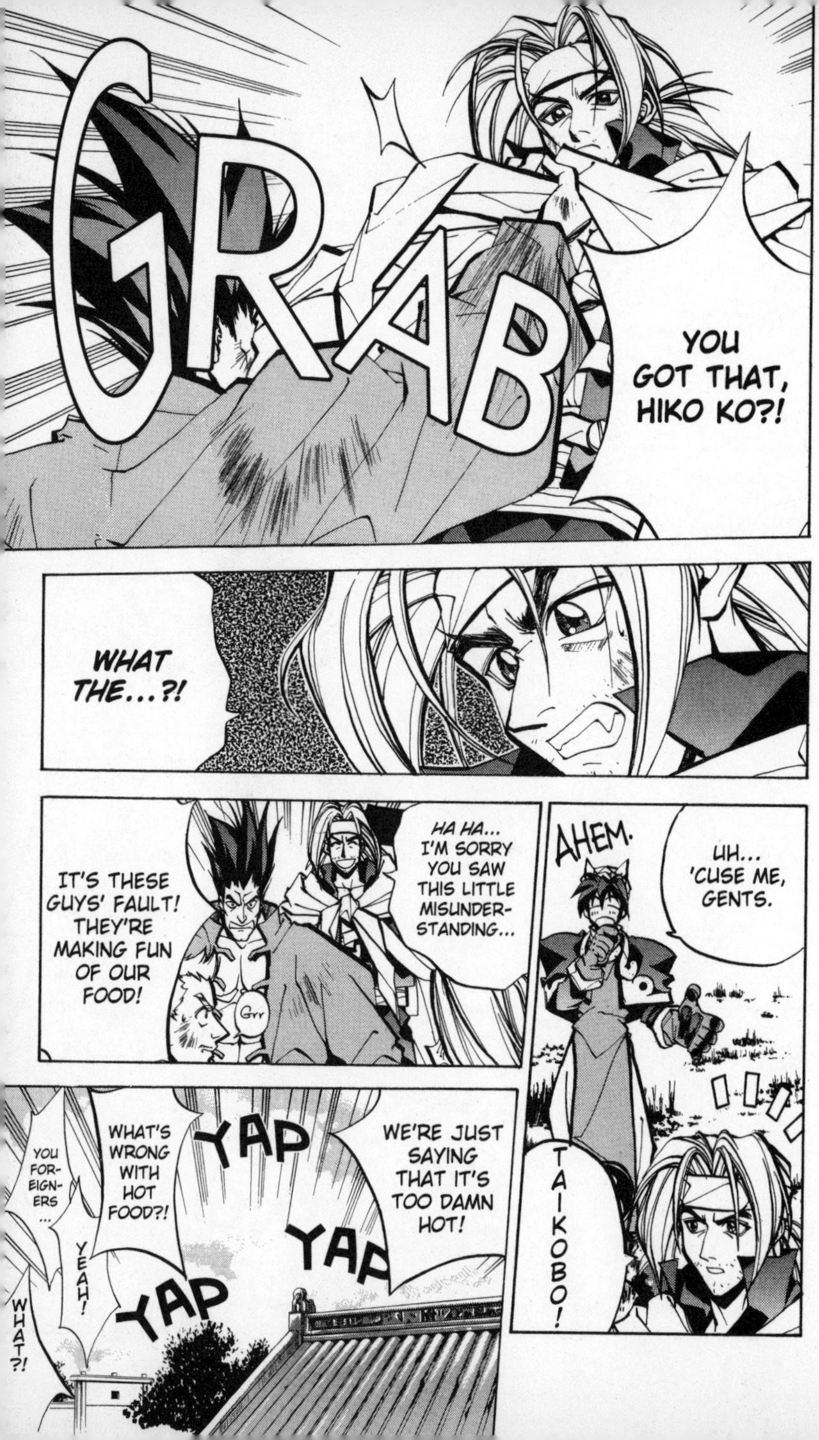
GRAB
YOU GOT THAT, HIKO KO?!
WHAT THE...?!
AHEM.
UH... 'CUSE ME, GENTS.
TAIKOBO!
HA HA... I'M SORRY YOU SAW THIS LITTLE MISUNDERSTANDING...
IT'S THESE GUYS' FAULT! THEY'RE MAKING FUN OF OUR FOOD!
Grr
WE'RE JUST SAYING THAT IT'S TOO DAMN HOT!
YAP
YAP
YAP
WHAT'S WRONG WITH HOT FOOD?!
YEAH!
YOU FOREIGNERS...
WHAT?!

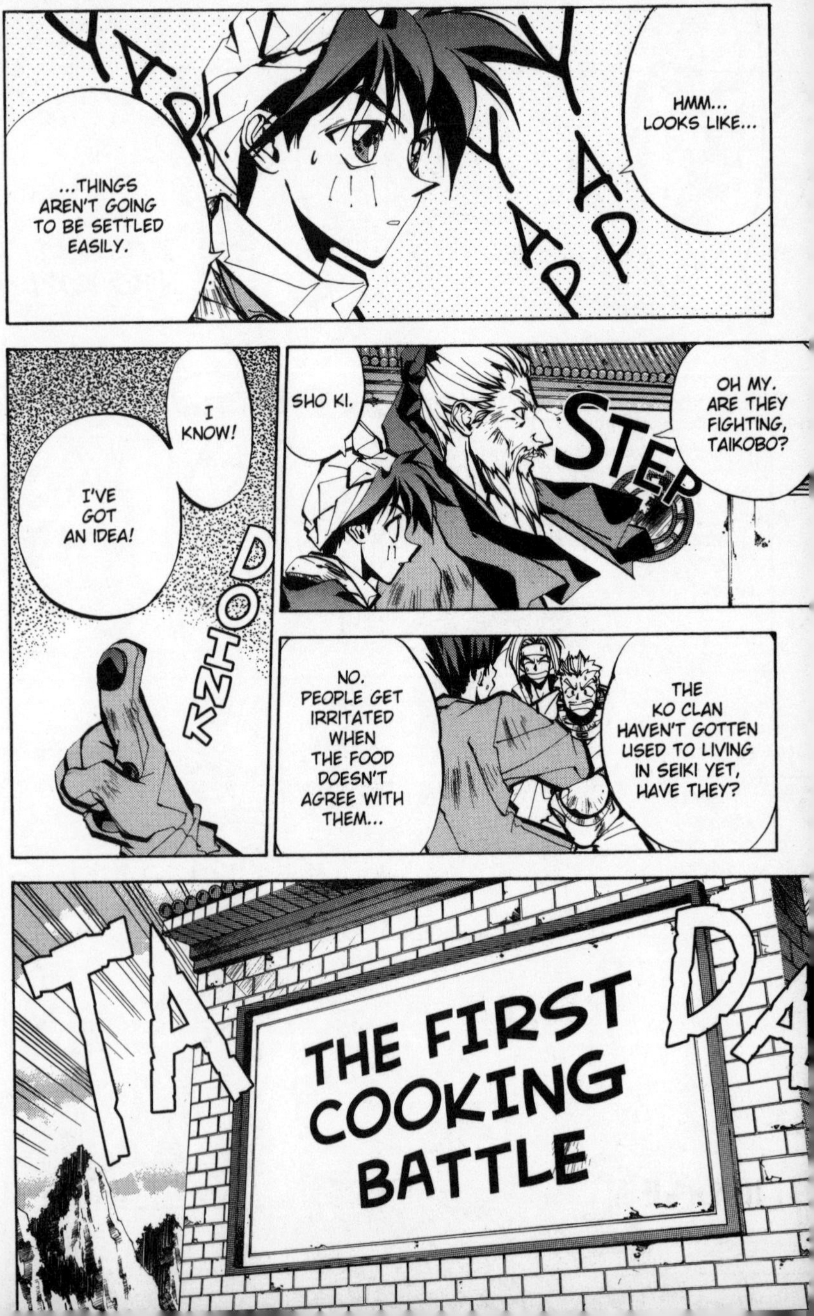
HMM... LOOKS LIKE...
YAP YAP YAP
...THINGS AREN'T GOING TO BE SETTLED EASILY.
OH MY. ARE THEY FIGHTING, TAIKOBO?
STEP
SHO KI.
I KNOW!
I'VE GOT AN IDEA!
DOINK
THE KO CLAN HAVEN'T GOTTEN USED TO LIVING IN SEIKI YET, HAVE THEY?
NO. PEOPLE GET IRRITATED WHEN THE FOOD DOESN'T AGREE WITH THEM...
TA DA
THE FIRST COOKING BATTLE

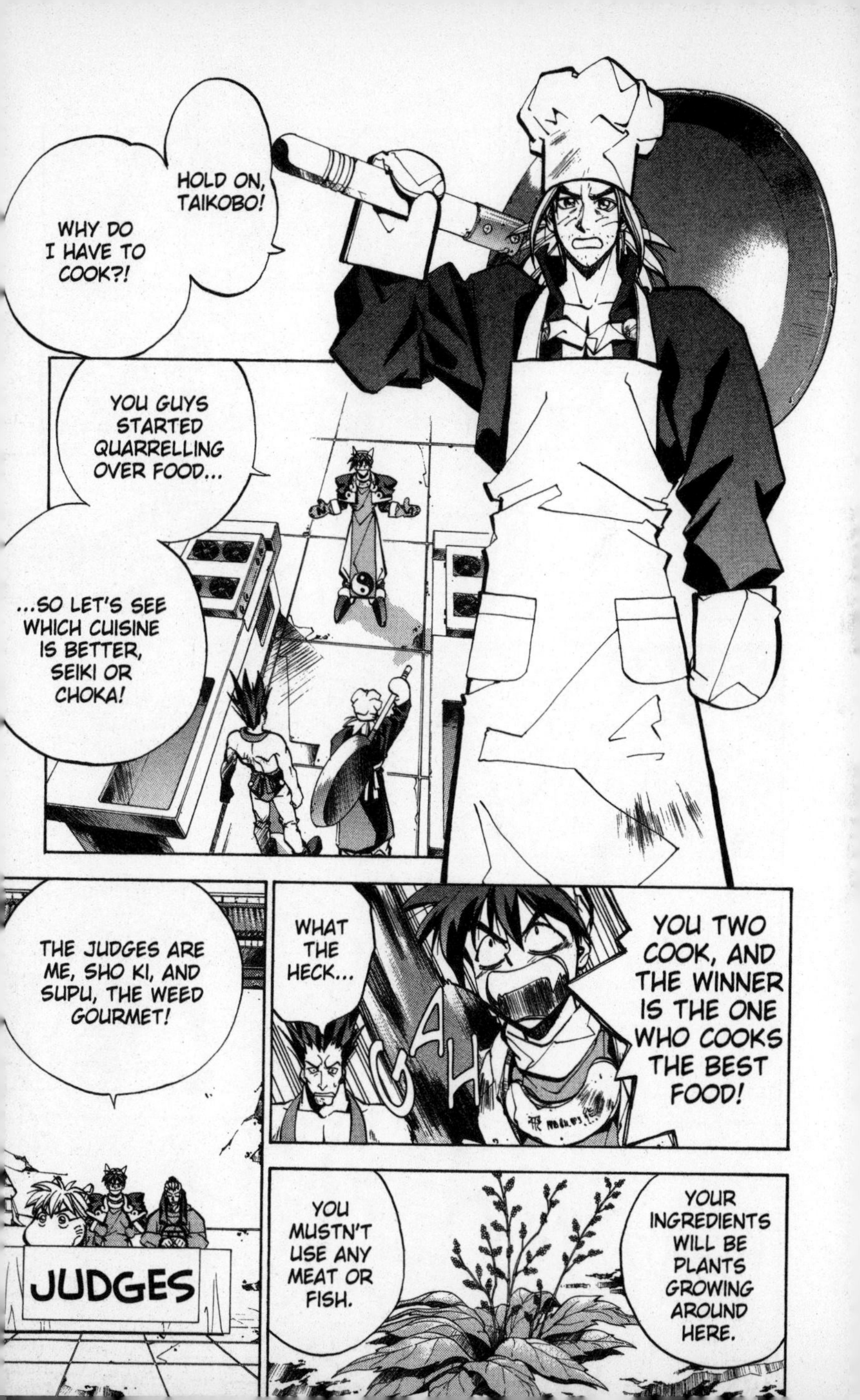
HOLD ON, TAIKOBO!
WHY DO I HAVE TO COOK?!
YOU GUYS STARTED QUARRELLING OVER FOOD...
...SO LET'S SEE WHICH CUISINE IS BETTER, SEIKI OR CHOKA!
YOU TWO COOK, AND THE WINNER IS THE ONE WHO COOKS THE BEST FOOD!
WHAT THE HECK...
YOUR INGREDIENTS WILL BE PLANTS GROWING AROUND HERE.
YOU MUSTN'T USE ANY MEAT OR FISH.
THE JUDGES ARE ME, SHO KI, AND SUPU, THE WEED GOURMET!
JUDGES

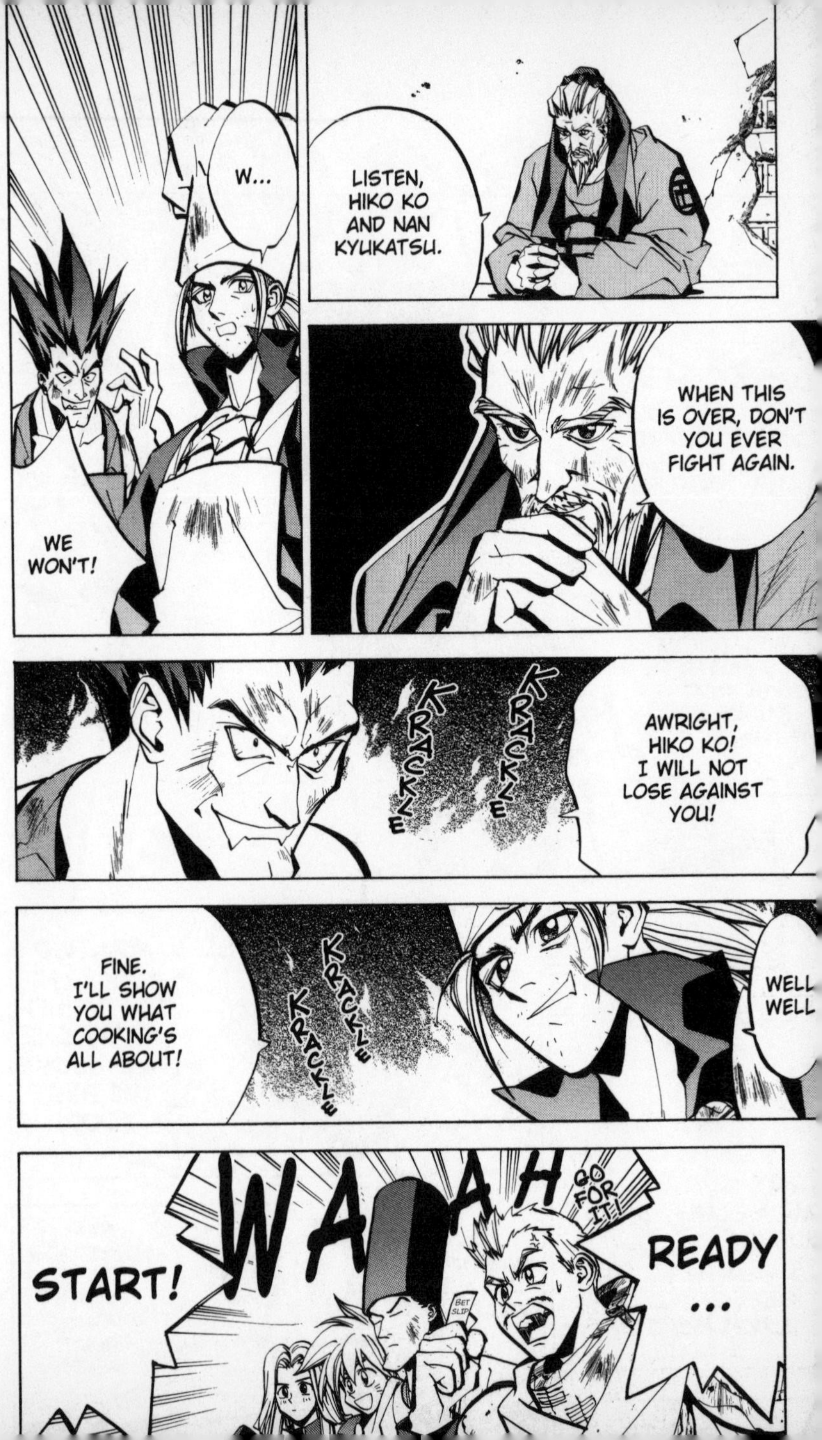
LISTEN, HIKO KO AND NAN KYUKATSU.
WHEN THIS IS OVER, DON'T YOU EVER FIGHT AGAIN.
W...
WE WON'T!
AWRIGHT, HIKO KO! I WILL NOT LOSE AGAINST YOU!
KRACKLE
KRACKLE
WELL WELL
FINE. I'LL SHOW YOU WHAT COOKING'S ALL ABOUT!
KRACKLE
KRACKLE
READY ...
GO FOR IT!
WAAH
BET SLIP
START!

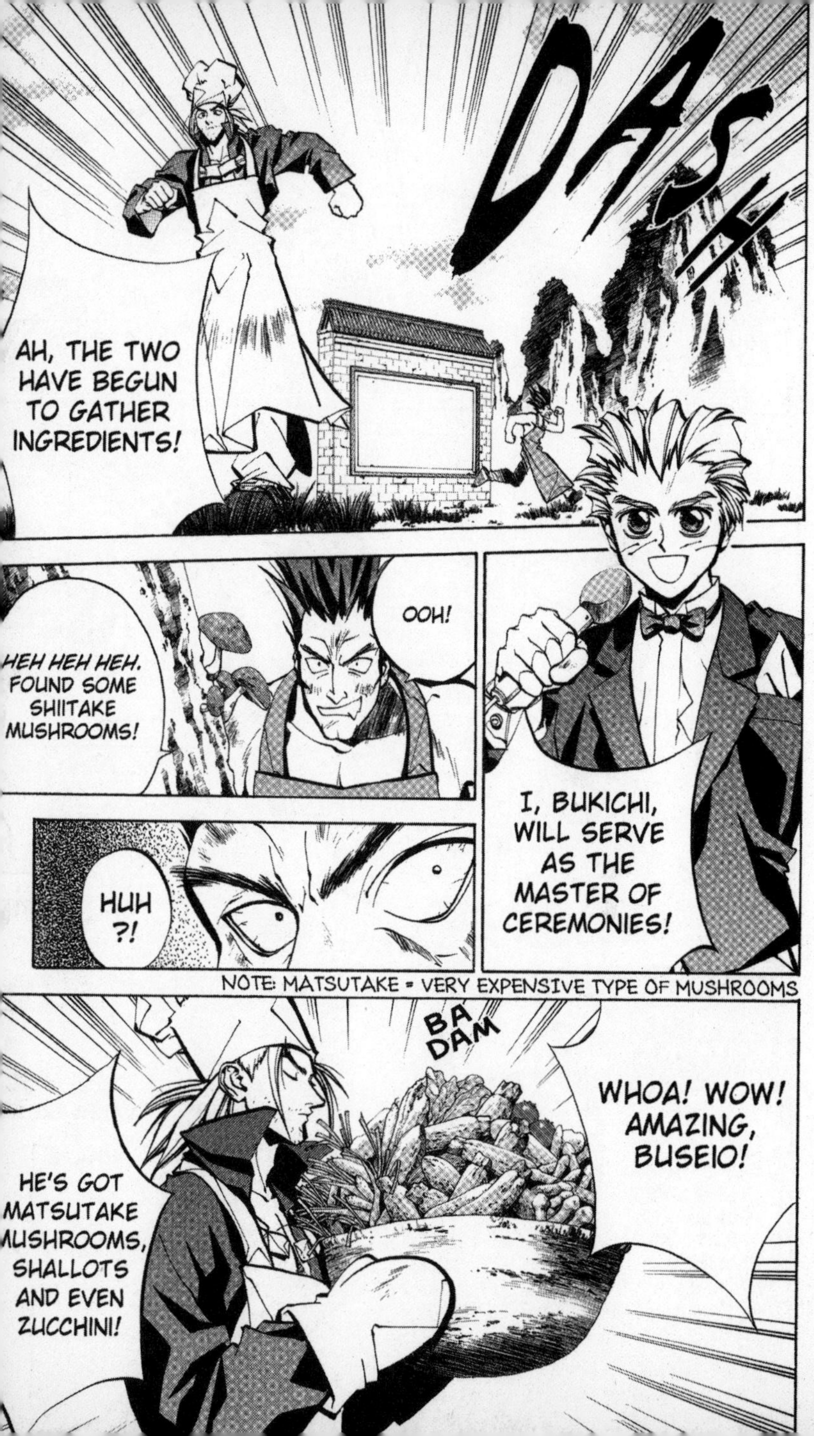
DASH
AH, THE TWO HAVE BEGUN TO GATHER INGREDIENTS!
I, BUKICHI, WILL SERVE AS THE MASTER OF CEREMONIES!
OOH!
HEH HEH HEH. FOUND SOME SHIITAKE MUSHROOMS!
HUH ?!
NOTE: MATSUTAKE = VERY EXPENSIVE TYPE OF MUSHROOMS
BA DAM
WHOA! WOW! AMAZING, BUSEIO!
HE'S GOT MATSUTAKE MUSHROOMS, SHALLOTS AND EVEN ZUCCHINI!

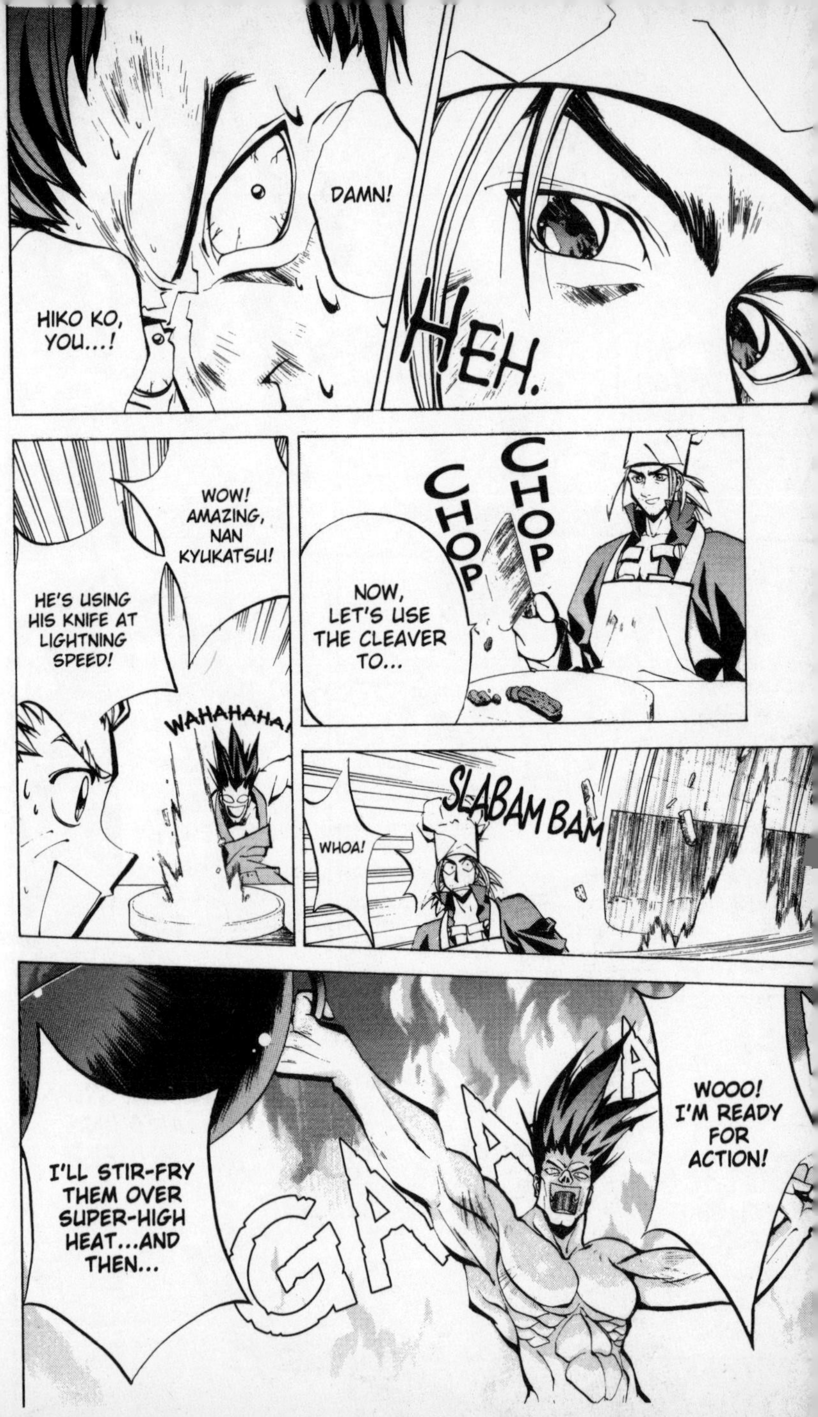
HEH.
DAMN!
HIKO KO, YOU...!
CHOP CHOP
NOW, LET'S USE THE CLEAVER TO...
SLABAM BAM
WHOA!
WOW! AMAZING, NAN KYUKATSU!
HE'S USING HIS KNIFE AT LIGHTNING SPEED!
WAHAHAHA!
WOOO! I'M READY FOR ACTION!
GAAAA
I'LL STIR-FRY THEM OVER SUPER-HIGH HEAT...AND THEN...

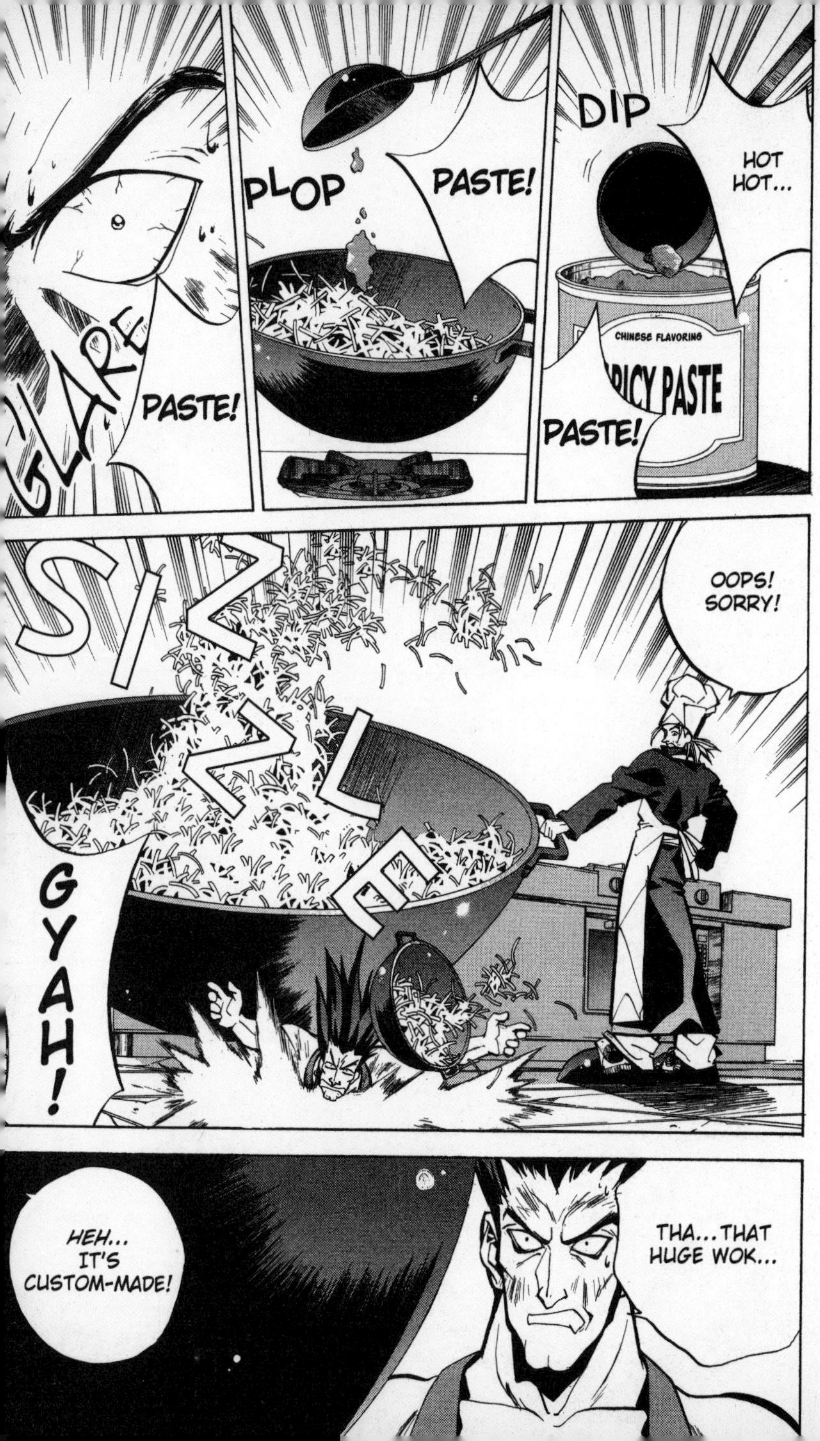
HOT HOT...
DIP
CHINESE FLAVORING
PICY PASTE
PASTE!
PASTE!
PLOP
GLARE
PASTE!
OOPS! SORRY!
SIZZLE
GYAH!
THA...THAT HUGE WOK...
HEH... IT'S CUSTOM-MADE!

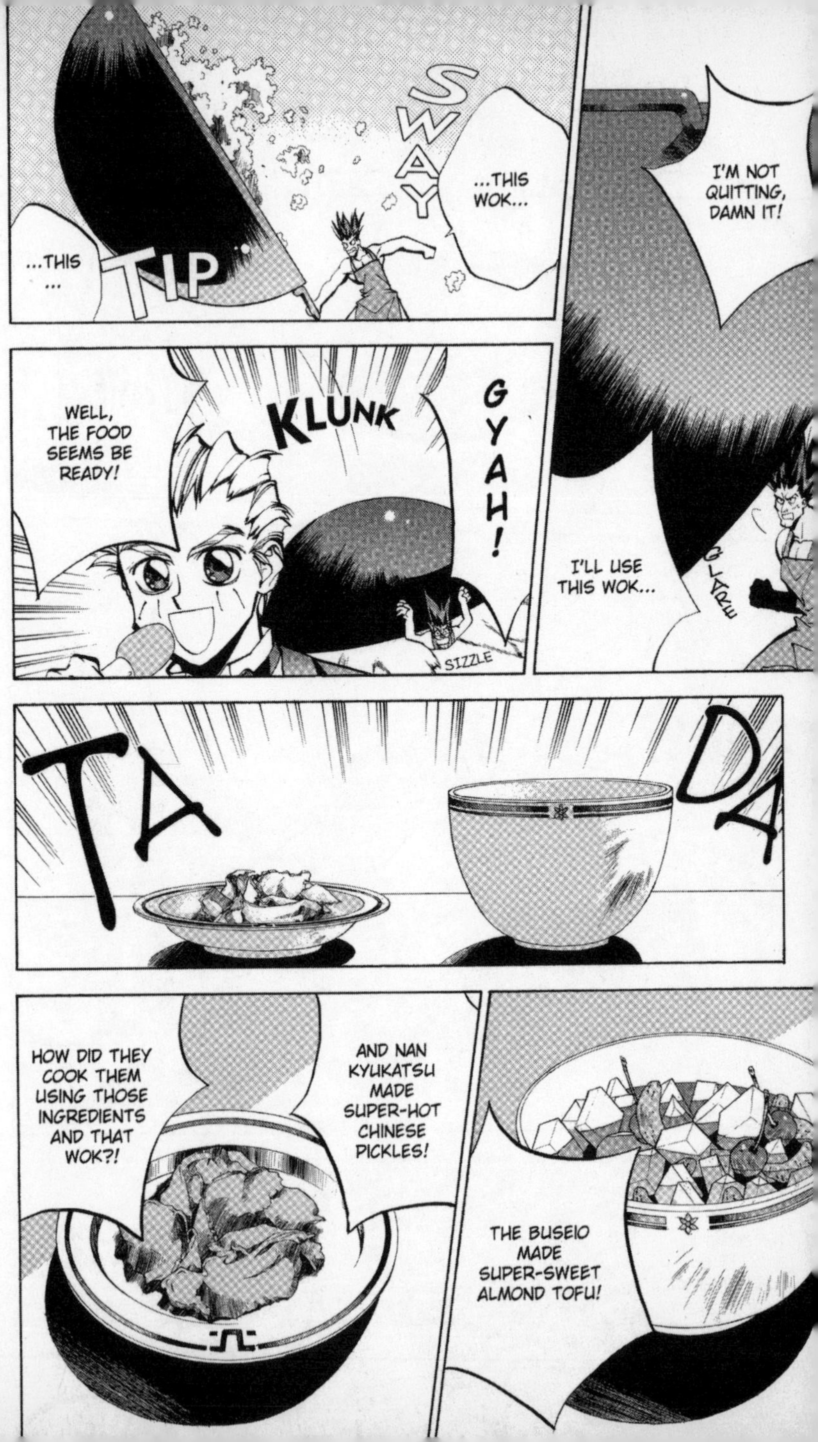
I'M NOT QUITTING, DAMN IT!
I'LL USE THIS WOK...
GLARE
...THIS WOK...
SWAY
...THIS ...
TIP
GYAH!
KLUNK
WELL, THE FOOD SEEMS BE READY!
SIZZLE
TA DA
THE BUSEIO MADE SUPER-SWEET ALMOND TOFU!
AND NAN KYUKATSU MADE SUPER-HOT CHINESE PICKLES!
HOW DID THEY COOK THEM USING THOSE INGREDIENTS AND THAT WOK?!

READ THIS WAY

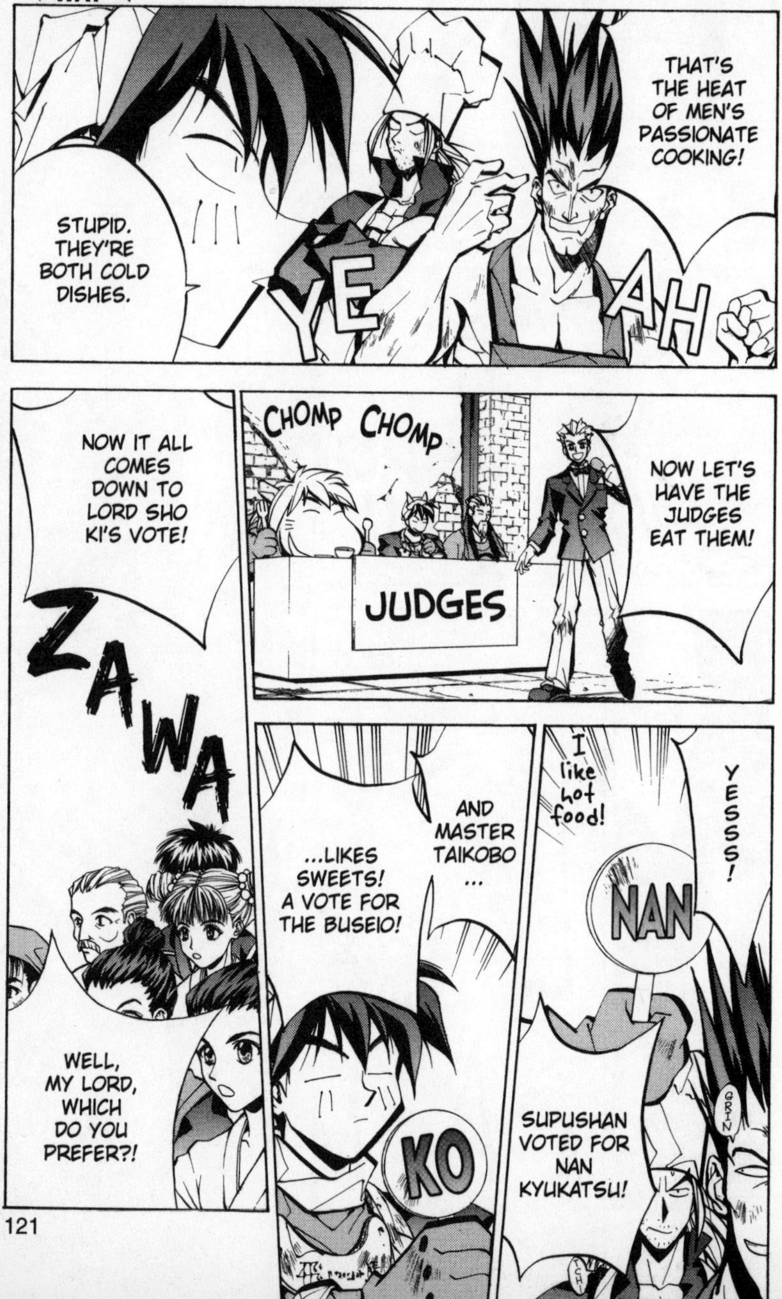

THAT'S THE HEAT OF MEN'S PASSIONATE COOKING!
YE AH
STUPID. THEY'RE BOTH COLD DISHES.
NOW LET'S HAVE THE JUDGES EAT THEM!
CHOMP CHOMP
JUDGES
YESSS!
I like hot food!
NAN
GRIN
SUPUSHAN VOTED FOR NAN KYUKATSU!
TCHI
AND MASTER TAIKOBO ...
...LIKES SWEETS! A VOTE FOR THE BUSEIO!
KO
NOW IT ALL COMES DOWN TO LORD SHO KI'S VOTE!
ZAWA
WELL, MY LORD, WHICH DO YOU PREFER?!

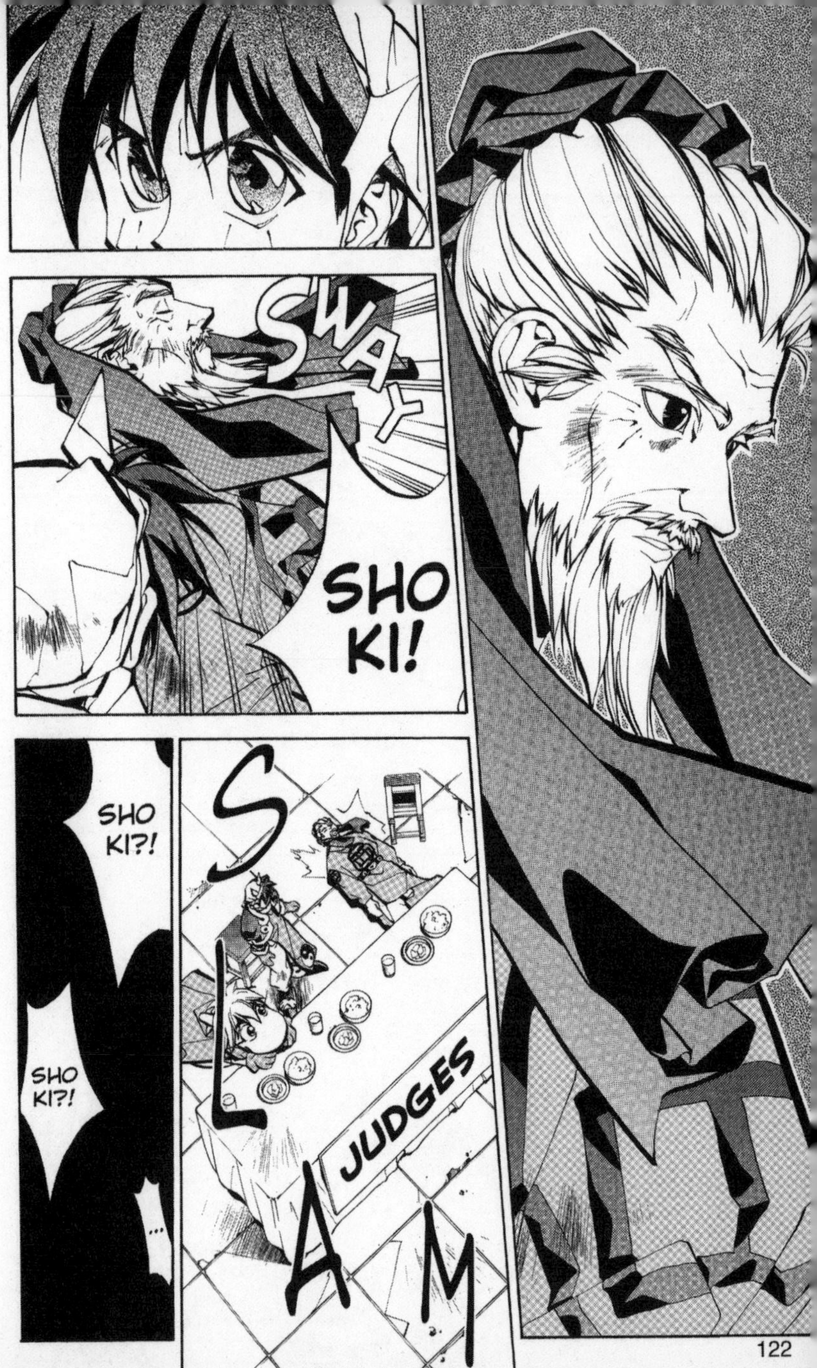
SWAY
SHO KI!
SLAM
JUDGES
SHO KI?!
SHO KI?!
...

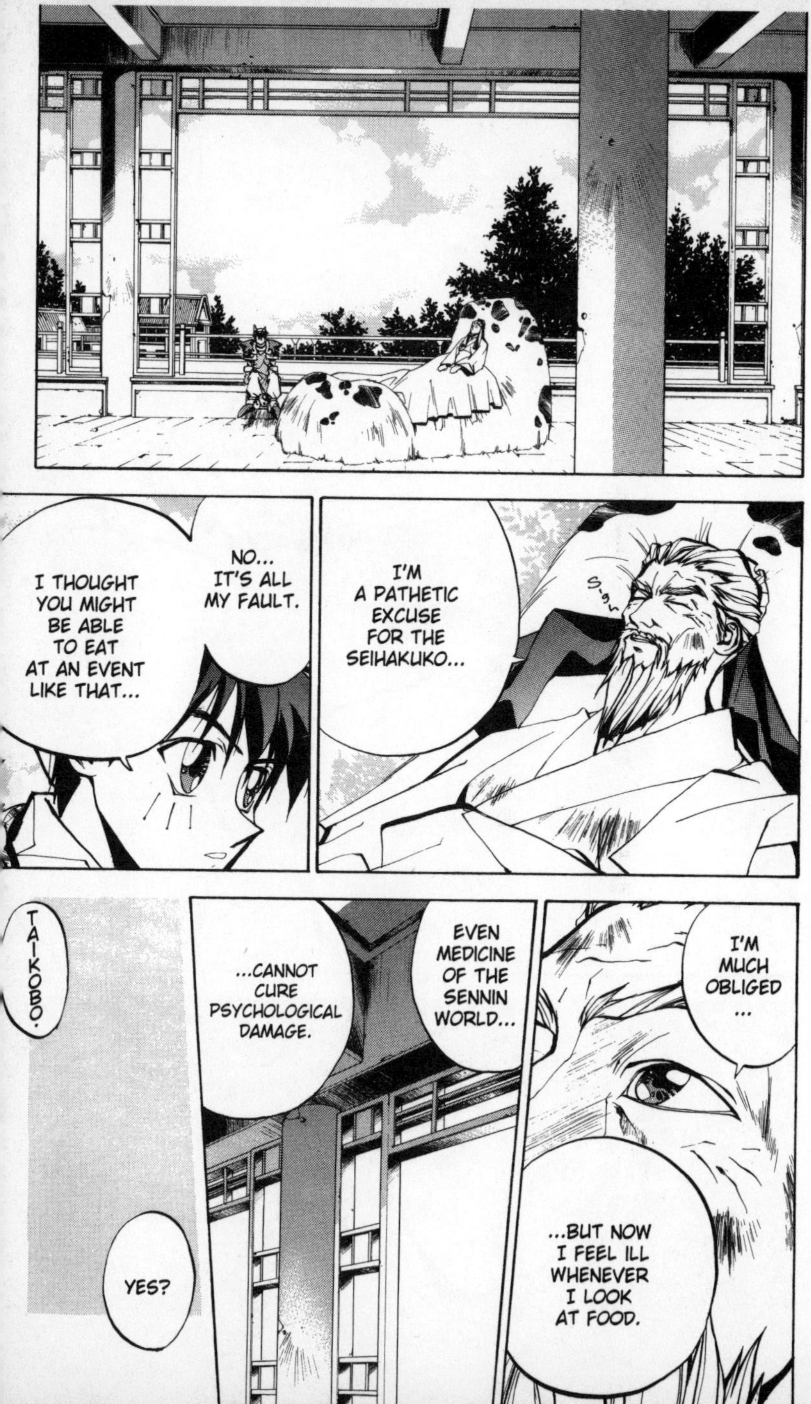
I'M A PATHETIC EXCUSE FOR THE SEIHAKUKO...
Sigh
NO... IT'S ALL MY FAULT.
I THOUGHT YOU MIGHT BE ABLE TO EAT AT AN EVENT LIKE THAT...
I'M MUCH OBLIGED ...
...BUT NOW I FEEL ILL WHENEVER I LOOK AT FOOD.
EVEN MEDICINE OF THE SENNIN WORLD...
...CANNOT CURE PSYCHOLOGICAL DAMAGE.
TAIKOBO.
YES?

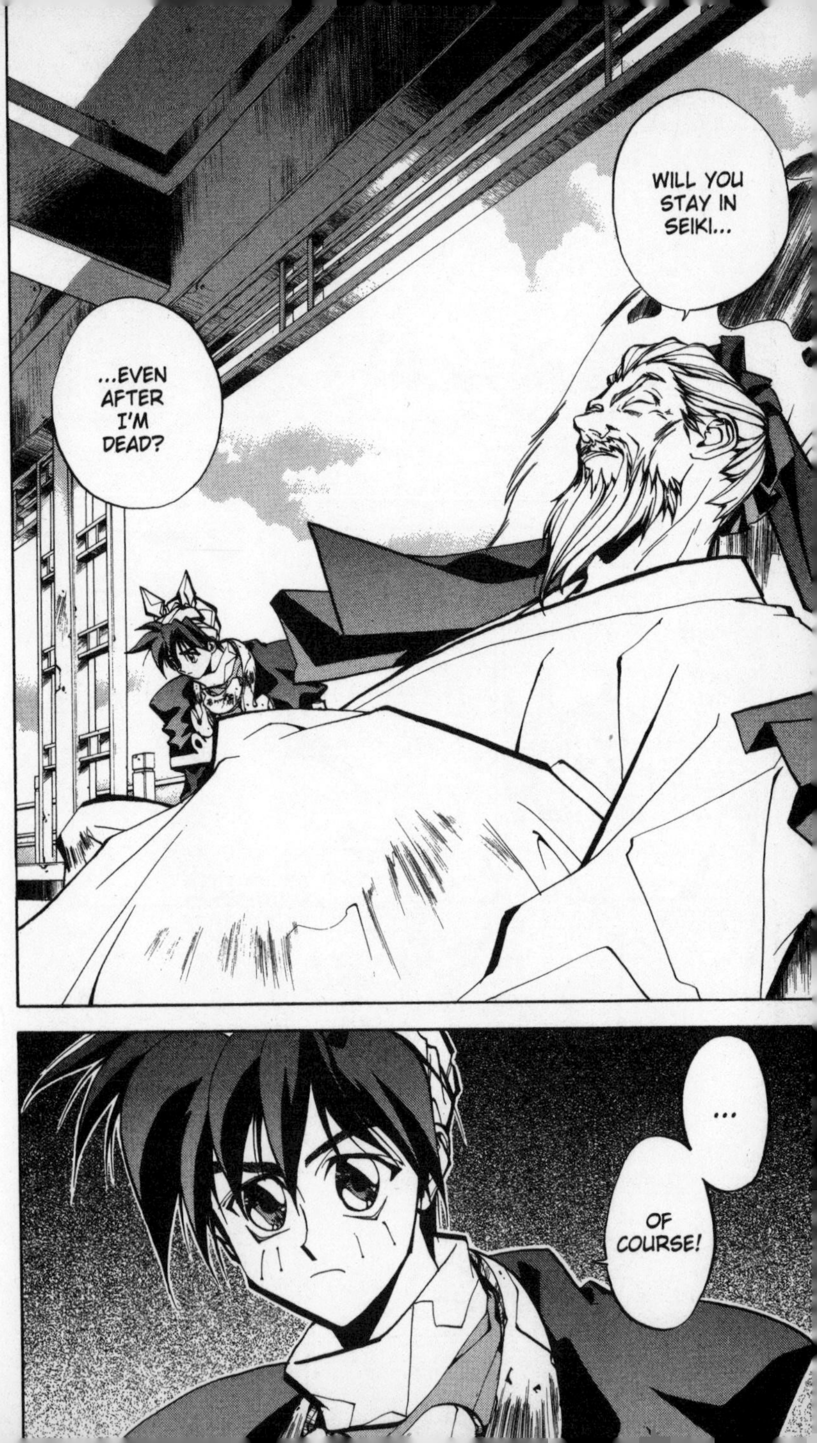
WILL YOU STAY IN SEIKI...
...EVEN AFTER I'M DEAD?
...
OF COURSE!

READ THIS WAY

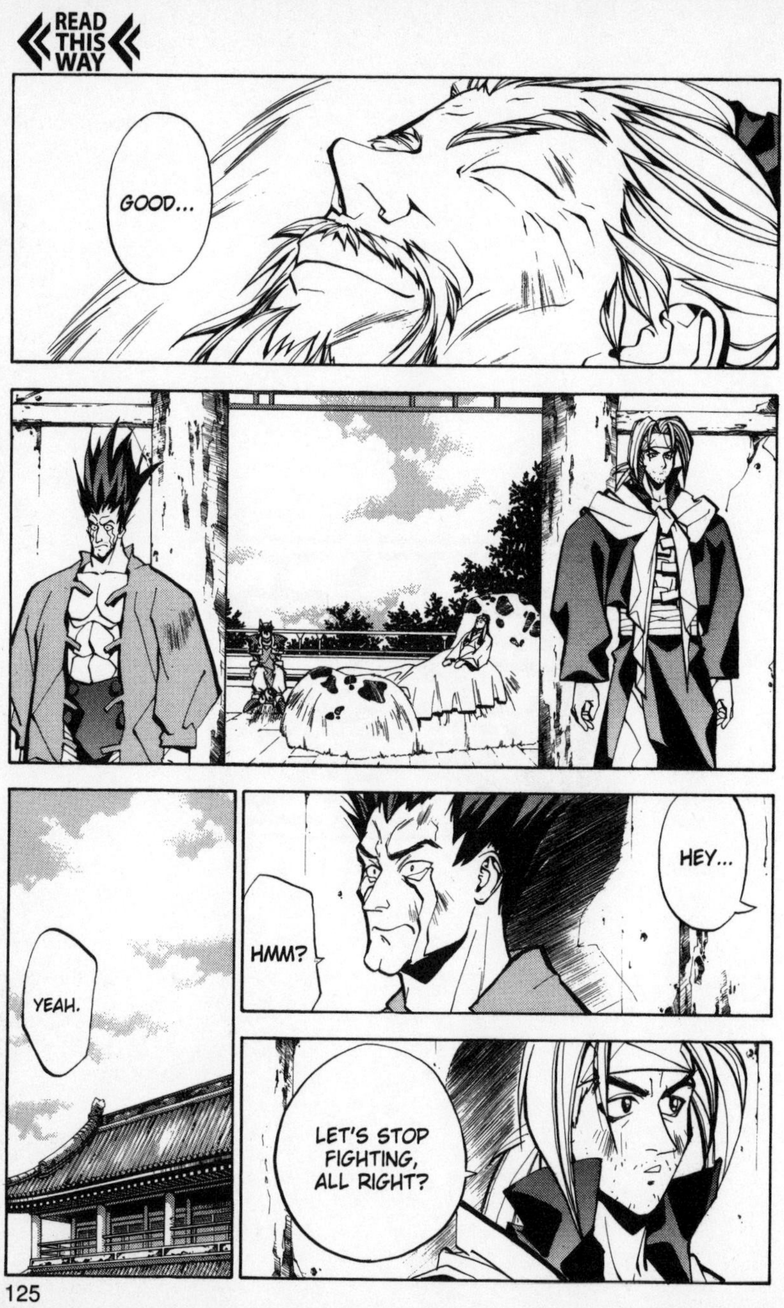
GOOD...
HEY...
HMM?
LET'S STOP FIGHTING, ALL RIGHT?
YEAH.

封神演義

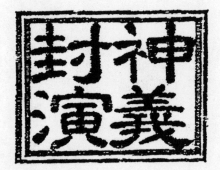

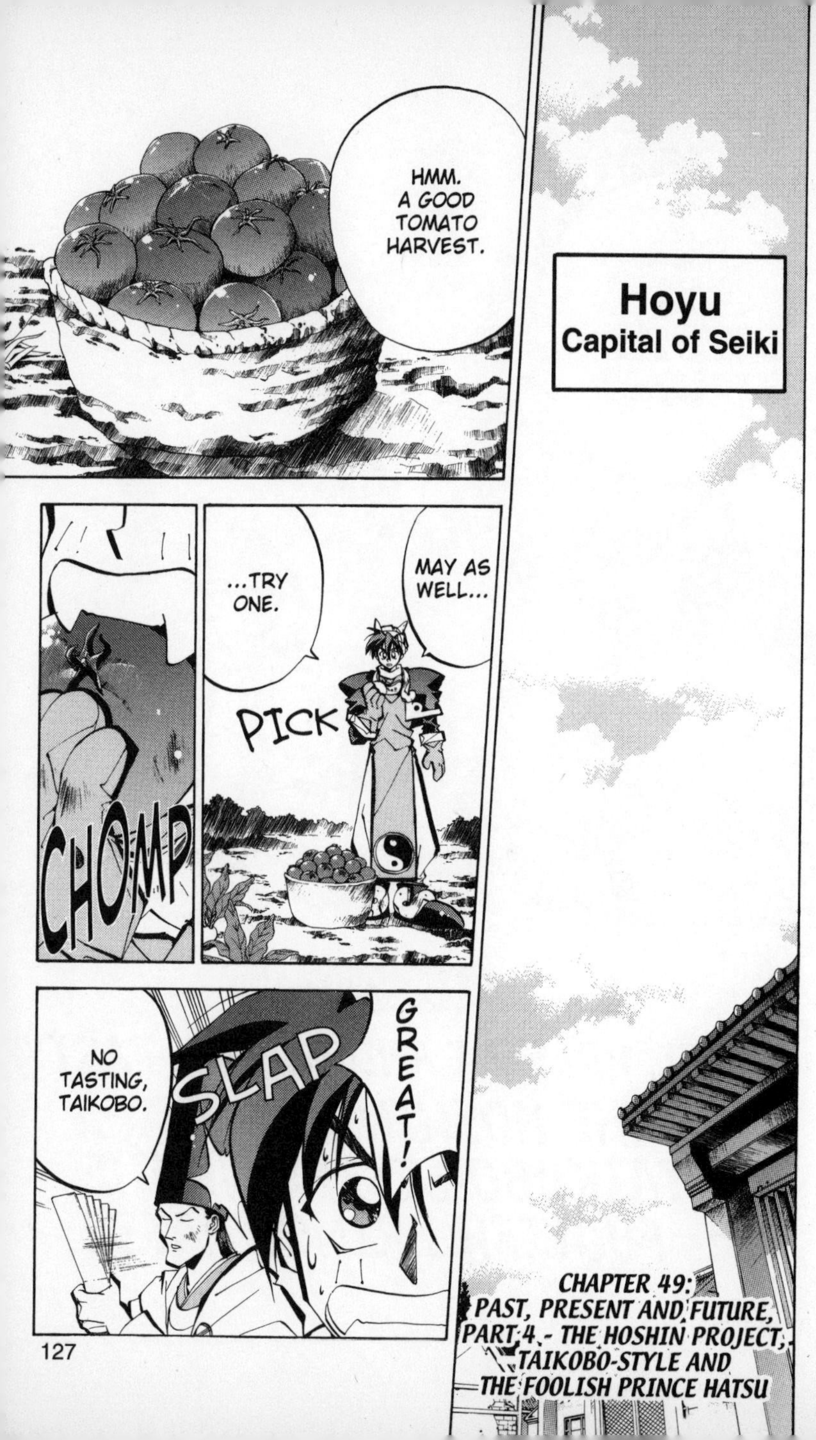
Hoyu
Capital of Seiki
CHAPTER 49:
PAST, PRESENT AND FUTURE,
PART 4 - THE HOSHIN PROJECT,
TAIKOBO-STYLE AND
THE FOOLISH PRINCE HATSU
HMM. A GOOD TOMATO HARVEST.
MAY AS WELL...
...TRY ONE.
PICK
CHOMP
GREAT!
SLAP
NO TASTING, TAIKOBO.

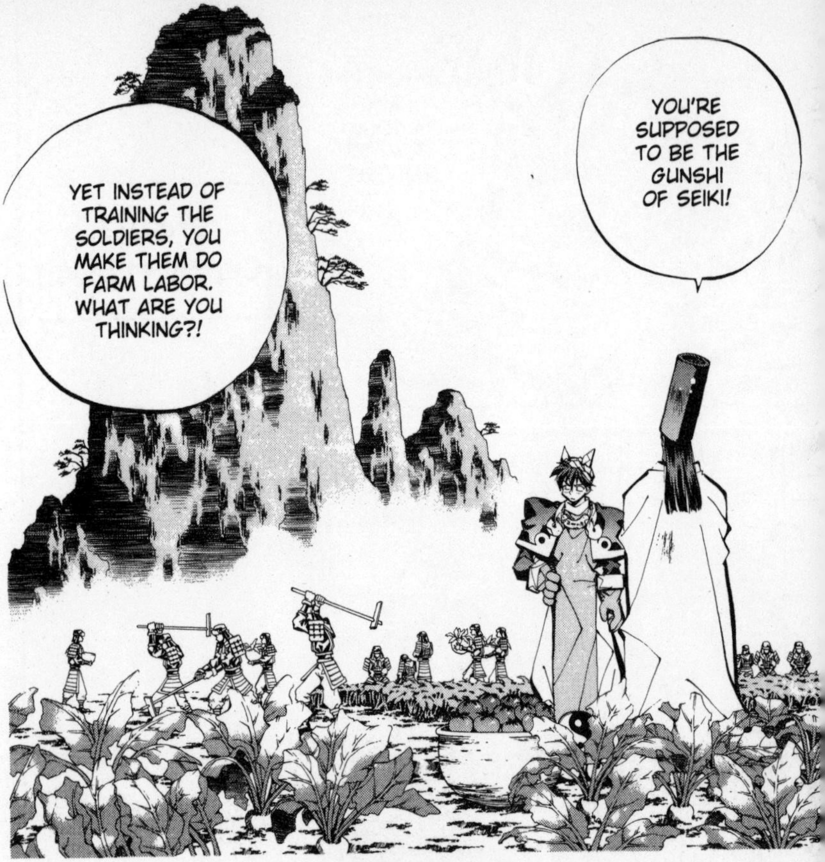
YOU'RE SUPPOSED TO BE THE GUNSHI OF SEIKI!
YET INSTEAD OF TRAINING THE SOLDIERS, YOU MAKE THEM DO FARM LABOR. WHAT ARE YOU THINKING?!

Chapter 49

PAST, PRESENT AND FUTURE, PART 4

THE HOSHIN PROJECT, TAIKOBO-STYLE AND THE FOOLISH PRINCE HATSU

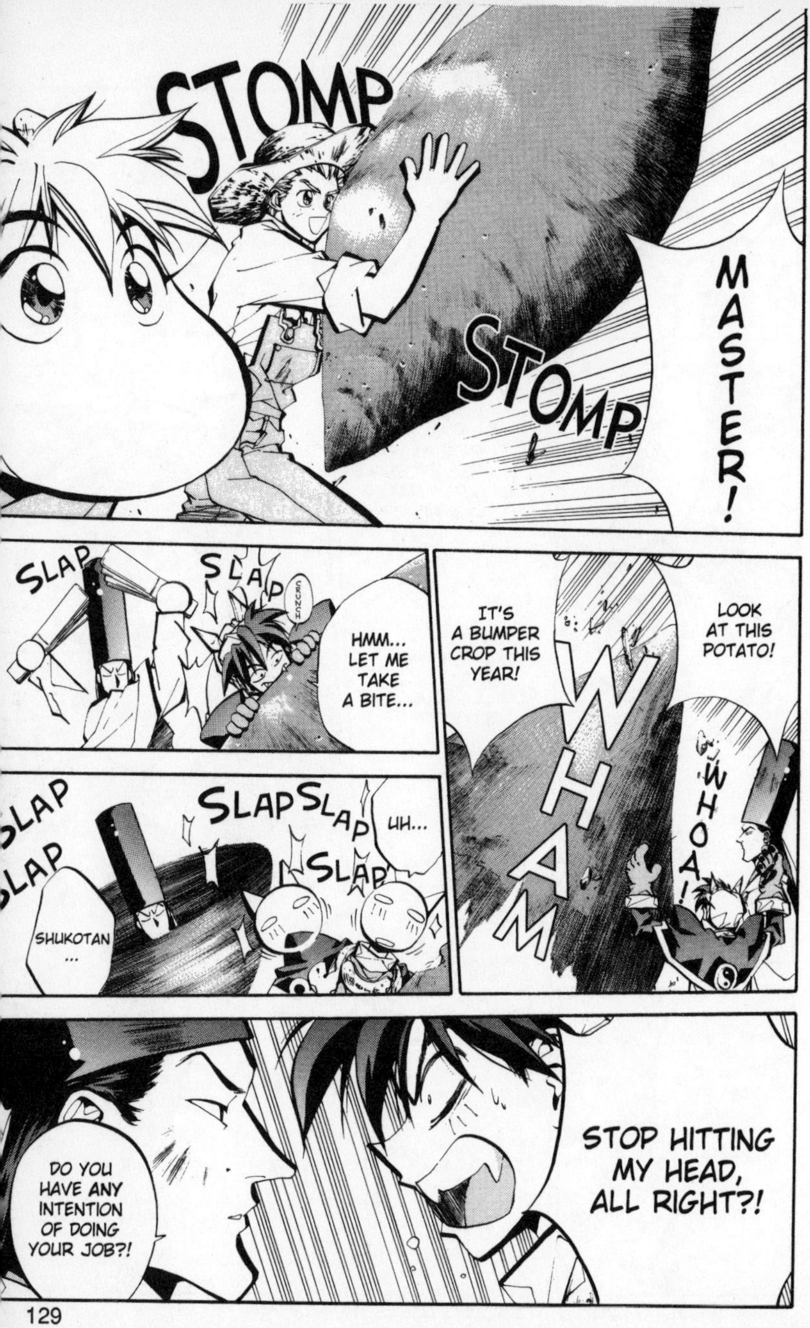
MASTER!
STOMP
STOMP
LOOK AT THIS POTATO!
IT'S A BUMPER CROP THIS YEAR!
WHAM
WHOA!
HMM... LET ME TAKE A BITE...
CRUNCH
SLAP
SLAP
UH...
SLAP
SLAP
SLAP
SLAP
SLAP
SHUKOTAN...
STOP HITTING MY HEAD, ALL RIGHT?!
DO YOU HAVE ANY INTENTION OF DOING YOUR JOB?!

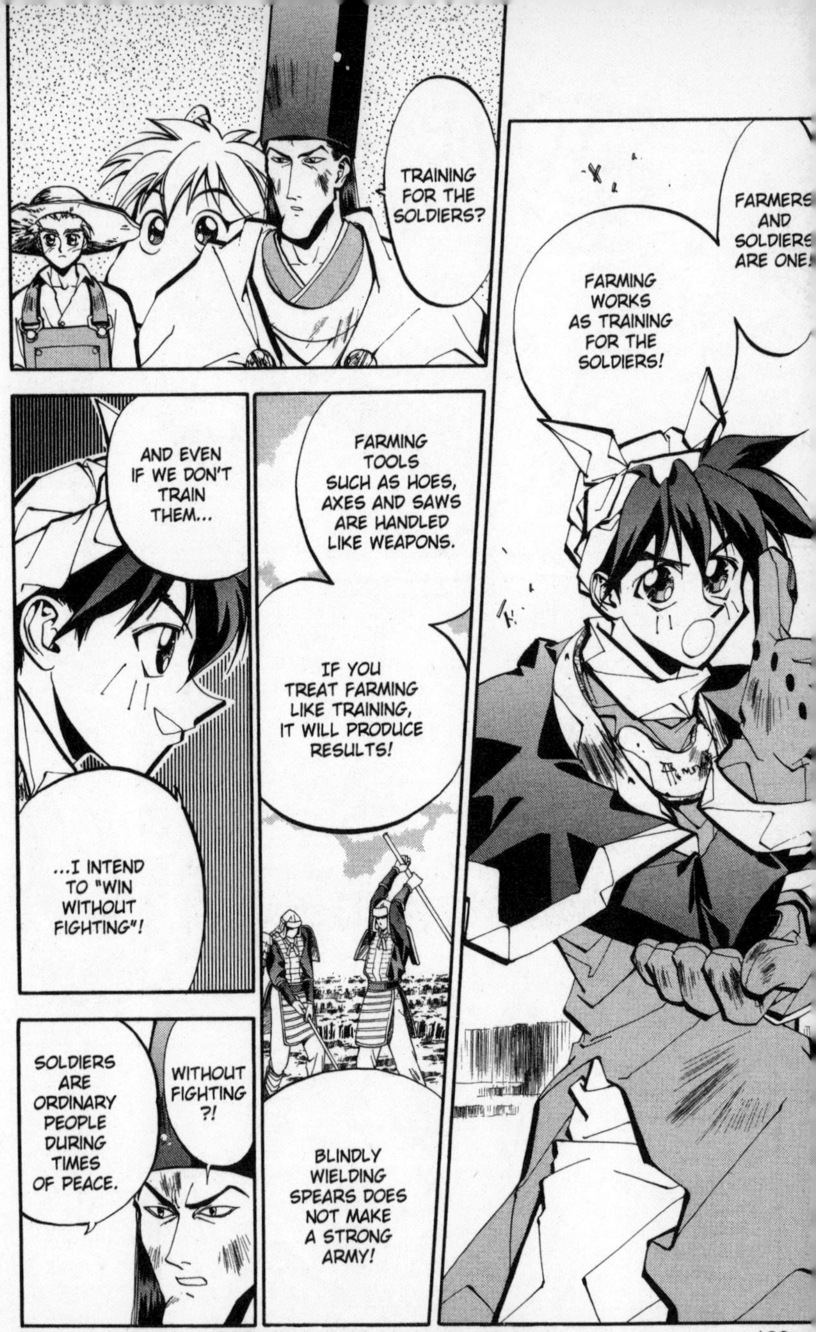
TRAINING FOR THE SOLDIERS?
FARMERS AND SOLDIERS ARE ONE!
FARMING WORKS AS TRAINING FOR THE SOLDIERS!
FARMING TOOLS SUCH AS HOES, AXES AND SAWS ARE HANDLED LIKE WEAPONS.
IF YOU TREAT FARMING LIKE TRAINING, IT WILL PRODUCE RESULTS!
BLINDLY WIELDING SPEARS DOES NOT MAKE A STRONG ARMY!
AND EVEN IF WE DON'T TRAIN THEM...
...I INTEND TO "WIN WITHOUT FIGHTING"!
WITHOUT FIGHTING ?!
SOLDIERS ARE ORDINARY PEOPLE DURING TIMES OF PEACE.

THERE WERE NO PROFESSIONAL SOLDIERS IN THIS ERA.
MEN WERE DRAFTED ONLY WHEN BATTLES WERE FOUGHT.

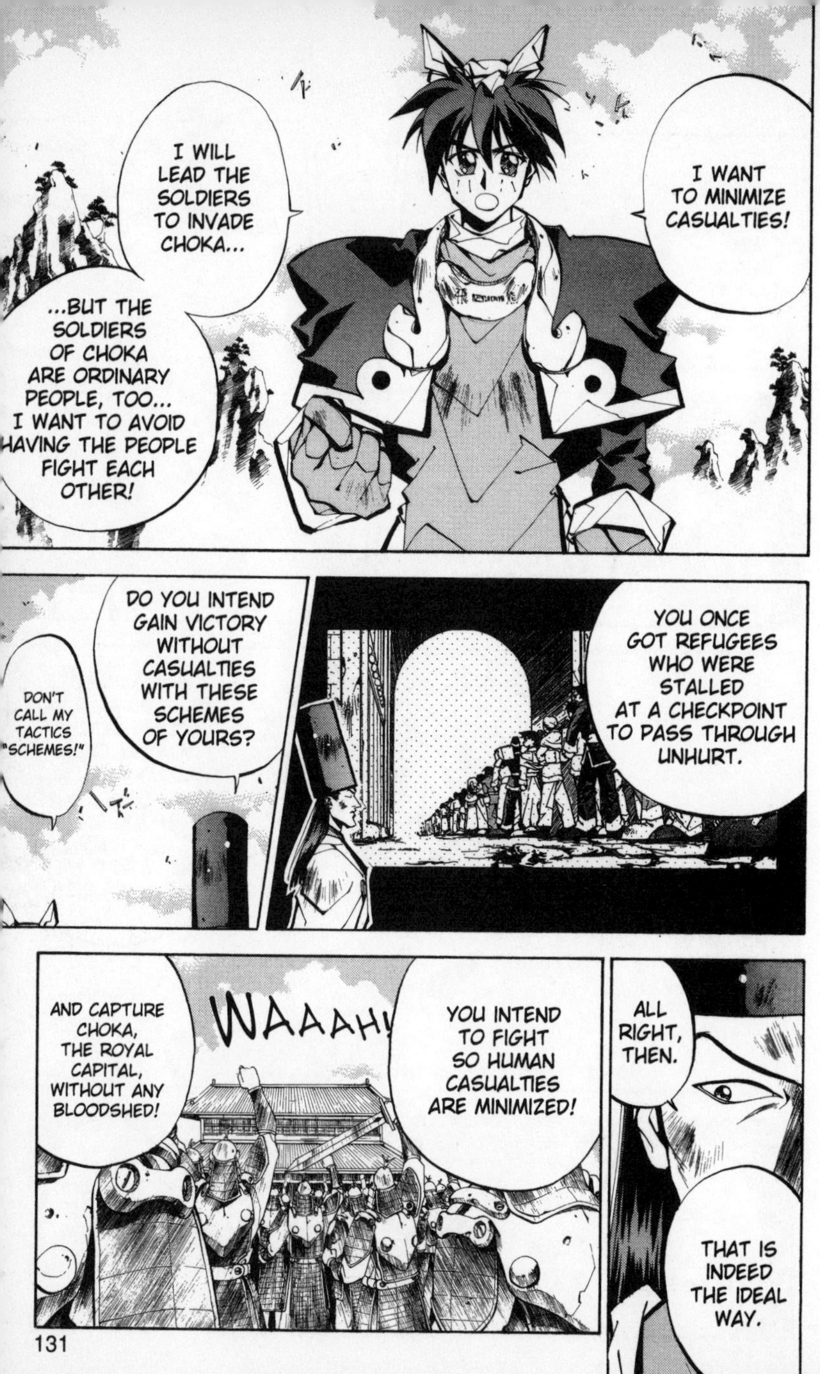
I WANT TO MINIMIZE CASUALTIES!
I WILL LEAD THE SOLDIERS TO INVADE CHOKA...
...BUT THE SOLDIERS OF CHOKA ARE ORDINARY PEOPLE, TOO... I WANT TO AVOID HAVING THE PEOPLE FIGHT EACH OTHER!
YOU ONCE GOT REFUGEES WHO WERE STALLED AT A CHECKPOINT TO PASS THROUGH UNHURT.
DO YOU INTEND GAIN VICTORY WITHOUT CASUALTIES WITH THESE SCHEMES OF YOURS?
DON'T CALL MY TACTICS "SCHEMES!"
ALL RIGHT, THEN.
THAT IS INDEED THE IDEAL WAY.
YOU INTEND TO FIGHT SO HUMAN CASUALTIES ARE MINIMIZED!
WAAAH!
AND CAPTURE CHOKA, THE ROYAL CAPITAL, WITHOUT ANY BLOODSHED!

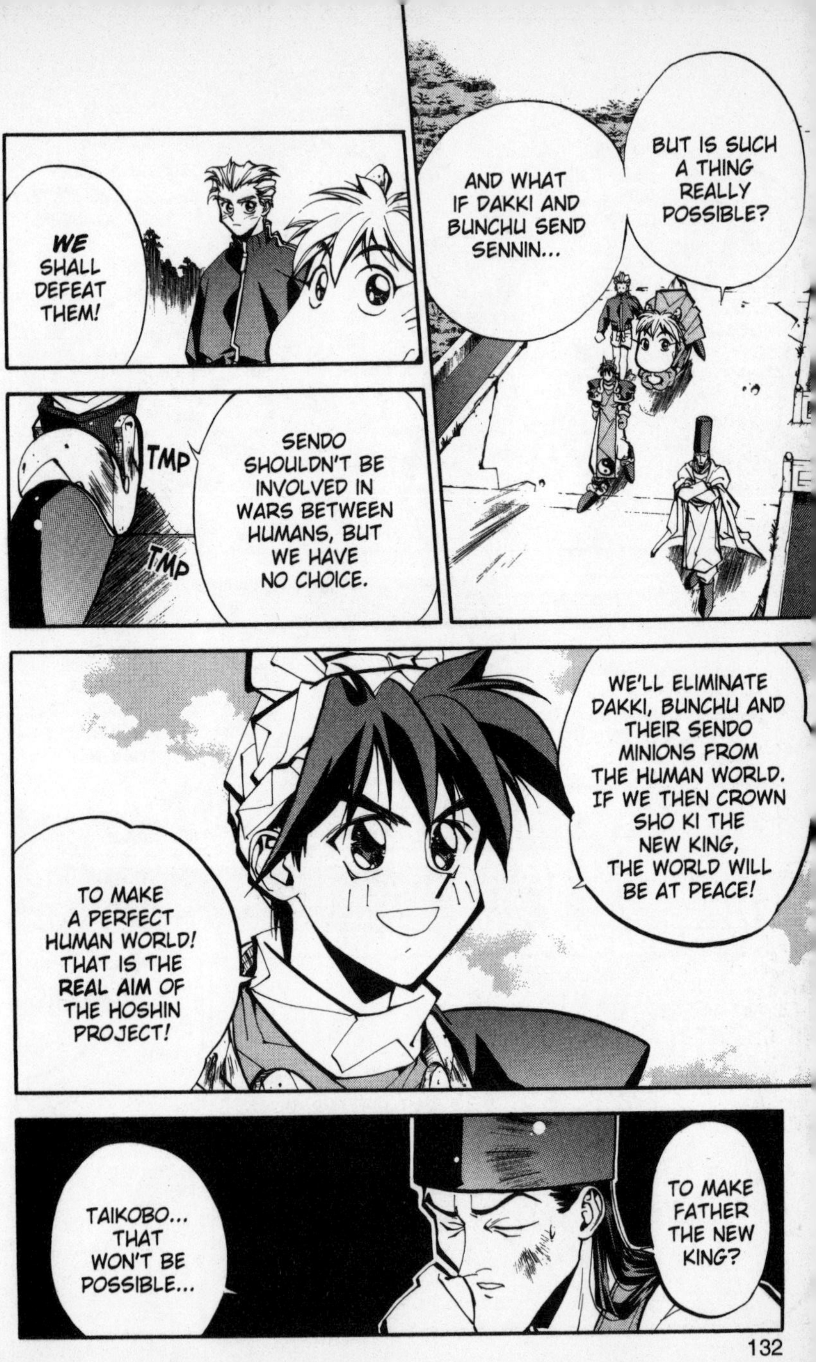

BUT IS SUCH A THING REALLY POSSIBLE?
AND WHAT IF DAKKI AND BUNCHU SEND SENNIN...
WE SHALL DEFEAT THEM!
SENDO SHOULDN'T BE INVOLVED IN WARS BETWEEN HUMANS, BUT WE HAVE NO CHOICE.
TMP
TMP
WE'LL ELIMINATE DAKKI, BUNCHU AND THEIR SENDO MINIONS FROM THE HUMAN WORLD. IF WE THEN CROWN SHO KI THE NEW KING, THE WORLD WILL BE AT PEACE!
TO MAKE A PERFECT HUMAN WORLD! THAT IS THE REAL AIM OF THE HOSHIN PROJECT!
TO MAKE FATHER THE NEW KING?
TAIKOBO... THAT WON'T BE POSSIBLE...

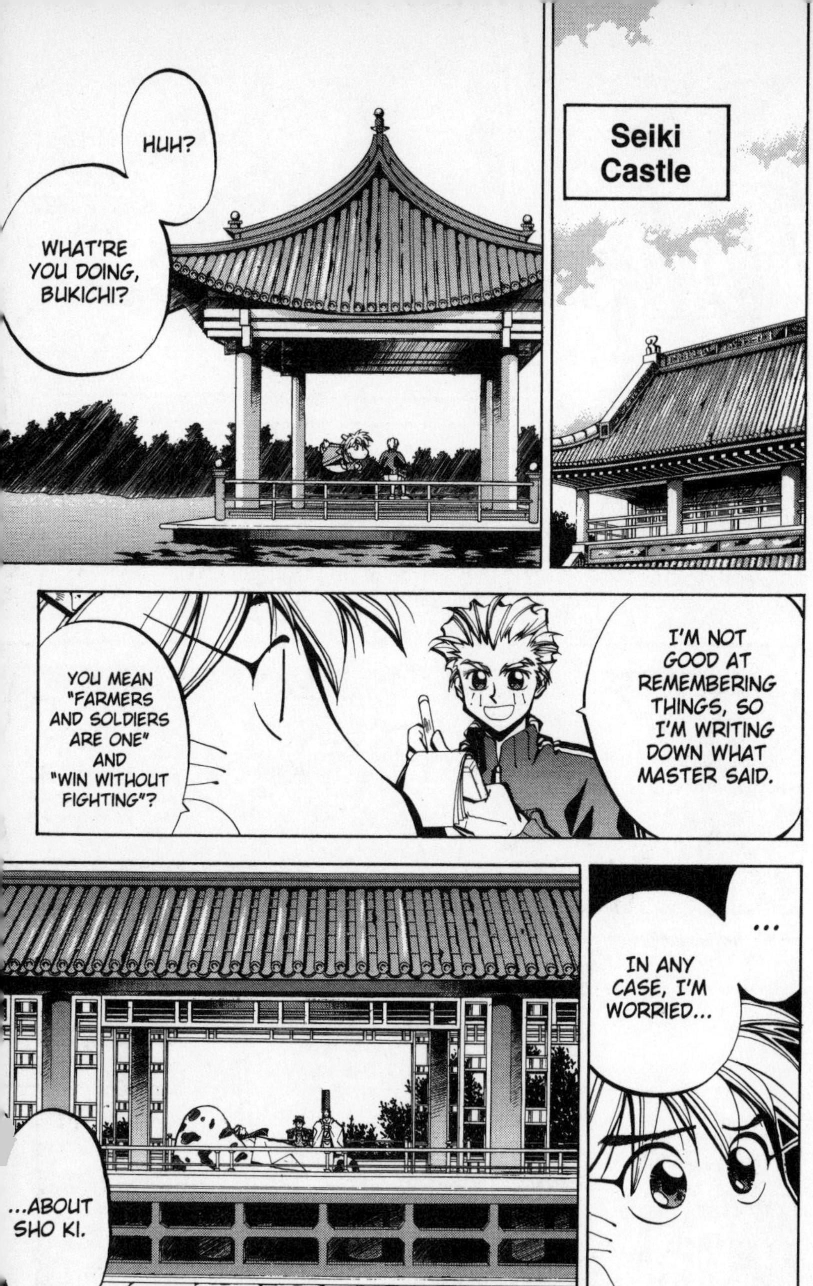
Seiki Castle
HUH?
WHAT'RE YOU DOING, BUKICHI?
I'M NOT GOOD AT REMEMBERING THINGS, SO I'M WRITING DOWN WHAT MASTER SAID.
YOU MEAN "FARMERS AND SOLDIERS ARE ONE" AND "WIN WITHOUT FIGHTING"?
...
IN ANY CASE, I'M WORRIED...
...ABOUT SHO KI.

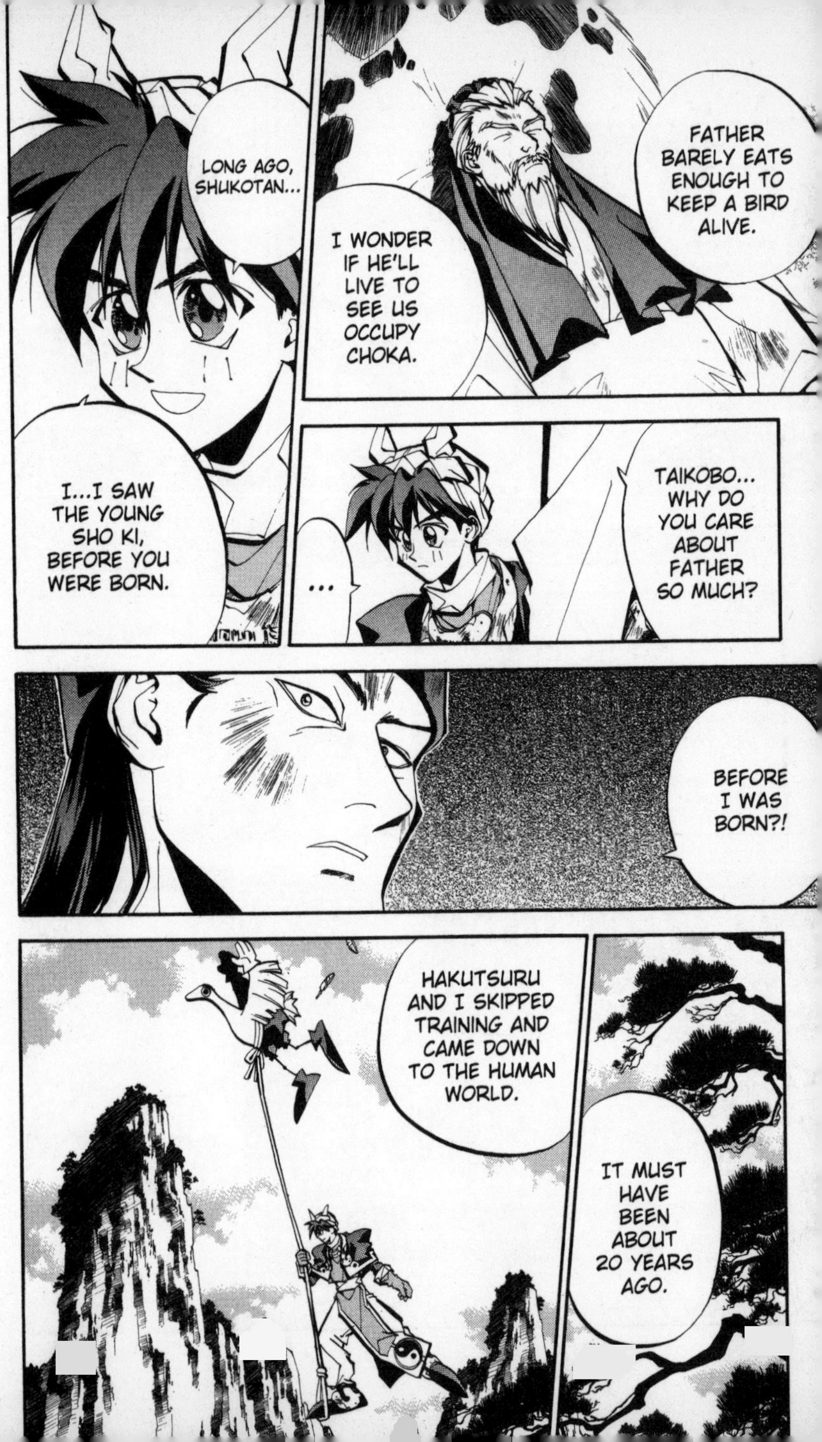
FATHER BARELY EATS ENOUGH TO KEEP A BIRD ALIVE.
I WONDER IF HE'LL LIVE TO SEE US OCCUPY CHOKA.
TAIKOBO... WHY DO YOU CARE ABOUT FATHER SO MUCH?
...
LONG AGO, SHUKOTAN...
I...I SAW THE YOUNG SHO KI, BEFORE YOU WERE BORN.
BEFORE I WAS BORN?!
IT MUST HAVE BEEN ABOUT 20 YEARS AGO.
HAKUTSURU AND I SKIPPED TRAINING AND CAME DOWN TO THE HUMAN WORLD.

READ THIS WAY

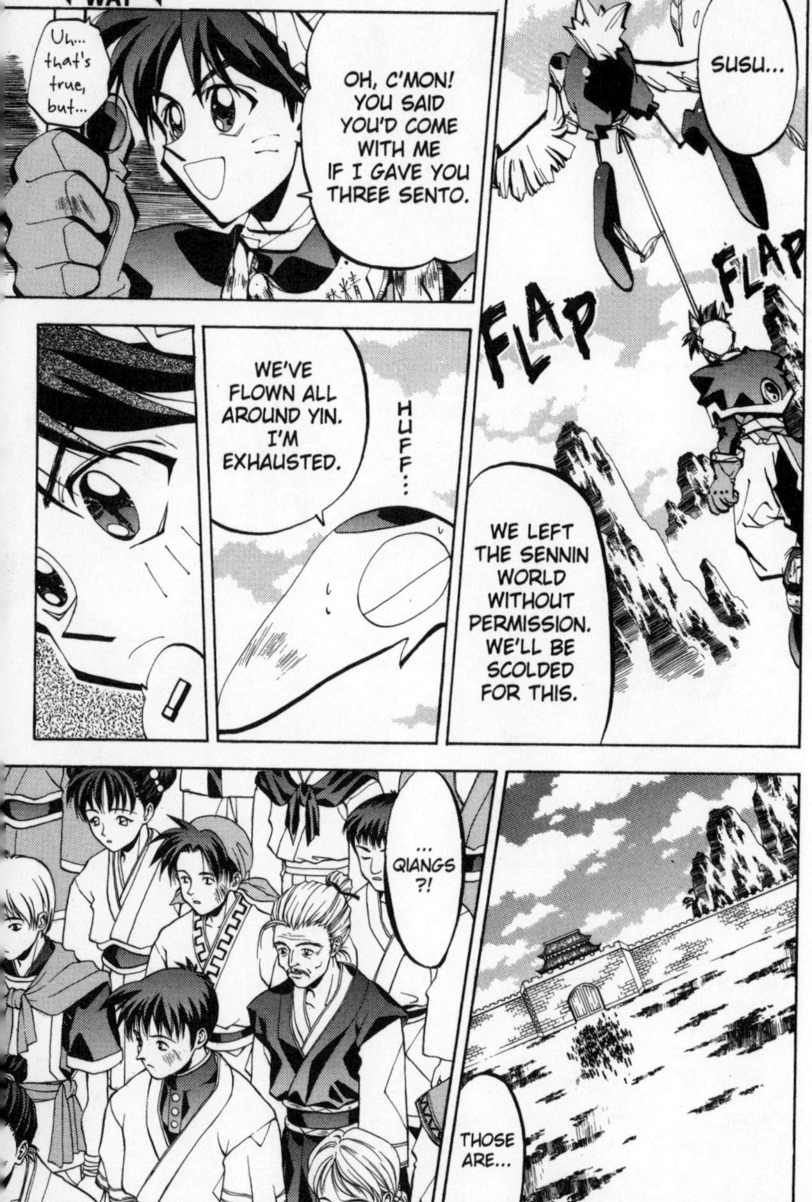
SUSU...
FLAP FLAP
WE LEFT THE SENNIN WORLD WITHOUT PERMISSION. WE'LL BE SCOLDED FOR THIS.
OH, C'MON! YOU SAID YOU'D COME WITH ME IF I GAVE YOU THREE SENTO.
Uh... that's true, but...
WE'VE FLOWN ALL AROUND YIN. I'M EXHAUSTED.
HUFF...
!
THOSE ARE...
...QIANGS?!

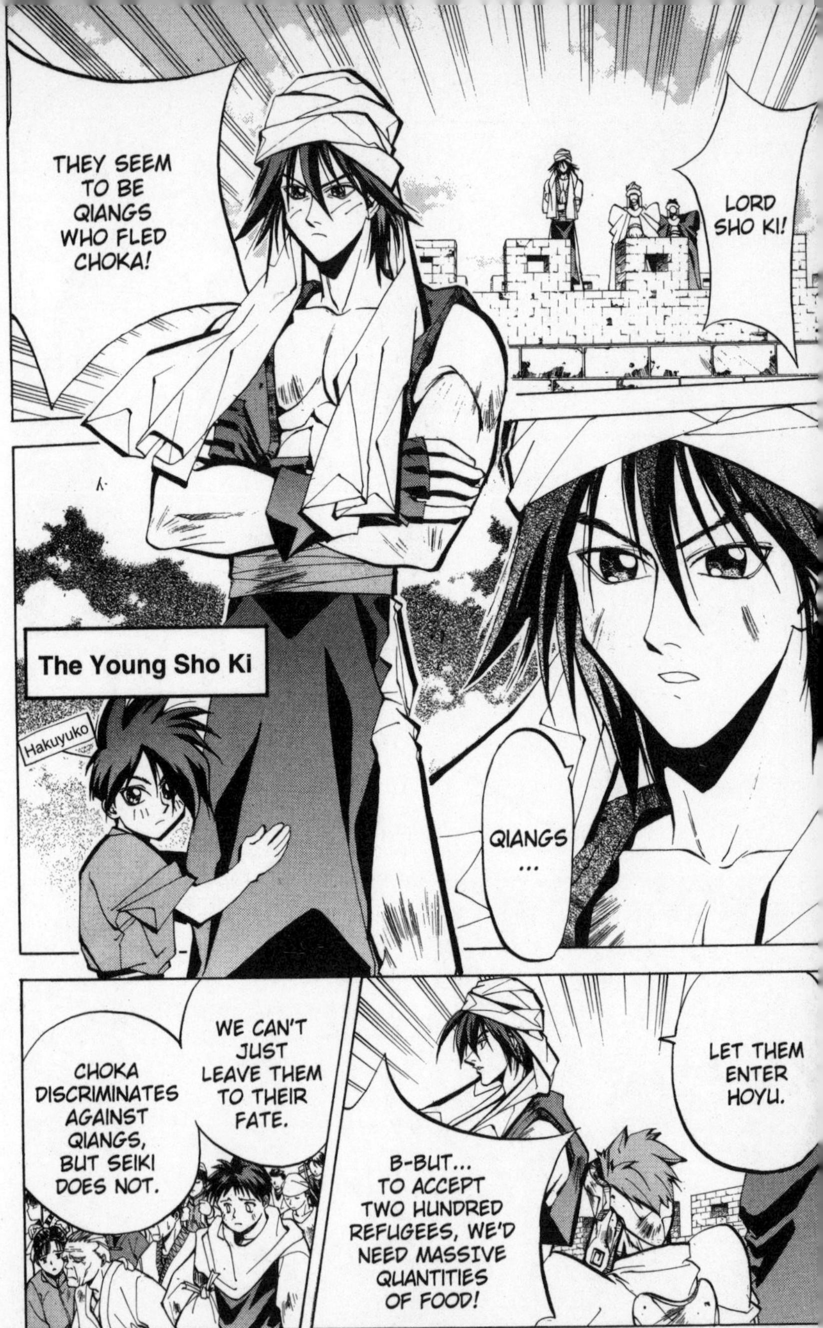
LORD SHO KI!
THEY SEEM TO BE QIANGS WHO FLED CHOKA!
QIANGS ...
The Young Sho Ki
Hakuyuko
LET THEM ENTER HOYU.
B-BUT... TO ACCEPT TWO HUNDRED REFUGEES, WE'D NEED MASSIVE QUANTITIES OF FOOD!
WE CAN'T JUST LEAVE THEM TO THEIR FATE.
CHOKA DISCRIMINATES AGAINST QIANGS, BUT SEIKI DOES NOT.

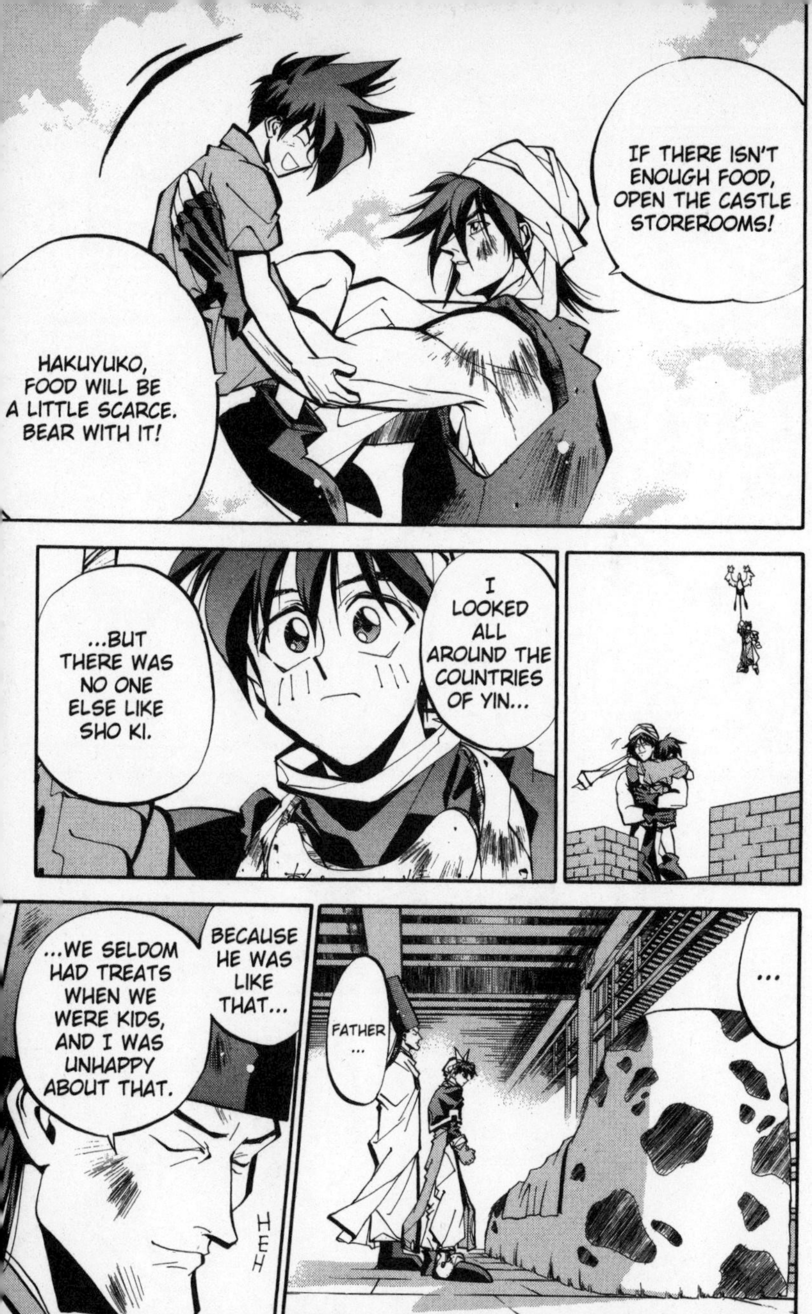
IF THERE ISN'T ENOUGH FOOD, OPEN THE CASTLE STOREROOMS!
HAKUYUKO, FOOD WILL BE A LITTLE SCARCE. BEAR WITH IT!
I LOOKED ALL AROUND THE COUNTRIES OF YIN...
...BUT THERE WAS NO ONE ELSE LIKE SHO KI.
...
FATHER ...
BECAUSE HE WAS LIKE THAT...
...WE SELDOM HAD TREATS WHEN WE WERE KIDS, AND I WAS UNHAPPY ABOUT THAT.
HEH

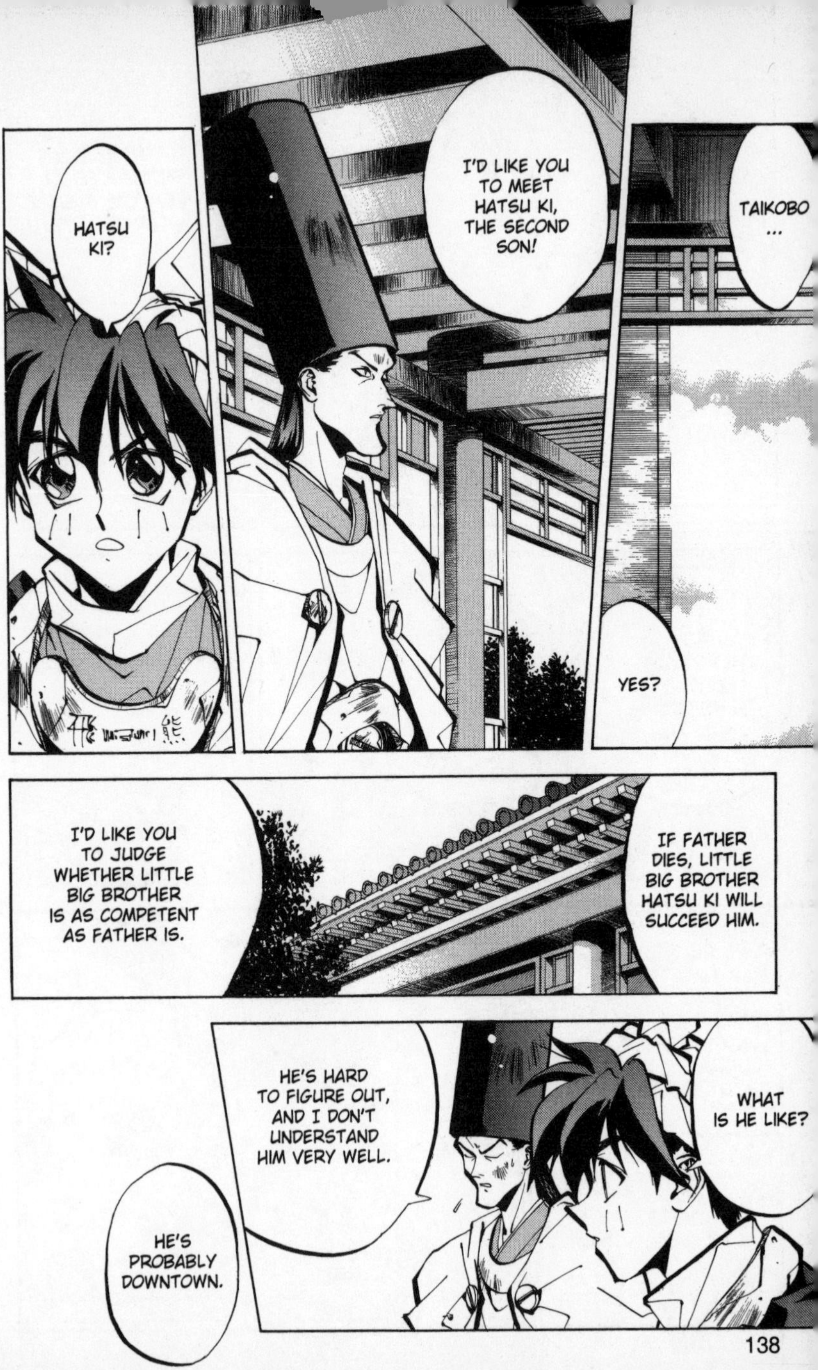
TAIKOBO ...
YES?
I'D LIKE YOU TO MEET HATSU KI, THE SECOND SON!
HATSU KI?
IF FATHER DIES, LITTLE BIG BROTHER HATSU KI WILL SUCCEED HIM.
I'D LIKE YOU TO JUDGE WHETHER LITTLE BIG BROTHER IS AS COMPETENT AS FATHER IS.
WHAT IS HE LIKE?
HE'S HARD TO FIGURE OUT, AND I DON'T UNDERSTAND HIM VERY WELL.
HE'S PROBABLY DOWNTOWN.

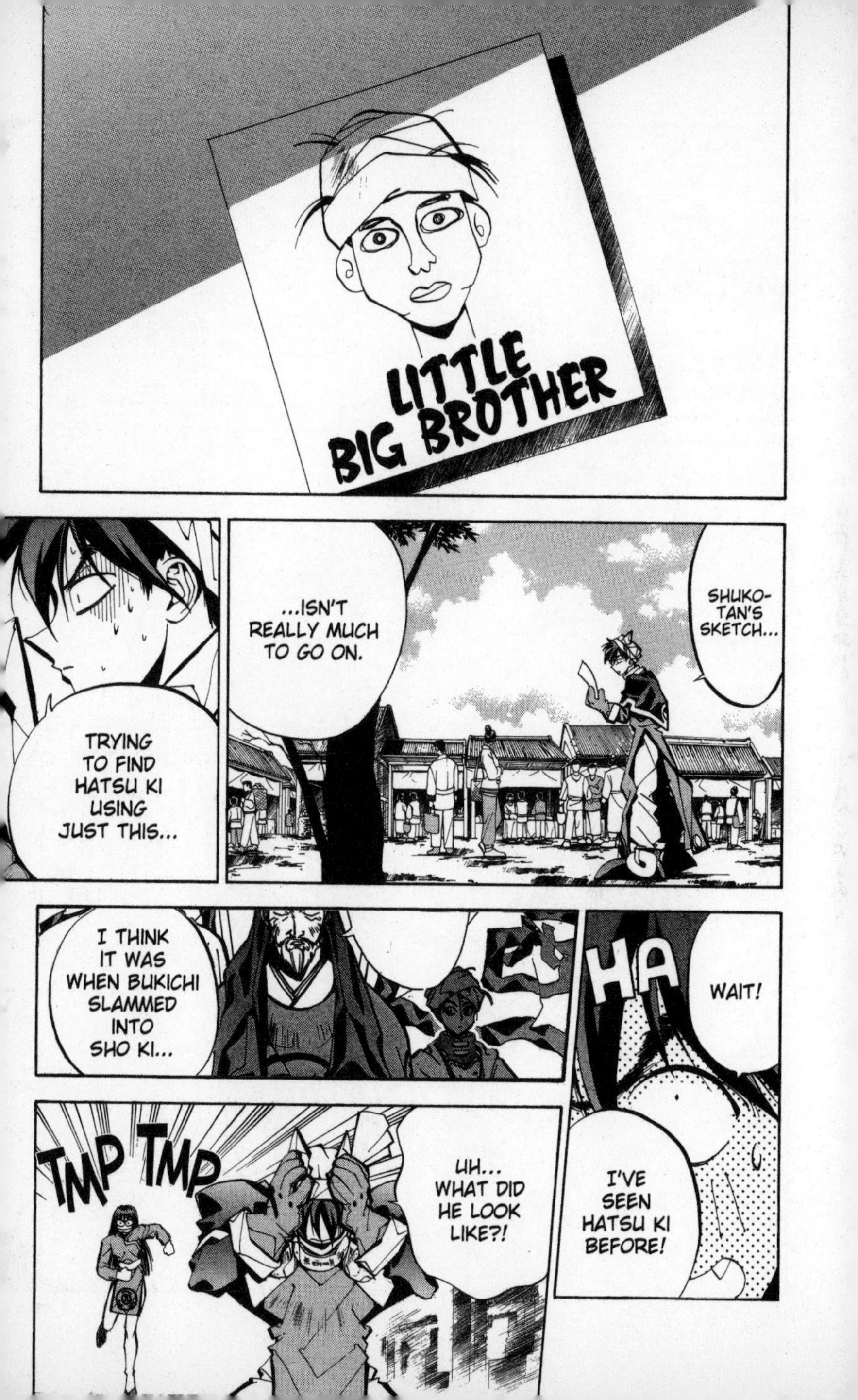
LITTLE
BIG BROTHER
SHUKO-TAN'S SKETCH...
...ISN'T REALLY MUCH TO GO ON.
TRYING TO FIND HATSU KI USING JUST THIS...
HA
WAIT!
I'VE SEEN HATSU KI BEFORE!
I THINK IT WAS WHEN BUKICHI SLAMMED INTO SHO KI...
TMP TMP
UH... WHAT DID HE LOOK LIKE?!

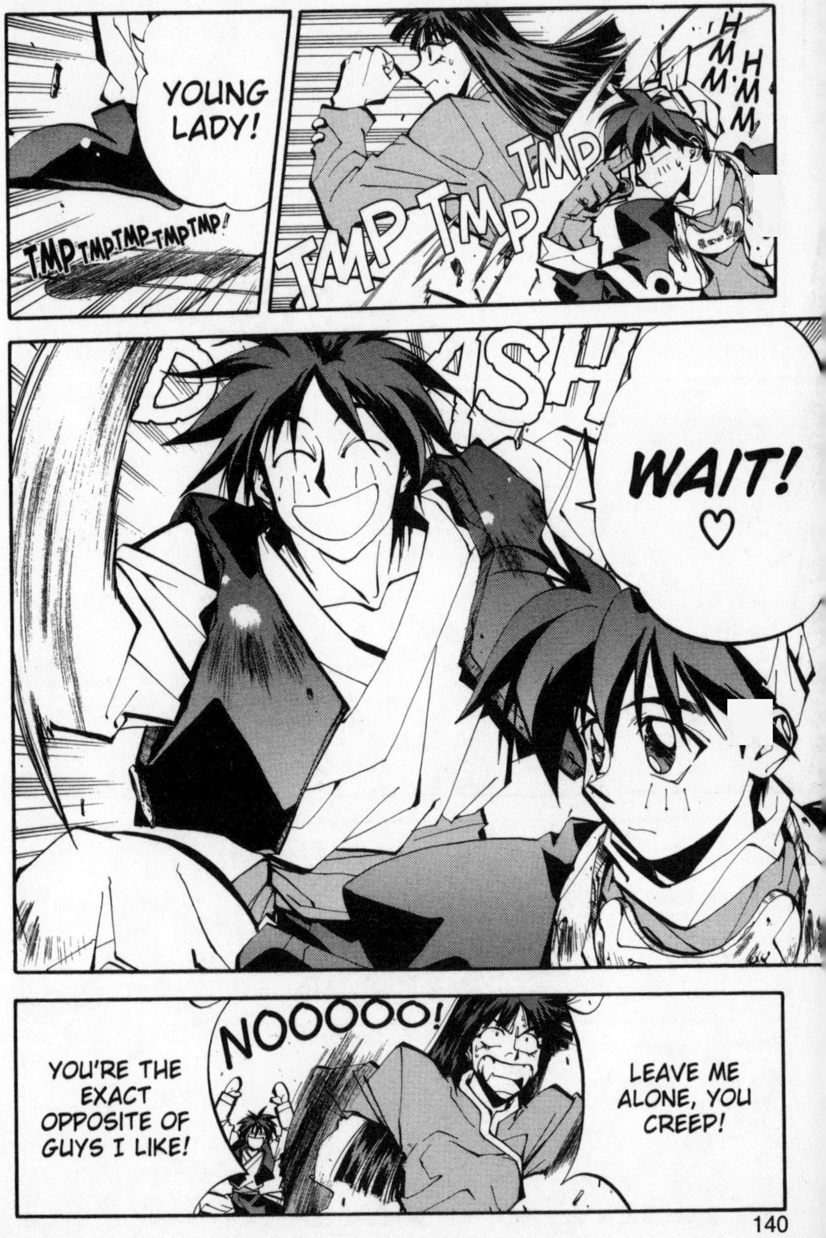
HMMM HMMM
TMP TMP TMP
YOUNG LADY!
TMP TMP TMP TMP TMP!
WAIT! ♡
LEAVE ME ALONE, YOU CREEP!
NOOOOO!
YOU'RE THE EXACT OPPOSITE OF GUYS I LIKE!

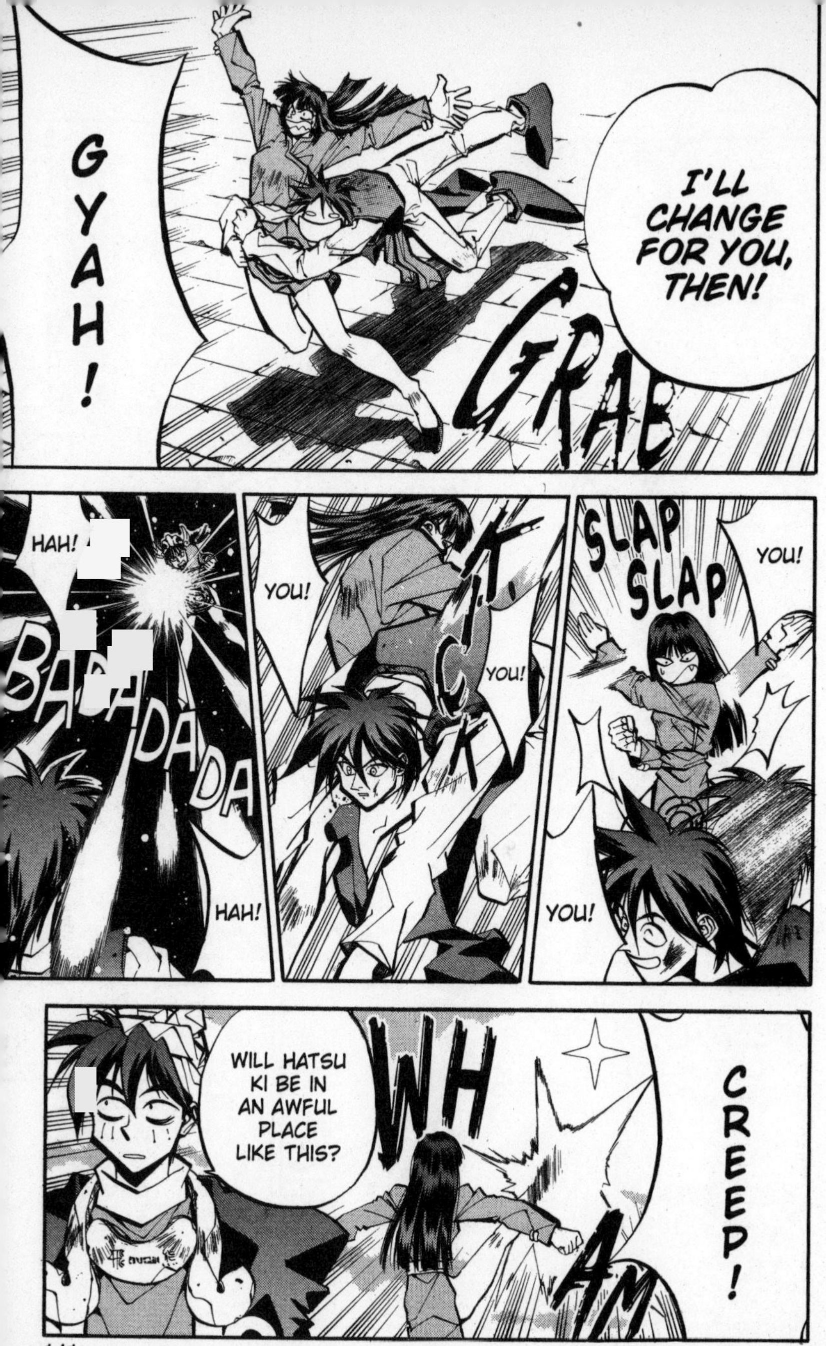
I'LL CHANGE FOR YOU, THEN!
GRAB
GYAH!
SLAP SLAP
YOU!
YOU!
KICK
YOU!
YOU!
HAH!
BADADADA
HAH!
CREEP!
WHAM
WILL HATSUKI BE IN AN AWFUL PLACE LIKE THIS?

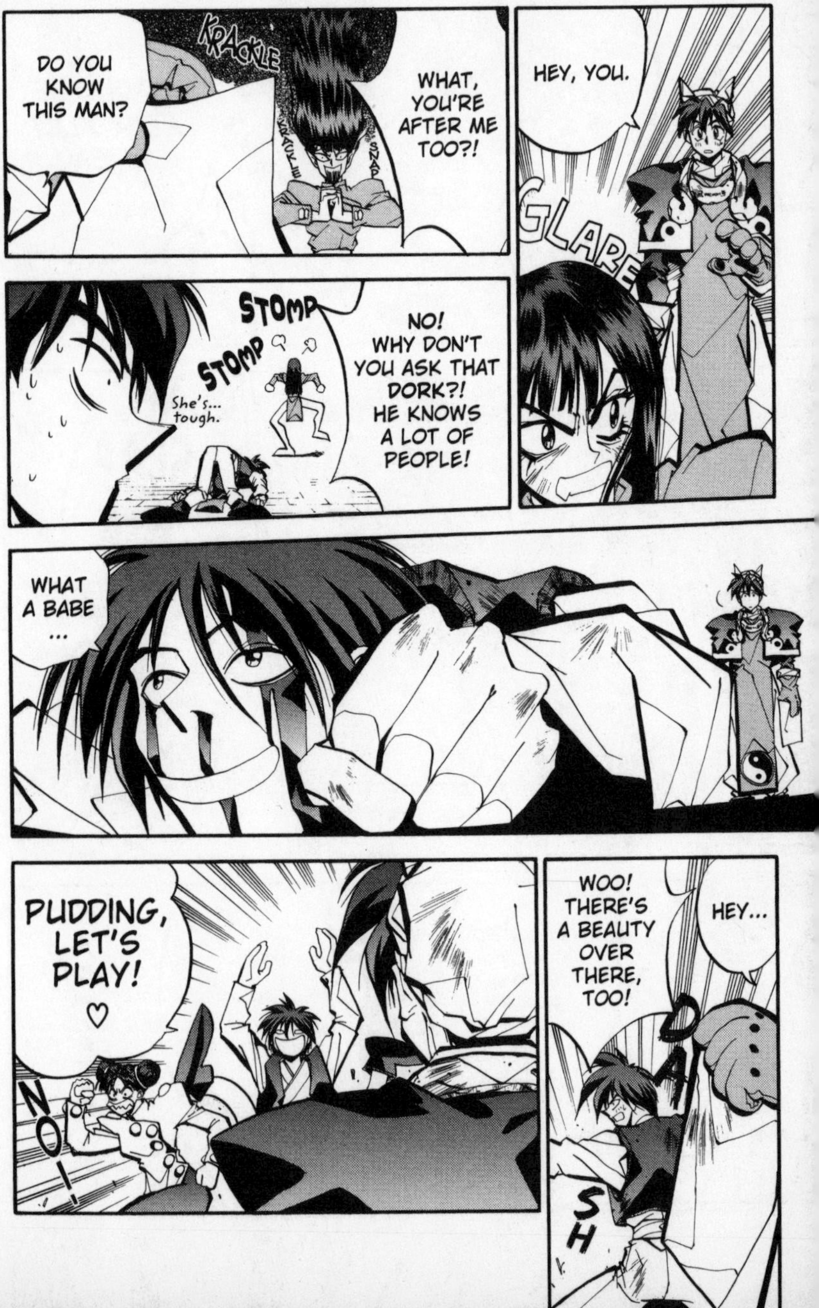
HEY, YOU.
GLARE
WHAT, YOU'RE AFTER ME TOO?!
KRACKLE
KRACKLE
SNAP
DO YOU KNOW THIS MAN?
NO! WHY DON'T YOU ASK THAT DORK?! HE KNOWS A LOT OF PEOPLE!
STOMP
STOMP
She's... tough.
WHAT A BABE ...
HEY...
WOO! THERE'S A BEAUTY OVER THERE, TOO!
DA
SH
PUDDING, LET'S PLAY! ♡
NO!!

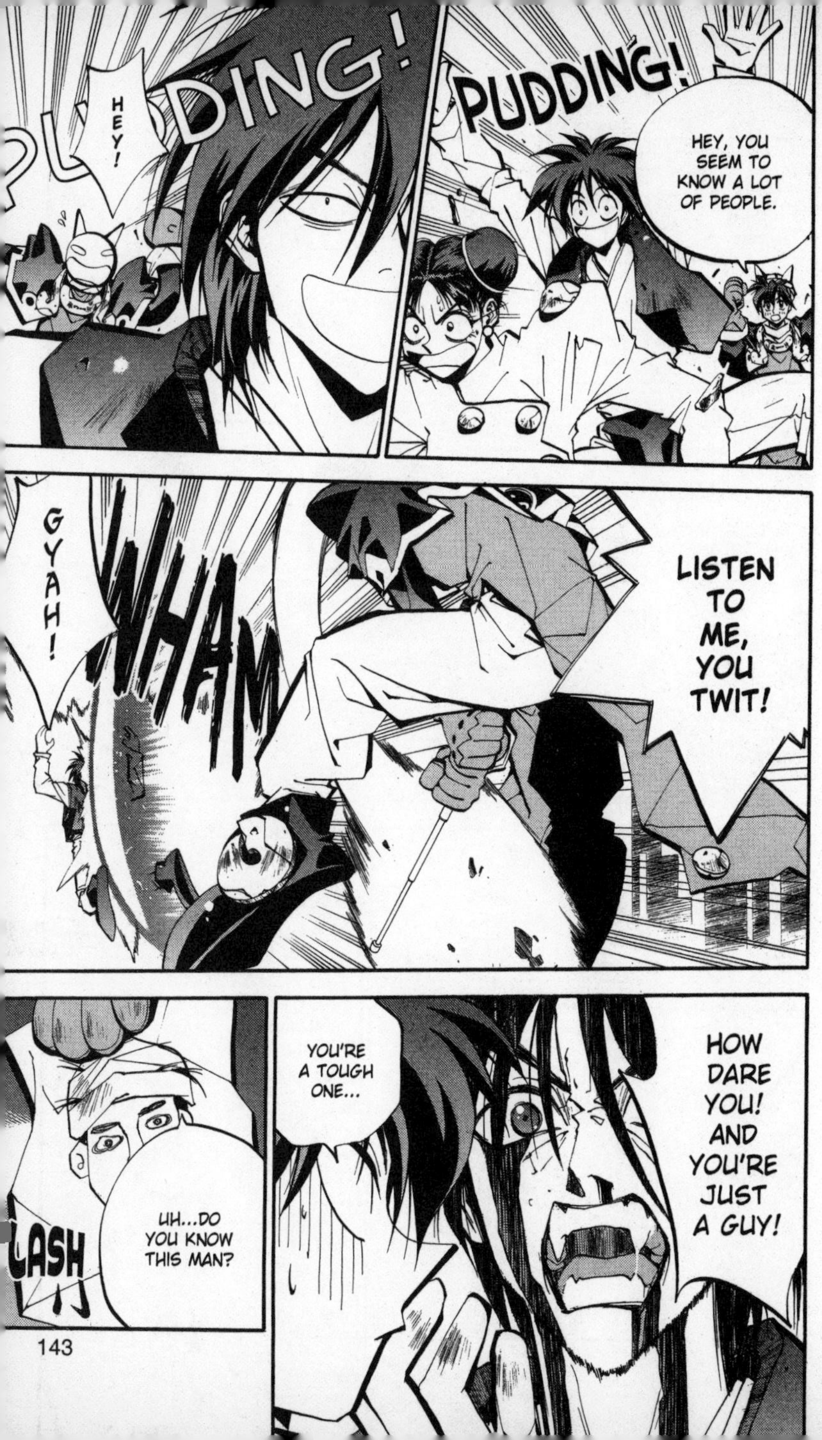
PUDDING!
HEY, YOU SEEM TO KNOW A LOT OF PEOPLE.
DING!
HEY!
LISTEN TO ME, YOU TWIT!
WHAM
GYAH!
HOW DARE YOU! AND YOU'RE JUST A GUY!
YOU'RE A TOUGH ONE...
UH...DO YOU KNOW THIS MAN?
LASH

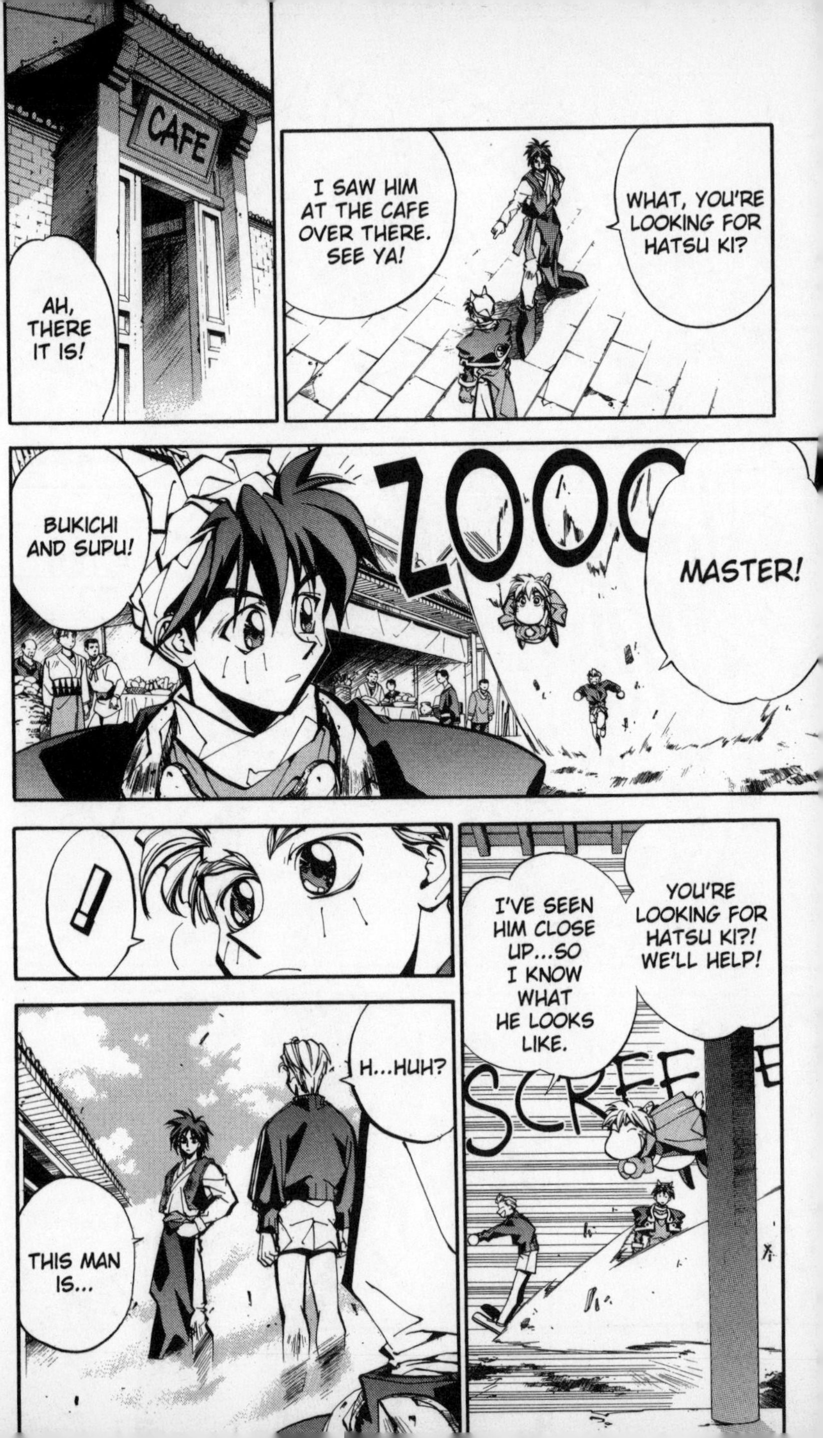
WHAT, YOU'RE LOOKING FOR HATSU KI?
I SAW HIM AT THE CAFE OVER THERE. SEE YA!
CAFE
AH, THERE IT IS!
MASTER!
ZOO
BUKICHI AND SUPU!
YOU'RE LOOKING FOR HATSU KI?! WE'LL HELP!
I'VE SEEN HIM CLOSE UP...SO I KNOW WHAT HE LOOKS LIKE.
SCREE
!
H...HUH?
THIS MAN IS...

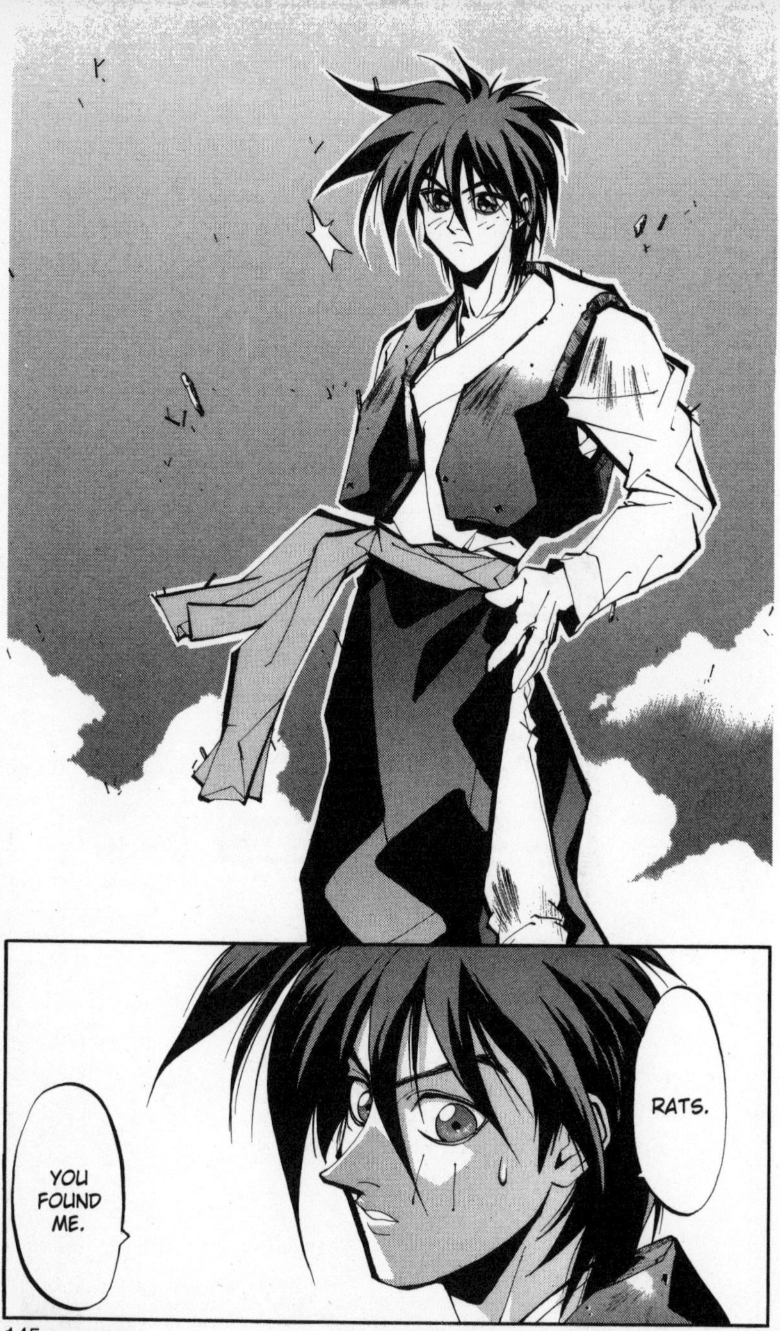
RATS.
YOU FOUND ME.

封神演義

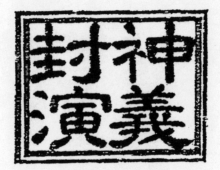

Chapter 50

PAST, PRESENT AND FUTURE, PART 5
THE ELEPHANT RACE

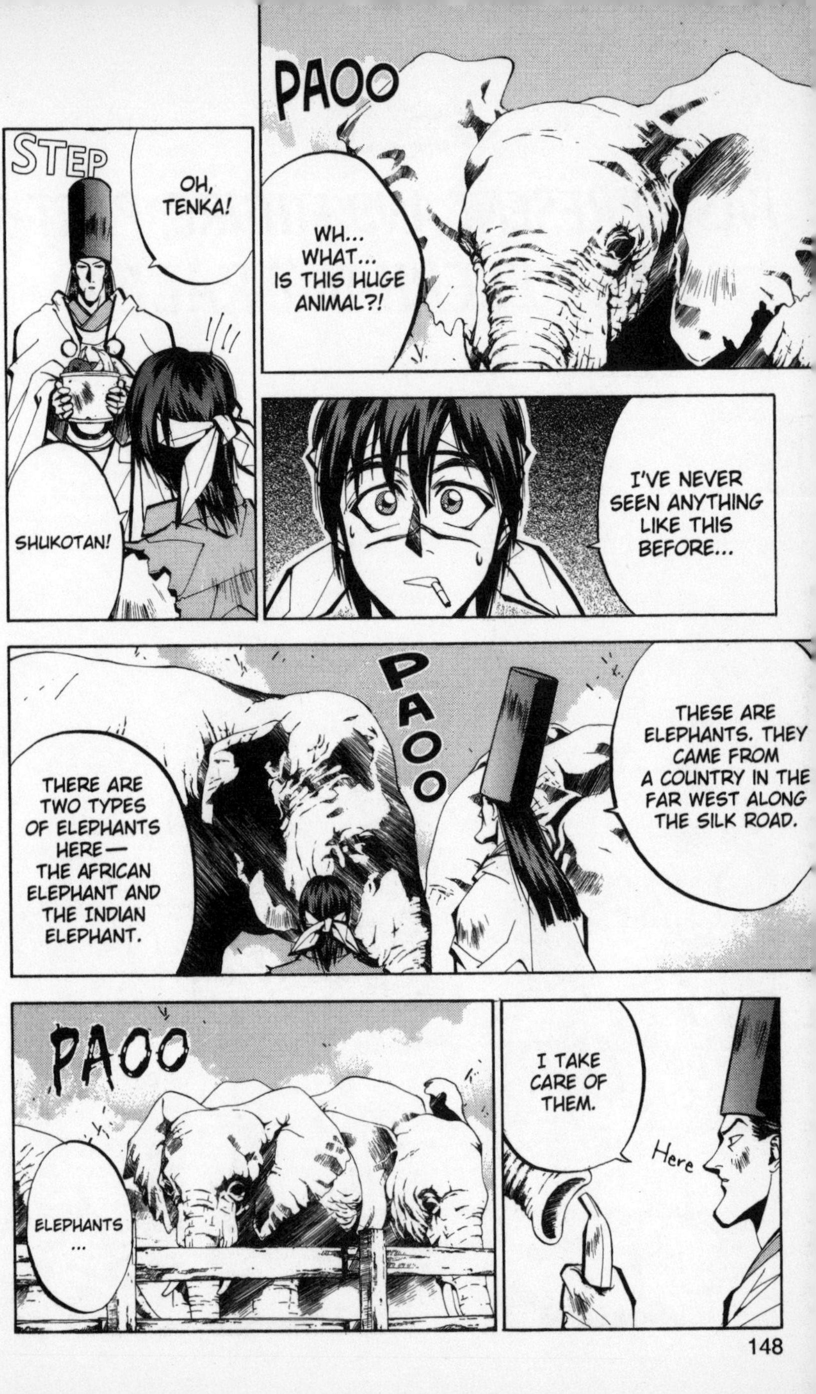
PAOO
WH... WHAT... IS THIS HUGE ANIMAL?!
I'VE NEVER SEEN ANYTHING LIKE THIS BEFORE...
STEP
OH, TENKA!
SHUKOTAN!
THESE ARE ELEPHANTS. THEY CAME FROM A COUNTRY IN THE FAR WEST ALONG THE SILK ROAD.
PAOO
THERE ARE TWO TYPES OF ELEPHANTS HERE— THE AFRICAN ELEPHANT AND THE INDIAN ELEPHANT.
I TAKE CARE OF THEM.
Here
PAOO
ELEPHANTS ...

READ THIS WAY

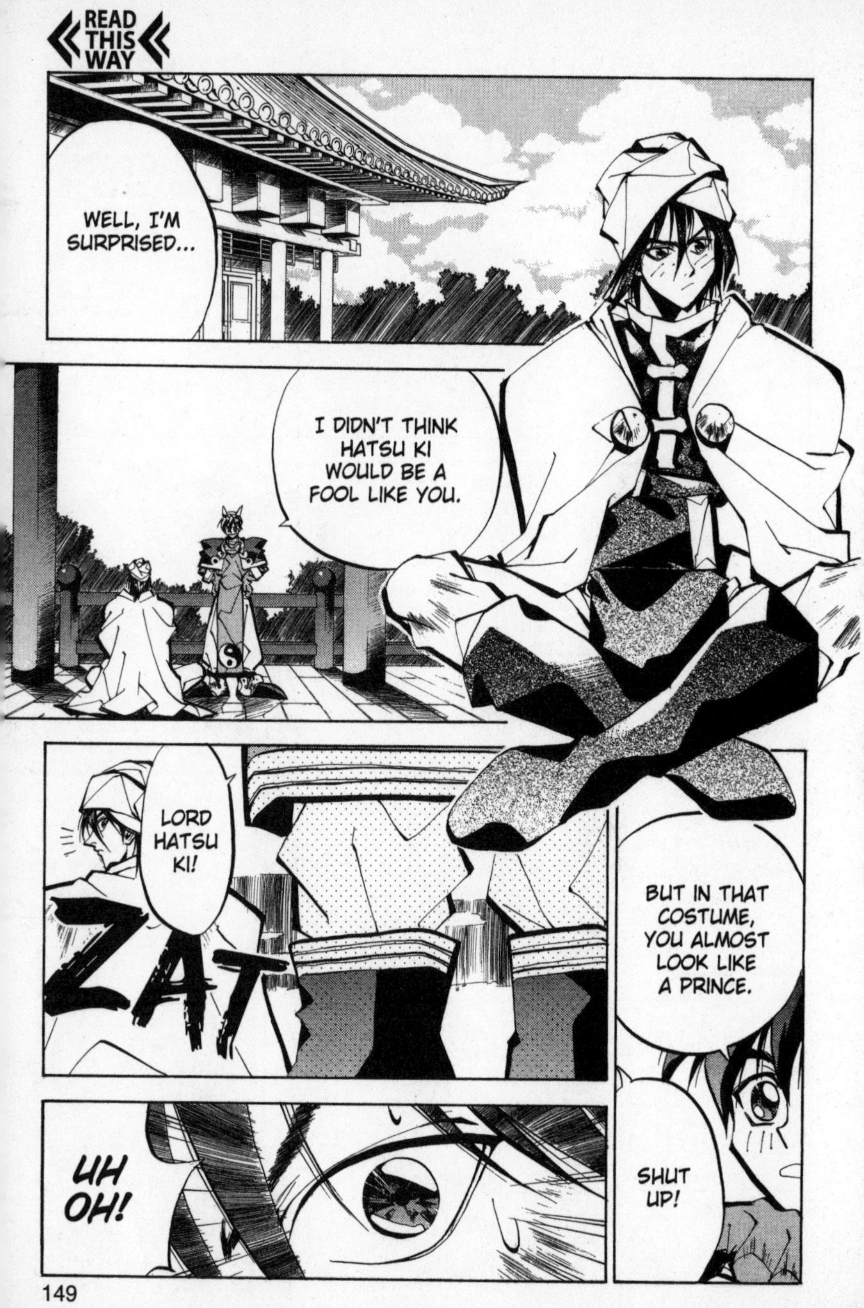
WELL, I'M SURPRISED...
I DIDN'T THINK HATSU KI WOULD BE A FOOL LIKE YOU.
BUT IN THAT COSTUME, YOU ALMOST LOOK LIKE A PRINCE.
SHUT UP!
LORD HATSU KI!
ZAT
UH OH!

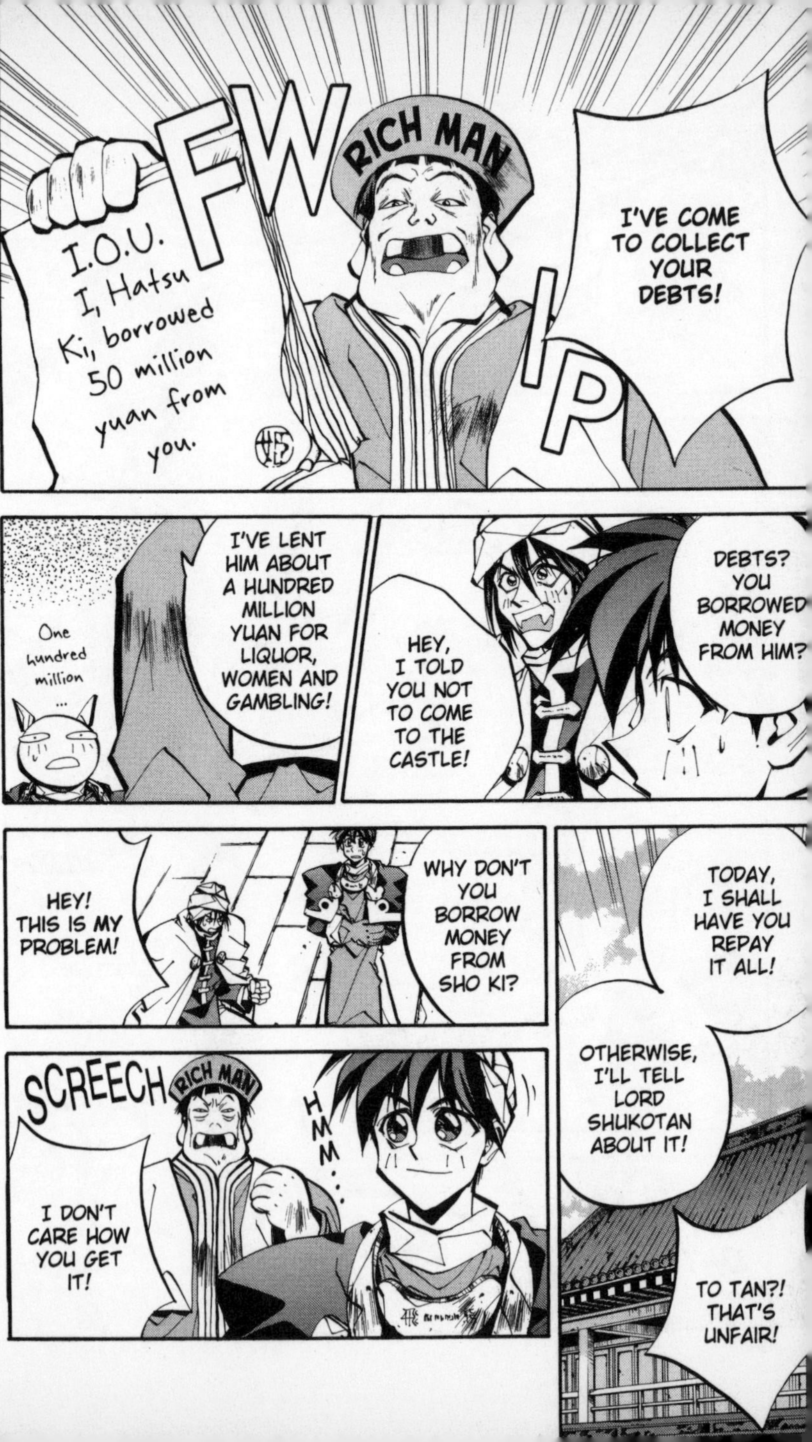
I'VE COME TO COLLECT YOUR DEBTS!
FWIP
RICH MAN
I.O.U. I, Hatsu Ki, borrowed 50 million yuan from you.
DEBTS? YOU BORROWED MONEY FROM HIM?
HEY, I TOLD YOU NOT TO COME TO THE CASTLE!
I'VE LENT HIM ABOUT A HUNDRED MILLION YUAN FOR LIQUOR, WOMEN AND GAMBLING!
One hundred million ...
TODAY, I SHALL HAVE YOU REPAY IT ALL!
OTHERWISE, I'LL TELL LORD SHUKOTAN ABOUT IT!
TO TAN?! THAT'S UNFAIR!
WHY DON'T YOU BORROW MONEY FROM SHO KI?
HEY! THIS IS MY PROBLEM!
HMM...
SCREECH
RICH MAN
I DON'T CARE HOW YOU GET IT!

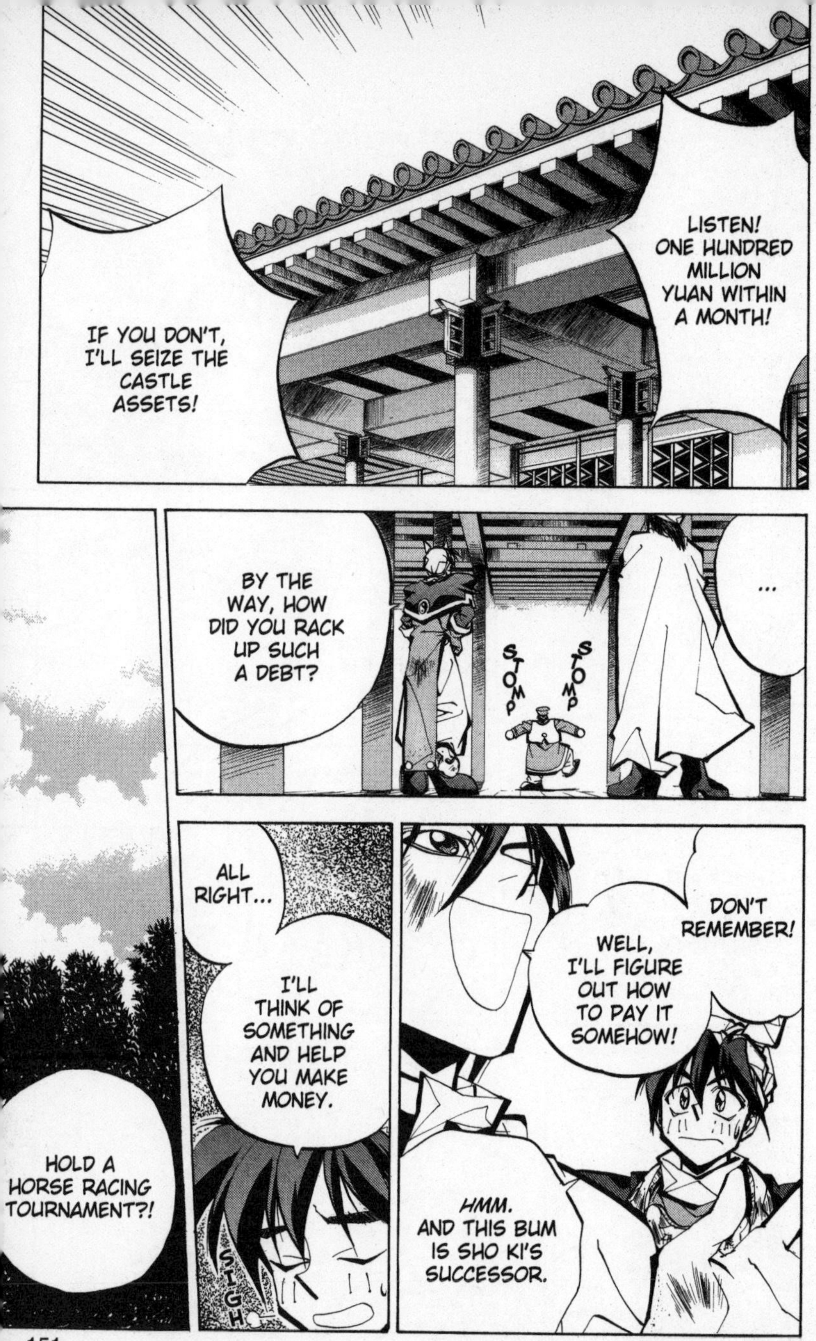

LISTEN! ONE HUNDRED MILLION YUAN WITHIN A MONTH!
IF YOU DON'T, I'LL SEIZE THE CASTLE ASSETS!
...
STOMP
STOMP
BY THE WAY, HOW DID YOU RACK UP SUCH A DEBT?
DON'T REMEMBER!
WELL, I'LL FIGURE OUT HOW TO PAY IT SOMEHOW!
HMM. AND THIS BUM IS SHO KI'S SUCCESSOR.
ALL RIGHT...
I'LL THINK OF SOMETHING AND HELP YOU MAKE MONEY.
SIGH
HOLD A HORSE RACING TOURNAMENT?!

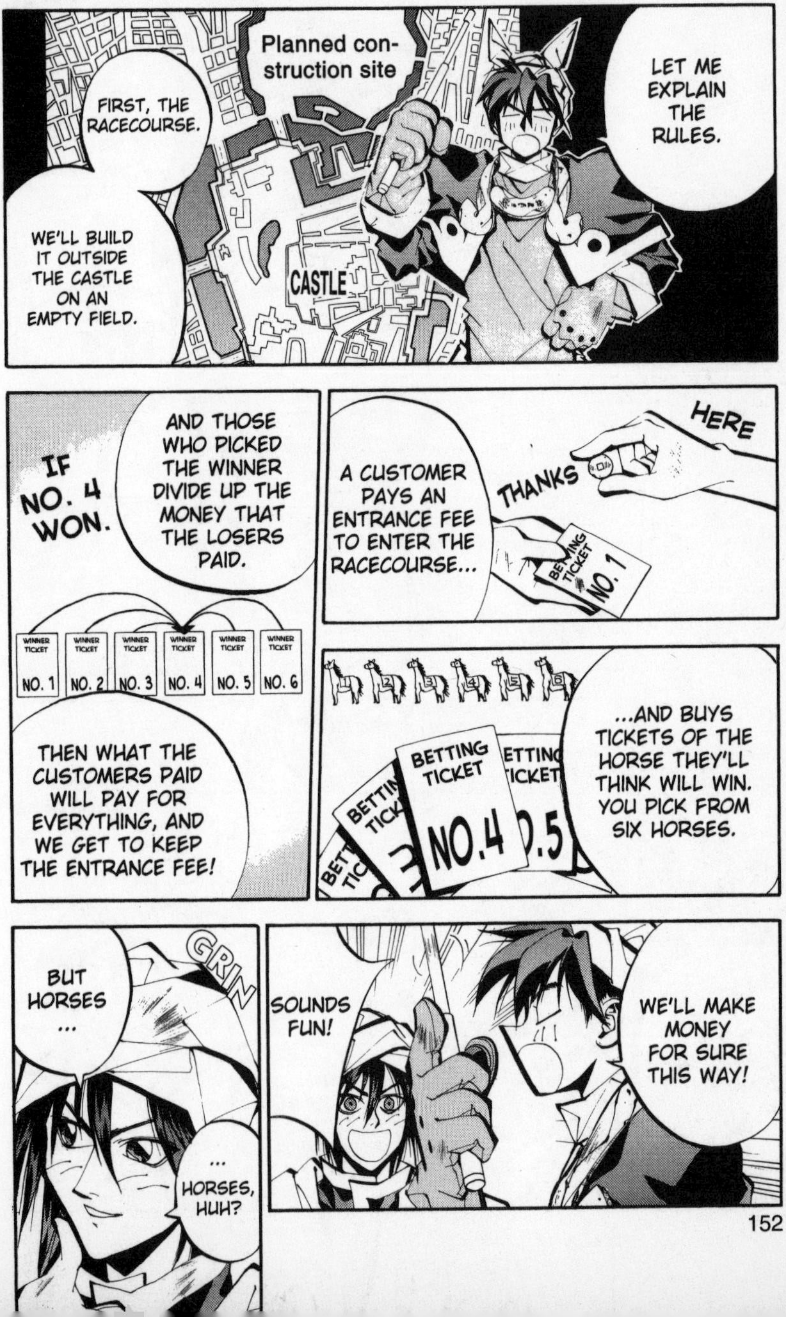

LET ME EXPLAIN THE RULES.
Planned construction site
FIRST, THE RACECOURSE.
WE'LL BUILD IT OUTSIDE THE CASTLE ON AN EMPTY FIELD.
CASTLE
HERE
THANKS
A CUSTOMER PAYS AN ENTRANCE FEE TO ENTER THE RACECOURSE...
BETTING TICKET NO. 1
...AND BUYS TICKETS OF THE HORSE THEY'LL THINK WILL WIN. YOU PICK FROM SIX HORSES.
BETTING TICKET NO.4
AND THOSE WHO PICKED THE WINNER DIVIDE UP THE MONEY THAT THE LOSERS PAID.
IF NO. 4 WON.
WINNER TICKET NO. 1
WINNER TICKET NO. 2
WINNER TICKET NO. 3
WINNER TICKET NO. 4
WINNER TICKET NO. 5
WINNER TICKET NO. 6
THEN WHAT THE CUSTOMERS PAID WILL PAY FOR EVERYTHING, AND WE GET TO KEEP THE ENTRANCE FEE!
WE'LL MAKE MONEY FOR SURE THIS WAY!
SOUNDS FUN!
GRIN
BUT HORSES ...
... HORSES, HUH?

A Few Days Later

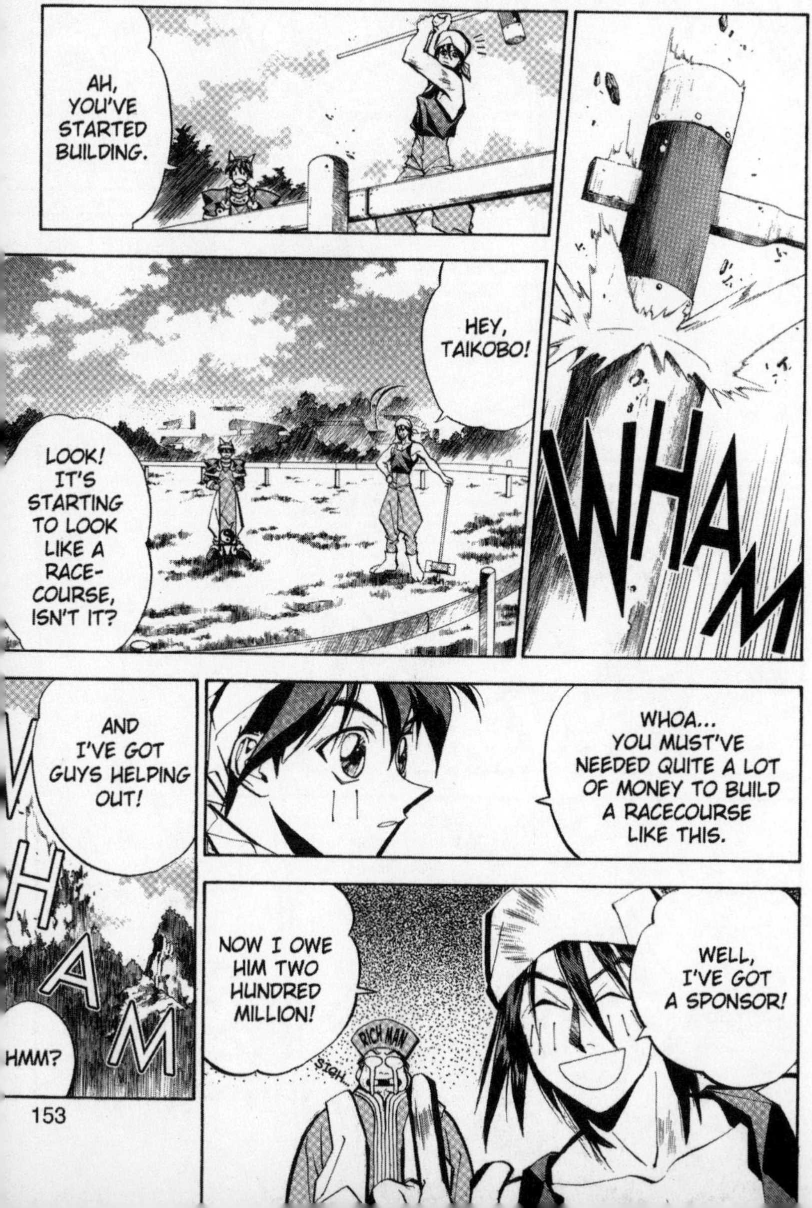

WHAM
AH, YOU'VE STARTED BUILDING.
HEY, TAIKOBO!
LOOK! IT'S STARTING TO LOOK LIKE A RACE-COURSE, ISN'T IT?
WHOA... YOU MUST'VE NEEDED QUITE A LOT OF MONEY TO BUILD A RACECOURSE LIKE THIS.
WELL, I'VE GOT A SPONSOR!
NOW I OWE HIM TWO HUNDRED MILLION!
RICH MAN
SIGH...
AND I'VE GOT GUYS HELPING OUT!
WHAM
HMM?

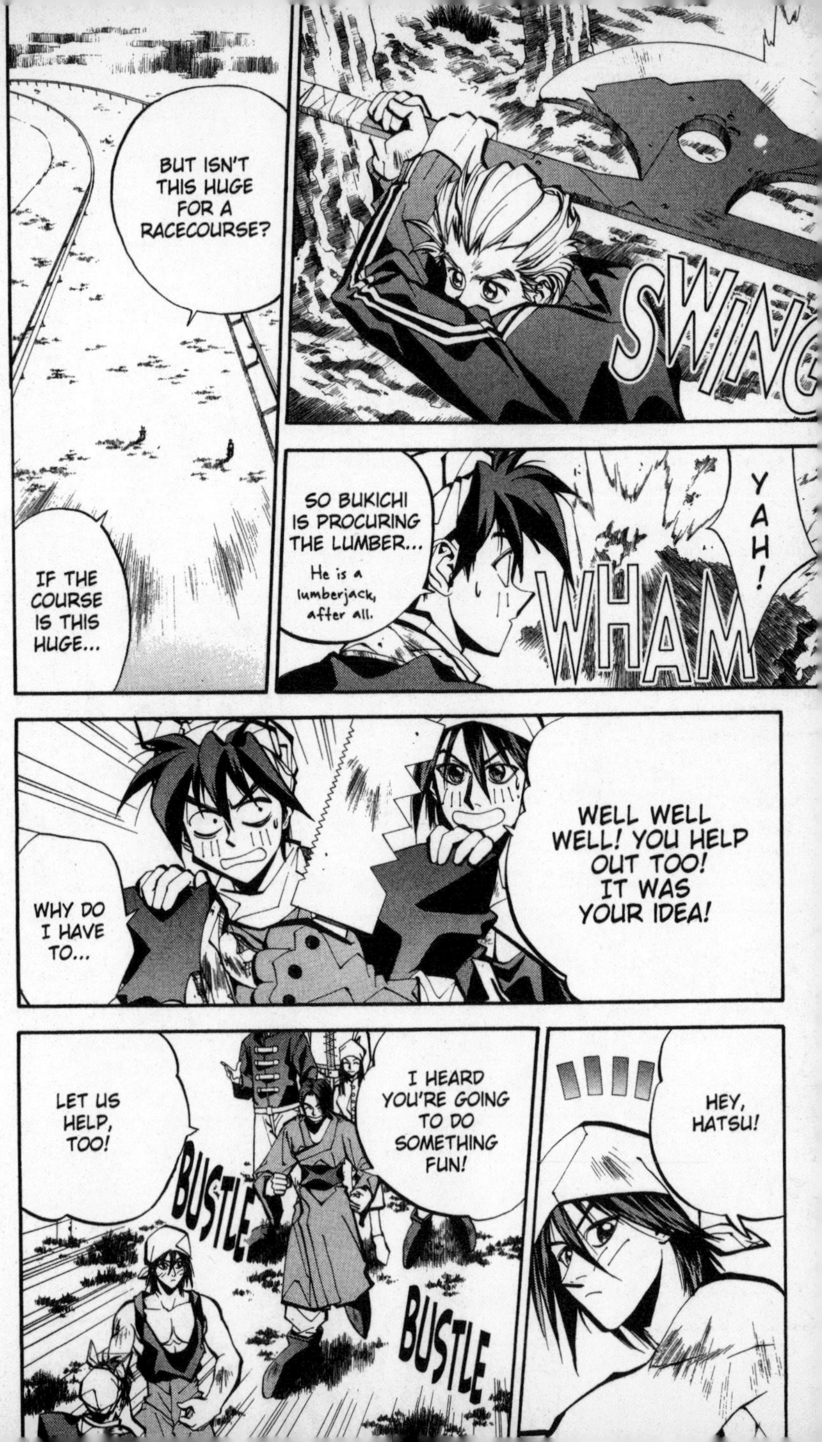
SWING
YAH!
WHAM
SO BUKICHI IS PROCURING THE LUMBER...
He is a lumberjack, after all.
BUT ISN'T THIS HUGE FOR A RACECOURSE?
IF THE COURSE IS THIS HUGE...
WELL WELL WELL! YOU HELP OUT TOO! IT WAS YOUR IDEA!
WHY DO I HAVE TO...
HEY, HATSU!
I HEARD YOU'RE GOING TO DO SOMETHING FUN!
BUSTLE
BUSTLE
LET US HELP, TOO!

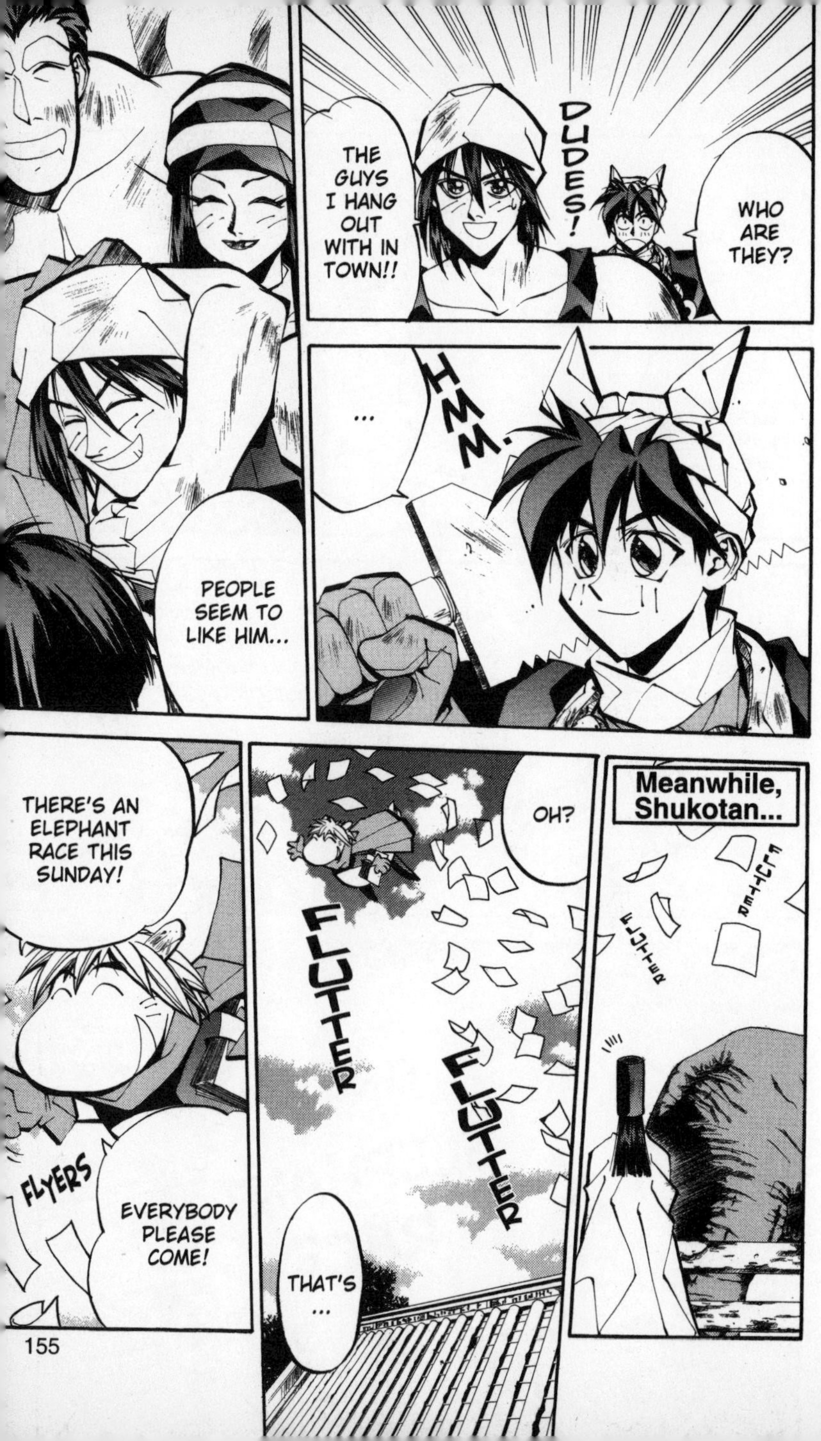
WHO ARE THEY?
DUDES!
THE GUYS I HANG OUT WITH IN TOWN!!
HMM.
...
PEOPLE SEEM TO LIKE HIM...
Meanwhile, Shukotan...
FLUTTER
FLUTTER
OH?
FLUTTER
FLUTTER
THAT'S ...
THERE'S AN ELEPHANT RACE THIS SUNDAY!
FLYERS
EVERYBODY PLEASE COME!

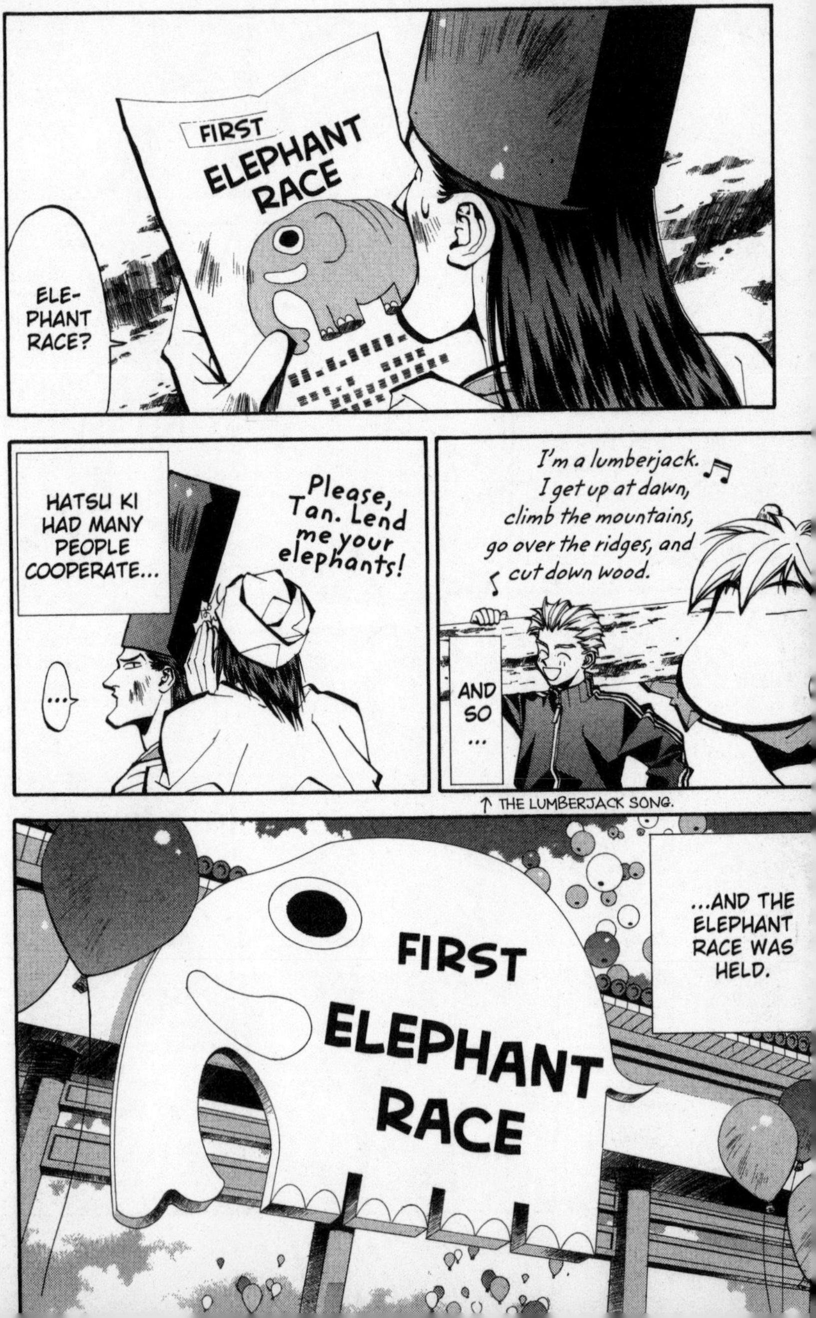
FIRST
ELEPHANT RACE
ELE-PHANT RACE?
I'm a lumberjack. I get up at dawn, climb the mountains, go over the ridges, and cut down wood.
AND SO ...
↑ THE LUMBERJACK SONG.
Please, Tan. Lend me your elephants!
HATSU KI HAD MANY PEOPLE COOPERATE...
...
...AND THE ELEPHANT RACE WAS HELD.
FIRST
ELEPHANT RACE

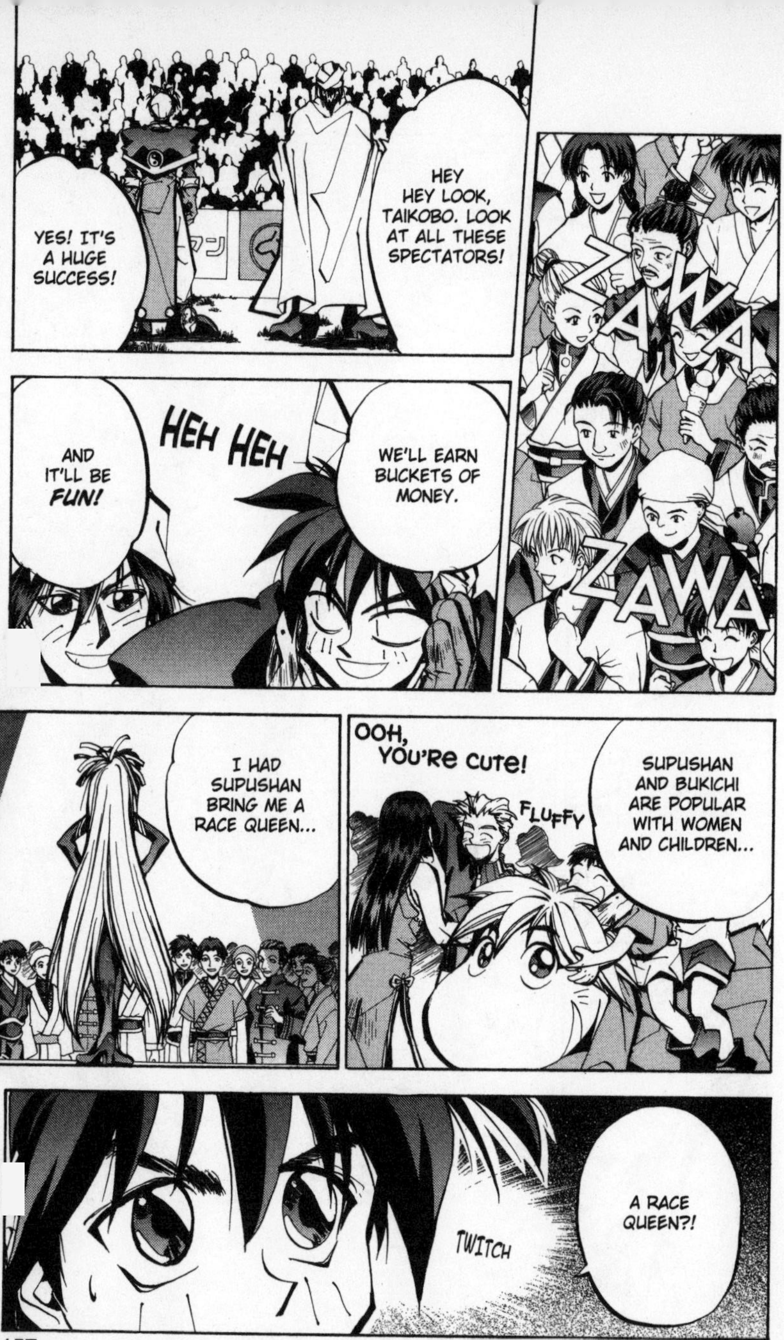
HEY HEY LOOK, TAIKOBO. LOOK AT ALL THESE SPECTATORS!
YES! IT'S A HUGE SUCCESS!
ZAWA
ZAWA
WE'LL EARN BUCKETS OF MONEY.
HEH HEH
AND IT'LL BE *FUN!*
SUPUSHAN AND BUKICHI ARE POPULAR WITH WOMEN AND CHILDREN...
FLUFFY
OOH, YOU'RE CUTE!
I HAD SUPUSHAN BRING ME A RACE QUEEN...
A RACE QUEEN?!
TWITCH

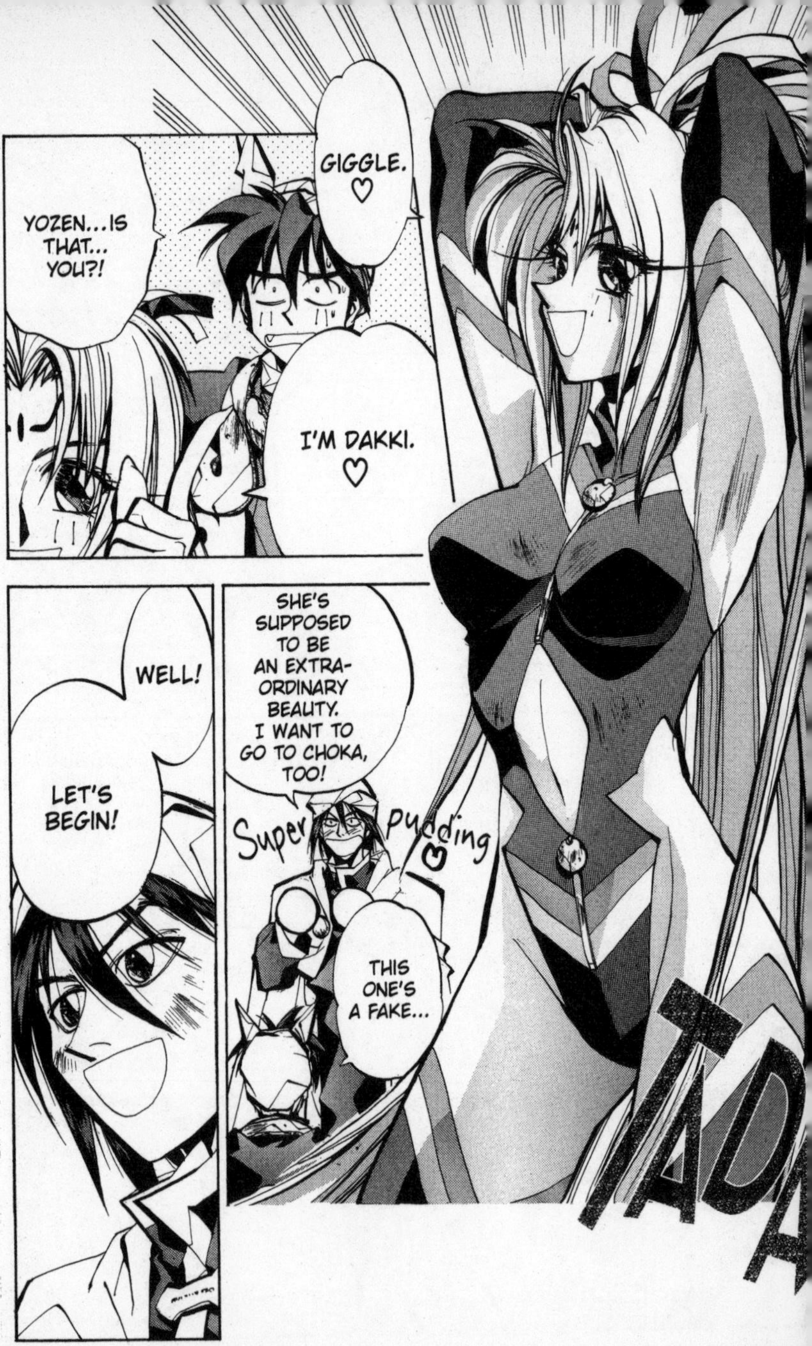
GIGGLE. ♡
TADA
YOZEN...IS THAT... YOU?!
I'M DAKKI. ♡
SHE'S SUPPOSED TO BE AN EXTRA-ORDINARY BEAUTY. I WANT TO GO TO CHOKA, TOO!
Super pudding ♡
THIS ONE'S A FAKE...
WELL!
LET'S BEGIN!

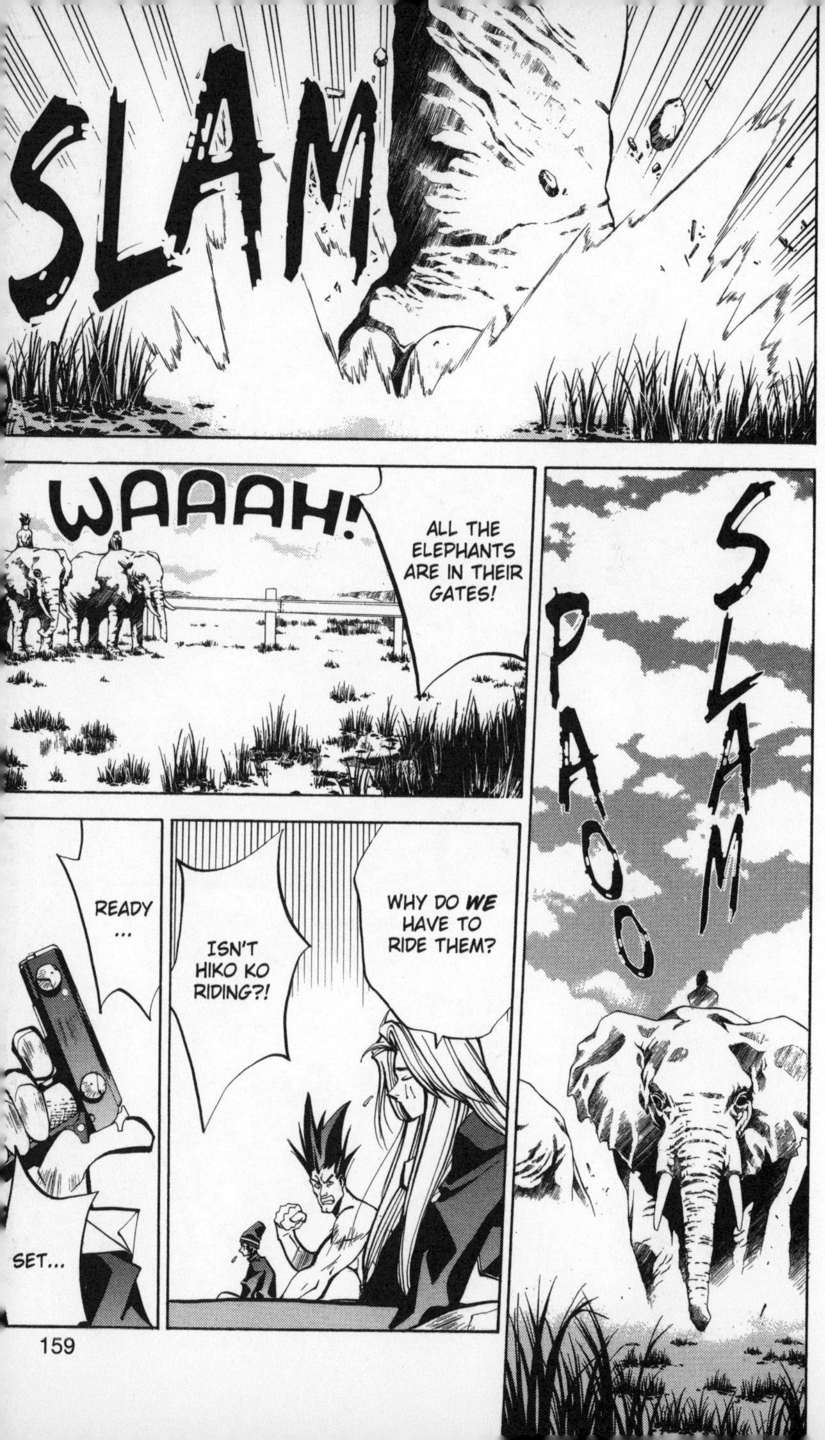
SLAM
SLAM
PAOOO
WAAAH!
ALL THE ELEPHANTS ARE IN THEIR GATES!
WHY DO *WE* HAVE TO RIDE THEM?
ISN'T HIKO KO RIDING?!
READY ...
SET...

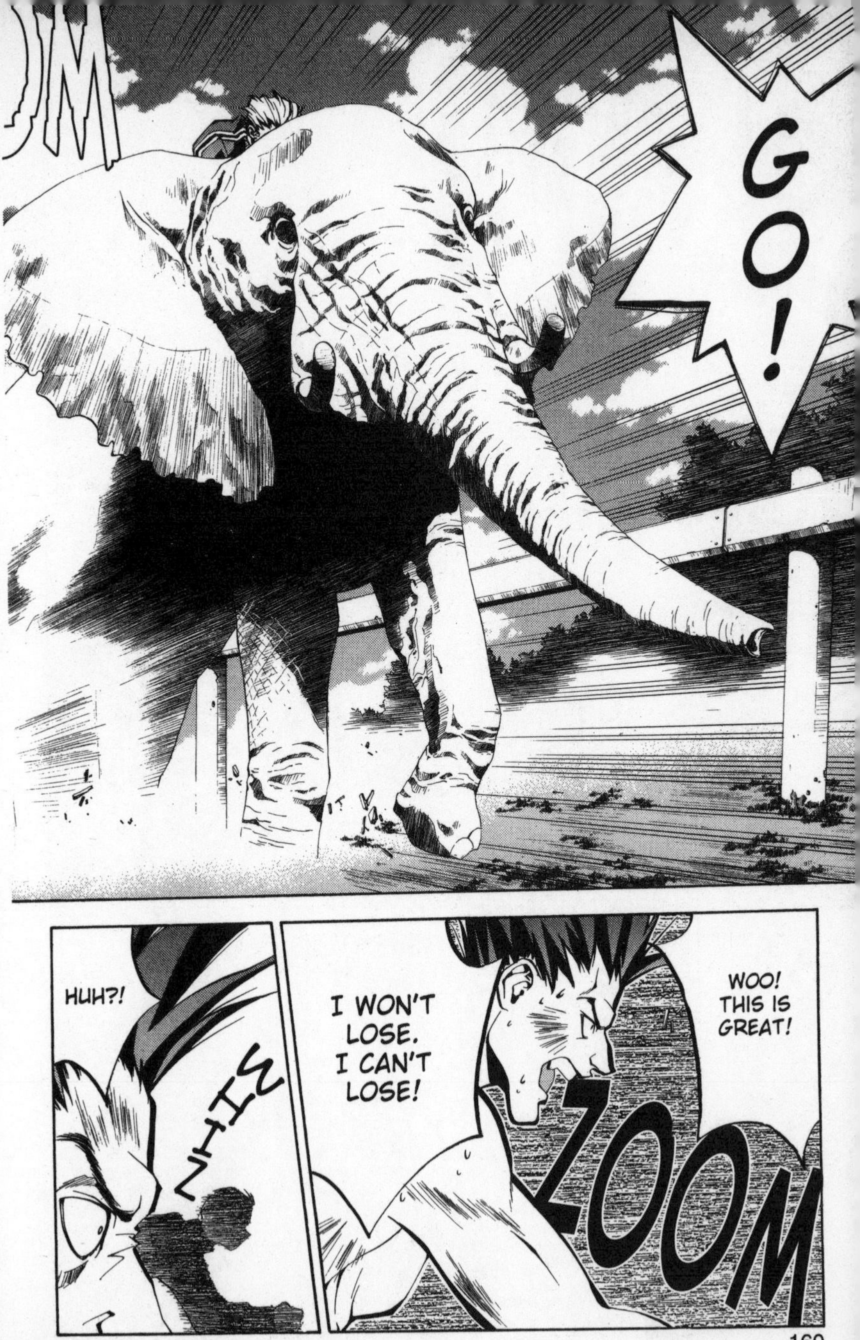
GO!
WOO! THIS IS GREAT!
I WON'T LOSE. I CAN'T LOSE!
ZOOM
HUH?!
WHIN

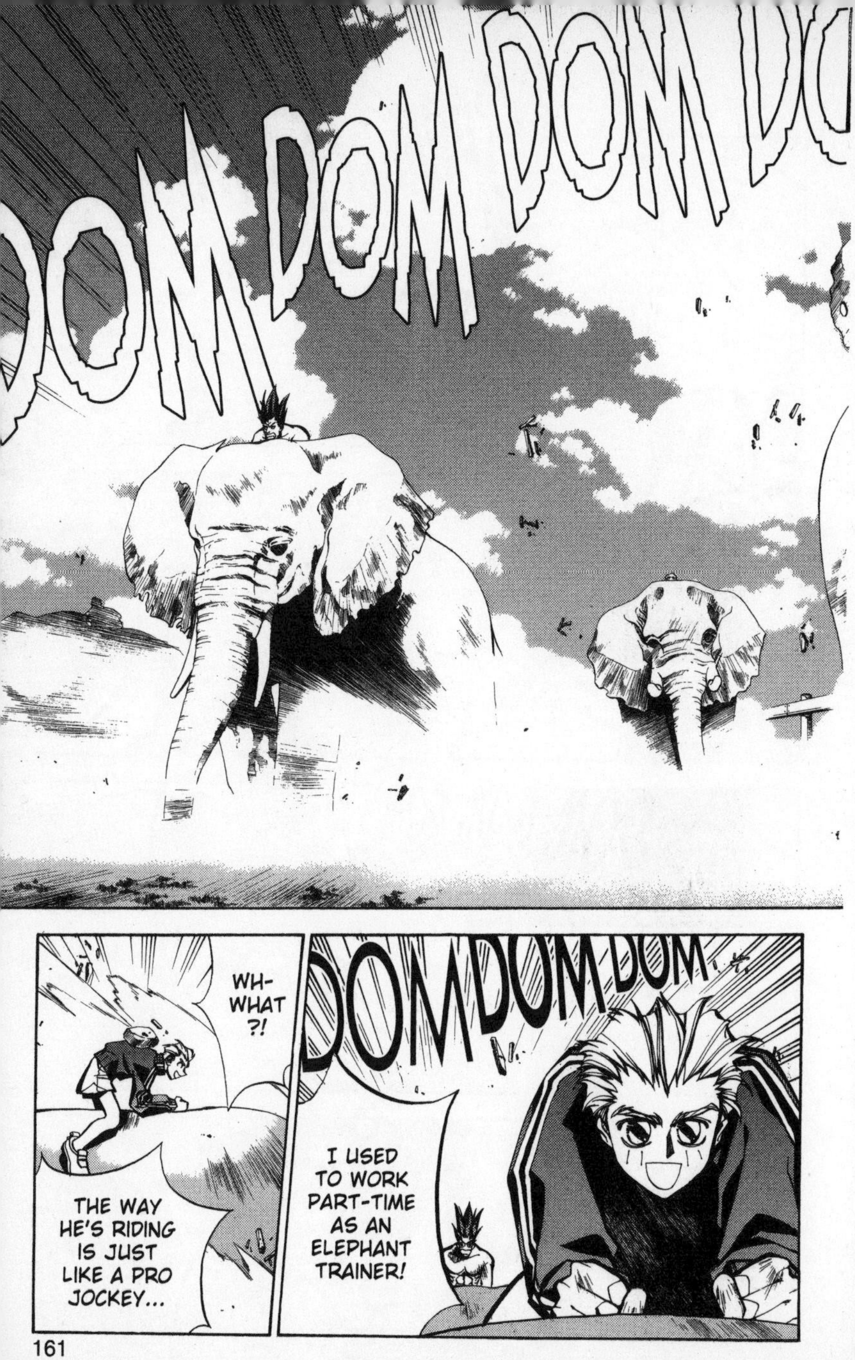
DOM DOM DOM DOM DO
DOM DOM DOM
I USED TO WORK PART-TIME AS AN ELEPHANT TRAINER!
WH- WHAT ?!
THE WAY HE'S RIDING IS JUST LIKE A PRO JOCKEY...

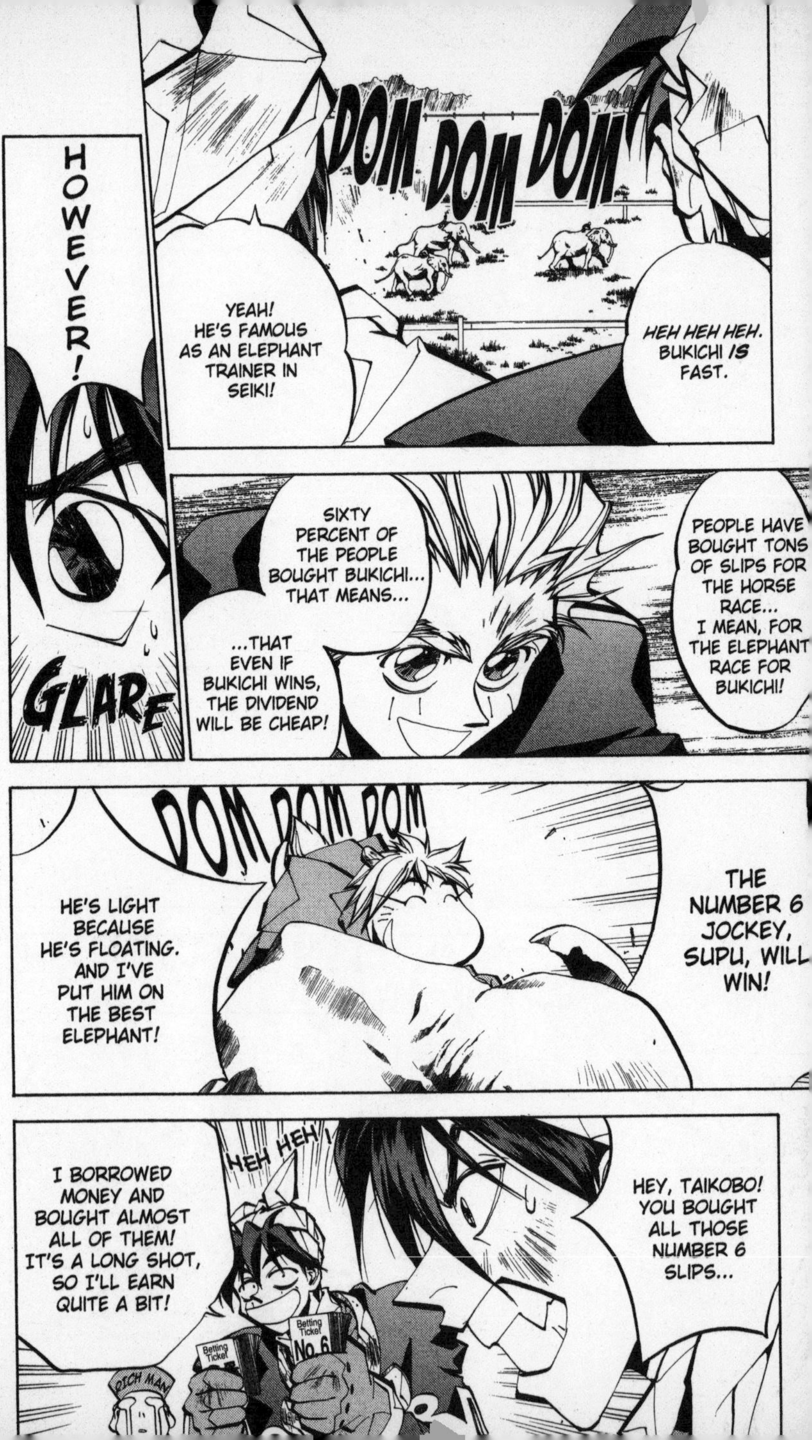
DOM DOM DOM
HEH HEH HEH. BUKICHI *IS* FAST.
YEAH! HE'S FAMOUS AS AN ELEPHANT TRAINER IN SEIKI!
PEOPLE HAVE BOUGHT TONS OF SLIPS FOR THE HORSE RACE... I MEAN, FOR THE ELEPHANT RACE FOR BUKICHI!
SIXTY PERCENT OF THE PEOPLE BOUGHT BUKICHI... THAT MEANS...
...THAT EVEN IF BUKICHI WINS, THE DIVIDEND WILL BE CHEAP!
HOWEVER!
GLARE
DOM DOM DOM
THE NUMBER 6 JOCKEY, SUPU, WILL WIN!
HE'S LIGHT BECAUSE HE'S FLOATING. AND I'VE PUT HIM ON THE BEST ELEPHANT!
HEY, TAIKOBO! YOU BOUGHT ALL THOSE NUMBER 6 SLIPS...
HEH HEH!
I BORROWED MONEY AND BOUGHT ALMOST ALL OF THEM! IT'S A LONG SHOT, SO I'LL EARN QUITE A BIT!
Betting Ticket No. 6
Betting Ticket
RICH MAN

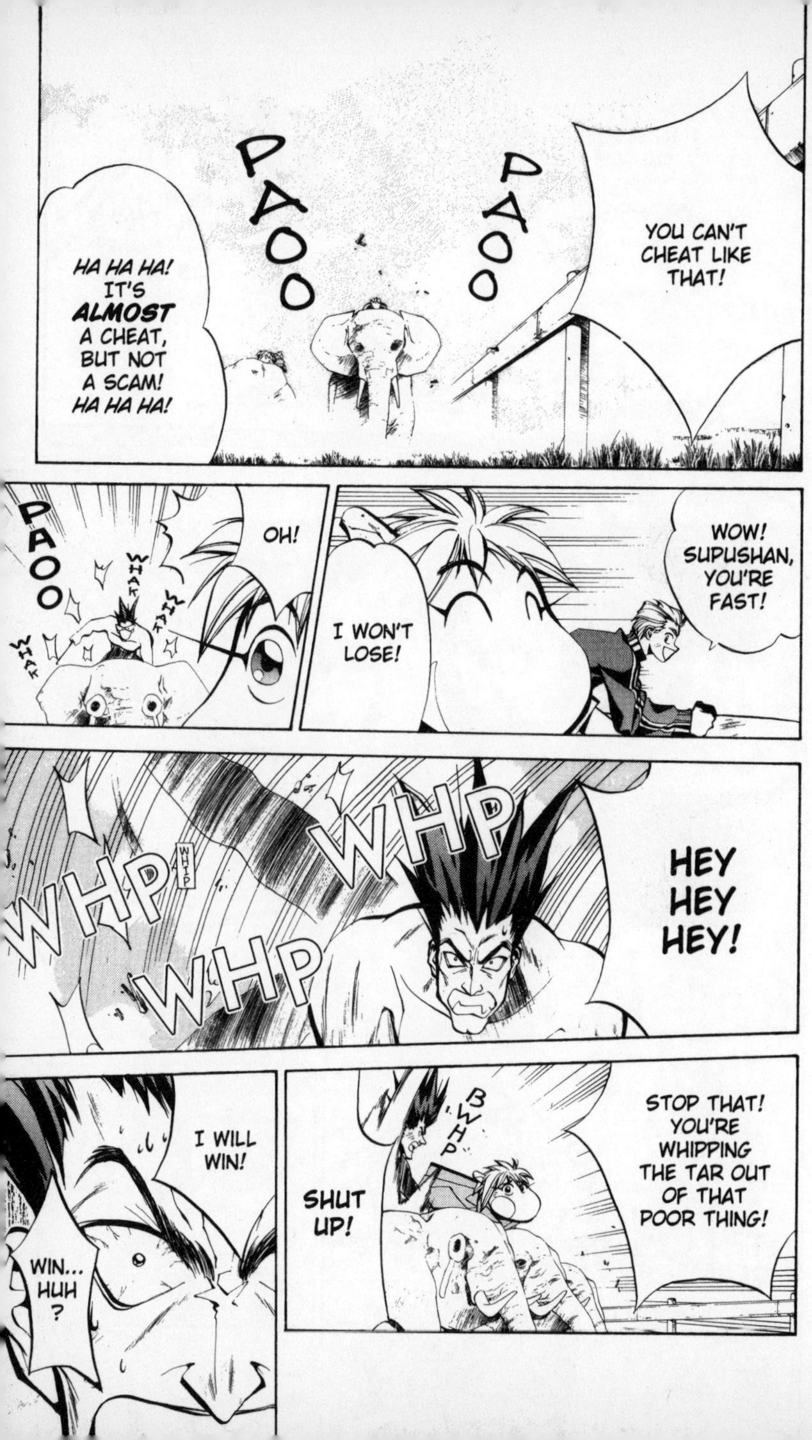
YOU CAN'T CHEAT LIKE THAT!
PAOO
PAOO
HA HA HA! IT'S **ALMOST** A CHEAT, BUT NOT A SCAM! HA HA HA!
WOW! SUPUSHAN, YOU'RE FAST!
I WON'T LOSE!
OH!
PAOO
WHAK
WHAK
WHAK
HEY HEY HEY!
WHP
WHP
WHIP
WHP
STOP THAT! YOU'RE WHIPPING THE TAR OUT OF THAT POOR THING!
BWHP
SHUT UP!
I WILL WIN!
WIN... HUH?

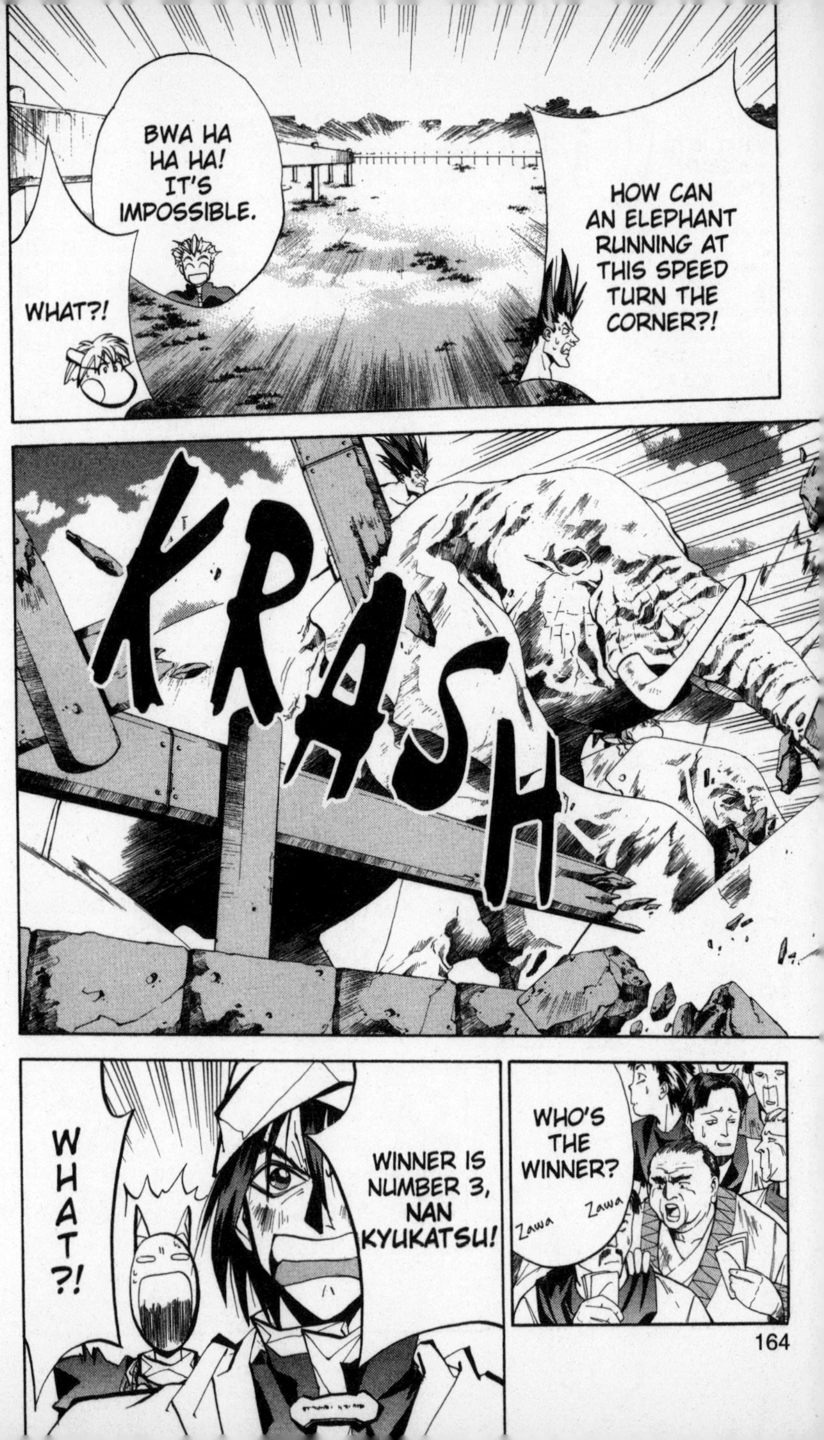
HOW CAN AN ELEPHANT RUNNING AT THIS SPEED TURN THE CORNER?!
BWA HA HA HA! IT'S IMPOSSIBLE.
WHAT?!
KRASH
WHO'S THE WINNER?
Zawa
Zawa
WINNER IS NUMBER 3, NAN KYUKATSU!
WHAT?!

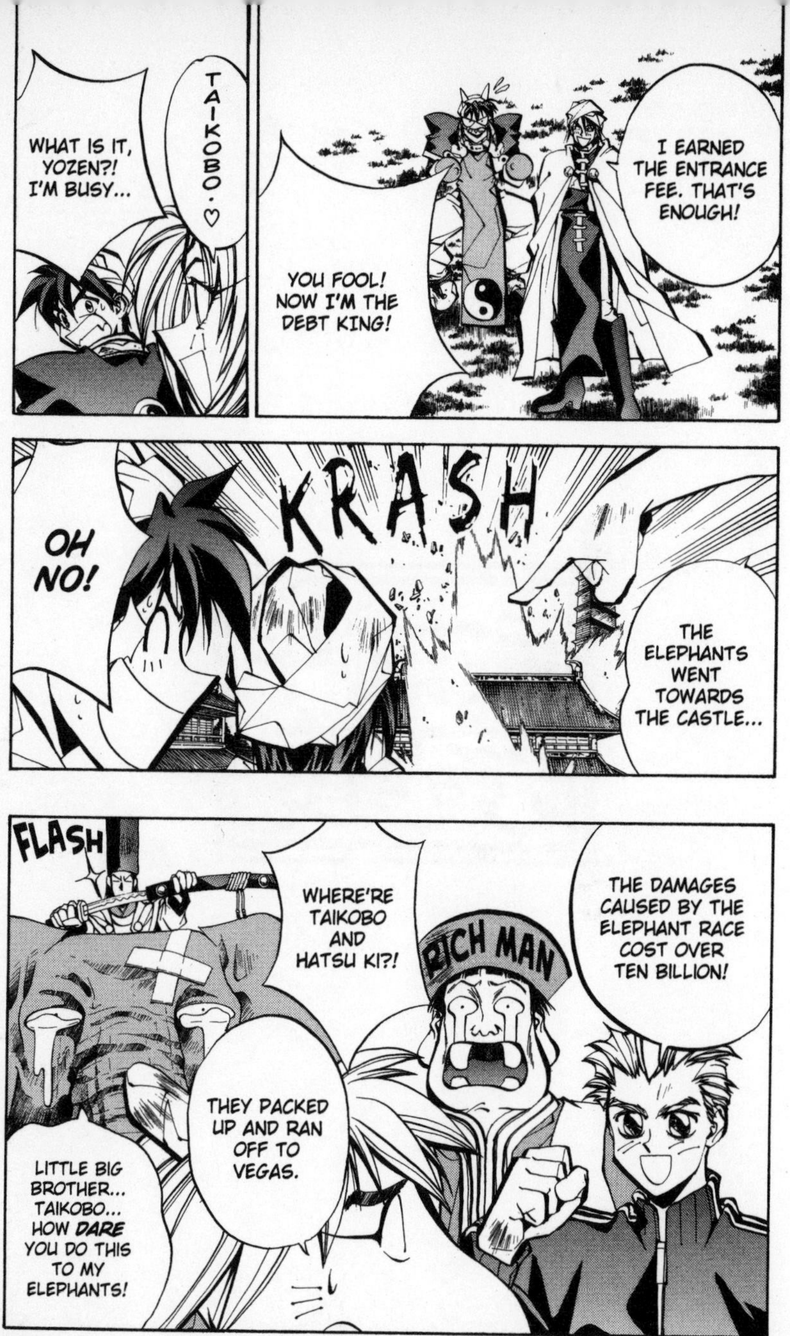
I EARNED THE ENTRANCE FEE. THAT'S ENOUGH!
YOU FOOL! NOW I'M THE DEBT KING!
TAIKOBO.♥
WHAT IS IT, YOZEN?! I'M BUSY...
THE ELEPHANTS WENT TOWARDS THE CASTLE...
KRASH
OH NO!
THE DAMAGES CAUSED BY THE ELEPHANT RACE COST OVER TEN BILLION!
WHERE'RE TAIKOBO AND HATSU KI?!
RICH MAN
THEY PACKED UP AND RAN OFF TO VEGAS.
LITTLE BIG BROTHER... TAIKOBO... HOW *DARE* YOU DO THIS TO MY ELEPHANTS!
FLASH

封神演義

CHAPTER 51:
PAST, PRESENT AND FUTURE, PART 6
THE BOND WITH THE LINEAGE

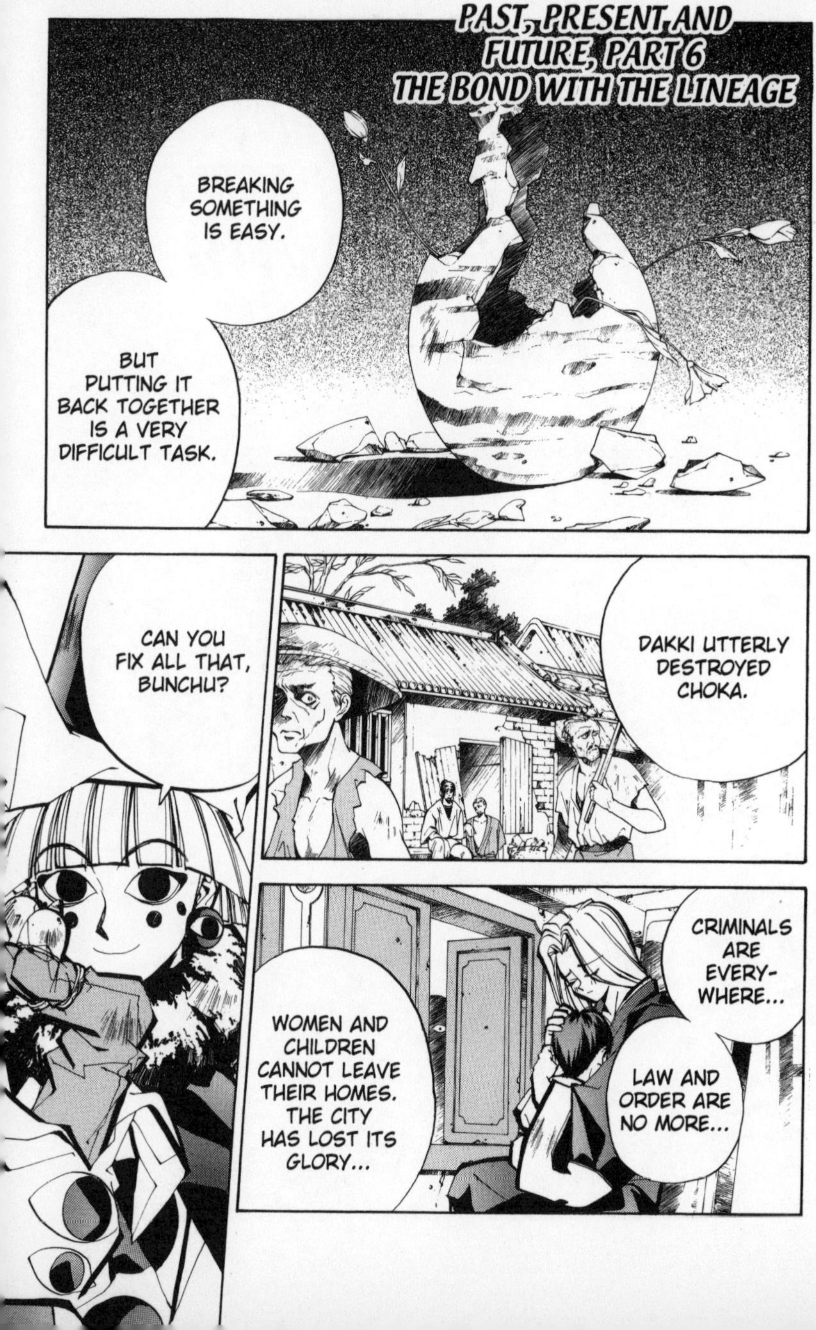
BREAKING SOMETHING IS EASY.
BUT PUTTING IT BACK TOGETHER IS A VERY DIFFICULT TASK.
DAKKI UTTERLY DESTROYED CHOKA.
CRIMINALS ARE EVERY-WHERE...
LAW AND ORDER ARE NO MORE...
WOMEN AND CHILDREN CANNOT LEAVE THEIR HOMES. THE CITY HAS LOST ITS GLORY...
CAN YOU FIX ALL THAT, BUNCHU?

Chapter 51

PAST, PRESENT AND FUTURE, PART 6
THE BOND WITH THE LINEAGE

OF COURSE, YOU CLOWN!
YIN *WILL* RECOVER!

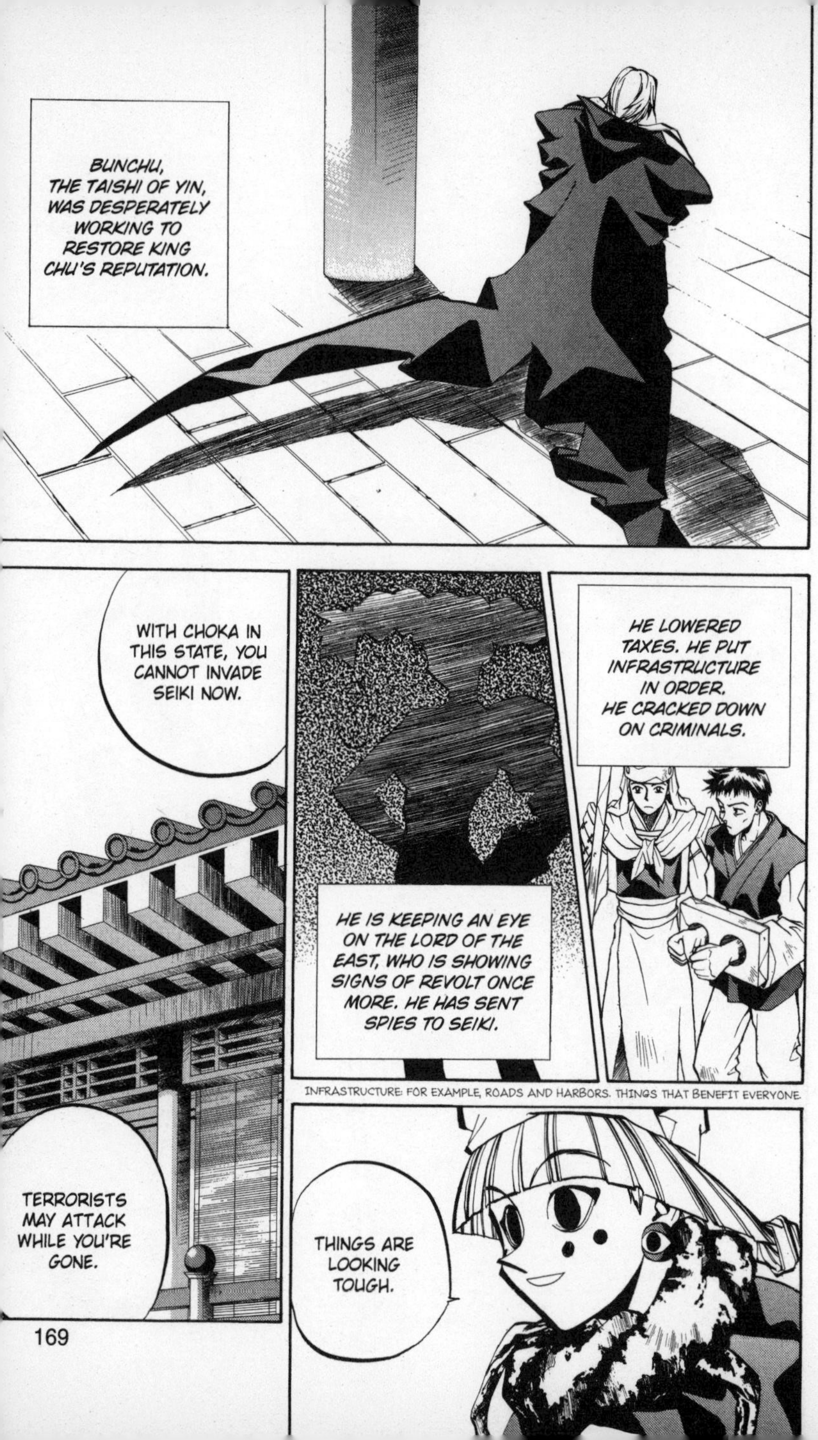
BUNCHU, THE TAISHI OF YIN, WAS DESPERATELY WORKING TO RESTORE KING CHU'S REPUTATION.
HE LOWERED TAXES. HE PUT INFRASTRUCTURE IN ORDER. HE CRACKED DOWN ON CRIMINALS.
INFRASTRUCTURE: FOR EXAMPLE, ROADS AND HARBORS. THINGS THAT BENEFIT EVERYONE.
HE IS KEEPING AN EYE ON THE LORD OF THE EAST, WHO IS SHOWING SIGNS OF REVOLT ONCE MORE. HE HAS SENT SPIES TO SEIKI.
THINGS ARE LOOKING TOUGH.
WITH CHOKA IN THIS STATE, YOU CANNOT INVADE SEIKI NOW.
TERRORISTS MAY ATTACK WHILE YOU'RE GONE.

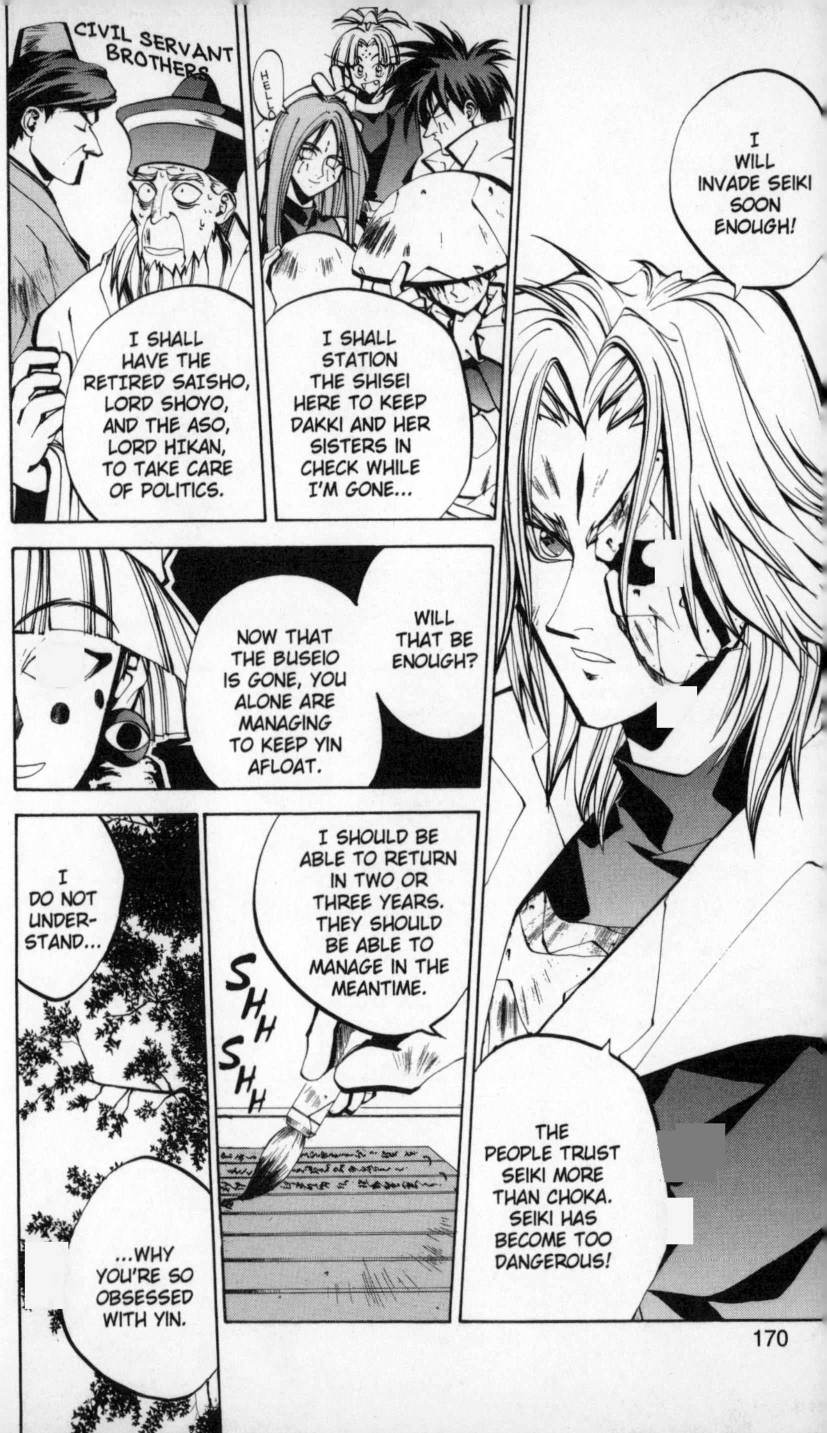
I WILL INVADE SEIKI SOON ENOUGH!
HELLO
I SHALL STATION THE SHISEI HERE TO KEEP DAKKI AND HER SISTERS IN CHECK WHILE I'M GONE...
CIVIL SERVANT BROTHERS
I SHALL HAVE THE RETIRED SAISHO, LORD SHOYO, AND THE ASO, LORD HIKAN, TO TAKE CARE OF POLITICS.
WILL THAT BE ENOUGH?
NOW THAT THE BUSEIO IS GONE, YOU ALONE ARE MANAGING TO KEEP YIN AFLOAT.
THE PEOPLE TRUST SEIKI MORE THAN CHOKA. SEIKI HAS BECOME TOO DANGEROUS!
I SHOULD BE ABLE TO RETURN IN TWO OR THREE YEARS. THEY SHOULD BE ABLE TO MANAGE IN THE MEANTIME.
SHH SHH
I DO NOT UNDER-STAND...
...WHY YOU'RE SO OBSESSED WITH YIN.

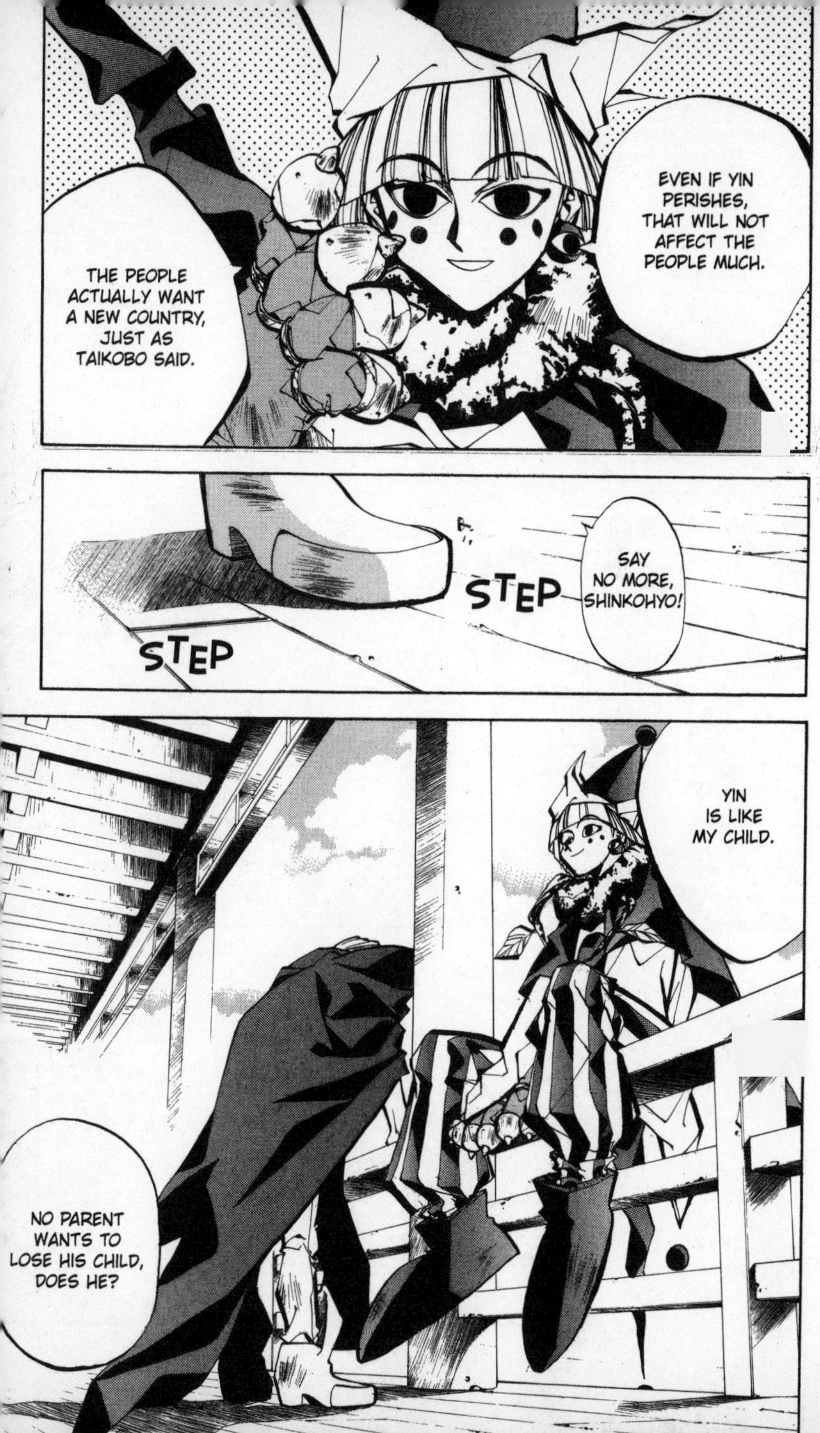
EVEN IF YIN PERISHES, THAT WILL NOT AFFECT THE PEOPLE MUCH.
THE PEOPLE ACTUALLY WANT A NEW COUNTRY, JUST AS TAIKOBO SAID.
SAY NO MORE, SHINKOHYO!
STEP
STEP
YIN IS LIKE MY CHILD.
NO PARENT WANTS TO LOSE HIS CHILD, DOES HE?

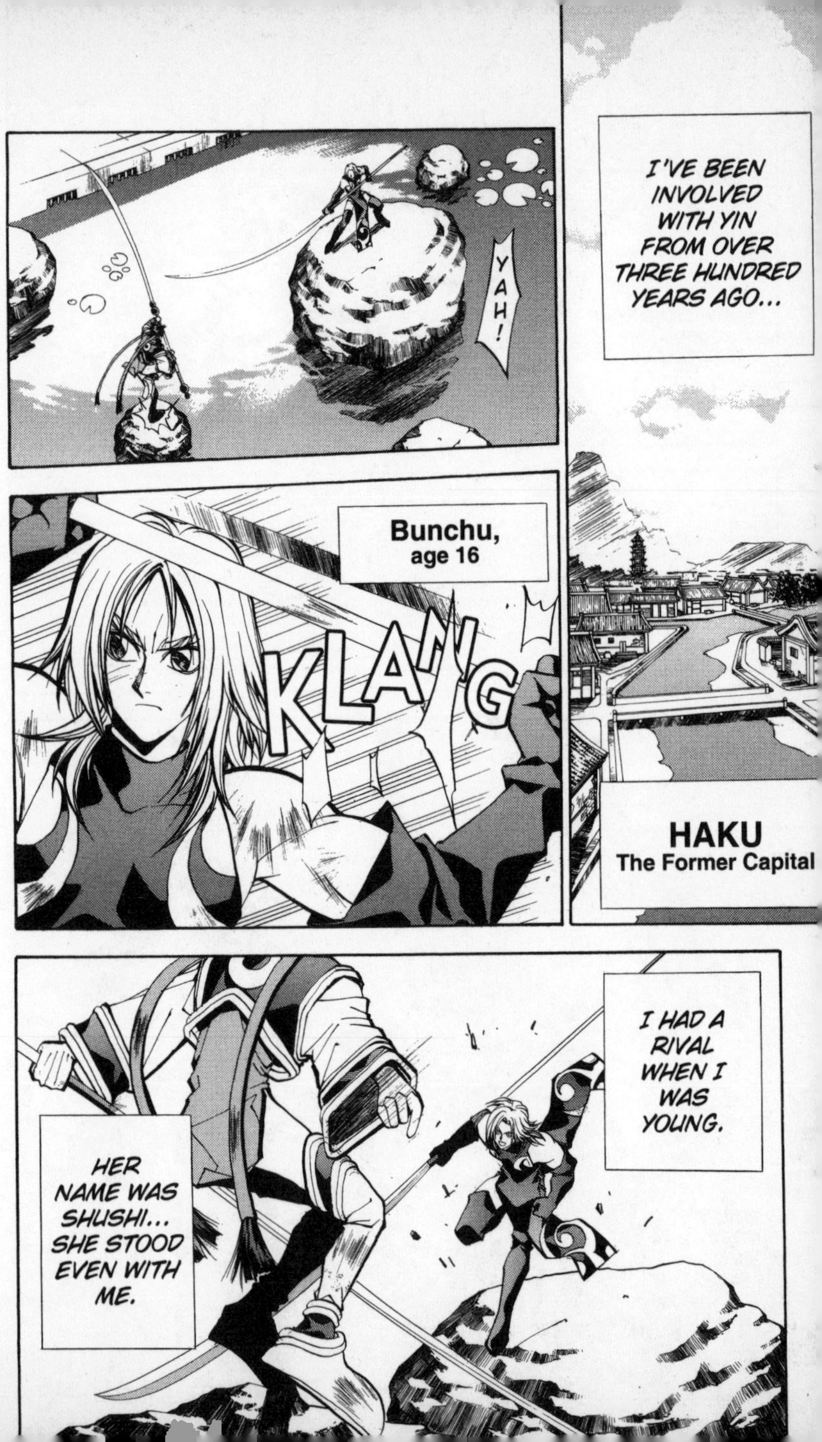
I'VE BEEN INVOLVED WITH YIN FROM OVER THREE HUNDRED YEARS AGO...
HAKU
The Former Capital
YAH!
Bunchu, age 16
KLANG
I HAD A RIVAL WHEN I WAS YOUNG.
HER NAME WAS SHUSHI... SHE STOOD EVEN WITH ME.

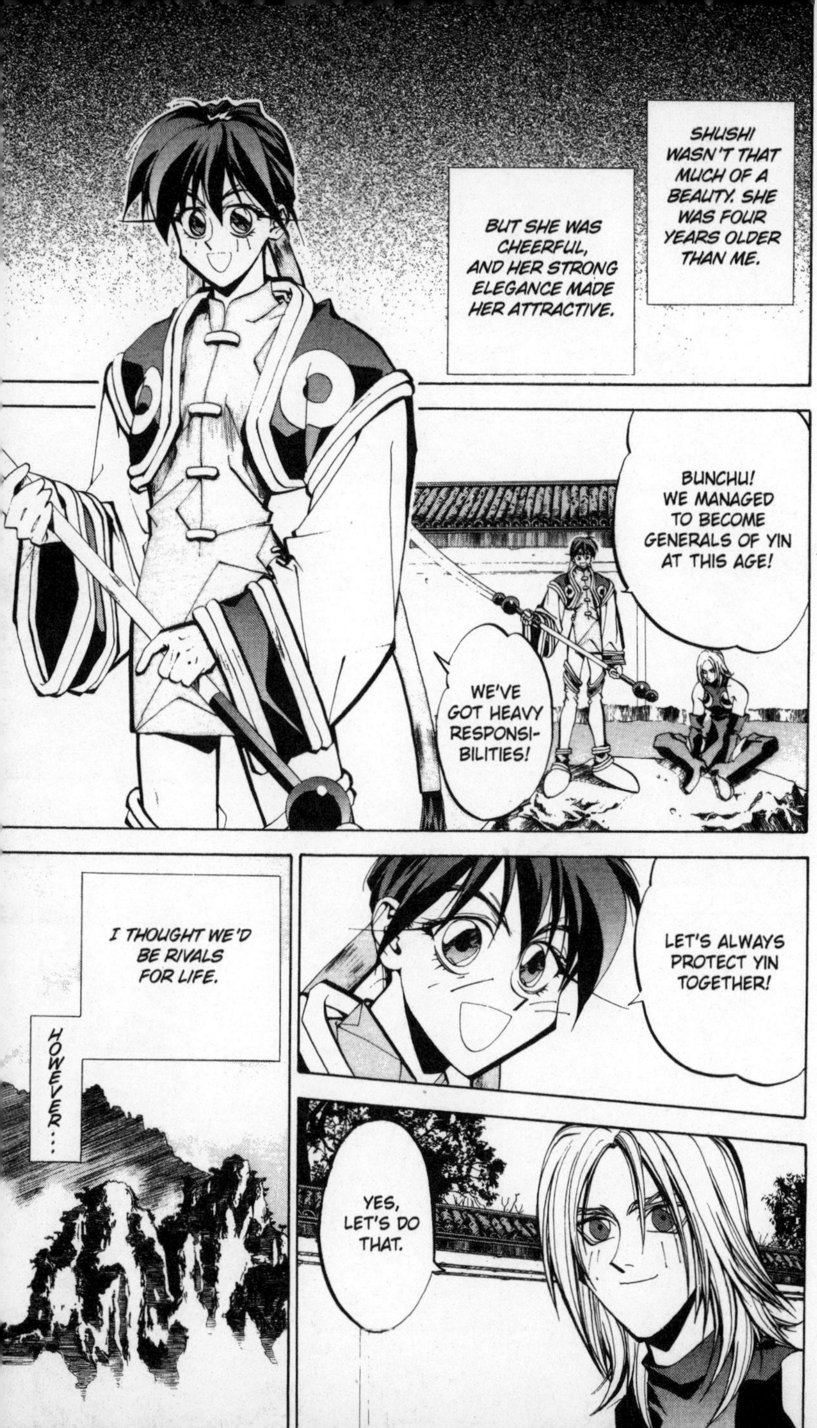
SHUSHI WASN'T THAT MUCH OF A BEAUTY. SHE WAS FOUR YEARS OLDER THAN ME.
BUT SHE WAS CHEERFUL, AND HER STRONG ELEGANCE MADE HER ATTRACTIVE.
BUNCHU! WE MANAGED TO BECOME GENERALS OF YIN AT THIS AGE!
WE'VE GOT HEAVY RESPONSI-BILITIES!
LET'S ALWAYS PROTECT YIN TOGETHER!
YES, LET'S DO THAT.
I THOUGHT WE'D BE RIVALS FOR LIFE.
HOWEVER...

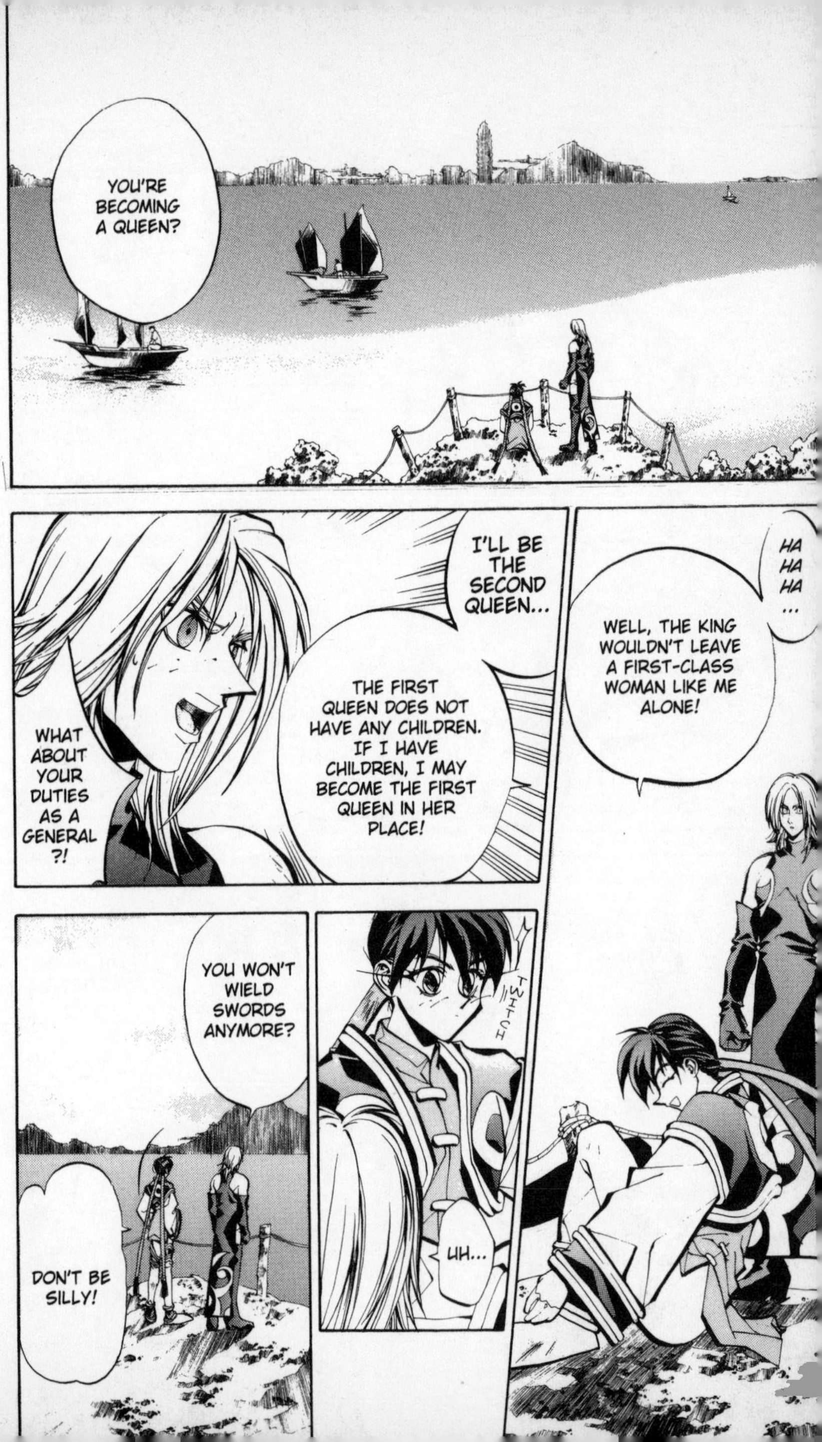
YOU'RE BECOMING A QUEEN?
HA HA HA ...
WELL, THE KING WOULDN'T LEAVE A FIRST-CLASS WOMAN LIKE ME ALONE!
I'LL BE THE SECOND QUEEN...
THE FIRST QUEEN DOES NOT HAVE ANY CHILDREN. IF I HAVE CHILDREN, I MAY BECOME THE FIRST QUEEN IN HER PLACE!
WHAT ABOUT YOUR DUTIES AS A GENERAL ?!
TWITCH
UH...
YOU WON'T WIELD SWORDS ANYMORE?
DON'T BE SILLY!

READ THIS WAY

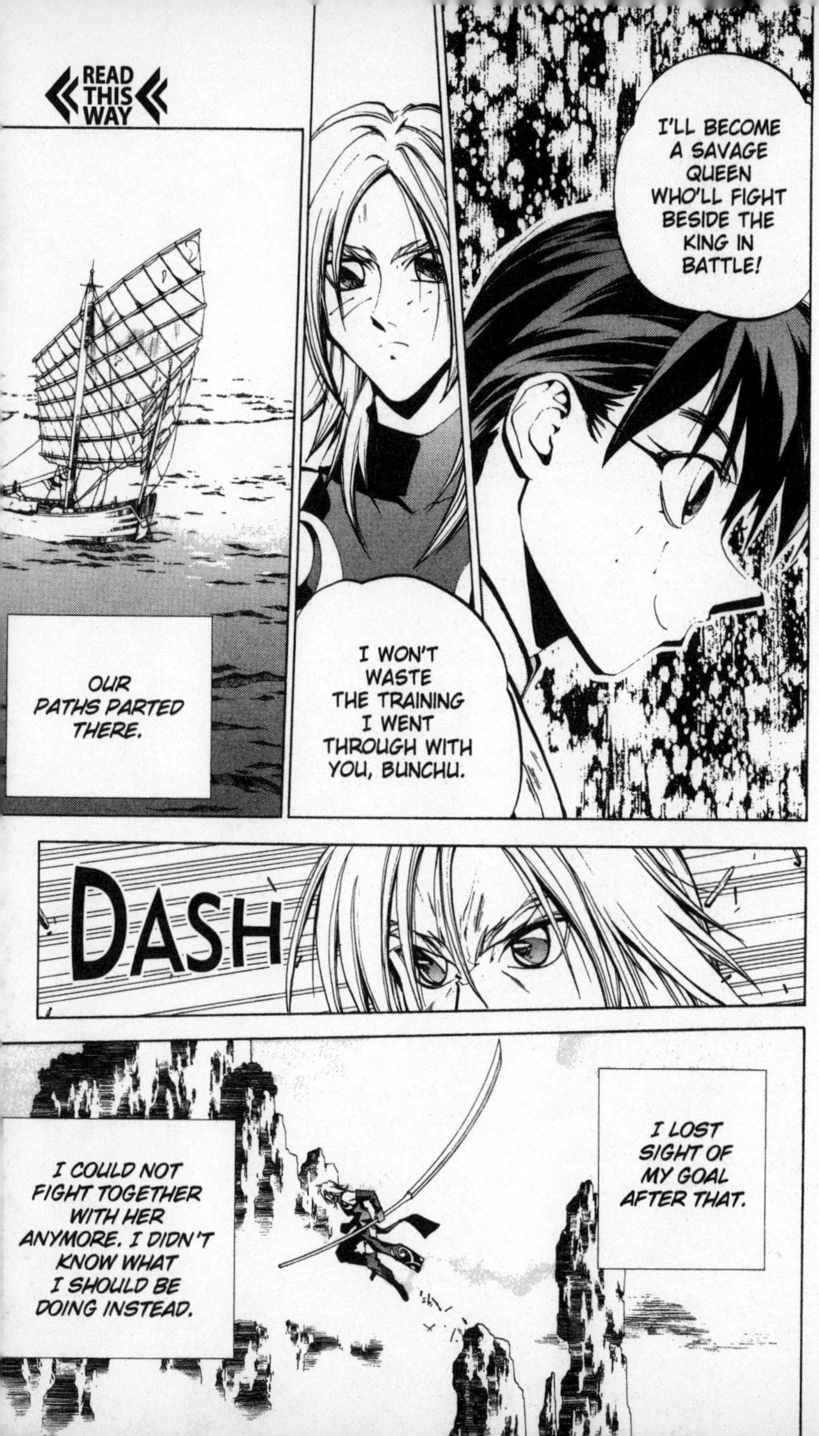
I'LL BECOME A SAVAGE QUEEN WHO'LL FIGHT BESIDE THE KING IN BATTLE!
I WON'T WASTE THE TRAINING I WENT THROUGH WITH YOU, BUNCHU.
OUR PATHS PARTED THERE.
DASH
I LOST SIGHT OF MY GOAL AFTER THAT.
I COULD NOT FIGHT TOGETHER WITH HER ANYMORE. I DIDN'T KNOW WHAT I SHOULD BE DOING INSTEAD.

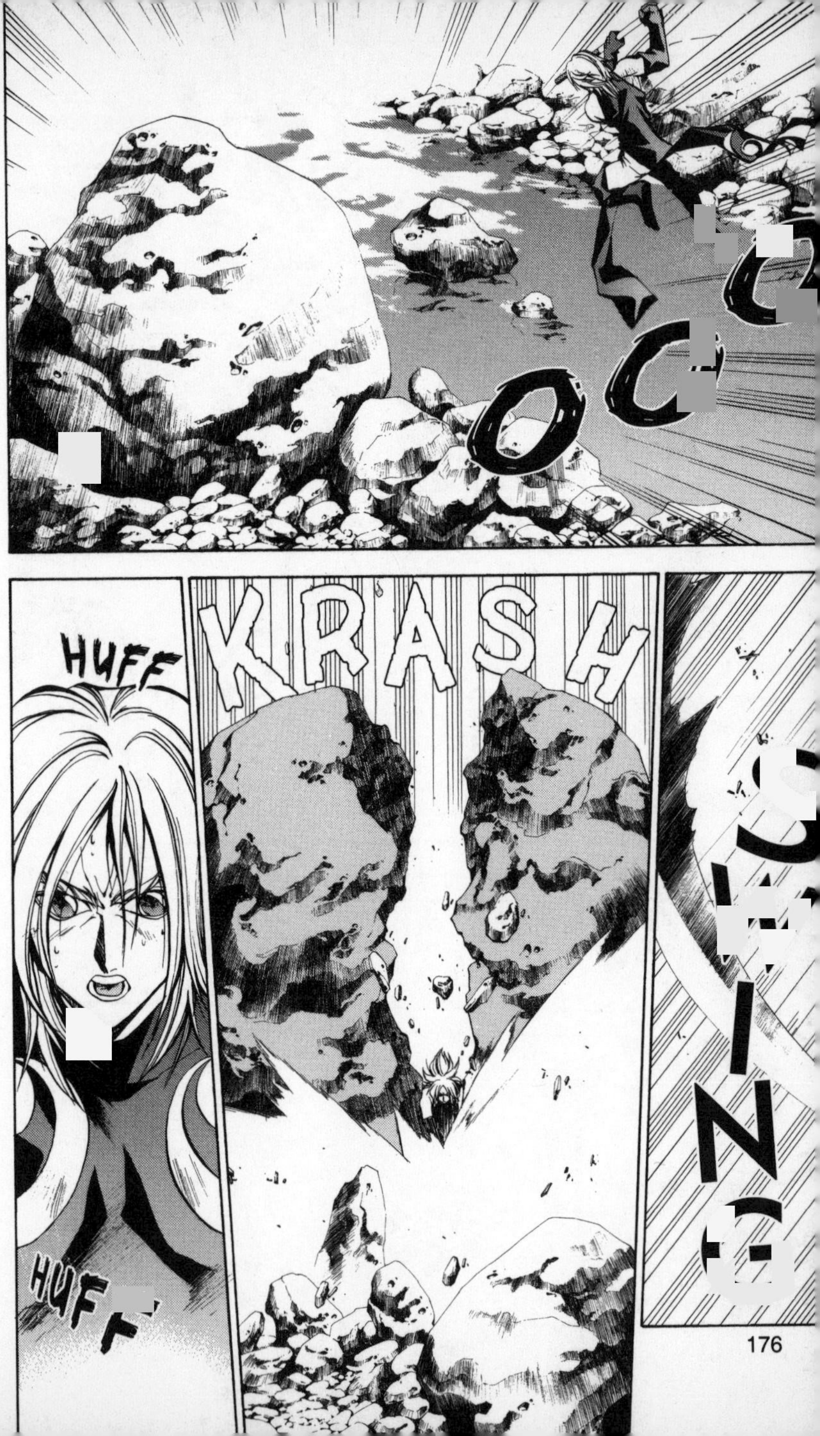
KRASH
HUFF
HUFF

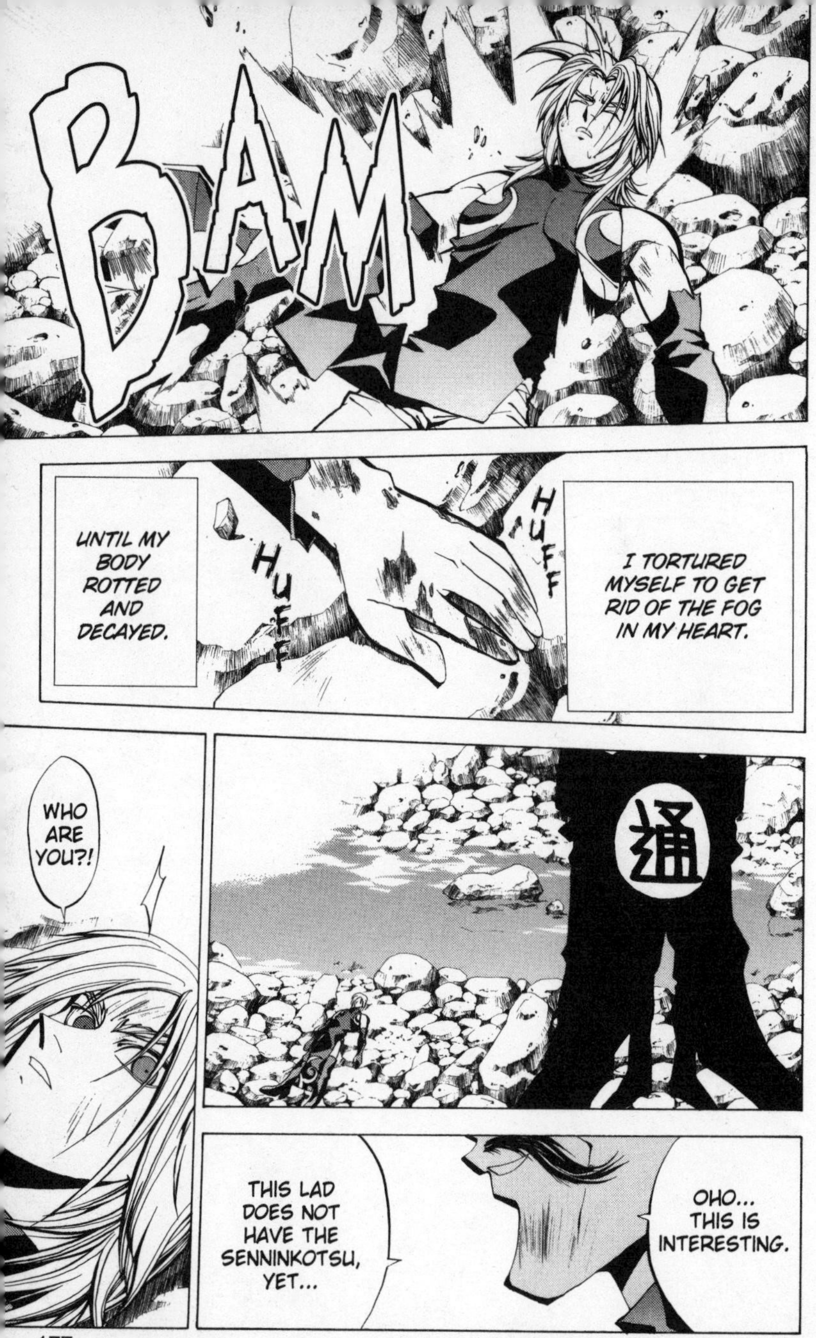
BAM
I TORTURED MYSELF TO GET RID OF THE FOG IN MY HEART.
HUFF
HUFF
UNTIL MY BODY ROTTED AND DECAYED.
通
OHO... THIS IS INTERESTING.
THIS LAD DOES NOT HAVE THE SENNINKOTSU, YET...
WHO ARE YOU?!

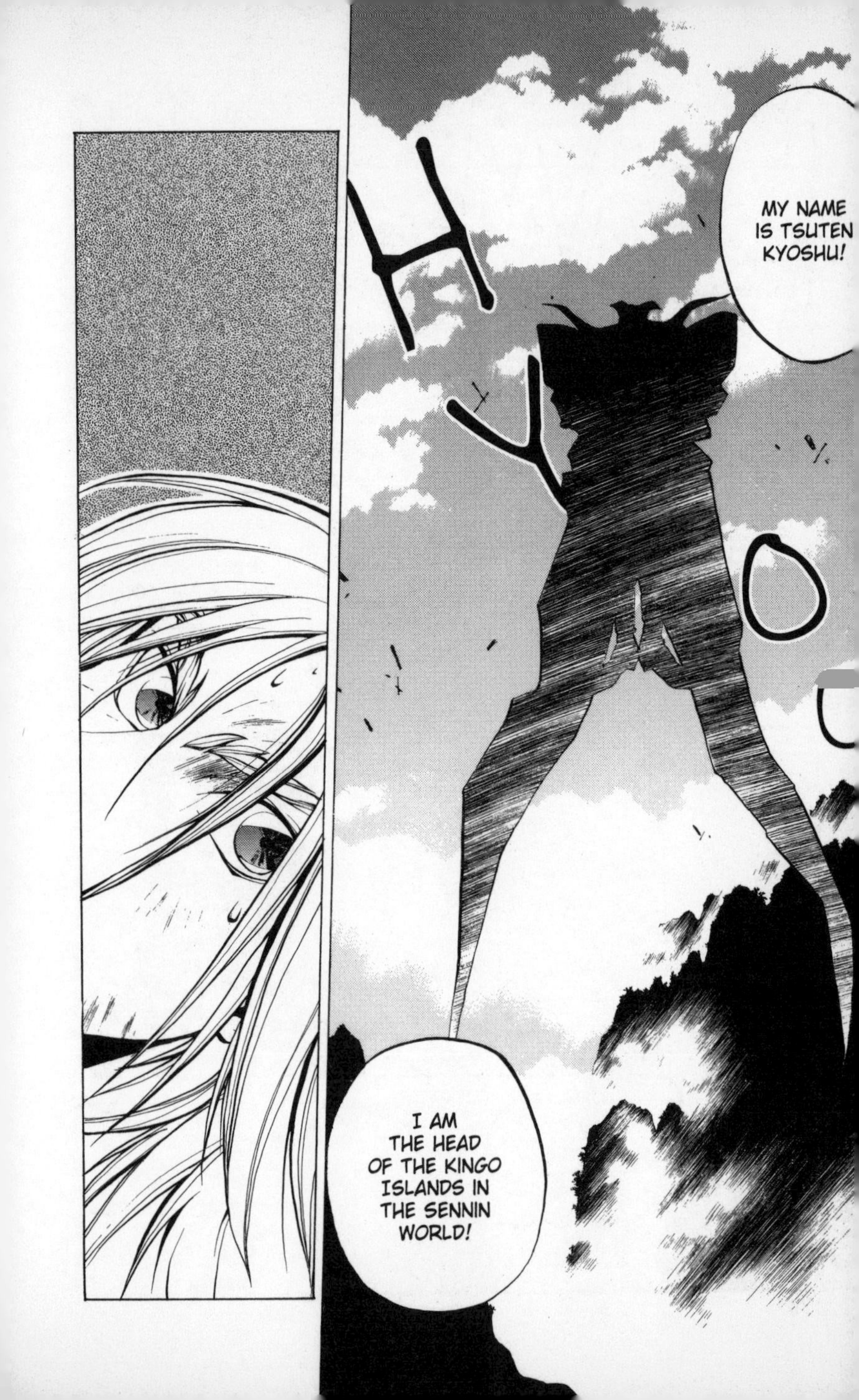
MY NAME IS TSUTEN KYOSHU!
HYO
I AM THE HEAD OF THE KINGO ISLANDS IN THE SENNIN WORLD!

READ THIS WAY

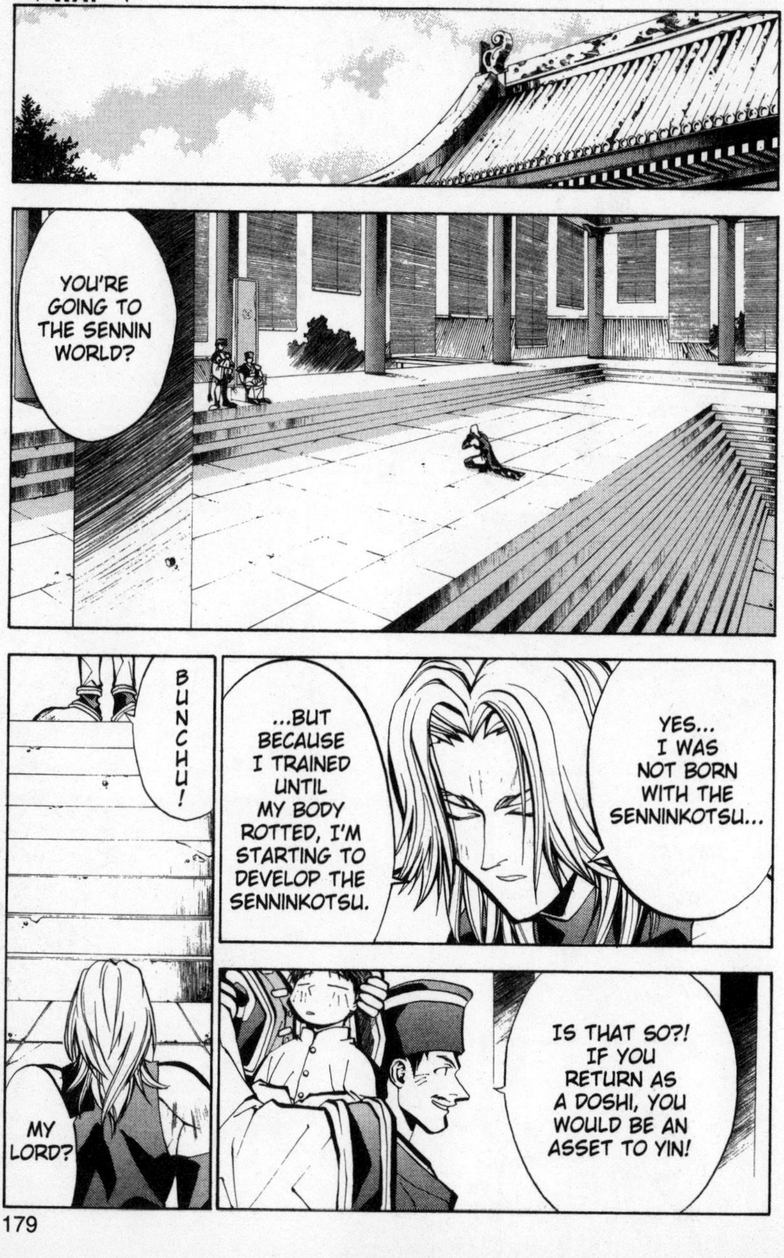

YOU'RE GOING TO THE SENNIN WORLD?
YES... I WAS NOT BORN WITH THE SENNINKOTSU...
...BUT BECAUSE I TRAINED UNTIL MY BODY ROTTED, I'M STARTING TO DEVELOP THE SENNINKOTSU.
IS THAT SO?! IF YOU RETURN AS A DOSHI, YOU WOULD BE AN ASSET TO YIN!
BUNCHU!
MY LORD?

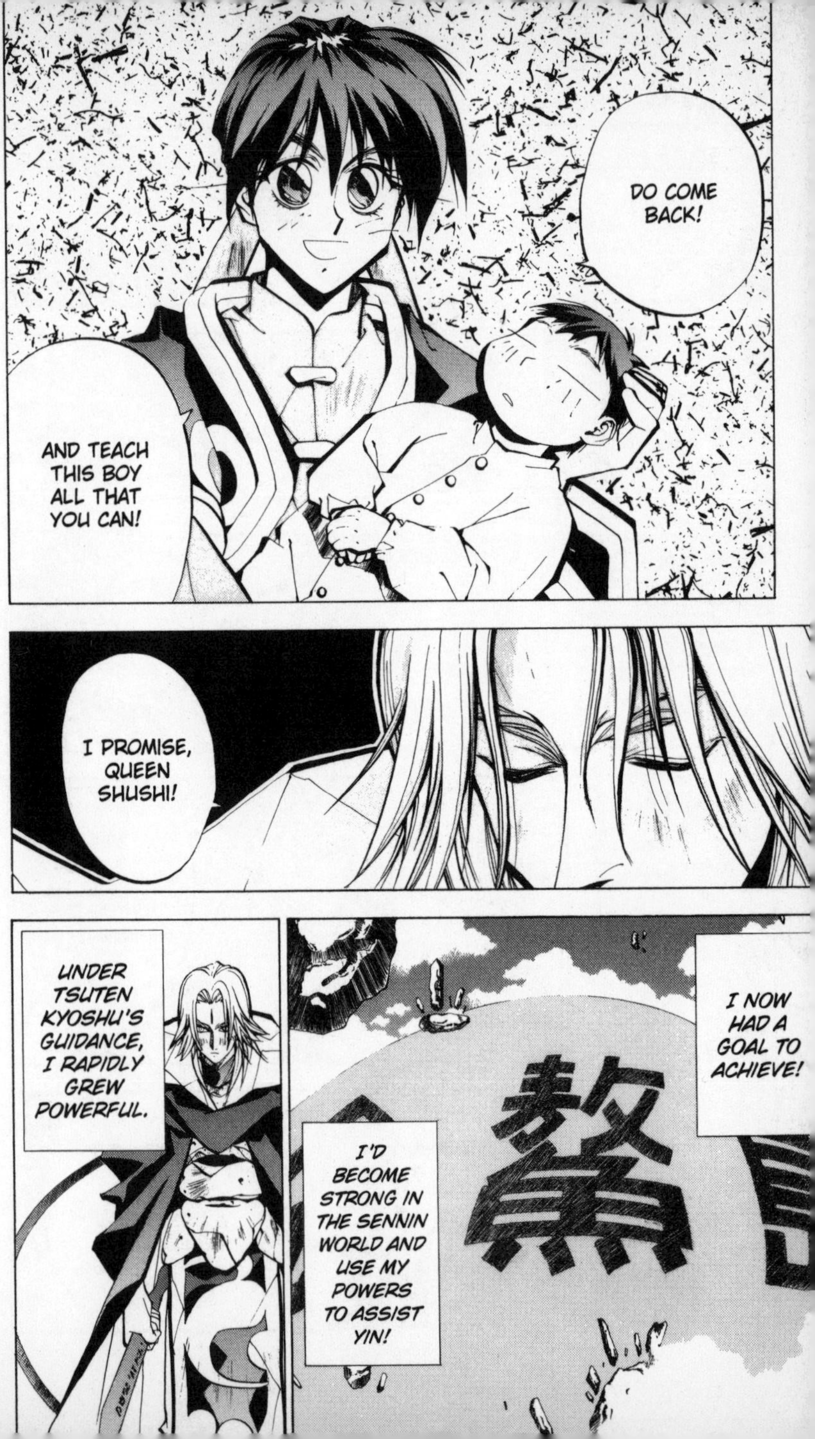
DO COME BACK!
AND TEACH THIS BOY ALL THAT YOU CAN!
I PROMISE, QUEEN SHUSHI!
I NOW HAD A GOAL TO ACHIEVE!
I'D BECOME STRONG IN THE SENNIN WORLD AND USE MY POWERS TO ASSIST YIN!
UNDER TSUTEN KYOSHU'S GUIDANCE, I RAPIDLY GREW POWERFUL.

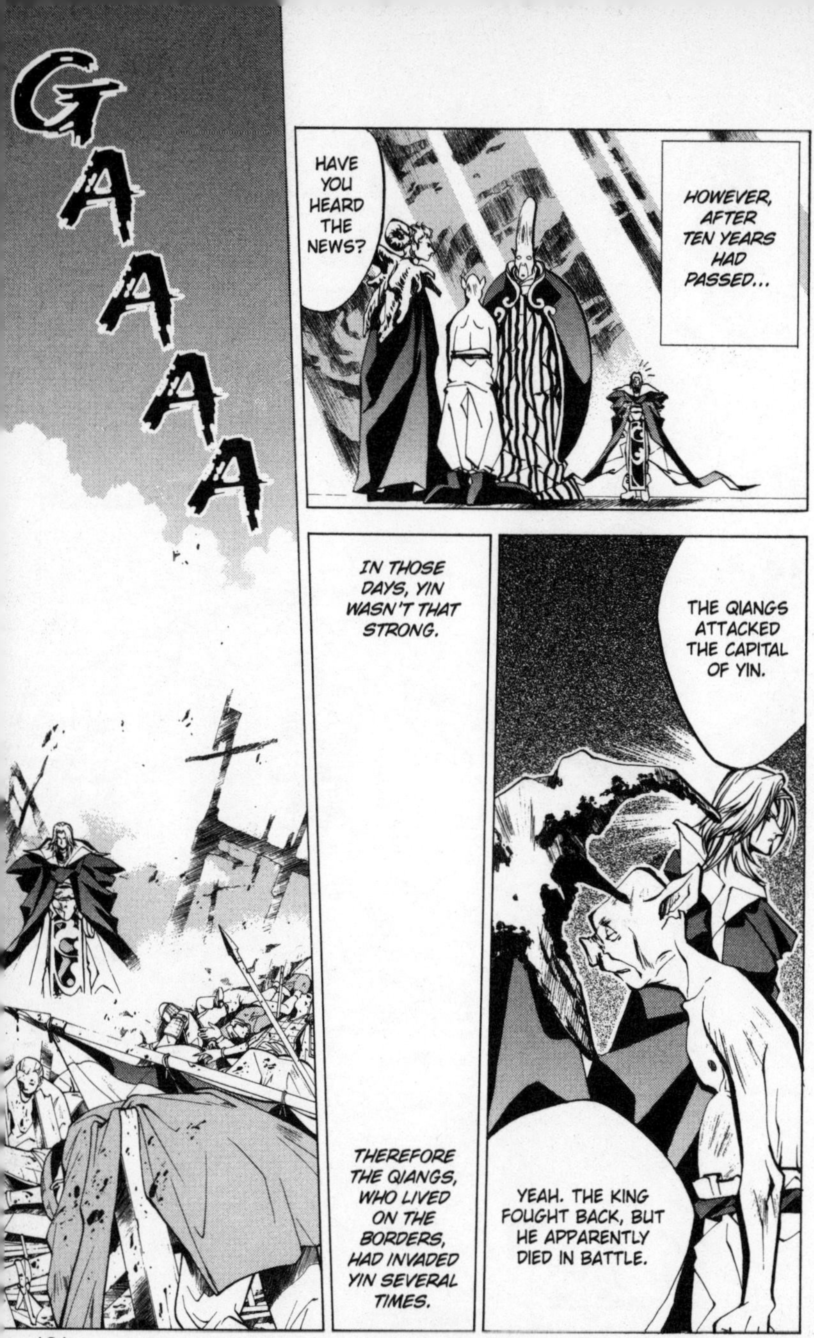
HOWEVER, AFTER TEN YEARS HAD PASSED...
HAVE YOU HEARD THE NEWS?
THE QIANGS ATTACKED THE CAPITAL OF YIN.
YEAH. THE KING FOUGHT BACK, BUT HE APPARENTLY DIED IN BATTLE.
IN THOSE DAYS, YIN WASN'T THAT STRONG.
THEREFORE THE QIANGS, WHO LIVED ON THE BORDERS, HAD INVADED YIN SEVERAL TIMES.
GAAAA

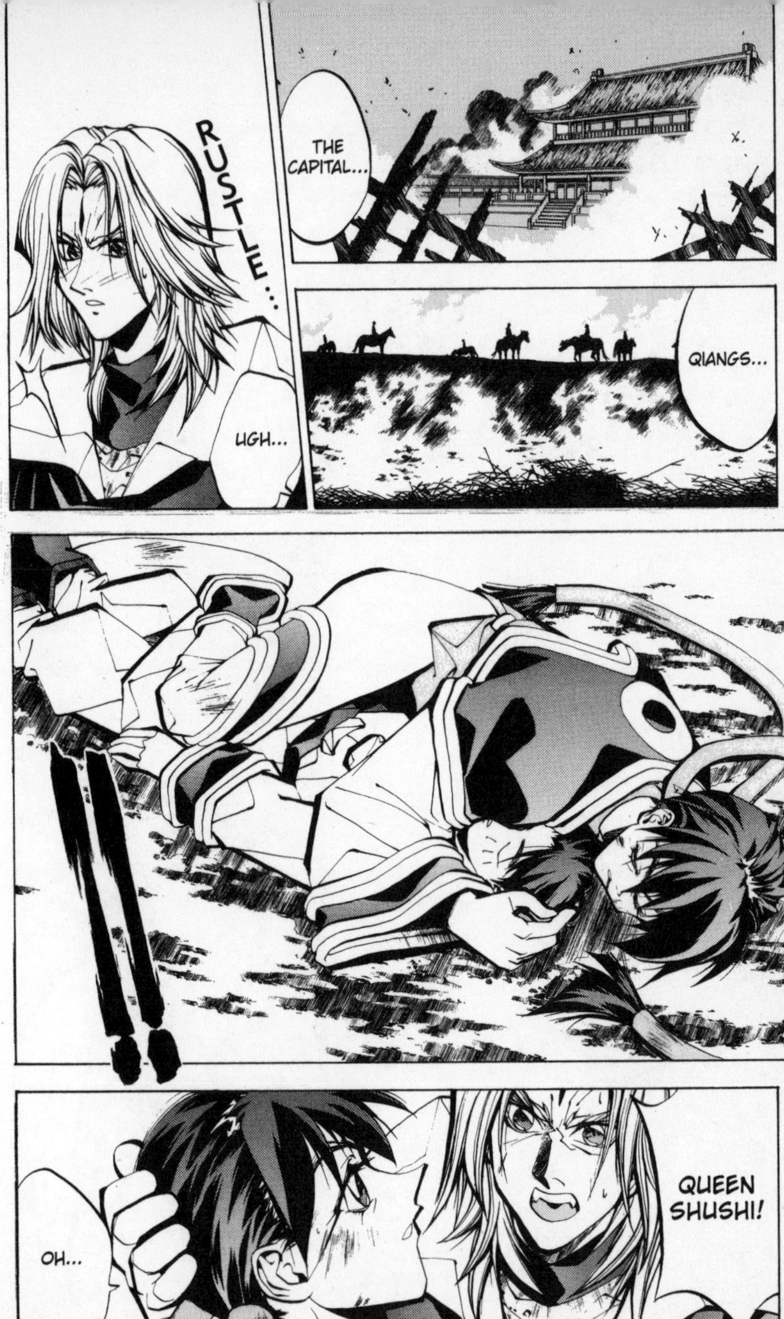
THE CAPITAL...
QIANGS...
RUSTLE...
UGH...
QUEEN SHUSHI!
OH...

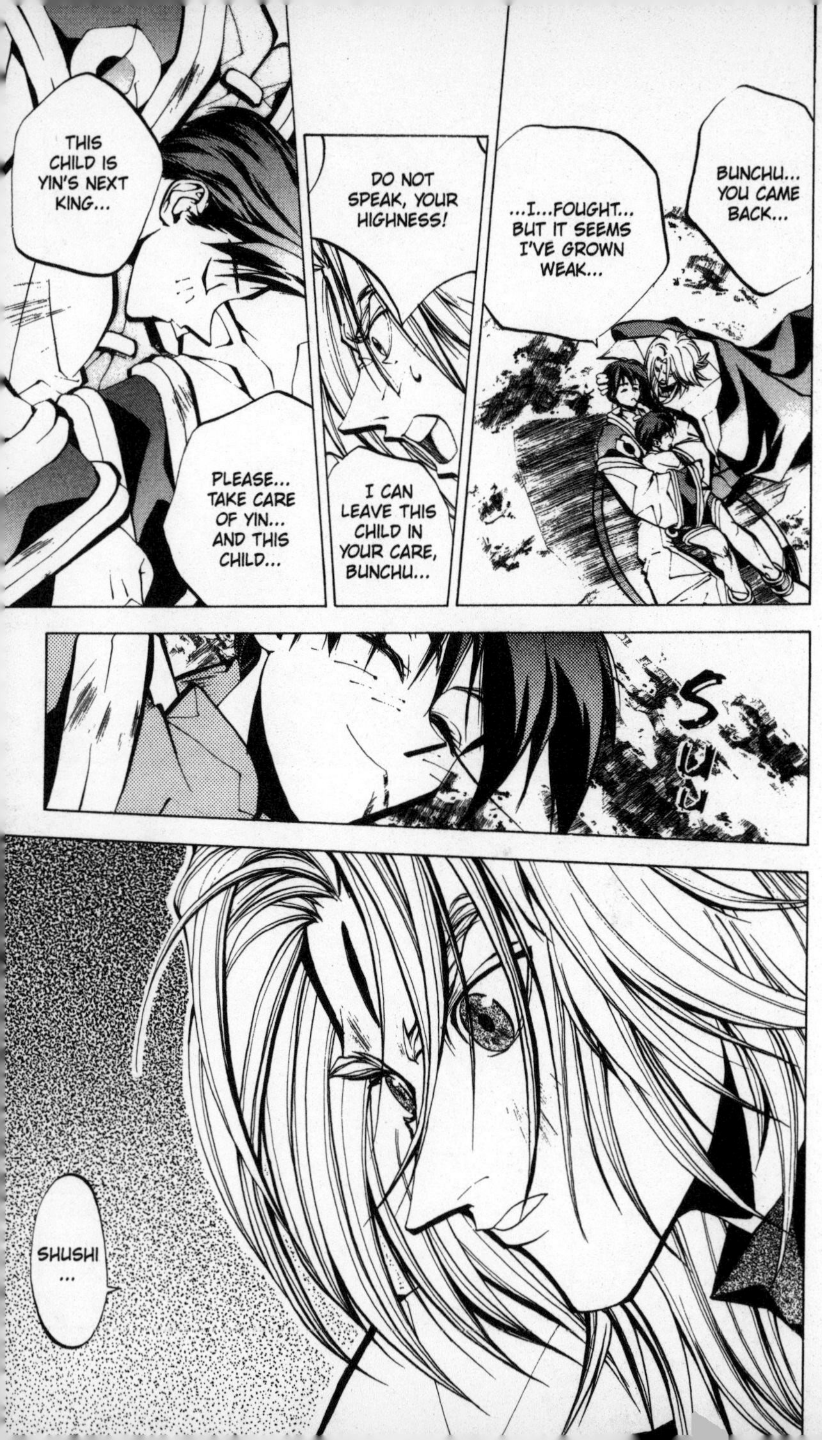
BUNCHU... YOU CAME BACK...
...I...FOUGHT... BUT IT SEEMS I'VE GROWN WEAK...
DO NOT SPEAK, YOUR HIGHNESS!
I CAN LEAVE THIS CHILD IN YOUR CARE, BUNCHU...
THIS CHILD IS YIN'S NEXT KING...
PLEASE... TAKE CARE OF YIN... AND THIS CHILD...
SUU
SHUSHI ...

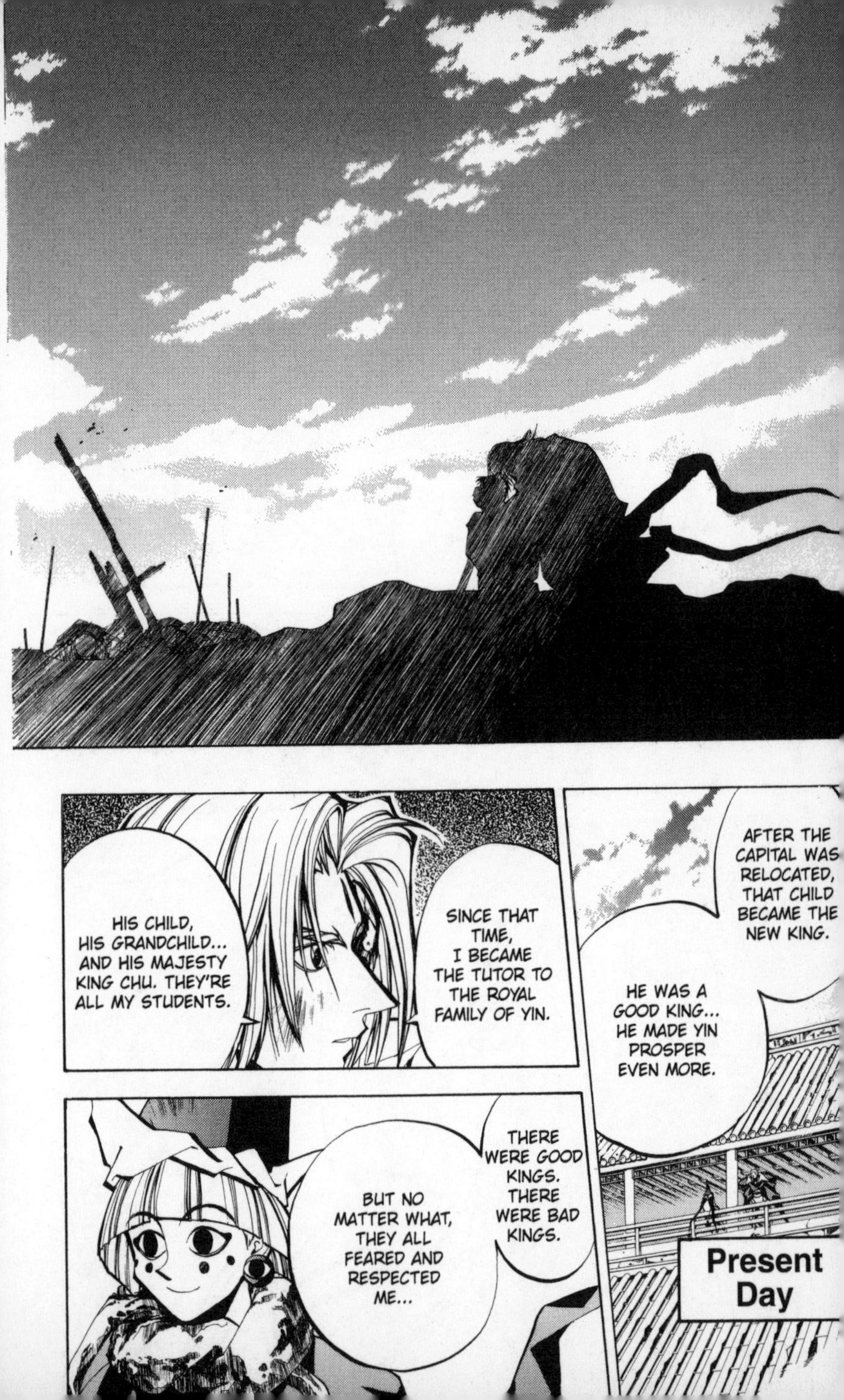
AFTER THE CAPITAL WAS RELOCATED, THAT CHILD BECAME THE NEW KING.
HE WAS A GOOD KING... HE MADE YIN PROSPER EVEN MORE.
Present Day
SINCE THAT TIME, I BECAME THE TUTOR TO THE ROYAL FAMILY OF YIN.
HIS CHILD, HIS GRANDCHILD... AND HIS MAJESTY KING CHU. THEY'RE ALL MY STUDENTS.
THERE WERE GOOD KINGS. THERE WERE BAD KINGS.
BUT NO MATTER WHAT, THEY ALL FEARED AND RESPECTED ME...

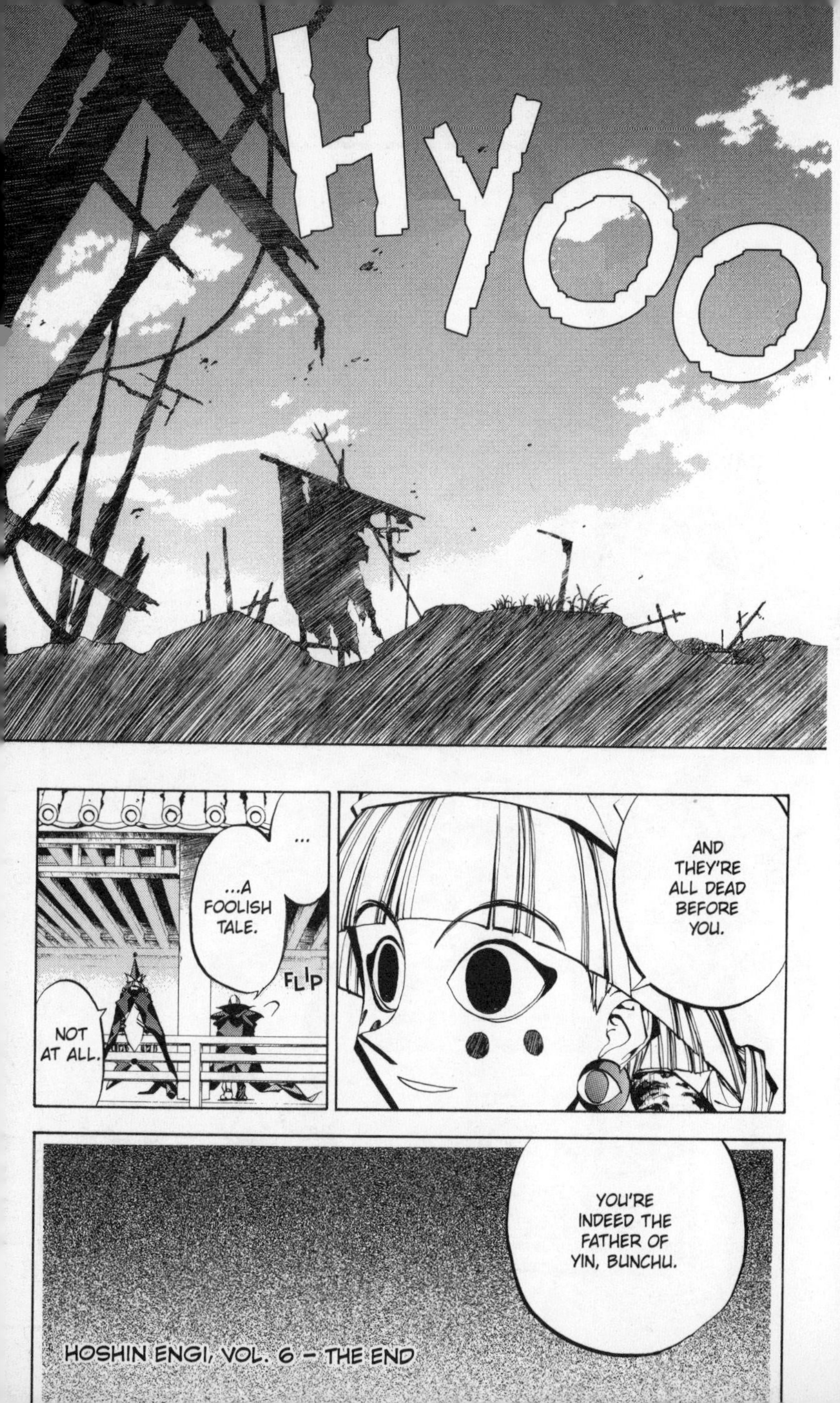
HYOO
AND THEY'RE ALL DEAD BEFORE YOU.
...
...A FOOLISH TALE.
FLIP
NOT AT ALL.
YOU'RE INDEED THE FATHER OF YIN, BUNCHU.
HOSHIN ENGI, VOL. 6 – THE END

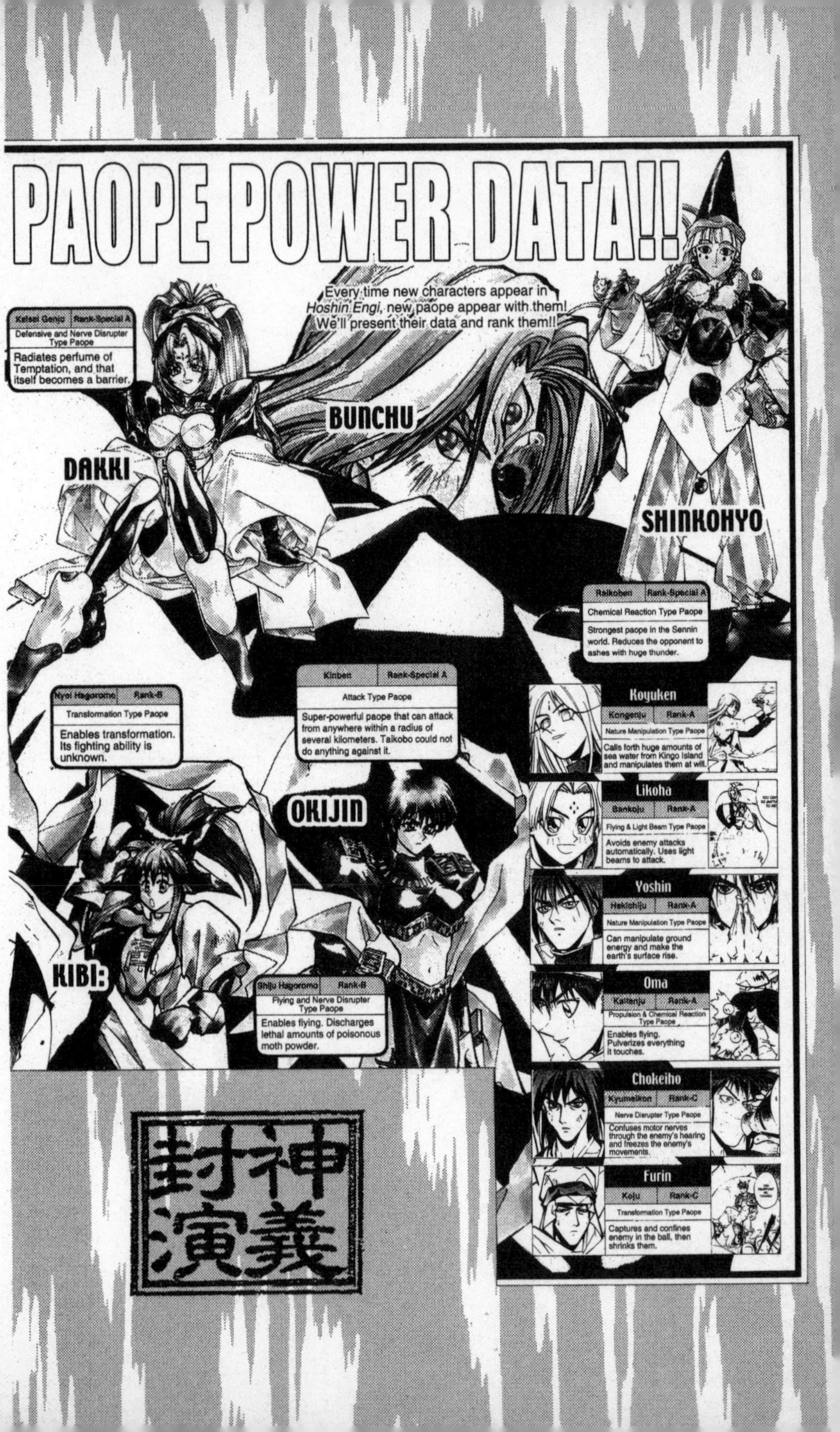
PAOPE POWER DATA!!
Every time new characters appear in *Hoshin Engi*, new paope appear with them! We'll present their data and rank them!!
SHINKOHYO
Raikoben | Rank-Special A
Chemical Reaction Type Paope
Strongest paope in the Sennin world. Reduces the opponent to ashes with huge thunder.
BUNCHU
Kinben | Rank-Special A
Attack Type Paope
Super-powerful paope that can attack from anywhere within a radius of several kilometers. Taikobo could not do anything against it.
DAKKI
Keisei Genjo | Rank-Special A
Defensive and Nerve Disrupter Type Paope
Radiates perfume of Temptation, and that itself becomes a barrier.
Koyuken
Kongenju | Rank-A
Nature Manipulation Type Paope
Calls forth huge amounts of sea water from Kingo Island and manipulates them at will.
Likoha
Bankoju | Rank-A
Flying & Light Beam Type Paope
Avoids enemy attacks automatically. Uses light beams to attack.
Yoshin
Hekichiju | Rank-A
Nature Manipulation Type Paope
Can manipulate ground energy and make the earth's surface rise.
Oma
Kaitenju | Rank-A
Propulsion & Chemical Reaction Type Paope
Enables flying. Pulverizes everything it touches.
Chokeiho
Kyumeikon | Rank-C
Nerve Disrupter Type Paope
Confuses motor nerves through the enemy's hearing and freezes the enemy's movements.
Furin
Koju | Rank-C
Transformation Type Paope
Captures and confines enemy in the ball, then shrinks them.
OKIJIN
Shiju Hagoromo | Rank-B
Flying and Nerve Disrupter Type Paope
Enables flying. Discharges lethal amounts of poisonous moth powder.
KIBI:
Nyoi Hagoromo | Rank-B
Transformation Type Paope
Enables transformation. Its fighting ability is unknown.

封神演義

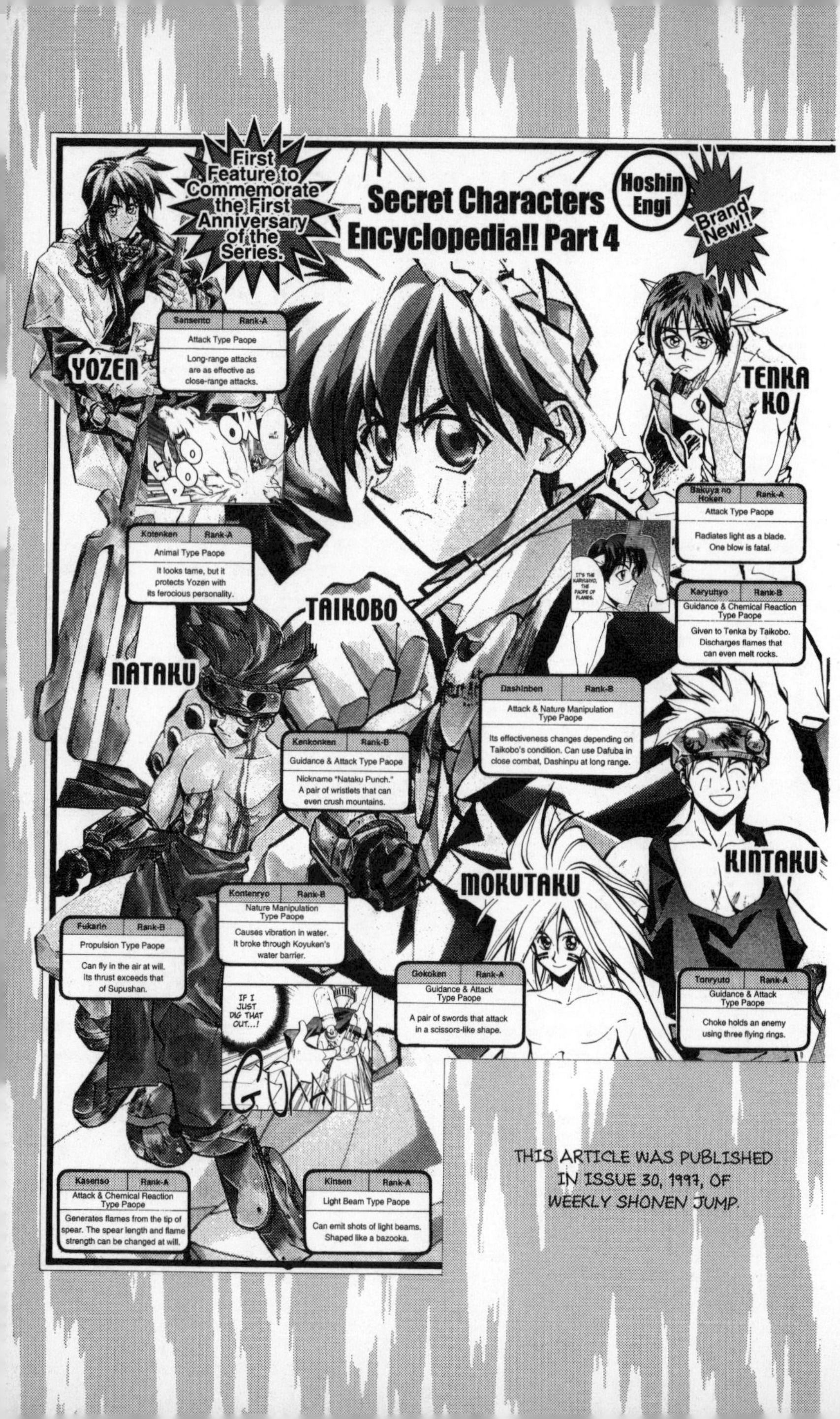

First Feature to Commemorate the First Anniversary of the Series.
Secret Characters Encyclopedia!! Part 4
Hoshin Engi
Brand New!!
TENKA KO
Bakuya no Hoken | Rank-A
Attack Type Paope
Radiates light as a blade. One blow is fatal.
IT'S THE KARYUHYO, THE PAOPE OF FLAMES.
Karyuhyo | Rank-B
Guidance & Chemical Reaction Type Paope
Given to Tenka by Taikobo. Discharges flames that can even melt rocks.
YOZEN
Sansento | Rank-A
Attack Type Paope
Long-range attacks are as effective as close-range attacks.
GOBOO
Kotenken | Rank-A
Animal Type Paope
It looks tame, but it protects Yozen with its ferocious personality.
TAIKOBO
Dashinben | Rank-B
Attack & Nature Manipulation Type Paope
Its effectiveness changes depending on Taikobo's condition. Can use Dafuba in close combat, Dashinpu at long range.
KINTAKU
Tonryuto | Rank-A
Guidance & Attack Type Paope
Choke holds an enemy using three flying rings.
MOKUTAKU
Gokoken | Rank-A
Guidance & Attack Type Paope
A pair of swords that attack in a scissors-like shape.
NATAKU
Kenkonken | Rank-B
Guidance & Attack Type Paope
Nickname "Nataku Punch." A pair of wristlets that can even crush mountains.
Kontenryo | Rank-B
Nature Manipulation Type Paope
Causes vibration in water. It broke through Koyuken's water barrier.
Fukarin | Rank-B
Propulsion Type Paope
Can fly in the air at will. Its thrust exceeds that of Supushan.
IF I JUST DIG THAT OUT...!
GUM
Kinsen | Rank-A
Light Beam Type Paope
Can emit shots of light beams. Shaped like a bazooka.
Kasenso | Rank-A
Attack & Chemical Reaction Type Paope
Generates flames from the tip of spear. The spear length and flame strength can be changed at will.

THIS ARTICLE WAS PUBLISHED IN ISSUE 30, 1997, OF WEEKLY SHONEN JUMP.

Fifteen Keywords to Decipher "Hoshin"!!

Reiju

Three reiju have appeared so far: Taikobo's Supushan, Shinohyo's Kokutenko and Bunchu's Kokukirin. Supushan assists Taikobo by acting as a "vehicle" and helping during battles with his quick movements. You couldn't imagine his speed from his looks. Kokutenko's body itself is suited for battle. Kokukirin acts as Bunchu's advisor. The roles that reiju play (besides being "vehicles") differ and are full of personality.

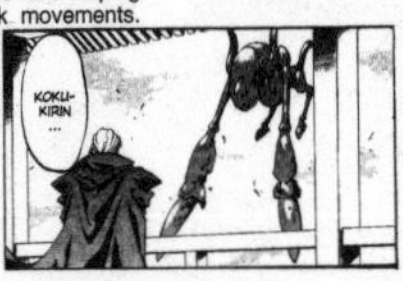
KOKU-KIRIN ...

▲ Kokukirin is a reiju that even the Shisei respects.

There have only been 48 episodes in the series, but mysteries keep popping up in *Hoshin Engi*. We'll explain 15 keywords in detail here! They're all important to the story so far, and to how the story will develop from now on, so please read them thoroughly and use them as hints!

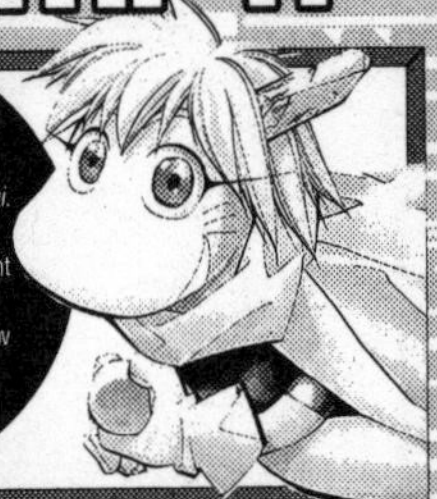

Taikobo and the Qiang Tribe

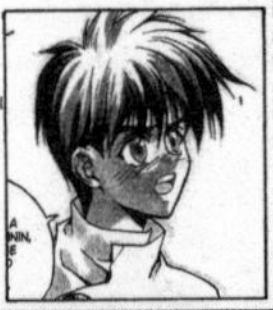

▶ Taikobo wishes for a peaceful world.

Taikobo and Dakki's connection goes back to when Taikobo was a teenager. Taikobo (Ryobo) was the son of the Qiang tribe chief. While he was grazing sheep, he found out that that his family, tribe and comrades had been captured by Yin soldiers. The captured Qiangs were buried alive as attendants to the dead King. Dakki was the one who ordered a hunt of a hundred times more attendants than usual. Humans other than Yin were treated like cattle then.

Hoshin Project (1)

The Hoshin Project was initially a project where Taikobo was to defeat Dakki, the Sennyo nesting in the Yin Dynasty, and other evil Sennin and Doshi, 365 in all, and seal them in "Shinkai," a new world created between the Sennin World and the Human World. Taikobo loses the battle against Dakki, but he gathers comrades to strike a second time...

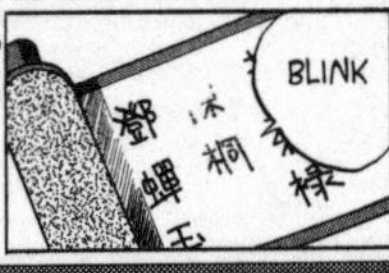
BLINK

▶ When someone is sealed, their name disappears from the Hoshin List.

Kongrong Mountains

The Kongrong Mountains are home to a school for training Doshi and Sennin run by Genshi Tenson. Taikobo is the direct disciple of Genshi Tenson. The 12 Elite Sennin are the highest executives under the command of Genshi Tenson. The 12 Elite Sennin have disciples such as Yozen, Nataku, and Tenka Ko. Sennin and Doshi such as Unchushi, who is not one of the 12 Elite Sennin, live independently as well. Shinkohyo is originally from the Kongrong Mountains, too...

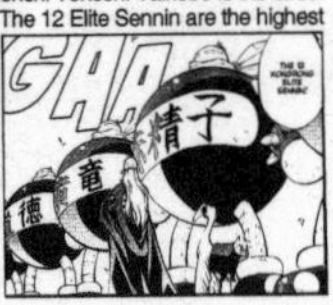
GAA

▲ The organization is stable under Genshi Tenson.

Hoshin Project (2)

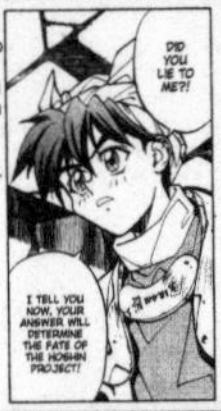
DID YOU LIE TO ME?!
I TELL YOU NOW, YOUR ANSWER WILL DETERMINE THE FATE OF THE HOSHIN PROJECT!

▶ Taikobo asks Genshi Tenson about his doubts.

The 365 who will be sealed are supposed to be evil Sennin such as Dakki's minions. However, the Hoshin List actually contains only about 180 names, and those who aren't Sennin, such as King Chu and the two princes, are also on the list. Taikobo goes back to ask Genshi Tenson about this, and finds out that the real Hoshin Project is to have Seihakuko Sho Ki defeat Choka and set up a new dynasty. Those with high abilities who die in the battle, regardless of whether they're Sendo or not, and regardless of whose side they're on, will be sealed in Shinkai, until 365 souls are sealed.

Choka vs. Seiki

Yin consists of 800 large and small countries in addition to the capital Choka. The Great Feudal Lords of the East, West, South, and North manage and govern those 800 countries. Due to King Chu and Dakki's misrule, refugees leave Choka and flock to Seiki, a good country governed by Seihakuko Sho Ki. Dakki assassinated both Tohakuko and Nanhakuko, and made Hokuhakuko her ally. She imprisoned Sho Ki, who had become strong, and even set a trap for his eldest son.

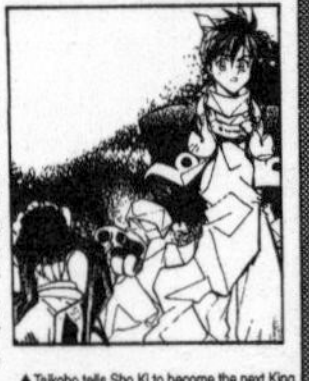

▲ Taikobo tells Sho Ki to become the next King.

Paope

Paope are secret battle weapons developed by Sennin and Doshi. Those who develop paope are highly-ranked Sennin such as the 12 Elite Sennin. Their direct disciples, who are suitable Doshi, tend to use those paope. A paope consumes the user's physical and mental powers to cause miracles, so the user needs to have enormous power to use a paope. Paope come in many shapes and forms. As the user matures, their paope become stronger.

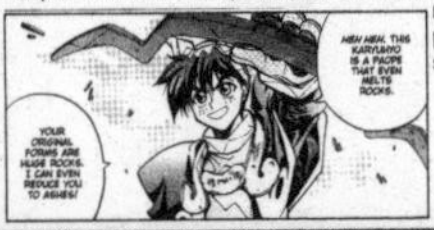
HEH HEH. THIS KARYUHYO IS A PAOPE THAT EVEN MELTS ROCKS.
YOUR ORIGINAL FORMS ARE HUGE ROCKS. I CAN EVEN REDUCE YOU TO ASHES!

◀ A paope that's not your own cannot be wielded effectively.

SECOND FEATURE TO COMMEMORATE THE FIRST ANNIVERSARY OF THE SERIES.

SECRET CHARACTERS ENCYCLOPEDIA!! PART 5

Hoshin Engi

The Sons of Sho Ki

Seihakuko Sho Ki is supposed to have a hundred sons. The eldest son, Hakuyuko, was killed by Dakki. The fourth son, Shukotan, assists Sho Ki to govern the land. However, as Sho Ki's health deteriorates, his successor is unknown... Hatsu Ki, who once appeared with Shukotan, is someone to watch...

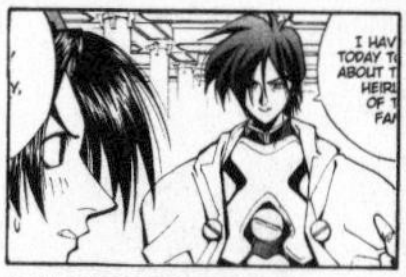

▲ Hakuyuko's death left a deep scar in Sho Ki's heart.

Yokai Sennin and their Original Forms

It's not just humans who can become Sennin. If animals and objects are exposed to moonlight and sunlight for over a thousand years, they become enchanted and become a "Yosei." They then become "Yogetsu," then "Sennin." The original form refers to a Yokai Sennin's origin. Dakki was a fox, Kibi was a pheasant, Okijin was a stone biwa lute. However, there are good Yokai Sennin (Doshi) like Hakutsuru Doji, so we cannot say that all Yokai Sennin are evil.

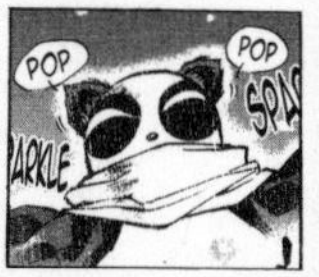
POP
POP

▲ A lot of Dakki's minions are Yokai Sennin.

History's Guidepost

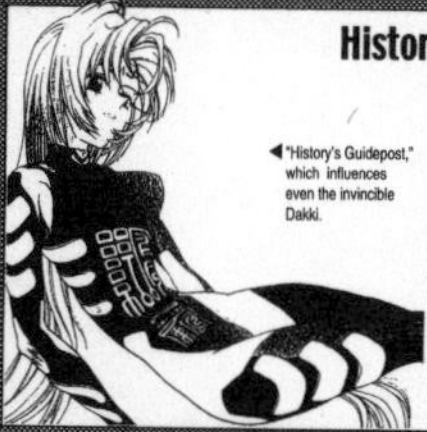

◀ "History's Guidepost," which influences even the invincible Dakki.

"History's Guidepost" is a term Shinkohyo used as a symbol for Dakki's whereabouts when she was absent from Choka (Kibi substituted as Dakki during this time). Dakki was supposed to have taken control of the Human World and be ruling the dynasty by her own will... "History's Guidepost" might be something that's influencing Dakki somehow...

Tennen Doshi

▶ Bukichi's speed helps in battle.

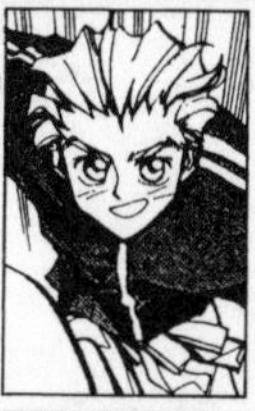

Tennen Doshi are humans who have the Senninkotsu but weren't scouted by the Sennin World. The Buseio Hiko Ko and Taikobo's self-described disciple Bukichi are Tennen Doshi. In Hiko Ko's case, he's one of the best masters of the martial arts and has superhuman powers. Bukichi can run as fast as Supushan can fly. He can also swim superhumanly, as shown in the battle against Koyuken, one of the Shisei. As comrades, they're very dependable.

Kingo Islands

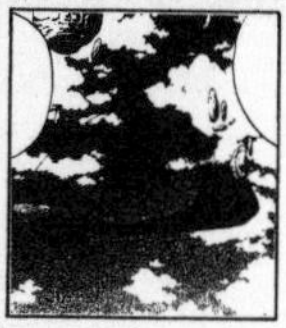

▲ Compared to Kongrong Mountains, there isn't much information about Kingo Islands.

In *Hoshin Engi* right now, Sennin and Doshi are trained in the Kongrong Mountains as well as the Kingo Islands. (Dakki's faction is another force?) Bunchu and his subordinates, the Shisei, are from the Kuryu Islands, which belong to the Kingo Islands. Genshi Tenson, the head of the Kongrong Mountains, considers the Kingo Islands their long-time rival, and that it is time they fight a decisive battle. In addition to the war between Seiki and Choka, it looks as if the Kongrong Mountains will be fighting the Kingo Islands.

Hiko Ko and Bunchu

Hiko Ko and Bunchu are now enemies, but they used to be the Buseio and Taishi of Yin. They worked in different places, one working on internal affairs and the other on foreign affairs, but because they were both warriors, they trusted each other. But Hiko Ko's dear wife and younger sister were led to their deaths by Dakki. Bunchu vowed loyalty to King Chu, who loved Dakki. There's no room for their relationship to recover.

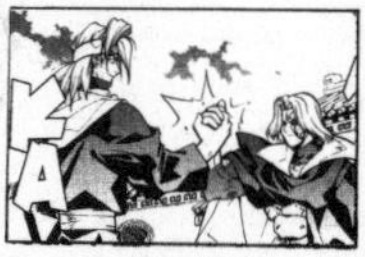

▲ They were a pair that could counter Dakki...

The Modification of King Chu

When the Buseio's wife and younger sister were killed, he asked King Chu to grant him a match. The Buseio is a Tennen Doshi, yet King Chu was an even match and even beat the Buseio at his own game. Shinkohyo, who was observing this match, pointed out the "modification of King Chu" to Dakki, and Dakki admitted to it, too. King Chu has maintained his youthfulness of his twenties and has superhuman power, so Dakki is probably modifying King Chu physically, something different from her Temptation jutsu. Dakki's final weapon is not her minions or her sisters, but could be King Chu himself.

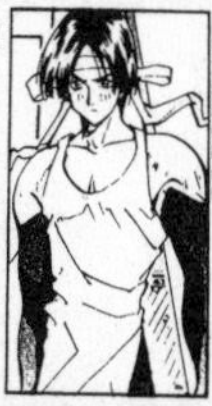

◀ Does King Chu realize he's being modified?

Shinkohyo's Philosophy

Shinkohyo hasn't done much recently. However, when King Chu's sons, the princes Inchon and Inchi, ran away from Choka and were rescued by Taikobo, Shinkohyo did not elegantly stand by as he usually does. He lectured the princes from the position of Choka and even tried to get them back by force. This was a rare moment where he showed his neutral position towards the Hoshin Project as well as his private values about a King's successors.

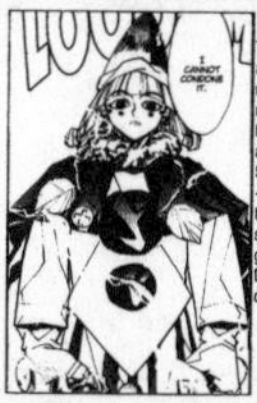

◀ There are many mysteries about Shinkohyo, the strongest Doshi of all.

THIS ARTICLE WAS PUBLISHED IN ISSUE 30, 1997, OF WEEKLY SHONEN JUMP.

THE SHEER PRECIPICE, WHERE IS IT NOW? 9

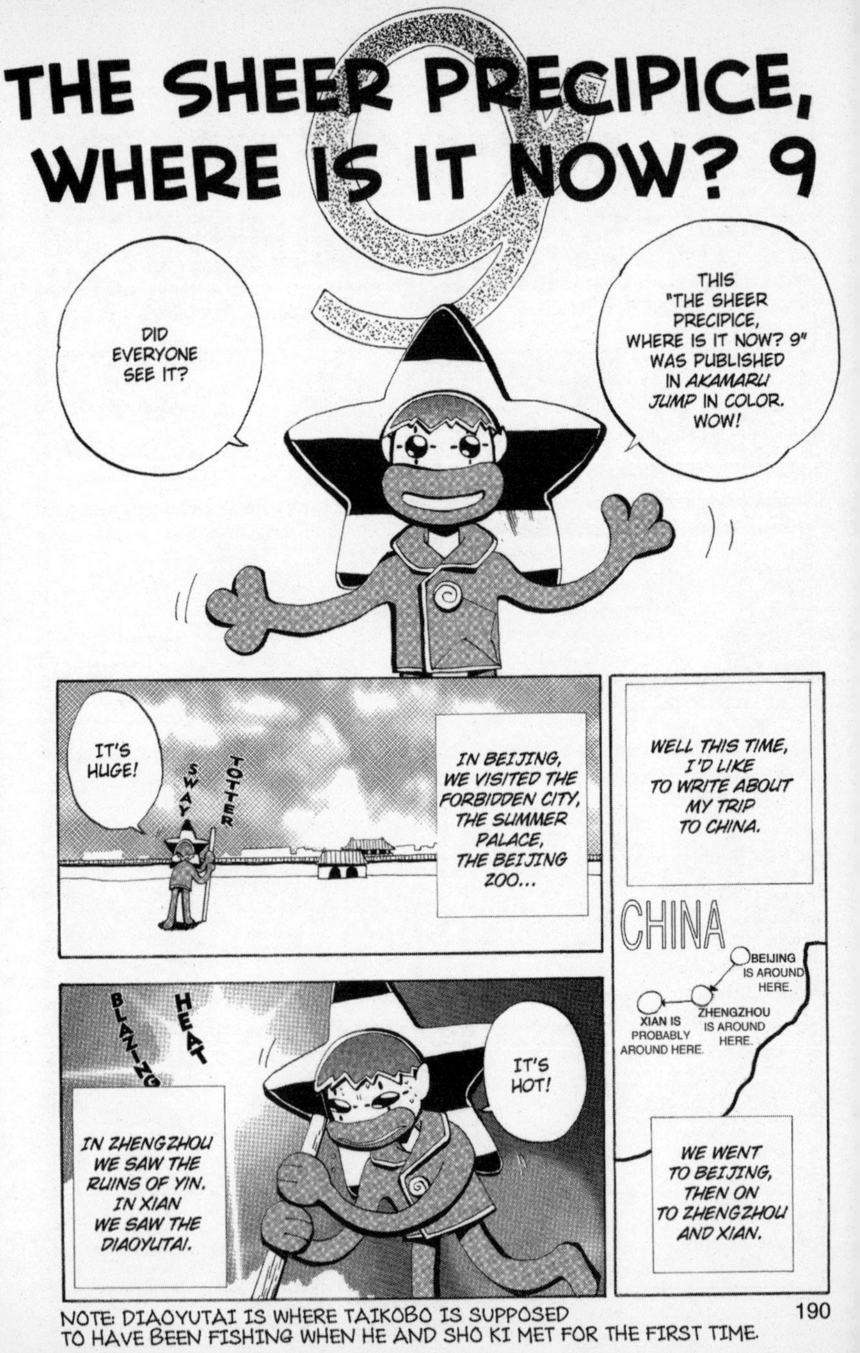
THIS "THE SHEER PRECIPICE, WHERE IS IT NOW? 9" WAS PUBLISHED IN AKAMARU JUMP IN COLOR. WOW!
DID EVERYONE SEE IT?
WELL THIS TIME, I'D LIKE TO WRITE ABOUT MY TRIP TO CHINA.
CHINA
BEIJING IS AROUND HERE.
ZHENGZHOU IS AROUND HERE.
XIAN IS PROBABLY AROUND HERE.
WE WENT TO BEIJING, THEN ON TO ZHENGZHOU AND XIAN.
IN BEIJING, WE VISITED THE FORBIDDEN CITY, THE SUMMER PALACE, THE BEIJING ZOO...
TOTTER
SWAY
IT'S HUGE!
IT'S HOT!
HEAT
BLAZING
IN ZHENGZHOU WE SAW THE RUINS OF YIN. IN XIAN WE SAW THE DIAOYUTAI.

NOTE: DIAOYUTAI IS WHERE TAIKOBO IS SUPPOSED TO HAVE BEEN FISHING WHEN HE AND SHO KI MET FOR THE FIRST TIME.

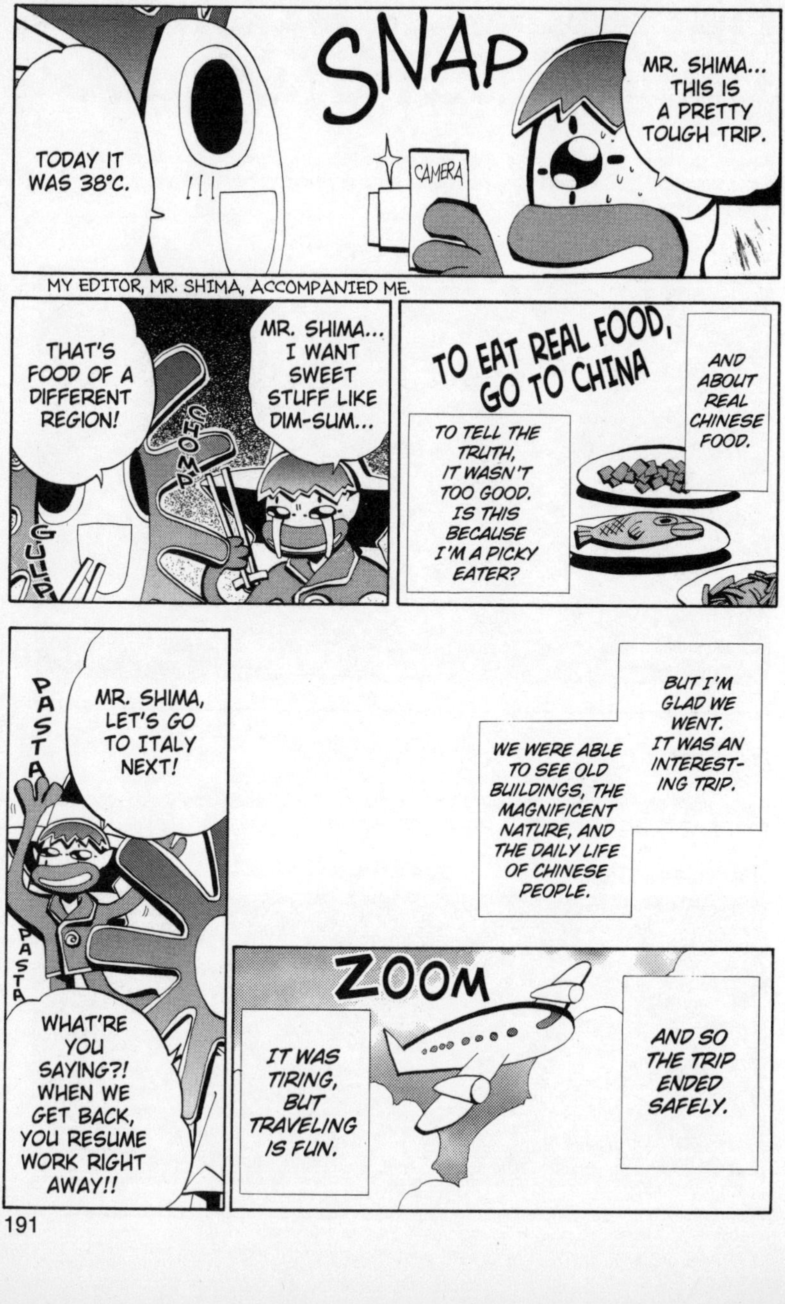
MR. SHIMA... THIS IS A PRETTY TOUGH TRIP.
SNAP
TODAY IT WAS 38°C.
MY EDITOR, MR. SHIMA, ACCOMPANIED ME.
AND ABOUT REAL CHINESE FOOD.
TO EAT REAL FOOD, GO TO CHINA
TO TELL THE TRUTH, IT WASN'T TOO GOOD. IS THIS BECAUSE I'M A PICKY EATER?
MR. SHIMA... I WANT SWEET STUFF LIKE DIM-SUM...
CHOMP
THAT'S FOOD OF A DIFFERENT REGION!
GULP
BUT I'M GLAD WE WENT. IT WAS AN INTEREST-ING TRIP.
WE WERE ABLE TO SEE OLD BUILDINGS, THE MAGNIFICENT NATURE, AND THE DAILY LIFE OF CHINESE PEOPLE.
AND SO THE TRIP ENDED SAFELY.
ZOOM
IT WAS TIRING, BUT TRAVELING IS FUN.
PASTA
MR. SHIMA, LET'S GO TO ITALY NEXT!
PASTA
WHAT'RE YOU SAYING?! WHEN WE GET BACK, YOU RESUME WORK RIGHT AWAY!!

Hoshin Engi: The Rank File!

You'll find as you read *Hoshin Engi* that there are titles and ranks that you are probably unfamiliar with. While it may seem confusing, there is an order to the madness that is pulled from ancient Chinese mythology, Japanese culture, other manga, and, of course, the incredible mind of *Hoshin Engi* creator Ryu Fujisaki.

Where we think it will help, we give you a hint in the margin on the page the name appears. But in addition, here's a quick primer on the titles you'll find in *Hoshin Engi* and what they mean:

Japanese	Title	Job Description
武成王	Buseio	Chief commanding officer
宰相	Saisho	Premier
太師	Taishi	The king's advisor/tutor
大金剛	Dai Kongo	Great Vassals
軍師	Gunshi	Military tactician
大諸侯	Daishoko	Great feudal lord
東伯侯	Tohakuko	Lord of the east region
西伯侯	Seihakuko	Lord of the west region
北伯侯	Hokuhakuko	Lord of the north region
南伯侯	Nanhakuko	Lord of the south region

Hoshin Engi: The Immortal File

Also, you'll probably find the hierarchy of the Sennin, Sendo and Doshi somewhat complicated. Here, we spell it out the easiest way possible!

Japanese	Title	Description
道士	Doshi	Someone training to become Sennin
仙道	Sendo	Used to describe both Sennin and Doshi
仙人	Sennin	Those who have mastered the way. Once you "go Sennin" you are forever changed.
妖孽	Yogetsu	A Yosei who can transform into a human
妖怪仙人	Yokai Sennin	A Sennin whose original form is not human
妖精	Yosei	An animal or object exposed to moonlight and sunlight for more than 1000 years

Hoshin Engi: The Magical File

Paope (宝貝) are powerful magical items used by Sennin and Doshi. Sometimes they look like regular objects, like a veil or hat. These are just a few of the magical items, both paope and otherwise, that you'll encounter in *Hoshin Engi!*

Japanese	Magic	Description
打神鞭	Dashinben	Known as the God-Striking Whip, Taikobo's paope manipulates the air and wind.
霊獣	Reiju	A magical flying beast that Sennin and Doshi use for transportation and support. Taikobo's reiju is his pal Supu.
雷公鞭	Raikoben	Reduces an opponent to ashes with a huge clap of thunder.
哮天犬	Kotenken	The Howling Dog can fly and be used as an attack Paope.
莫邪宝剣	Bakuya no Hoken	Tenka's weapon, a light saber.
叫名槌	Kyumeikon	An object that can freeze someone's movements when their name is shouted.
紅珠	Koju	Buddhist rosary beads that can capture an enemy.
混元珠	Kongenju	A gem that can control water, it is connected to a similar gem beneath the sea.
劈地珠	Hekichiju	An object that uses the Earth's power to heal allies.
拌黄珠	Bankoju	A vehicle that shoots energy beams.
開天珠	Kaitenju	A missile that destroys anything it touches. Allows the user to fly.
禁鞭	Kinben	A powerful whip that can attack anything in a diameter of several kilometers.
紫綬羽衣	Shiju Hagoromo	Allows the user to fly, and emits a lethal poison moth powder.
傾世元禳	Keisei Genjo	An object that radiates the perfume of temptation.
如意羽衣	Nyoi Hagoromo	A cloak that enables the wearer to transform his or her appearance.

Coming Next Volume:
The Curtain Falls

With Sho Ki on the verge of death, the forces of Seiki struggle to find a new leader. Meanwhile, Taikobo and his allies must fight their strongest opponent yet—the Maka Yonsho!

AVAILABLE JUNE 2008!

Read Any Good Books Lately?

Hoshin Engi is based on *Fengshen Yanji* (*The Creation of the Gods*, written in the 1500s by Xu Zhonglin) one of China's four classical fantastical novels of adventure, magic and mystery. The other three are *Saiyuki* (*Journey to the West* by Cheng'en Wu, late 1500s), *Sangokushi Engi* (*Romance of the Three Kingdoms* by Guanzhong Luo), and *Shui Hu Zhuan* (*Outlaws of the Marsh*, by Shi Nai'an, mid-1500s).

Want to read these books? You can! They're all still in print, more than 500 years later!

These books are North American in-print editions only.

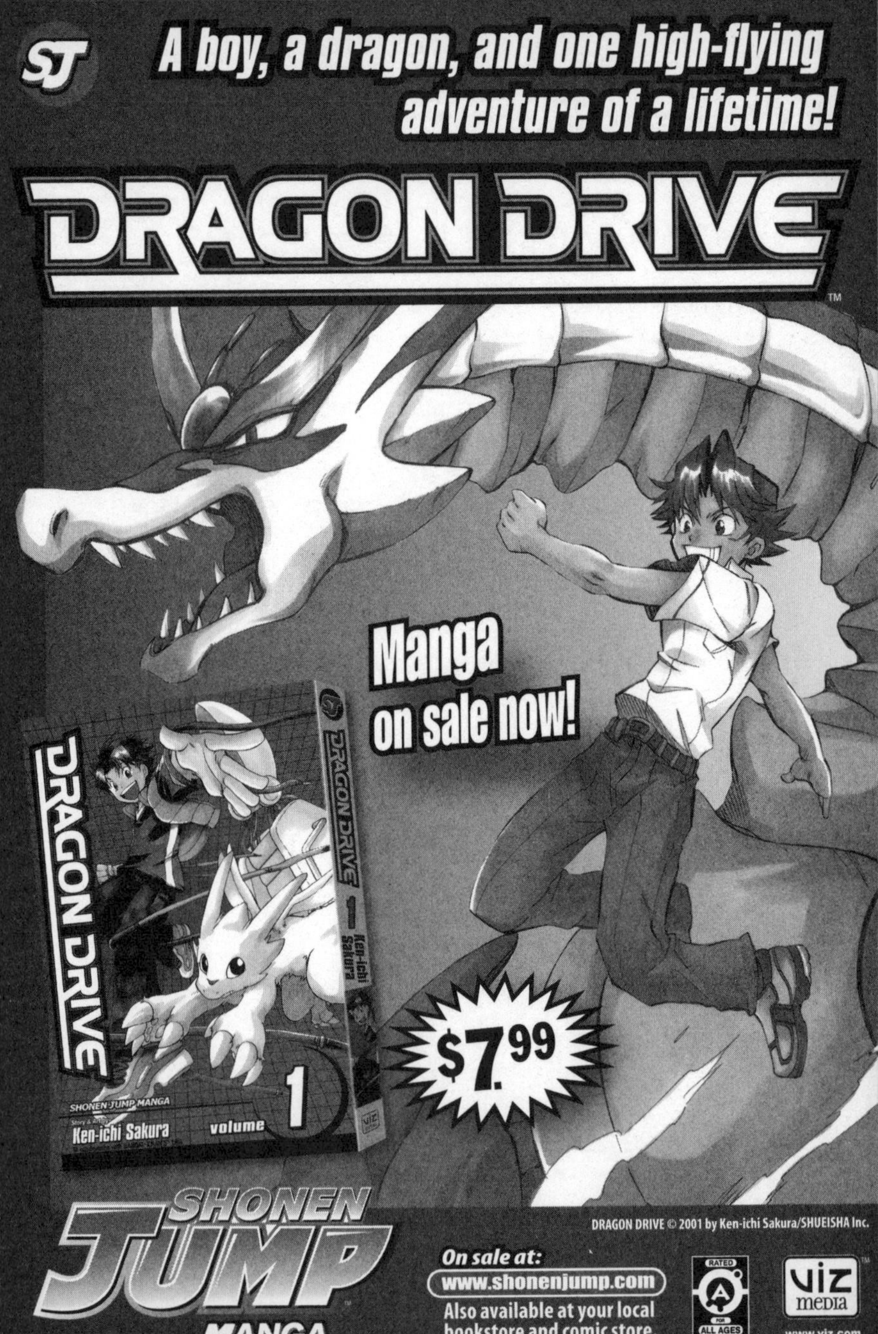

SJ
A boy, a dragon, and one high-flying adventure of a lifetime!
DRAGON DRIVE™
Manga on sale now!
DRAGON DRIVE
1 Ken-ichi Sakura
SHONEN JUMP MANGA
Ken-ichi Sakura
volume 1
$7.99
SHONEN JUMP MANGA
DRAGON DRIVE © 2001 by Ken-ichi Sakura/SHUEISHA Inc.
On sale at:
www.shonenjump.com
Also available at your local bookstore and comic store.
RATED A FOR ALL AGES
VIZ media
www.viz.com

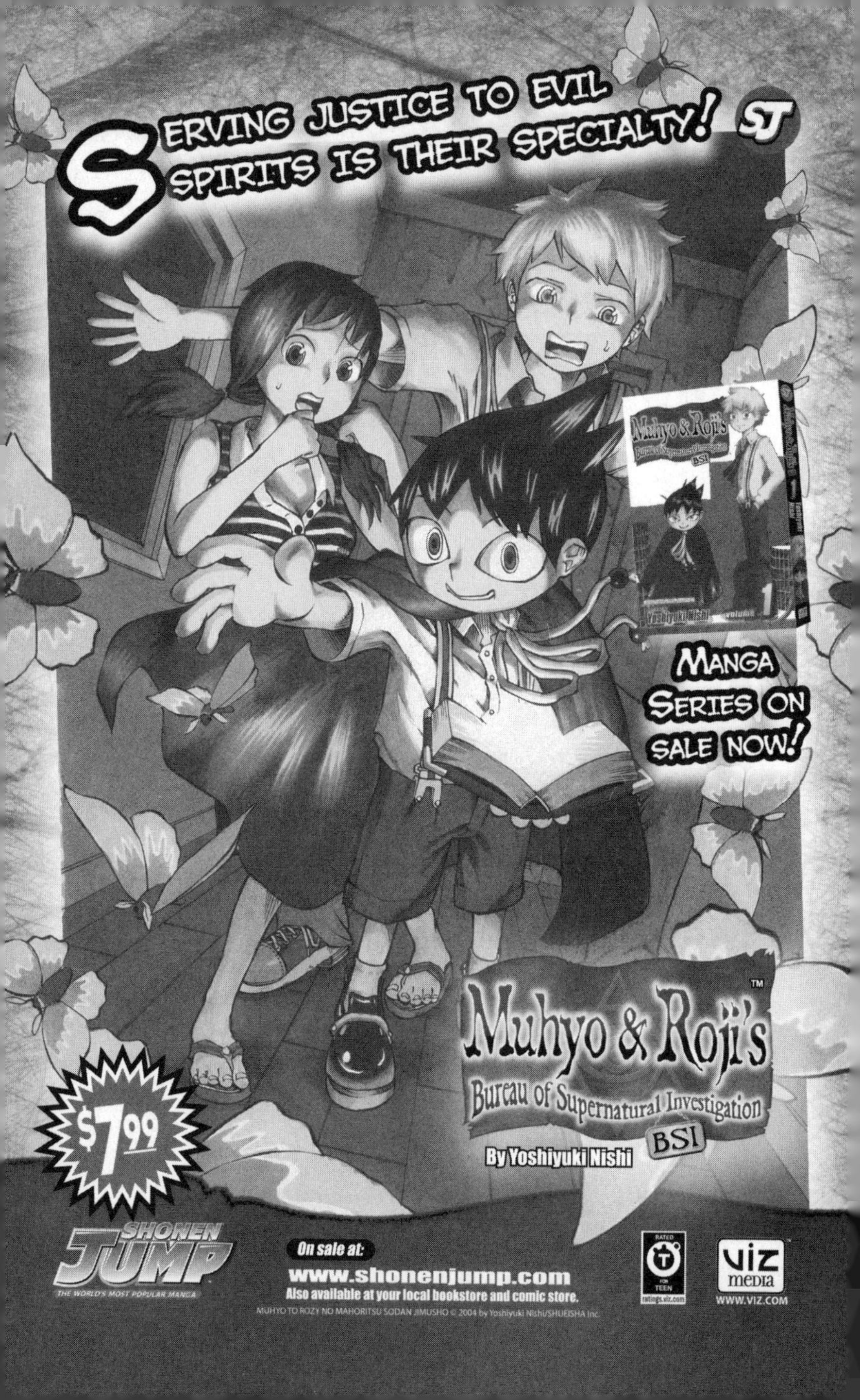
SERVING JUSTICE TO EVIL SPIRITS IS THEIR SPECIALTY!
SJ
MANGA SERIES ON SALE NOW!
Muhyo & Roji's
Bureau of Supernatural Investigation
BSI
By Yoshiyuki Nishi
$7.99
SHONEN JUMP
THE WORLD'S MOST POPULAR MANGA
On sale at:
www.shonenjump.com
Also available at your local bookstore and comic store.
MUHYO TO ROZY NO MAHORITSU SODAN JIMUSHO © 2004 by Yoshiyuki Nishi/SHUEISHA Inc.
RATED T FOR TEEN
ratings.viz.com
VIZ media
WWW.VIZ.COM

Tell us what you think about SHONEN JUMP manga!

Our survey is now available online.
Go to: **www.SHONENJUMP.com/mangasurvey**

Help us make our product offering better!